The Manager's Casebook
of Business Strategy

The Manager's Casebook of Business Strategy

Bernard Taylor, *Professor of Business Policy,*
Henley Management College
and
John Harrison, *Principal,*
Knight Wendling, London

Butterworth-Heinemann Ltd
Halley Court, Jordan Hill, Oxford OX2 8EJ

 PART OF REED INTERNATIONAL BOOKS

OXFORD LONDON GUILDFORD BOSTON
MUNICH NEW DELHI SINGAPORE SYDNEY
TOKYO TORONTO WELLINGTON

First published 1990
First published as a paperback edition 1991

British Library Cataloguing in Publication Data
The manager's casebook of business strategy
  1. Corporate planning
  I. Taylor, Bernard   II. Harrison, John
  658.4'012

ISBN 0 7506 0055 1

Printed and bound in Great Britain by
Billing & Sons Ltd, Worcester

Contents

Acknowledgements   viii

Introduction – Successful strategic planning: a managers' casebook   ix

Synopses of chapters   xvii

**Part One   Setting corporate direction in an uncertain
              environment**   1

1 **Using scenarios to develop strategies at Shell**   5
   J. P. Leemhuis
   Manager, Corporate Planning, Shell Nederland B.V.

2 **Analysing the business portfolio in Black & Decker Europe** 19
   Robert Walker
   Corporate Planning Officer, Black & Decker Europe

3 **Setting corporate objectives and operational targets for the
   British Airports Authority**   37
   Don Turner
   Privatization Director, British Airports Authority

4 **Assessing country risk and business potential at National
   Westminster Bank**   47
   David Kern
   Manager and Chief Economist, National Westminster Bank plc

5 **Using issues management to deal with public issues**   63
   C. B. Arrington Jr. and *R. N. Sawaya*
   Public Affairs Department, Atlantic Richfield Company

Part Two   Crisis and recovery: managing radical change   77

6 **Creating a productive organizational culture at Shell
   Chemicals**   81
   Ian A. Thornley
   Personnel Director, Shell UK Ltd

7 **The turnaround at MFI: From troubled mail-order firm to
   leading furniture retailer**   93
   Jack Seabright
   Joint Managing Director, MFI Furniture Group

8 ICL: Crisis and swift recovery   105
   D. C. L. Marwood
   Company Secretary, ICL Ltd

9 Getting FIAT back on the road   127
   Fabrizio Galimberti
   Chief Economist, FIAT Group

Part Three Implementing profitable growth strategies   139

10 Strategic leadership through corporate planning at ICI   143
   Alan I. H. Pink
   General Planning Manager, Imperial Chemical Industries plc

11 Successful strategies: The story of Singapore Airlines   157
   Karmjit Singh
   Company Planning Manager, Singapore Airlines Ltd

12 Implementing corporate strategy: The story of International
   Thomson   168
   Gordon C. Brunton
   President, International Thomson Organisation Ltd

13 Strategic planning for the World Wildlife Fund   183
   George J. Medley
   Director, World Wildlife Fund, UK

14 Strategic planning in the Thomas Cook Group   194
   Adrian H. T. Davies
   Director, Group Planning and Business Development, Thomas Cook
   Group Ltd

*Part Four Transforming company cultures and achieving
            excellence*   217

15 Achieving Japanese productivity and quality levels at a US
   plant   221
   Kazuo Ishikure
   President and Chief Executive Officer, Bridgestone USA

16 The quest for quality at Philips   235
   Kees van Ham and *Roger Williams*
   Senior Director of Corporate Organisation and Efficiency at Philips
   International, Eindhoven, and Erasmus University, Rotterdam

17 Changing the corporate culture of Rank Xerox   246
Paul Chapman
Director of Business Management Systems, Rank Xerox (UK) Ltd

18 Creating a new organization and culture at Scandinavian Airlines   258
Olle Stiwenius
Senior Consultant, SAS Management Consultants

19 Woolworth's drive for excellence   274
Don Rose
Personnel Director, Woolworths plc

20 From organization development to corporate development at Trebor   281
Arthur Chapman
Personnel Director, Trebor Ltd

21 A management strategy for information processing: the Segas case   289
Alfred C. Collins
Director of Corporate Planning and Management Services, South Eastern Gas

Part Five   Responding to deregulation and privatization   317

22 Competing with AT & T   321
Kathleen Reichert Smith
Vice-President, Staff Operations, GTE Sprint Communications Corporation

23 The transformation of the Trustee Savings Banks   332
Ian Marshall
Group Strategic Planner, TSB Group Central Executive

24 The NFC employee buy-out: A new form of industrial enterprise   340
Sir Peter Thompson
Chairman, National Freight Consortium

List of *Long Range Planning* journal articles   354

Index   355

Acknowledgements

This book records some of the outstanding business achievements of the last decade – written down not by academics or journalists, but by the businessmen themselves. They would be the first to admit that they are not professional writers. But any shortcomings in style are more than made up for in the realism that comes from direct experience on the job. The managers involved come from different countries around the world – Sweden, Japan, Holland, USA, Italy, Belgium, Singapore – as well as Britain. They come from various businesses, from chemicals to confectionary, from airlines to automobiles, from travel to telecommunications, and from furniture to fund-raising. They have one characteristic in common which all our readers will value. They are not advisers, or writers. Like their readers, they are businessmen and managers. They have 'been there'. They have held the responsibilities, taken the decisions and, in many cases, suffered the consequences.

The stories they tell are not the 'trivial pursuits' that appear every day in business magazines and financial newspapers. Some tell of the struggles for survival which occurred in businesses across the world in the early 1980s. How FIAT laid off 23,000 workers in 1979 – 15 per cent of their labour force, introduced automation and increased labour productivity by 50 per cent. They also reduced their debt/equity ratio by 90 per cent and pushed their margin from a loss of 3 per cent on turnover to a profit of 2 per cent. At the same time their share of the Italian market rose from 51 per cent in 1981 to 54 per cent in 1984. How ICL cut its work force by 10,000, and doubled their turnover per employee from £18,000 in 1979 to £37,000 in 1983, and with financial re-structuring, re-organization, a new joint venture with Fujitsu, clever marketing and a massive investment in training moved from a £50 million loss in 1981 to a profit of £40 million in 1983 – all in two and a half years. Also, how a Shell Chemicals plant in Manchester, having slimmed down from 2700 to 1150 staff in five years, then achieved a *further* 57 per cent reduction in manpower to 500 and survived by 'creating a more productive company culture' in barely a year. But these 'headlines' cannot tell the full story: the re-training courses that were necessary to produce multi-skilled technicians, the communications programme that was mounted to keep people informed, the Redeployment Unit that helped to place 76 per cent of the workforce in new jobs.

Other company case histories describe a dramatic record of growth. For instance, how Singapore Airlines became a world class airline in just ten years. From 1974 to 1984 the total revenue grew sixfold from $400m to $2,600m. Meanwhile staff numbers only doubled from 5000 to 10,600. Consequently, Singapore Airlines' productivity is one of the highest in the airline league. Also, the aircraft are consistently over 70 per cent full, and the organization has an international reputation for high quality service.

Another engaging story is the tale of the World Wildlife Fund UK – and how George Medley joined the Fund from Glaxo and proceeded to apply modern business methods to a non-profit organization. The graphs tell their own story. Net funds grew from £600,000 in 1977 to £3,600,000 in 1986. Income per employee rose from around £10,000 in 1977 to over £60,000 in 1986. Meanwhile, membership increased nearly tenfold from 12,000 to 110,000 and the donor list expanded from 25,000 to 450,000. As with the other case studies, the real interest is in learning how it was done, from one of the people who planned it, and helped to make it happen.

The National Freight Consortium is another exceptional, possibly unique, case. In this final chapter, Sir Peter Thompson describes how, via an employee buy-out, 'a new form of industrial enterprise', Britain's largest road transport and distribution business was transformed in three years from a state-owned company with a poor profit record and unhappy industrial relations to a very profitable and highly productive private business in which the 25,000 employees held 83 per cent of the shares. Trading profit increased from £4m in 1981–2 to £23m in 1983–4 – and pilfering stopped overnight! Meanwhile, the price of the shares grew from £100 to £12,400 in just three years. The directors and the staff of NFC wonder why more companies do not follow their example. Why, for instance, management teams arrange management buy-outs but do not follow through and sell the shares to the workforce, treating them like genuine employee shareholders so that management and the workers can both benefit from achieving higher productivity.

All too often business strategy is thought of as an esoteric art practised in ivory towers by groups of analysts and financial specialists. In this book, business strategy is seen for what it should be – part of business leadership which, when pursued with drive and energy, and backed up by teamwork, entrepreneurial flair and strong operational management, can achieve remarkable results – often from the least promising material or in a hostile environment. The cases illustrate the theme of strategic leadership, explaining how leaders and teams of managers thought out their strategy and then implemented it vigorously and with imagination. Of course, they had luck. But then as Pasteur said 'Chance favours the prepared mind'.

As editors of this book we would like to express our gratitude and our admiration to the authors who have written these chapters for us. For taking the time out of their very busy schedules to produce a blow-by-blow account, not just to tell what was achieved but to explain what strategies they pursued, and what action was taken to implement these strategies. We also wish to say how much we appreciate the candid way in which these pieces have been written. Company names are quoted, dates and times are given, techniques are described, and results are recorded. This adds greatly to the credibility of the case studies and we wish to thank the companies concerned for allowing them to be published in full.

We wish particularly to thank Pergamon Press, the publishers of the *Long Range Planning*, of which Bernard Taylor is Editor. This book was conceived in 1984 as a joint venture between Heinemann and Pergamon, and the majority of the chapters have already appeared individually over the past few years in the pages of the journal. These articles are listed on page 354.

'Implementing Corporate Strategy: The Story of International Thomson' is reprinted by permission from the *Journal of Business Strategy*, Fall 1984. Copyright 1984, Warren, Gorham & Lamont Inc., Boston, Mass. All rights reserved.

Finally, we wish to record our thanks to Mrs Julia Lewis who for the past ten years has been editorial assistant to the Editor of *Long Range Planning* and who has brought these chapters to the point of publication, though at times it seemed that the book would never emerge.

Introduction
Successful strategic planning – a managers' casebook

This casebook is a unique collection of case histories written by practising managers and describing how they have put strategic planning into operation, with what results and with the conclusions they have drawn.

In twenty years' experience of editing *Long Range Planning Journal* Bernard Taylor has found a continuing demand from readers (mainly senior managers and corporate planners) for company cases, written by practitioners, explaining their use of Strategic Planning approaches and techniques in achieving business success.

Managers operate in an environment where there is a good deal of uncertainty and they are often called upon to make decisions and take action with incomplete information. They therefore have little time for theoretical articles, based on hypotheses and assumptions, which offer no explanation of how the theory is applied.

In addition, professional managers appreciate that there is no unique and prescriptive solution to their own business situation; each organization must develop its own tailor-made solutions. They are looking for models, ideas and lessons from other people's experience.

There is a large unmet demand for case studies, not so much of the 'open ended' Harvard Business School type, but more case histories of the type that appear in *Management Today* and *Fortune*. These tend to be written by talented journalists or are produced, with great effort, by the managers themselves.

A manager usually experiences only two or three of these major cases in his or her own career. It usually takes considerable time to make organizational changes and achieve the required results: success in corporate strategy may well take five to ten years to be realized in a particular company.

Based on this knowledge, we felt that there was a need for a book of this kind. The casebook contains twenty-four case histories from well-known organizations, mostly commercial businesses but including a few public utilities and a charity. Each case history features an important aspect of strategic management as described by a manager directly involved in the process. The authors write with first hand knowledge of what problems were faced, how they were overcome, and what lessons were learned from the experience.

The book has been some time in development as more than fifty companies were originally approached as potential candidates for inclusion. In the event it has not been possible to use all the cases produced: we have chosen those we believe to be the best. Some were excluded because they were not comprehensive enough; others were eliminated because they formed one of a number with similar experiences. For example, we received more examples of turnarounds than we needed, and had several similar banking and telephone company cases from which to choose.

Planning for operating managers

This is a good time for operating managers to have access to these cases because corporate planning is being taken over by boards of directors and line managers and there is a tremendous training job to be done.

In the early 1980s many large planning departments were disbanded and headquarters offices closed as companies sought for more cost effectiveness. This meant that planning ceased to be a staff activity and the responsibility was handed over to management teams in newly formed profit centres or strategic business units. This move towards profit centre management has not only affected the private sector but has also become widespread in the public sector.

In addition, many public sector organizations like British Gas, British Airports Authority and National Freight Corporation, all included in this volume, were privatized. Trustee Savings Bank also were floated on the stock exchange. In all these cases the process of privatization was the subject of careful and successful strategic planning.

This means that many people such as sales managers, engineers, production managers, designers, local government officers and the like are now charged with operating business enterprises. Few had previous experience in the planning and implementation of business strategy and many could clearly benefit from guidance.

What we are offering, therefore, is a book which distils the experience of managers using modern planning techniques in a variety of business situations for those directors and managers who would like to learn from their peers. The book covers success stories, turnarounds and the development of new ventures. It also demonstrates how companies have used planning to raise their performance and change their cultures and deals with a range of organizations from the private, public and the voluntary sector.

The book is also intended for more junior managers and post-graduate students who want to expand their knowledge of business. It provides 'packaged experience' to such readers whereby they can think their way into a real situation and mentally sit alongside a management team at a level to which they would not normally have access. Business strategy is a core part of BA, MBA and MSc business programmes and is difficult to teach to those inexperienced in business at a senior level.

Increasingly, junior managers who are given the task of managing projects, products or brands are required to apply a strategic perspective to their jobs. They have to relate their own activity to the broader business context.

The structure of the book

In bringing the cases together a number of common themes emerged which represent key strategic issues for the 1980s and the 1990s. The five themes are:

- Setting a strategic direction in an uncertain environment
- Crisis and recovery: Managing turnaround situations
- Implementing strategies for profitable growth
- Transforming company cultures and achieving excellence
- Responding to deregulation and privatization

These themes provide the framework for the five parts of the book.

The cases should provide practical pointers to those involved in developing and implementing corporate strategies in their own businesses.

They illustrate that, for many successful businesses, strategy development and implementation now play a central role. This has required the creation of a robust and flexible strategy review process, led by management, but operating throughout the business. We are seeing the emergence of the *strategy-driven business*.

The evolution of corporate planning

Corporate planning in western industrialized countries has had to deal with many changing issues during the past thirty years as described in Figure 1.

As a result, the style of corporate planning has moved through several phases since its widespread introduction in the 1960s. The dominant style of planning in large sophisticated companies has broadly followed the pattern shown in Figure 2.

1960s: Long range planning

This decade was a period of relative stability as the post-war boom continued. Leading industrial companies were extending their annual

Planning for a period of stability and growth	Planning for business under attack	Planning for cutback and rationalization	Planning for: 1 Profitable growth 2 Cultural transformation 3 Deregulation and privatisation 4 Global markets
1960s	1970s	Early 1980s	Late 1980s

Figure 1 *Development of corporate planning: the key issues*

one-year budgeting processes to include a five-year operating plan and a long-range forecast. Planning at this time was usually about expansion and growth through means such as diversification, internal expansion, acquisition and merger. It was also concerned with the allocation of resources to support the development. Often in the corporate planning process little attention was paid to improving competitive performance and increasing the level of service to existing customers in the traditional industries.

Most of the five-year plans were based on a simple extrapolation of past trends. The underlying assumption was that the economic boom would continue ad infinitum. This assumption was to undermine the plans of many businesses during the following decade.

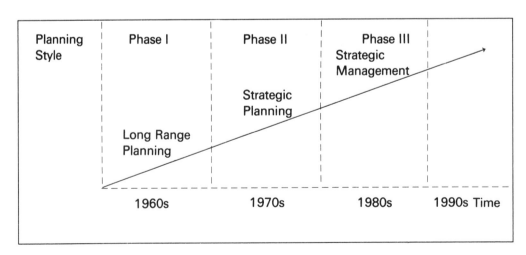

Figure 2 *Development of corporate planning styles*

1970s: Strategic planning

In the mid-1970s a new range of planning techniques was developed which encouraged debate about Corporate and Business Strategy before preparing detailed operating plans. The energy crisis of 1973–4 brought the period of stable economic growth to an abrupt end. In many western countries, the crisis introduced a period of high inflation, turbulent industrial relations and large scale public investment. At the same time the Japanese were spearheading a new wave of competition based on new standards of product quality, consumer service and aggressive marketing.

The late 1970s was characterized by widespread cutback and rationalization as firms struggled to cope with the first stages of the recession. One major problem was that managers were just not used to dealing with stagnant and declining markets and were ill-prepared to make tough decisions quickly. As a result many firms found themselves in a downward spiral which some failed to survive.

1980s: Strategic management

Early in the 1980s positive action began to turn the economic tide. In the USA and Western Europe right-wing governments were voted in and immediately began to support business through confronting the unions, reducing the level of government bureaucracy and bringing a new commercialization to the public sector. For many businesses this was a difficult time as cutbacks and rationalizations were continued in order to restore businesses to a stable financial state.

Professional managers were brought in by many businesses to 'break the traditional mould' and make the drastic changes necessary. People like Jan Carlzon at SAS, Wisse Dekker at Philips, and Carlo de Benedetti at Olivetti led the change in continental Europe. Likewise, in the UK, Ralph Halpern at Burtons, John Harvey-Jones at ICI, Ian MacGregor at British Coal and British Steel were among those heading the UK turnaround.

Following the period of cutback and rationalization, confidence has been restored in many of the companies that survived the recession. The strategy question then facing the survivors was how to grow and prosper in an uncertain environment and how to transform corporate cultures to meet competitive standards in productivity, quality and customer service.

Some of the key differences between the long-range planning, strategic planning and strategic management styles are shown in Figure 3.

The uncertain environment

The speed and extent of the changes which have occurred in the 1970s and 1980s have required businesses to be much more adaptable to the chang-

1960s: Long-range planning	1970s: Strategic planning	1980s: Strategic management
Main elements	*Main elements*	*Main elements*
• Long-term forecasts • Five-year budgets • Detailed operational plans • Strategies for growth and diversification	• Explicit company strategy • Division into strategic business units • Exploratory forecasting • Planning for social and political change • Simulation of alternative strategies	• Top management in charge of strategy • Total business approach – strategy formation and implementation • Attempt to manage strategic change • Visible leadership by top management • Staff involvement at all levels • Massive investments in new technology
Techniques	*Techniques*	*Techniques*
• Technological forecasting • Manpower planning • Programme budgeting • Gap analysis • Product – market matrix	• Scenario planning • Political risk assessment • Social forecasting • Environmental impact assessment • Business portfolio analysis • Experience curves • Sensitivity and risk analysis • Zero-base budgeting	• Competitive bench-making • Explicit business philosophy and objectives • Technology and resource portfolios • Employee shareholding and profit sharing • Internal marketing and service training • Company-wide quality improvement programmes • Internal and external databases
Problems	*Problems*	*Problems*
• Inflexible for fluctuating markets • Over-optimistic in a low-growth environment • Inadequate assessment of risk • Too little discussion of alternatives • No assessment of social and political factors	• Too centralized and remote • Too elaborate analysis • No process for implementation • Not designed to cope with crisis • Portfolio approach underestimates linkages between businesses	• How to maintain momentum once the crisis is over? • How to find the huge investments required for new technology? • Employee and union backlash against bonuses to executives. • Cultural change programmes have a short-term effect. • It is rarely possible to develop an integrated programme of corporate development. • Heavy demands on staff training and management development.

Figure 3 *Different planning styles*

ing environment. Some of the pressures for change have resulted from factors such as:

- widespread deregulation and privatization,
- the development of global markets, and direct investment by companies overseas,
- the concentration and restructuring of retail and wholesale markets,
- the decline of the manufacturing and heavy industry sector and a switch to high value-added products and service industries,
- the emergence of corporate raiders ready to pick up both those with poor financial records ripe for asset stripping and those with good potential,
- a shortage of key skills, despite a continuing high level of unemployment, in areas such as electronics, computers and systems design, marketing and finance,

In summary there is much **more competition** and pressure to raise performance.

Pressure for short term performance improvement has produced tension as short term results may be achieved at the expense of longer term investment in market development, new technology, new products, new systems and people. Organic growth has sometimes been neglected in favour of an acquisition strategy by which growth is 'bought' quickly.

Investing institutions and corporate raiders in the capital markets have increased the demand for short-term financial performance. Shareholder loyalty seems to be a thing of the past as the pressure is on pension funds and investment groups to 'perform'. In the market place too, customers are looking for new products *now*, and a quick response to their changing needs.

These trends are all at odds with the long-term planning approach which used to be the norm.

Cases in strategic management
The cases reflect various ways in which 'strategic management' has been applied. They are assembled and presented in five sections, each section having its own introduction.

These cases have been chosen because they demonstrate the use of strategic planning in:

- setting strategic direction in an uncertain environment for example, using scenarios, contingency planning and risk analysis;
- dealing with crisis and recovery in turnaround situations;
- implementing strategies for profitable growth, and managing the process of corporate development;

- transforming company cultures in order to meet changed circumstances and to maintain a competitive edge, using programmes of training, employee communication and internal marketing;
- responding to deregulation and privatization by adapting to a more commercial environment and applying new expertise in such areas as marketing and finance to raise the performance and effectiveness of 'non-commercial' organizations.

In addition to these themes, readers will also recognize many of the hallmarks of successful management. Success is invariably linked with 'getting the simple things right', such as: having positive leadership, setting clear objectives and paying close attention to customer needs. These simple things are easier to describe than to put into practice. Many company turnarounds and transformations are needed when companies get over-sophisticated and lose sight of the basics. A restoration of sound management and a return to fundamentals, enable strategic changes to be implemented efficiently and effectively. The result is the type of dramatic change in business fortunes seen in many of the businesses illustrated in the book.

We hope that readers will enjoy reading these cases and will draw from them practical approaches that can be applied in their own businesses.

Bernard Taylor and John Harrison
Henley Management College
July 1989

Synopses of chapters

1 Using scenarios to develop strategies at Shell

J. P. Leemhuis

Ideally, a scenario should be a description of a possible future in which social, political, economic and technological developments evolve in an internally consistent order. The initial task in the development of scenarios is to describe and analyse how these components of the business world interact. Scenarios are not forecasts. They provide a picture of possible futures in which the consequences of alternative strategic choices made today may be examined.

Strategies can be defined as 'ways to achieve a specific goal'. In business terms, this goal may be a statement of a long-term objective, such as improvement of market share. To select a strategy, a scenario/strategy payoff matrix may be utilized. In the matrix, the result of each strategy in different scenarios is calculated and compared, for example on the basis of net present value. However, from a practical decision-making point of view, this simple linkage of scenarios and strategies leaves a number of unsolved problems. In taking strategic decisions, management has to deal firstly with uncertainty in an explicit way in order to reveal risks. Secondly, they must treat the business on an integral basis rather than just on an incremental project by project basis. Thirdly, they should review the criteria for decision-making, such as the reward and risk criteria. For this, a process is required which is based on the identification of the perceptions of top management, the decision-makers themselves. It must be a simple process which deals with both key uncertainties and key elements of strategy. The process should enable direct interaction to take place between bottom-up and top-down decision-makers, in which the corporate planning staff can play a facilitating role.

Shell Nederland has experimented with such a process of strategy development over the last few years. Corporate planners must gear their activities towards the strategic decision-making needs of the company's management. The experience gained at Shell Nederland has shown that these needs are more effectively met by the use of flexible planning. Scenarios play a role in those processes as one of the key elements of a coherent planning framework in which risk and reward are central.

2 Analysing the business portfolio in Black & Decker Europe

Robert Walker

This case study describes the successful application of Portfolio Analysis in Black & Decker Europe without the assistance of external consultants. The author describes the problems encountered in installing the system and how these difficulties were turned to advantage by adapting and extending the original Boston Consulting Group Growth Share Matrix.

The BCG matrix was used as a basis for allocating resources among a diverse range of businesses and among the different European countries. Operating managers found the collection of data time-consuming, but the BCG analyses stimulated strategic thinking in the European office and provided a framework for planning and a way of validating and controlling plans throughout the group.

3 Setting corporate objectives and operational targets for the British Airports

Don Turner

The British Airports Authority (BAA) is constrained by the Airports Authority Act (1975) which states the duty to provide the required level of necessary services and facilities. This effectively sets parameters for the BAA's corporate strategy. In addition, it has to operate within the general framework of the relationship between nationalized industries and government.

In 1982, it was agreed that corporate planning should become proactive: a stimulant for new ideas and developing options. At the start of the cycle, the BAA has two major inputs: the government-agreed targets and the traffic forecasts. Airports, it must be remembered, are natural monopolies; true intra-competition cannot occur. Their development and operations are highly capital intensive. Thus, long-term forecasts are of vital importance. Traffic is broken down according to whether domestic, European, intercontinental, scheduled, charter, business or leisure. Annual forecasts are readied for each airport and the end result are forecasts of throughput, aircraft movement, etc over the next five years. The process begins each year in May with Board agreement to the BAA's objectives. Senior Management meets in June to agree the overall framework. The two key requirements are the responsibilities of management in achieving goals and the need to recognize the trend to decentralization and deregulation. Each of the seven airports is a discrete business unit. Each airport has to prepare a business plan which is submitted in early autumn and forms essential updating of the Corporate Plan.

The preparation of budgets and financial forecasts takes place integrally with the Business Plans and, then, the Corporate Plan. It is hoped to reduce the post first year level of detail in the five-year plan. The Corporate Plan, after all, represents the heart of BAA's forward planning, setting the overall objectives, policies and strategies. These are set out in the first section. The Plan's second section considers the possible options and detailed strategies. The financial effects are contained in a detailed five-year forecast. The Plan is presented to the Board for approval in March. One especial feature is that the Plan is part of the ongoing management process. Its production and monitoring is inextricably woven into the entire management of the business.

Editors' note: BAA was successfully privatized in July 1987. The value at issue was £1,225m. The shares were floated at 245p and quickly rose to 282p. The value after the first day's dealing rose to £1,460m.

4 Assessing country risk and economic potential at National Westminster Bank

David Kern

At a practical level, the growing use of structural analyses for assessing country risks can be seen as a natural reaction to the increasingly difficult and complex problems facing those involved in international activities. Essentially, this type of systematic approach attempts to identify explicitly and to quantify the international risks arising from business operations.

The extensive literature on country risk assessment shows a very wide variety of approaches to this subject, ranging from highly complex mathematical models used by academics to very simplified frameworks, often preferred by those involved in practical business situations. In view of the enormous complexity of the economic environment, it is naturally tempting to try and incorporate all possible factors which may be relevant. However, experience shows that it is simply not practical to try and capture the entire spectrum of possible variables in any one model. A more sensible and fruitful approach is to analyse carefully the specific requirements of the organization undertaking the risk exercise, and focus attention on a small number of factors which appear to be particularly relevant. These factors can then be evaluated in a medium-term risk model which assumes a risk spectrum ranging from 0 (nil risk) to 100 (maximum risk). Each category is given a maximum level of 'possible risk' associated with the particular factor, and the figure chosen reflects its perceived relative importance. The overall score for each country simply reflects the sum of its separate scores in each category.

Trying to quantify risk numerically, with reference to a small number of identifiable factors, is inevitably rather mechanistic. Some of the more subtle and complicated risks will deliberately be over-simplified in such an analysis. Clearly, calculating a risk score which ranges from nil to maximum risk must involve some element of artificiality. Nevertheless, if the results of such an analysis are used properly, they can be an invaluable aid to those involved in making decisions, providing them with a necessary analytical framework for communicating ideas in a logical and explicit manner.

5   Using issues management to deal with public issues

C. B. Arrington, Jr and R. N. Sawaya

Issues management is a process using many disciplines to tackle possible discontinuities in the external environment, helping organizations anticipate and respond to change. To be effective, it needs to link staff and line expertise and it must have executive commitment. The process consists of three linked activities. One is foresight, the use of pragmatic judgment about external factors vital to company success. It is essential to link the readily available external information with an internal consistent company viewpoint on the issue.

At the core is policy development, based on the making of coherent positions on specific issues. Exposures and opportunities need to be identified clearly and strategies formulated. Without this, the third element, advocacy, is not possible. Largely the responsibility of the public affairs department, advocacy can be undertaken by the top executive. It must always include feedback.

Evaluation of the total processes should take place on a regular and qualitative basis. Lack of surprise can be a good indicator of effective issues management. But, just as important, is the need to liaise with planning. In this way, public policy issues can be integrated into company planning. Issues management parallels and contributes to strategic planning. People involved in it need to have a collective synthesizing habit of thinking.

Issues management should ensure coherent participation in external advocacy and relationships. The function should remain small and non-hierarchical, and be at the heart of the company's strategic thinking.

6 Creating a productive organizational culture at Shell Chemicals

Ian A. Thornley

Despite five years of continuous retrenchment, in 1985 Shell Chemicals UK's Carrington site still needed to reduce its fixed costs and its manpower. It was recognized that conventional approaches to manpower reduction would be insufficient: a change in the site's culture was required. Management believed that Carrington's competitive edge lay in the knowledge and commitment of its people. The key to a productive environment was identified as consistency in values and systems.

The organization's previous structure was 'flattened' to improve communications and allow more scope within each job. Unprofitable plants were shut down and the site was changed into one based on four performance-accountable plant centres. Old demarcations between groups of workers were abolished and the new multi-skilled technicians both operated and maintained the plant centres, in teams co-ordinated by a shift manager, on a six-month cycle which combined shift operation and day maintenance (supported by specialists). Personal training programmes, leading to nationally-recognized qualifications, were carried out for each technician. There was rationalization of union agreements, terms and conditions, and incident payments.

The change process had five aspects: a high degree of resolve coupled with high integrity; attention paid to the individual's needs, by keeping him informed and offering counselling; precise and thorough communication using modern techniques; a tight schedule, which was adhered to; and visible management leadership by the line function. A full-time Redeployment Unit provided practical and emotional support for those leaving Carrington. Target levels of site manpower were achieved and there was a high success rate in redeployment and additional skills training for those seeking alternative work.

7 Turnaround at MFI: From troubled mail order firm to leading furniture retailer

J. W. Seabright

MFI was set up in the early 1960s. The company flourished and, in 1971, went public. By 1973, margins were under pressure and the company's response was to reduce prices and extend credit. 1975 saw profits at £78,000 (1973: £2·2m). Mail order was performing poorly and that side of the business was shut down in September 1975. At the same time, a hard look was taken at all aspects of the business.

The company had strengths; it also had weaknesses. Yet it had identified a gap in the market which could be exploited. It had a record of successful advertising, low overheads, and cash for investment. It was determined to become the Marks and Spencer of the furniture industry. To do this required a new organization.

The entrepreneurs had to be removed from day-to-day management. A team was created which had common objectives. Four policy groups (the retail group, the merchandise group, the warehouse group and the Chairman's sub-committee) were set up as sub-committees of the Board, the most important being the retail group. The members were directors and line managers and were encouraged to take a broad company view. The resultant organization was designed to be efficient: flexible yet allowing detailed management control.

Manager training and development was seen as a key priority, as was careful merchandise selection and control. The installation of a computer provided the basis for better and more frequent pricing decisions. Quality control, though difficult, was maintained, as was customer service. The turnaround strategy proved a success. The management team goes from strength to strength. The company now dominates the retail furniture sector. And, as so often is the case, the change depended on people.

8   ICL: Crisis and swift recovery

D. C. L. Marwood

During the late 1970s, ICL's financial strategy was based on high revenue growth to cover its swiftly rising cost base and to leave a steady profit progression. This was a high risk strategy; the mainframe market might not grow fast enough, costs were leaping ahead, and margins were being squeezed by competition. The effort to reduce manufacturing costs led to the decision, in October 1979, to close the plant at Dukinfield, Manchester, and management began special measures to reduce overheads, such as recruitment bans.

In June 1980, there were clear signs of a sharp fall in profitability for the whole of 1979–80. The position continued to deteriorate and the Board decided upon a second major manpower reduction involving the closure of the plant at Winsford, Cheshire. With further losses forecast for 1980–81, the Board moved to a policy of seeking an outright bid or some form of joint venture which included a substantial equity injection. Finally, it became necessary for the government to step in and the management team was changed.

The aim of the new team was to stem the losses, restore confidence and ensure ICL's independent survival. As a result, all partnership discussions were abandoned. Part of the new strategy was to seek collaborative ventures aimed at improving ICL's future products, especially those aimed at providing synergy with the ICL product range and markets. A number of collaborative agreements were eventually concluded, most notably one with Fujitsu.

The successful completion of a Rights Issue to raise £32m in January 1982 provided the first indication that ICL was undergoing a recovery. With losses being substantially reduced over the year and with the company beginning to move out of its survival period into one of renewed profitability and growth, the Board decided to go ahead with a fresh Rights Issue and to redeem the Preference shares in four instalments. The issue was launched in conjunction with the 1981–2 results, which showed a pre-tax profit of $23.7m, and was an immediate success.

The position of ICL continued to improve throughout 1982–3 as the company became involved in a number of major programmes, notably ESPRIT. By the end of the period, ICL announced pre-tax profits nearly double the level for 1981–2. All the major targets set two-and-a-half years earlier had been accomplished. With trading conditions still difficult and highly competitive, growth had been restored and the Group's financial base secured. Finally, in September 1984, ICL accepted a bid from Standard Telephones and Cables (STC), with STC holding over 81 per cent of ICL's equity. A new and even more profitable ICL future had begun.

9 Getting FIAT back on the road

Fabrizio Galimberti

The last five years for FIAT have shown that things at times have to get worse before they improve and cost cutting is essential for survival. Market and political developments in the 1970s forced the company into a position which threatened its survival. The slowdown in economic growth faced a company which was geared to high output and high growth. The adjustment process was a long and arduous one.

In 1980, FIAT announced plans for a massive lay off and a massive capital injection. The scale of the former (15 per cent of the labour force) was staggering. There was a long battle with the unions who lost, largely due to the loyalty of most workers. The recapitalization was basically for an extensive re-tooling of production lines following a radical re-think of strategy. This latter was due to three factors: the second oil crisis, slower growth combined with a fall in car demand, increasing and intensifying competitive pressures.

Costs had to come down. Product innovation was essential. It was essential to produce at costs lower than competitors. Unit wages could not be significantly reduced, so one answer was to 'lose' workers. Another was to modernize and automate, all the while ensuring flexibility. It became important to offer more variety and the 'customized car' was now a possibility. Automation has proceeded relentlessly in the last five years.

In addition, it was realized that FIAT was geographically over-extended and the company's presence in different markets was reviewed. Europe's importance was confirmed. It was decided to pull out of the USA; FIAT's activities in Latin America were cut back. Four other items were reviewed: inventories, dealers, suppliers and finances. Working capital was reduced.

FIAT aims not just to survive, but to grow and prosper. It needs to widen its presence in non-Italian markets. The 'phase two' strategy is aimed at making the company a leading car manufacturer which can successfully meet the challenges of the 1990s.

10 Strategic leadership through corporate planning at ICI

Alan I. H. Pink

The challenge within a large complex company such as ICI is to allow the development of individual businesses while maintaining the coherence of the Group. A profit crisis arising from problems in the external environment led to a reassessment of short-term objectives and long-term strategy, and brought about fundamental changes in the company's management style and direction. The broad strategy was to achieve two major thrusts: to improve competitiveness, in terms of both costs and added value, and to change Group shape in respect of both products and territorial spread.

The new approach is based around a smaller, more closely-knit Executive Team which has a strong strategic planning role. There is a quantitative vision of the Group ten years ahead and a process for setting corporate objectives and identifying potential shortcomings in achievement, and strategic identification and justification of acquisitions. The team draws up strategies for each unit with its Chief Executive, to whom operating responsibility is delegated, which include short-term profit and cash budgets, using strategic milestones to provide a linkage with long-term strategies. The Corporate Planning and Finance Departments work closely together, using a simple, flexible and essentially qualitative portfolio management tool.

The Planning Department has the dual role of developing corporate and business strategies, and assessing changes in the external environment and their implications, including the activities of competitors. Changes in business shape must be reflected by changes in employee skills, and there must also be strategies for maintaining excellence in the important skills of innovation.

11 Successful strategies: the story of Singapore Airlines

Karmjit Singh

Singapore Airlines has had a remarkable success considering that the country is small, has a population of two-and-a-half million and few natural resources. External factors have played a part. Singapore is strategically located. It is the most prosperous Asian country after Japan. The Government has deliberately encouraged its development as an entrepot. In addition, the airline itself realized the need for effective marketing.

Always after careful evaluation, it has equipped itself with the most up-to-date aircraft. The technologically obsolete and fuel inefficient planes were put on the scrapheap. Investing in the latest technology was taken at the bottom of the business cycle. A major emphasis has also been placed on service, style and personnel. One result is that its passenger load factors have averaged 70 per cent and over since 1973. It has maintained productivity and a reputation for innovation combined with prudent financial management.

Corporate planning plays an important role. The responsible department acts as a facilitator and monitor. In order to ensure effective strategy formulation, it uses issue analysis to provide the basis of strategic thought. The airline is now concerned as to how to maintain profitability at a time of rising costs. It feels confident, nonetheless, about the future.

12 Implementing corporate strategy: The story of International Thomson

Gordon C. Brunton

How does a small British-based publishing company grow to a diverse $2.5 billion company with world-wide interests? The story told by Gordon Brunton, the President of Thomson International, offers insights into the management of growth and diversification on an international scale.

This chapter describes the process of growth from 1961–84, with predictions to 1988. Phase 1: 1961–5 was a move into related areas of information and publishing. Phase 2: 1965–71 was concerned with the creation of two new profit centres in directory publishing and in holidays and travel. Phase 3: 1971–7 was an opportunistic move into oil and gas production in the North Sea. Phase 4: 1977–88 saw the attempt to develop operations in the United States, in information and publishing, travel, oil and gas.

George Brunton summarizes the lessons learned, and concludes that the secret is a combination of strategic planning and sheer opportunism.

13 Strategic planning for the World Wildlife Fund, UK

George J. Medley

The national organization of the World Wildlife Fund in the United Kingdom (WWF UK) was founded in 1961 to promote education and research on the conservation of world fauna, flora and other natural resources. In 1977 a new Chairman of the Trustees identified the need to manage the charity on a business basis and therefore recruited a successful businessman for the position of Chief Executive Officer. The new CEO's changes took the form of a structural reorganization, to ensure that fund raising areas were manned by business professionals, and the introduction of strategic planning based on a 'management by objectives' process.

The first need was to define the purpose of the organization in order to formulate objectives. Areas of the organization which had particular influence on its success were identified, and these turned out to match the designations of a similar process to industry. Each key area was subjected to a review of its strengths, weaknesses, opportunities and threats, which led to the formulation of strategy. Each department was asked to state the action it proposed to take to achieve the strategy (a collation of which became the organization's plans) and to produce budgets to meet the objectives. WWF UK's financial management was strengthened.

The success of the planning process can be demonstrated via the growth in net funds, productivity, the size of the donor list and the achievement of projected net funds. The initial scepticism within the organization towards strategic planning was converted into commitment to the process which, combined with team work, has produced excellent results.

14 Strategic planning in the Thomas Cook Group

Adrian H. T. Davies

Thomas Cook started in 1841 organizing outings for groups of working people. It developed quickly. In 1929 Wagons Lits took over. After the fall of France it was nationalized. The Midland Bank became sole owner in 1972 and thoroughly reorganized the company. In the last five years it has expanded.

There are planning problems. The travel industry is extremely diverse, involving cars, parking, air travel, hotels, restaurants, etc and the 'product' is, of course, intangible. Customers' requirements vary and public taste itself changes. In addition, operating margins are narrow and the volumes of transactions are high.

Planning in the Group has vastly improved. The annual planning cycle is geared to that of its parent, Midland Bank Group, and begins with the emphasis on the strategic dimension. The first step is the Group Strategic Conference which takes a medium- to long-term view. This is followed by a strategic review of the previous plan and a Group Planning Conference attended by operating company managers with their draft plans. A planning manual provides a detailed guide to the process.

The five-year plan contains a detailed first year operating plan, the next four being only a broad strategic framework. Each company will have its own approach, the emphasis being on results and on 'bottom up' planning. When approved by Group Management, Plan figures are consolidated and subjected to sensitivity analysis and the final Group Plan presented for Board approval.

Strategic planning is of crucial importance to the Group. Detailed operating plans form the basis of monthly management reporting; indeed reviews play an increasingly important role.

New developments are in branch and departmental productivity, manpower and marketing planning. Targeting will be refined and planning by passenger numbers will be introduced. For the future more attention will be given to business development, resource allocation and strategic management.

15 Achieving Japanese productivity and quality levels at a US plant

Kazuo Ishikure

Bridgestone Corporation of Japan began manufacturing in the United States by taking over a troubled tyre plant from a US corporation. Production, productivity and quality levels were low; profits were nonexistent.

Bridgestone took various steps in order to turn the plant around. One was to discover why demand for the tyres was so poor. A survey of customers identified a poor image, derived from poor product quality. Redressing this became the top priority. The first step was to clean up the plant by making each worker responsible for cleaning up after himself. Next was the use of the so-called '4M' approach, addressing problems with machines, materials, methods and manpower. Machines were continuously improved and became preventively maintained. Materials suppliers were subjected to scrutiny on their own process controls and product quality. Adjusting methods to Japanese standards proved more difficult because of the different capital equipment and materials. Not surprisingly, manpower proved to be the most difficult.

Steps were taken to reduce the difference between blue- and white-collar workers. An opinion poll of the work-force, management seminars and interviews with the President were instituted to help build 'mutual trust'. Training, including visits to Japan, quality control management, mistake reporting, quality circles and management by objectives were all introduced. The net result of these actions was a three-fold increase in output, a doubling of productivity, and a reduction of defective tyres by about half.

16 The quest for quality at Philips

Kees van Ham and Roger Williams

In the post-war period, there were shortages particularly in consumer goods. Now, the situation has changed. Manufacturers have to be aware of customer wishes. They have to contend with the demand for low prices and the consequent insistence on economies of scale. Product quality and reliability have become essential as markets have become global. Innovation and variety in product range are increasingly expected. As a result, within Philips as elsewhere, many long-established and previously highly successful practices have had to be changed. Management has realized that it has to take risks in taking the lead. But there are no standard techniques.

In 1983, the President issued a policy statement that set the direction for the future of the Company. This went to all senior executives who were asked to communicate the message to their own organizations. There were nine key points: customer satisfaction, leadership, total involvement, integrated approach, systematic approach, defect prevention, continuous improvement, maximum quality and, lastly, education and training. In all approaches, five main activities were identified and used. These were awareness and commitment, organization and planning, implementation and action, continuous renewal, and control and maintenance. Once a year a major evaluation is carried out for the Board of Management. Two-and-a-half years later, the results are encouraging. Improvements have been achieved.

This is seen as the start of a long-term learning strategy based on legitimacy, practicality and value. Improvement in quality is, of course, worth achieving. In addition to this natural 'desire', the Company has introduced the Philips Quality Award system. This gives management something extra to strive for.

Several lessons have been learned. The top-down cascade model has proved successful. Management 'ownership' of the strategy has proved absolutely essential, as has involvement. There must be consistency throughout. Perseverence is vital as is preparedness to accept frustration at times. And, at the end of the day, there is no standard way.

17 Changing the corporate culture of Rank Xerox

Paul Chapman

The major strategic objective in 1986 of Rank Xerox (UK)'s new Managing Director, David O'Brien, was to exploit the technological opportunities offered by Xerox's range of office equipment products. He decided that the challenge lay in two areas: the company's strategy and marketing, which had evolved as a style suited to the selling of stand-alone copiers rather than office systems, and its organization and management processes, which reflected its position as leader in the copier/duplicator market.

O'Brien perceived that different skills, strategies and programmes would be needed, and these could also have a beneficial effect on the 'traditional' areas of the business. Rather than replacing those executive directors whose experience reflected the company's earlier needs, O'Brien retained them and appointed as facilitators of change two new ones, for strategic business development and business management systems.

During the subsequent development process a valuable component was the company's own Leadership Through Quality Programme. This emphasized the needs of the customer, and caused some confusion and conflict arising from cultural clashes. The process needed a framework, and O'Brien introduced one tailored to the company's needs.

The emphasis was on consensus and teamwork, and, although decisions initially took longer to reach by this method, the time taken represented an investment which was repaid in the form of quality. The next step was to see how to apply technology to the process both for internal use and to show customers how to apply the approach. Already there have been some major successes both in sales and producing a better understanding of customer needs.

18 Creating a new organization and culture at Scandinavian Airlines

Olle Stiwenus

For a long time SAS operated in a steadily growing market protected by international airline agreements. Profitability was maintained by keeping costs down and reciprocally dividing the markets. However, increased fuel prices, rising costs, price wars, dwindling demand and liberalization of air-transport competition placed SAS in a loss-making position. It became apparent that the competitive market called for an entirely new corporate philosophy.

The new aim was to adapt to market preferences. This meant that SAS had to become attractive to its passengers by meeting their demands. In order that consumer tastes could be monitored, greater emphasis was placed on feedback from 'front-line' employees. This basic change called for a reorganization which achieved the greatest possible market contact and the greatest possible delegation of responsibility and authority to the 'front-line'.

One of the basic facts in business is that a deficit will arise if costs are higher than revenues. So, to reverse the situation, one either has to reduce cost or increase income. SAS decided to do both simultaneously. To increase revenues, efforts were made to become a more market-orientated organization, offering customers those services they were prepared to pay for. As a result SAS created the 'businessman's airline', offering the business traveller a product to suit their needs. To reduce costs, the initiative was decentralized to managers closer to the market, so that costs could be controlled without adverse effects on the quality of service offered.

The new SAS organization is adjusted to market-demand and is based on widespread delegation. This kind of structure encourages the customer-orientation and flexibility required to meet changing consumer demands. It opens up possibilities for competent personnel to develop quickly and take responsibility for results without direct supervision.

It is important that corporate culture should harmonize with the commercial environment. When the latter changes, the culture has to change as well, if the company is to survive. This change took place and is still taking place in SAS. To match the new strategy, a culture has been developed where the customer is the centre where opportunities are created for individual initiative and commitment that invests in market segments and 'backs winners'.

19 Woolworth's drive for excellence

Don Rose

F. W. Woolworth's decline in British retailing was a result of problems rooted in its outmoded style in both management and service. On acquiring the retailer, the Paternoster consortium launched a rescue mission dubbed 'Operation Focus'. Broadly it was to involve a streamlining, rationalization and modernization of operations, with renewed focus on staff training, geared towards customer service and satisfaction. Further investigation revealed inherent attitude and procedural problems at all levels, which had led to indications of inflexibility and inadequacy.

Changes included a hierarchical restructure and the adoption of a new philosophy based on the concept 'People serving people': retraining, recruitment, a redefinition of the role of personnel management and an increased emphasis on standards. Merchandise was rationalized and concentrated into five 'Focus Areas' around which new management teams were built. The new structure placed more emphasis on personal responsibility, aiming for clearly defined roles through simplification. Staff were made aware of their role in the company, and how they could contribute to its general philosophy and drive for success. The Excellence programme was introduced as part of this process, designed to motivate and reward.

The changes introduced appear to have paid off. Increased customer satisfaction and increased sales have led to a rise in profits, while restructuring of management and training have brought renewed confidence and improved service.

20   From organization development to corporate development at Trebor

Arthur Chapman

As Trebor moved from its 'pioneer' phase into a 'differentiated' phase, it became necessary to adopt a more formal, planned approach to the future. While corporate planning itself was found to be unreliable, Organization Development (OD) has enjoyed a degree of success, leading ultimately to the emergence of a new Corporate Development function.

At the outset of the OD project in 1973, the Executive Board produced a document called 'Our Picture of the Future' listing the key aims and policies of the company. The document was issued and discussed around the company. Then, at a two-day conference, heads of functions listed the major issues facing the company, selecting two which offered potential for learning as well as benefit from a satisfactory outcome. One was a severe labour turnover problem on a major site, and the other the difficulty a new service division was encountering in participating fully in the decision-making processes of its line department clients. At the same time, a Steering Committee of directors and senior managers was set up to support the new projects and to register and disseminate what was learned from them.

After a year in which much progress was achieved on both projects, the Steering Committee realized that its role was counselling and not directive, and it was considered necessary to move on to a new phase. This was to be a phase in which new concepts and a new culture were developed and shared amongst a wider group of managers. The vehicle for this was a one-week residential management course in which all levels of management and supervision were mixed. At the end of the series of courses, a further meeting of heads of functions took place to appraise the OD work, and selected five products for the next phase of work. The most significant development project at that meeting was the construction of a new factory which is now on-line and running at a high level of efficiency.

In 1980, however, a severe recession in the confectionery market made clear the need for restructuring. As a result, a small Corporate Development unit was set up alongside Organization Development. Its primary role was to help identify and develop long-term future profit opportunities. There followed a stage of intensive staff work which led to a Board review of possible futures for the market; an analysis of opportunities and barriers; the development of options and assessment criteria: all of which produced a clear picture of the path for future business development and the selection of three critical projects.

The latest chapter in Trebor's corporate development includes the deliberate ending of the OD Steering Committee, as the Executive Group takes over responsibility for its work, and a sharp change of course on structure, with the devolution of the company into four profit centres. The purpose of these changes is to increase the scope for initiative and develop the climate in which it will flourish.

21 A management strategy for information processing: the Segas case

Alfred C. Collins

In implementing information processing systems the main influences are business priorities, industrial relations, management awareness, responsibility chains and user involvement. The Segas (South-Eastern Gas) experience in introducing computerization is a good example of how these environmental factors can profitably be handled.

A major emphasis was placed on on-line computing using mainframe computers. A three-phase strategy was undertaken. Systems deficiencies were first resolved. The initial foundation was then laid, based on the IBM Business Systems planning methodology of introducing systems as a top-down exercise. The third phase (that of full scale implementation) is still in process. For instance, the education of all levels of management, staff and trade unions is part of the continuing process and the Business Systems Committee continue to co-ordinate the development of IT systems throughout the company.

From the outset Segas wanted a common network to serve both word and data processing at all levels of management and operations. Segas wanted a technological philosophy which would accommodate a grafting on of a variety of cost-effective services without being indefinitely tied to one supplier. Any equipment used had therefore to have the capability of connecting via IBM network architecture. Types of facilities sought were those serving best the various levels of management which would also yield identifiable productivity improvements: for assisting future systems design and justifying the existing system. Rigorous pool investment appraisal has been applied to all projects. After a period when major investments were made (as expected) without immediate or short-term pay-back, the profit per computing employee used in Segas was calculated as £9000.

Editors' note: British Gas was privatized in December 1986. The company's value at issue was £5,434m. The minimum amount payable was £50 and the value after the first day's dealing was £62.50p.

In 1987 British Gas bought Bow Valley for £350m, and in 1988 the company bought Arce Oil for £370m, and Tenneco Oil and Gas for £113m.

22   Competing at AT & T

Kathleen Reichert Smith

The telecommunications industry has undergone dramatic structural change in response to increasing competition arising from changes in regulation, technology and the market place. Regulatory changes have been the predominant force in the restructuring of the industry, which has moved rapidly from a classic monopoly structure, through an environment of emerging competition and regulatory protection, to a position now moving toward deregulation and free market competition.

GTE Sprint has evolved along with these changes. The company's strategic position has evolved, over a compressed period of time, from that of an entrepreneurial start-up company to that of a major billion-dollar corporation. The initial mission of the company in the regulated environment, was to attract customers away from the dominant Bell System. This remained the strategic directive of the company until divestiture changed the competitive environment and thus required a new orientation.

GTE Sprint is at present developing a competitive strategy to optimize its resources and strengthen its position in the post-divestiture environment. One of the major thrusts of this strategy is to enhance and develop the network, expanding capacity in both existing and new areas. Another major thrust is to gain market share rapidly. Attention is also being focused on creating a basis for competition on attributes other than price. Management is taking measures to differentiate its service from that of its competitors and to develop a brand identity. In addition to its basic marketing and technology thrusts, GTE Sprint is continuing to plan for the future. New products are being considered and developed.

It is also recognized that, in the deregulated environment, effective strategic planning plays a pivotal role in determining the future of the company. As a result, strategic planning is evolving to better meet the needs of management in assessing external factors and implementing and tracking critical strategic programmes. The company is also attempting to integrate strategic planning better into the day-to-day management process.

23 Transformation of the Trustee Savings Banks

Ian Marshall

Since the mid-1970s, the TSB Group has changed from a group of seventy-three savings banks, offering basic deposit services, to one of the UK's leading financial service groups. It has done this at a time when the traditional boundaries between institutions and the financial markets are rapidly breaking down, a process which is expected to gather pace over the next decade. With this in mind TSB has developed a sound foundation for its future growth in the 1980s and 1990s.

Throughout the last ten years, TSB management has continuously needed to look ahead to manage the shift from savings bank to financial services group. Planning in its widest sense has, therefore, received a high priority in the Group. In the period since the mid-1970s, the precise conceptual framework has evolved to suit the style of senior management. Certain underlying principles are stressed. The planning process is driven by senior management. The plans are based on a simple group wide segmentation of the market and each emphasizes intended 'action steps' needed to achieve the plan. The process is supported by modelling techniques and competitor and economic analysis.

In forming plans for the 1980s and 1990s, key questions arise for TSB in common with other financial groups. Firstly, what are the proper boundaries of a financial institution's business? In the financial revolution of the mid-1980s, organizations are rushing to create the 'international financial supermarket'. As they meet this challenge, it is necessary for banks to decide whether they are 'high tech' retailers or conveyors of financial services.

Secondly, banks must consider what customers want from financial organizations. Advances in technology will allow new entrants into the financial services world. The successful organizations will be those who can provide – at a profit – the services the customer wants.

Thirdly, the pace of technological change must be assessed. An organization needs to be in the forefront of technological developments but, at the same time, must not alienate its existing customer-base by introducing untried systems that the customer is not convinced he or she actually wants. Finally, and most important of all, banks must consider how the style of management will adapt to the changing market place. As barriers between institutions become blurred, the banker may need to become more innovative, more market-orientated and perhaps closer to the retailer. This change is not easily achieved, and the winners in the year 2000 will be those organizations which have effected the change.

As the TSB moves into the next decade, the challenge is how to combine the characteristics of a modern, competitive financial services group with the qualities of care and concern which have always been denoted by the symbols TSB.

Editors' note: TSB was floated by legislation in September 1986. The value at issue was £1,300m. In 1987 the bank acquired Hill Samuel, Britain's largest merchant bank, for £777m, and Target Life, a major life insurance company, for £229m.

24 The NFC employee buy out – a new form of industrial enterprise

Sir Peter Thompson

Management had in 1982 a vision for the future of National Freight Corporation (NFC). It believed that, by creating a company controlled and owned mainly by employees, it was launching a new kind of industrial enterprise. Commercial success was, of course, to be essential and the results for 1983–4, the third year of operation, demonstrated that the NFC was a strong, profitable and expanding business. Employee-ownership and professional management proved a very powerful combination, not least because those who bought shares in 1982 saw their holdings increase more than tenfold in value by 1985. All outgoings last year (1985) were covered from trading profit alone. Investments have been made in operations abroad as well as in the UK.

It had been decided early on that the business needed to be controlled by employee-investors. All employees must have an equal right to invest and investors should receive dividends in proportion to their investment. The business would be professionally managed. These principles met with internal approval and gained the support of the bankers. The Secretary of State gave the idea the government's blessing. At this point, it became important to ascertain the reactions of employees, the trade unions and the press. That of the trade unions was less enthusiastic than others. The company then had the task of educating, informing and persuading a large and geographically widespread audience. Video was the main medium chosen. The application lists for buying NFC shares opened on 25 January 1982 and closed on 16 February. Despite the slow initial response, the move was eventually very successful.

Now the new 'owners' are deeply involved. Shareholders, most of them employees, are given opportunities to tell management their views. They have been quick to comment, but also are ready to be guided by the Board. One topic, which has been agreed, is the widening of the shareholding among employees. Another is the strategy for the next five to ten years. It is one for growth, for high service levels and improved job opportunities, and for a better balanced business.

Editors' note: National Freight Corporation was sold by the Government to the National Freight Consortium as an employee buy-out in 1982 for £7m. In the stock market introduction in January 1989 the company was valued at £588m. The share price had increased 74-fold in seven years.

Part One

Setting corporate direction in an uncertain environment

Part One Setting corporate direction in an uncertain environment

Part One is concerned with setting corporate direction. In the pre-oil crisis world forecasting seemed easy in an environment which offered stable and steady business growth. The five-year plan seemed a natural process to use. But now continual change is the norm for many businesses and there is a constant need to rethink the business strategy. The strategy-making process involves a continual 'dialogue about the future' and this is illustrated by the cases in this first section. In each case we see techniques applied in order to develop a sense of direction or a strategic vision in an era of uncertainty and discontinuity.

A major source of uncertainty has been the volatility of commodity markets. Commodities such as gold, coal, copper, agricultural products (such as wheat and the 'EEC mountains') and of course oil, have all fluctuated. The Shell case shows how *scenario planning* can be employed in order to enable management to consider the level of uncertainty and its likely impact on the business.

One of the ways in which companies have dealt with uncertainty is by spreading risk through diversification of the business into different industries, new product-markets, new technologies and additional geographic areas. *Portfolio management* has been used by highly diversified organizations as a means of allocating resources between different businesses. This technique has been used at the corporate level in order to start a dialogue between headquarters and divisions about the level of investment required. The Black & Decker case illustrates how portfolio management can be used to assess the strategic future of a set of businesses: what they should buy, hold and sell in their business portfolio.

Another issue facing many organizations is how to create an integrated set of corporate objectives, strategies and operational targets. It is relatively easy to set objectives at the corporate level. These are commonly expressed as ROI (Return on Investment), ROA (Return on Assets), revenue growth percentages, or similar measures. It is then much more difficult to turn these measures into *operational targets* for the utilization of facilities, deployment of staff, levels of customer service, unit costs and so on.

The British Airports Authority (BAA) case shows how a new agency faced with imminent privatization handled the problem of *setting corporate objectives*, which incorporated standards of performance, and expressed them in operational terms. BAA monitored its own operations against these standards and published the results over a ten-year period in prize-winning Annual Reports.

Increased instability has also been apparent in the financial markets. Events such as the 'Big Bang' and the Stock Market Crash of November 1987 have contributed to this instability, as has the exposure of major clearing banks to third world debt. This last item illustrates the banks' vulnerability to credit risks arising from high levels of inflation and the associated currency fluctuations as well as the ultimate threat of sovereign risk – the threat that a bank's assets will be nationalized without compensation. National Westminster Bank's approach to *evaluating country risk* provides an example of the banking industry's response to the risk.

The final case in this first part features Atlantic Richfield's approach to dealing with uncertainty in public policy using *issue analysis* and *issue management*. Public issues such as the disposal of nuclear waste, acid rain, drinking and driving, smoking and education can have major impacts on business performance. By monitoring public issues – following the issue life-cycle – an organization can react quickly when there are implications for businesses within its own portfolio. This is a dimension of planning that is best grafted on to a standard planning process.

1 Using scenarios to develop strategies at Shell

J. P. Leemhuis, Manager Corporate Planning, Shell Nederland B.V.

Scenarios have been part of the planner's tool-kit in Industrial and Government organizations for more than a decade. Various publications have stressed how much better scenarios are than forecasts, extrapolations and other mechanisms used to look into the future. The introduction of multiple scenarios reflected a desire to cope with the instability and uncertainty of business environments. How, in a practical sense, apart from 'improving the quality of the debate', they can be used to improve strategy development and with that the quality of strategic decisions has so far remained a somewhat mysterious subject.

This chapter describes the linkage between scenarios and strategies. Through this linkage we obtain a structural way of evaluating risks and rewards which enable decision-makers to choose strategic options against an explicit background of uncertainty.

Scenarios

The word scenario is most frequently used in the film industry to describe a detailed description of the action of a film. For a good film the scenario will be a coherent story developing out of a plausible initial situation. Similarly, in strategic planning, a scenario is a coherent story about the business environment with the world of today as the starting point. Many good films can be made from the same initial situation. So it is impossible to know at the start how a film will develop. The business environment is also impossible to forecast, but with carefully chosen scenarios a range of alternative lines of development can be described and considered.

Ideally a scenario should be a description of a possible future in which social, political, economic and technological developments evolve in an internally consistent order. The initial task in the development of scenarios is to describe and analyse how these components of the business environment interact. Scenarios cannot be constructed as an aid to thinking about the future without our first gaining a proper understanding of how these interactions have taken place in the past (Figure 1.1). A scenario is not a forecast. Scenarios are descriptions of possible future worlds: worlds in which the consequences of alternative strategic choices made today must be examined.

For the purposes of the planning process we can distinguish three planning horizons (Figure 1.2): a shorter-term period of say five years, using business-cycle scenarios; a horizon of ten to fifteen years with archetype scenarios; and very long-term periods for which exploratory scenarios are used. For investment strategy development the focus is on the archetype scenarios with the ten to fifteen year horizon.

Archetype scenarios are scenarios which describe alternative developments of socio-political and economic structures. The word 'archetype' refers to a fundmental change in the development going in distinctly different directions. For example, in one scenario a society may go through a period of painful restructuring of the economy allowing increased innovation and entrepreneurship and thereby creating a new platform for growth. A complementary archetype would be a development in which opportunities are not identified, tough choices are not made and the economy muddles through at a lower level.

Strategy

Strategies can be defined as 'ways to achieve a specific goal'. Thinking about strategy is rather fruitless if the ultimate goal has not been clearly identified. In business terms this goal may be a statement of a long-term objective such as improvement of market share or continued partici-

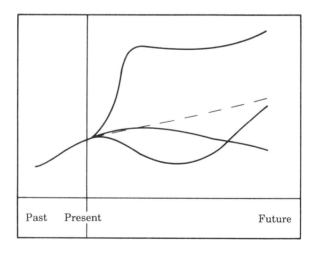

Figure 1.1 *Extrapolation and scenarios*

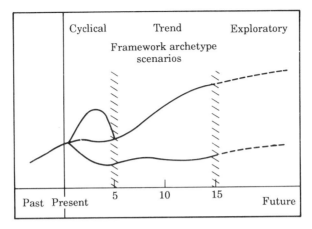

Figure 1.2   *Planning horizons*

pation in a business on the basis of a profitability criterion. A variety of different objectives are possible and it is pointless to consider strategies without first understanding what the longer term objective is.

Within the context of each overall business strategy hierarchical levels of strategies can be defined. This involves the translation of the overall business strategy into a marketing strategy, a product strategy, a processing strategy, a transport strategy and so on. Examples of various strategies leading to the same objective are to invest, to disinvest, to rationalize, to obtain short-term deals or long-term contracts, and to change the product mix. Together they should form a coherent and internally consistent business strategy.

Payoff matrix

The attractiveness of a strategy is judged against a multitude of criteria. The correct choice of criteria can be a difficult task for top management.

For each criterion the scenarios and the strategies can be ordered in a scenario/strategy payoff matrix. In this matrix the result of each strategy in different scenarios is calculated (for example on the basis of the net present value, Figure 1.3).

From this table it could be argued that strategy D is the most resilient or 'scenario independent' plan for the one criterion. From a decision-making point of view, however, one is still faced with an unsatisfactory evaluation. Amongst the questions which have been left unanswered are:

- Do the scenarios describe all possible futures as seen by the decision-makers?
- What are the probabilities of the various scenarios as perceived by the decision-makers?

	Scenario 1	Scenario 2	Scenario 3
Strategy A	100	-10	-30
Strategy B	-20	40	-50
Strategy C	-10	-50	400
Strategy D	30	10	50

Figure 1.3 *Scenario/strategy payoff matrix*

- What is the trade-off between criteria?
- What is the risk-taking attitude of the decision-makers?

Strategy C for example could be a preferred strategy if the decision-maker attaches a high probability to scenario 3 and is prepared to take the downside risks of scenarios 1 and 2. So, from a practical decision-making point of view, this first simple linkage of scenarios and strategies leaves us with a number of unsolved problems.

Strategic decisions

As indicated earlier, we are primarily interested in the process by which major decisions about the continuity, structure and direction of the corporation are taken. These decisions are called 'strategic decisions' and together they embody the chosen strategy. They normally involve a sizeable allocation of resources (both human and financial) which will be hard to reverse and to which the whole organization needs to be committed. Normally these decisions cannot be taken without board approval or sometimes the approval of government institutions. If we consider decision-making processes in large corporations a distinction can be made between bottom-up and top-down.

Bottom-Up
At the operating level of the organization, investment ideas are initiated and these move upwards in a level-by-level management decision process.

This process is often visible and systemized via budget procedures, known and clear expenditure approval mechanisms and so on.

These bottom-up proposals only enter the domain of strategic decisions once they have been received, discussed and approved by the top of the organization, so that a resource allocation can take place.

Top-Down

Proposals are made by top management and these have to be translated or interpreted by the organization so as to give lower management specific guidance within their own more limited span of control. It is only after this interpretation that the strategic nature of the proposal becomes clear.

A board which wishes to cut 10 per cent off total capital expenditure for the whole of the enterprise may have a very good reason for doing so, but the strategic consequences can only be measured after thorough investigation for each activity down the line.

Strategic decisions are made at the interface between top-down and bottom-up, where proper communication should take place. There are two problem areas in this regard: one is related to the *domain* in which these decisions take place; the other to the *language* which is used for these decisions.

The domain problem exists because the area of responsibility and perspective of the people who create innovative options in the bottom-up process is generally smaller than the domain of the top-down decision makers. A man who proposes an investment for efficiency in a manufacturing plant perceives his factory as the domain, whilst the manager

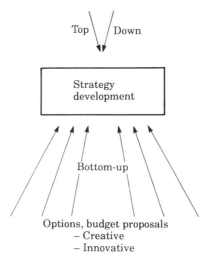

Figure 1.4 *'Planning' –decision routes*

who is responsible for the integrated manufacturing and marketing operation, and who cares about the total budget of that operation, has a much wider domain.

Secondly there is the language problem. Top-down proposals are qualitative or only broadly quantitative in nature and are based on the desired strategy. Bottom-up proposals, on the other hand, are specified in quantitative terms and are not necessarily based on the desired strategy. The bottom-up process deals with risk and reward in a quantitative way (for example by using discounted cash flow and sensitivities) whilst a top-down strategic proposal initially deals with them more qualitatively.

Both bottom-up and top-down are vulnerable to champions for ideas, stimulated by the 'designer-genes' working in the direction of project and technology push. We all know examples of this type of process. The Concorde example from the aircraft industry could serve as a very valid one. The counterforce to this type of planning and decision-making process needs to be a dispassionate review of the options.

Strategy development takes place at the interface of top-down and bottom-up and should be based on a proper communication in a non-advocative atmosphere in which risks and rewards play a central role. The process followed to realize this is described after a few comments on the notions of risk and reward.

Risk and reward

Risk and reward are a function of the long-term goals and the uncertainty in our business environment. The greater the uncertainty in the environment the greater the potential risk we are taking in achieving that goal. Higher rewards unfortunately call for more risk taking. Let us reflect for a moment on how this is dealt with in bottom-up decision-making processes. There the most widely used instrument is the 'discounted cash flow method' which leads to the 'earning power' of an investment. In order to complete the calculation of an earning power the following variables, amongst others, have to be used:

- Phasing and amount of investment
- Fixed and variable costs
- Service life assumed for the investment
- Fiscal depreciation rates
- Tax rate
- Inflation rates during the service life
- Residual value of investment
- Proceeds
- Interest rates

For all the variables assumptions reflecting a variable degree of uncertainty have to be made. The resultant earning power figure is based on an accumulation of uncertainties. Of course calculations can be done which will measure the change in the earning power if one of the assumptions is altered, but this methodology has shortcomings. The calculation allows for one uncertainty at a time to be introduced into the base case, ignoring the fact that if one variable changes others will change as well. Despite this there is a tendency to talk about earning powers as if they are firm indications of future rewards. We tend to ignore the uncertainties in the world which we have defined around the project. It is not intended to throw the discounted cash flow (DCF) method out of the window. It has validity, not least because it provides us with a way of communicating about investment choices. However, capital budgeting models based on projections of discounted cash flows are not the best way to make investment decisions in large organizations.

There are three principal reasons why these models are insufficient. Firstly, it is rather easy to find the right planning assumptions to give projects the required earning power. (If you do not like the result of the first calculation, just change one of the assumptions until the result is acceptable!) Secondly, projects are normally only evaluated on an incremental basis rather than on an integral basis also. Thirdly, proposed budgets in themselves are often a reflection of unrelated, available investment options, rather than a selection which is derived from the strategy of the corporation.

In taking strategic decisions, management has to deal firstly with uncertainty in an explicit way in order to reveal risks. Secondly, they must deal with the business on an integral basis rather than just on an incremental project-by-project basis. Thirdly, they should deal with the criteria for decision-making such as reward and risk criteria. For this a process is required which is based on the identification of the perceptions of top management, the decision-makers themselves. It must be a simple process which deals with key uncertainties and key elements of strategy. The process should enable a direct interaction between the bottom-up and the top-down decision-makers in which the corporate planning staff can play a facilitating role.

The Shell experience

Shell Nederland is a sizeable member of the Shell Group of companies having large oil and gas exploration and production activities and substantial oil and chemicals manufacturing and marketing operations. It has experimented with such a process of strategy development over the last few years. Figure 1.5 gives a schematic presentation of all the elements which we wish to mobilize in what can be called a 'Strategy Review'. The right hand side deals with the long-term objectives: the strategies which

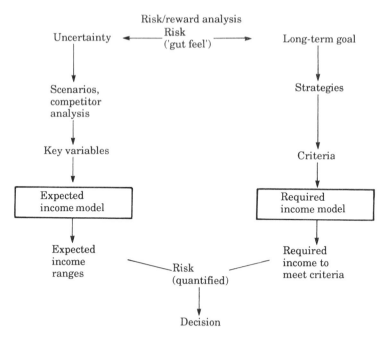

Figure 1.5   *Strategic decision method*

are available in order to achieve those objectives and the relevant criteria to choose between the strategies. This side is normative and should help to answer the question: 'What income levels are required for the strategies to achieve the corporate objective?'

The left hand side covers the company's business environment. Uncertainty is dealt with first by developing archetype scenarios. These are not specific to the evaluation of individual projects or strategic options but are broadbrush economic environments valid for the total company. In a second phase the important factors for a project are defined. They are called the 'key variables' of the project and are defined within each scenario. Historic price and cost analyses, industry modelling and competitor analysis all play an important part in choosing the key variables and their possible ranges.

The experience is that most businesses' income variations are determined by changes in only a small number of key variables. For example, whilst a scenario would describe a possible future development of exchange rates, the key variable approach will identify the impact of an exchange rate fluctuation of x per cent on the business result. With the introduction of this concept the ability to mobilize the perceptions of the management has been realized. Each member of the management team contributes his own perception of how each of the key variables might develop within each scenario over the planning period. The result of the process will be that the expected income will not give a forecast of income in the traditional form of a single line (the 'illusion of certainty') but will result in a range of income expectations based on an explicit statement of the key uncertainties as seen by the decision-makers. The resultant range can be compared with the company norms resulting from the right hand side to obtain a broad indication of risks and rewards.

Summing up
On the right hand side the vision of the decision-makers has been mobilized by an explicit statement of their own objectives. All the strategic options are reviewed in an ordered fashion in alternative strategies. Criteria which are consistent with the long-term objectives and strategic options have been reviewed and selected.

On the left hand side the uncertainty in the business environment has been reviewed and the decision-makers have offered their perceptions about future developments of the relevant uncertainty through the combination of key variables and scenarios.

Both sides lead to expressions of results: on the right hand side in the form of requirements and on the left hand side in the form of expectations expressed in a range. Iterations between the left hand side and the right hand side show how options tackle the relevant uncertainty in a different way.

It is possible now to review the various strategies against the same background of uncertainty and make a rough comparison of the risk and reward profiles which will enable management to select their preferred strategy.

Table 1.1 below provides a Case Example which illustrates the use of scenario/strategy payoff matrix.

The link with the formal Business Plan

What has been described is a new planning process which is flexible and somewhat informal. It better supports strategic decision-making require-ments because it is based on a high degree of top management involvement. A distinction can be made between formal business planning and these flexible processes. Formal planning responds to basic company reporting requirements. The larger the company the heavier the burden of the formal planning process will become. Budgets also form a part of the formal business plan and are expressed within a single, formal 'scenario' of budget premises. Although the investment proposals are presented and consoli-dated in terms of the budget premises they remain strategic options. As such they are not judged against the premises. They have been tested against a set of archetype scenarios, further developed by project-specific

Table 1.1   *The scenario/strategy payoff matrix*
A Case Example:

Business:	Manufacturing and Marketing
Long-term objective:	To continue to participate in this business on a profitable basis
Investment criterion:	10 per cent rate of return on net assets after tax
Key variables:	7, which can be identified and which describe actual income variances with a 95 per cent accuracy. They are descriptions of: ● raw material cost ● product prices ● level of activity (sales volume)
Alternative strategies:	Base Case. No further investment, let existing business run. (Figure 1.6: Base Case) Strategy A. Replacement of capacity to manufacture products from raw materials on a more efficient basis than with present configuration, combined with an investment which will increase number of marketing outlets. (Figure 1.7: Strategy).
Base Case:	The expected income range is calculated on the basis of the present configuration (no further investment). The managers' perceptions about the future development of the key variables are mobilized by questionnaires and become the input of the expected income model. (Exhibit: Base Case, Figure 1.6a, expected income model.) The required income depends on the expected fixed costs and a 10 per cent charge on the existing net assets. (Figure 1.6b: Base Case, required income model.)

Comparing the expected income range with the required income, it is clear that this business is unlikely to meet its longer term objective without a change of strategy (Figure 1.6c and d.)

Strategy A:

The expected income range is calculated on the basis of the present configuration until the new investment is operational, and on the revised configuration thereafter. As a result of the plant change and the increased number of outlets the income expectations are improved against the same background of uncertainty. (Figure 1.7a: Strategy A, expected income model.)

The required income depends on the expected fixed costs and a 10 per cent charge on the existing net assets at present, and on the additional investment of Strategy A. (Figure 1.7b: Strategy A, required income model.)

Comparing the expected income range with the required income, there appears to be a good chance that the long term objective will be met by following Strategy A. (Figure 1.7c and d: Strategy A.)

Comparison of strategies:

Against the same background of uncertainty as perceived by the decision makers the question to invest (Strategy A) or not to invest (Base Case) is answered by a clear indictation of a better risk and reward profile for the investment case. As a result of a better processing configuration and more outlets, both volume and income expectations have improved and show a better position in comparison with the new income requirement.

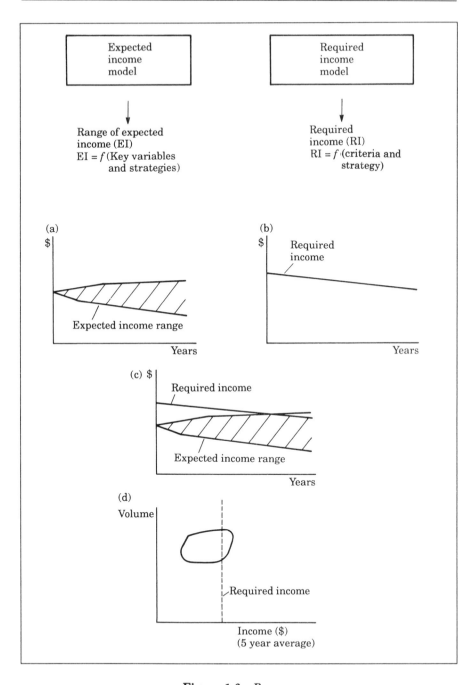

Figure 1.6 *Base case*

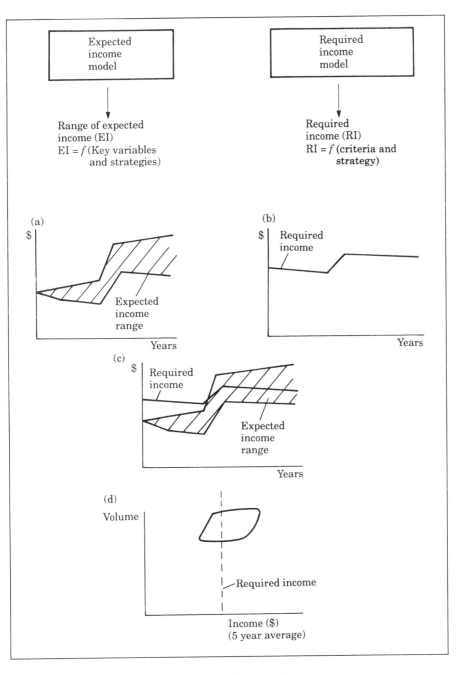

Expected
income
model

Required
income
model

Range of expected
income (EI)
EI = *f* (Key variables
          and strategies)

Required
income (RI)
RI = *f* (criteria and
          strategy)

(a)

$

Expected
income
range

Years

(b)

$ Required
     income

Years

(c) $ Required
          income

Expected
income
range

Years

(d)

Volume

Required income

Income ($)
(5 year average)

Figure 1.7   *Strategy A*

Formal planning process	Flexible planning process
Implict company objective (financial)	Management chooses explicit objectives
Implicit criterion is financial	Management chooses criteria to assess strategic options against achievement
Strategy formulation is merely addition of separate, good proposals	Strategy formulation is a coherent coherent process aiming to achieve explicit objectives
Proposals evaluated against single set of budget premises	Strategic options evaluated within set of archetype scenarios
Fixed values assumed within the budget premises	Specific key variables chosen within scenarios
Accountant's reflection of future results (single values)	Management's reflection of future results (range of uncertainty)
All aspects of risk hidden in a general discount factor	The trade-offs between criteria and risk/reward explicitly made
Supports the production of company reports	Supports the making of strategic decisions

Figure 1.8   *Formal and flexible planning processes*

key variables, and have been approved. The budget procedure is followed after the decisions have been made to link the chosen company strategy with formal reporting requirements.

Conclusion

Formal planning restricts the use of flexible planning processes. This is more likely in large companies with heavy reporting requirements and bureaucratic overloads. Attempting to introduce scenarios into formal planning may only add to the confusion.

Corporate planners must gear their activities towards the strategic decision-making needs of the company's management. The experience gained in Shell Nederland has shown that these needs are more effectively met by the use of flexible planning. Scenarios play a role in these processes as one of the key elements of a coherent framework in which reward and risk are central.

The successful introduction of flexible planning processes will enable management to adopt planning again as an integral part of their own responsibility.

2 Analysing the business portfolio in Black & Decker Europe

Robert Walker, Corporate Planning Officer, Black & Decker Europe

This case study deals with the implementation of the portfolio management technique in Black & Decker's European operations. The adaptation and development of the charts described in the case study were carried out in Black & Decker's European headquarters. However, the examples and figures described below are for illustration only and are not related in any way to Black & Decker's own performance or any part of its business. Although the basic growth share matrix was introduced to the Corporation by a firm of consultants in the mid 1970s, it was decided after a trial period not to continue with the technique at a Corporate level. However, while European management was initially sceptical as to the value of using portfolio management as an aid for making strategic decisions, it did recognize that the classic Boston Consulting Group portfolio chart was a useful method of displaying the characteristics and market environment experienced by a number of different product groups.

The European Policy Board therefore agreed that the Corporate Planning Officer (European Operations) could examine the possibility of using portfolio analysis as part of the established Long Range Planning cycle. The Board stated that use of portfolio management would have to:

- Be accepted and understood by operating managers as a useful planning tool.
- Be implemented internally without external consultants.
- Be adapted to the specific requirements and circumstances of the Group.
- Have demonstrable benefits to the Group beyond being purely a strategic planning technique.

Organization

Throughout the Corporation Black & Decker operated with a very decentralized management structure and had a philosophy of having 'strength at the periphery'. Thus European Operations had an autonomy which was unusual among major US companies. Beyond this, within European Operations, the managers of the thirty or so companies in the group also had a high degree of independence. This philosophy was a major contributor to the successful operation of the Group from its early days and throughout the period under discussion.

Nevertheless, as the company grew, some degree of coordination at a European level was required. By the early 1970s there were over thirty companies in the Group operating not only in Western Europe but also in Africa and the Middle East, and joint ventures in Eastern Europe and India. In Western Europe there were thirteen major marketing companies, eleven manufacturing sites in six countries and an increasing amount of cross-sourcing between the marketing companies and manufacturers.

Corporate planning

Corporate planning in the European Group was coordinated by the Corporate Planning Officer working in the small European headquarters in Brussels. This position was initially set up to collect and review the information required to establish the long-term sourcing requirements for the various factories. This exercise quickly developed into a full long-range plan which included forecasts of sales and thus product gaps, of profits and of capital expenditure requirements. A simple planning model was developed for testing the impact of various alternative forecasts and eventually the long-range plan covering four years became the preliminary exercise from which the annual budgets were developed.

This was very successful as a Long Range Forecast and provided useful guidance to management and operations. However, without full consideration of the market and competitive situation and the company's response, the forecast could not be considered as a Strategic Planning Document. It was for this additional analysis that the Portfolio Management technique was adapted and developed specifically for Black & Decker in Europe by the Corporate Planning Officer.

Practical Portfolio Management

When considering the practical application of portfolio management for Black & Decker Europe it was of paramount importance to remember at all times that the business was run by the management of the company, and not by a technique, or a series of charts.

Once this principle was recognized many of the management's objections to portfolio analysis and also many of the pitfalls associated with theory disappeared. These problems were however replaced by a host of practical difficulties many of which are experienced in implementing any planning system. This case study seeks to show how these difficulties were dealt with at Black & Decker and, indeed, how these problems were in several instances turned to good effect.

Initially the technique was considered in order to stimulate strategic thought within the top management group. However in Black & Decker the technique was expanded into a broader planning system, and not only was the quality of the long-range plans of the operating companies and the Group as a whole greatly improved, but in addition both staff and operating managers were provided with a valuable data bank on market and competitive conditions across a wide range of products and geographical areas.

By emphasizing the practical benefits of arraying the different characteristic of businesses on the original growth share matrix rather than the theory behind the technique, it was possible to show operating managers that there was a purpose in the exercise and a validity in the conclusions which could be drawn from such a display. The technique was extended to become a series of four charts to portray visually not only the current environment but also the managers' proposed response to the situation. Thus operating managers became involved in the planning system as a whole.

This set of four planning charts (which will be described below) became the focal point to the planning cycle in the Group. This not only stimulated strategic thinking in the European office but also provided a system which became the framework for planning throughout operations and a method by which to validate and control the plans throughout the Group.

The collection of a mass of data on markets and competitors is a necessary part of preparing a valid portfolio analysis. This heavy workload is frequently underestimated and underplayed in any description of portfolio planning. However the ways in which this data can be displayed and used by staff and operating management can, if done properly, turn what could be an exercise in 'paralysis by analysis' into a display of 'information for innovation'. The benefit of such a base of data to operations was an additional way of obtaining the commitment of operating managers to both the long range plans and also to the continuing improvement of the quality of the data supplied.

Without the goodwill, assistance, experience and commitment of the operating managers any portfolio analysis will run the risk of being grossly inaccurate and any strategies resulting from it will be invalid and impractical to implement. At Black & Decker these risks were minimized by maintaining a practical approach to portfolio management.

Constraints on Portfolio Analysis

Before describing the set of four planning charts themselves it is worth-while examining the reasons why it was necessary and advantageous to expand the original portfolio analysis technique in the light of the experience gained in practice. The Business Portfolio Concept[1] and the underlying 'experience curve effect'[2] were described and illustrated by Barry Hedley in two articles published in *Long Range Planning Journal* some years ago.

The limitations of the concept and theory have been discussed in various articles. However some of the specific problems that had to be overcome when adapting the technique to be a practical operating planning system were:

- The business units have to be defined.
- The validity of the data is at best variable.
- The growth share matrix does not by itself show how the company intends to respond to the environment in terms of sales.
- The response in terms of returns and profits is similarly not portrayed.
- Only one competitor is considered in each business unit in the growth share matrix.
- A full profile of competitors is not provided.
- The different characteristics of fragmented, as opposed to concentrated, markets are not differentiated.
- Differing market and competitive situations in a multinational environment are not considered.

Business unit definition

This is a critical requirement for any business, not only those wishing to use the portfolio analysis technique. To the theorist the task is very complex and much has been written on the problems of definition and the importance of making the right grouping for strategic business units. Abell and Hammond give a very good example of the problems of defining business units in their book *Strategic Market Planning*[3].

The important factors from a practical point of view are:

- that each business unit has some unique market characteristics, such as growth, competitive position, or of course, in the nature of the product itself;
- that management recognize and agree the unit definitions;
- that data is readily available on the agreed business units.

In practice most companies have business grouping for reporting and managerial purposes. For the theorist again these may sometimes not be what he regards as ideal. Nevertheless they do represent current management thinking and frequently offer the only easily obtainable analysis of data available within the company. To use any other groups not only implies a questioning of management's abilities but also requires a large amount of effort to restate the current information. This causes antagonism to the exercise from operating managers and makes the information upon which the analyses are based increasingly suspect. This is because it will be unrecognizable to operating managers and inevitably suffer from inaccuracies caused by using the data in combinations other than those for which they are normally used and checked in the day-to-day operating environment. For these reasons it was decided to keep the existing business groups and definitions used in Black & Decker's operating companies.

It was also decided to limit the number of business units that each chart should display to a maximum of twelve to fifteen. More than this and the charts became incomprehensible, and in any case managers would have had extreme difficulty trying to assess alternatives impacting on more than this number of units. In practice most companies limit the number of groupings for which managers are responsible and receive information. Obviously each of the dozen businesses for which the Board of Directors is responsible may in turn contain a dozen 'sub-businesses'. These of course can be the subject of another series of charts for use by the next level of management.

Validity of data

For strategic planning it was agreed that the data used did not have to be 100 per cent 'accountancy' accurate. What was required was consistent information upon which to identify the differences between business units and upon which to assess strategic alternatives.

The charts themselves were therefore designed and used to show trends and comparative positions rather than fine accuracy. The only proviso was that it was important that operating management could recognize the information displayed. Even though the information used in the first planning cycle was weak, management recognized the value of the exercise, and accuracy was later improved by use of cross checks both against competitive data and against data collected from a number of locations. For instance as well as normal market research, which was accurate to a greater or lesser extent depending on the product, market and geographical area, use was also made of data from import–export statistics and trade associations. Even though these sources were not wholly satisfactory the trends were what was more important than the raw data itself.

Planning Charts

Growth share matrix
In Black & Decker this chart was considered more of a method of displaying the positioning of a number of businesses rather than a panacea for running the corporation. For this reason, the well-known growth share matrix was slightly modified (Figure 2.1). In many papers on the technique the break point on the horizontal axis is plotted at the point where the company is equal to the largest competitor. In practice this share position can be highly competitive and unprofitable. Therefore the

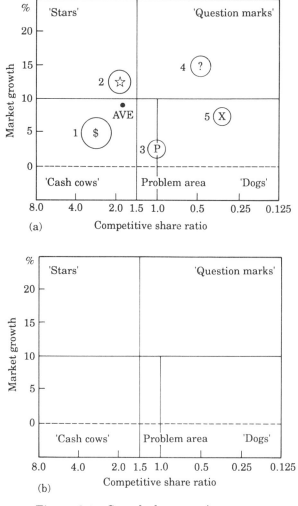

Figure 2.1 *Growth share matrix*

major break line was moved to one and one-half times the nearest competitor. Positions better than this can more truly be considered dominant. The line at one times is left however for reference. This format is in fact that described by Barry Hedley[1].

The company's overall growth objective was set by senior management once they had considered what they wanted the company to be in the future. It depended on the markets in which the company did or would have liked to participate, on the economic environment, what was required to capitalize on productivity increases, etc. In adapting the original growth share matrix it was found useful to define the break on the vertical axis as the company's overall growth objective, rather than a theoretical break between high and low growth markets. In the example the line is 10% which, in fact, equates to what many consider the break between high and low growth.

If the 'centre of gravity' of all the businesses in the company's portfolio falls along this line, or above it, the company has only to keep pace with the overall market to achieve its growth objectives. However, as is more likely, if it falls below the line, the company has to respond in some more positive way. It is this response that is portrayed on the sales growth share gain chart which will be described later.

The technique does not differentiate between fragmented markets and concentrated markets. For instance, a company could be the market leader with twice the sales of its nearest rival and only have, say, a 15% brand share, whereas for another product a company might have to have over 50% market share to be twice the size of its nearest rival. On the portfolio chart both businesses would be plotted at the same point on the comparative share scale.

Next, when forecasting market share changes it is most important to consider competitive reaction. Gains may come from the number one competitor or they may come from other major competitors or again from a shake out amongst the smaller companies. At the same time a significant change in share between competitors may be anticipated, which of itself may not affect the plotting on the portfolio chart but is nevertheless of strategic importance. Note how Japanese companies have come from insignificant share positions to relentlessly take share over the years. The growth share matrix would not consider the activities of such companies until they have already become the major competitors.

Finally, under this heading the technique takes no account of the comparative market sizes of the businesses being plotted. Although the contribution to sales of the company itself are portrayed by the size of the circles this may bear no relationship at all to the size of the market and the opportunity it represents.

It was for these reasons that having decided to use portfolio management it was apparent that data would have to be collected on all major competitors and on the total market itself for each of the business units. Only in this way would management feel happy that the data summarized on the growth share matrix had a firm detailed base which could be used to support the strategic decisions being made.

Market and competitor analysis chart
Even with twelve business units each with say five major competitors and some local competitors and reports from ten geographical locations, around 750 pieces of information would be collected. In Black & Decker, with more competitors and data both in value and units as well as subdivisions of the unit data into products within business units, over 5000 data items were collected each year within European Operations.

One reason for the expansion of the data base, which could perhaps have been maintained at under 1000 data items, was the uses that both staff and operational management found for the information, particularly once it had been collected for a number of years.

By keeping the data on computer, a wide variety of analyses and graphical representations of trends and of strengths and weaknesses of competitors became possible. The market/competitor analysis chart (Figure 2.2) was found particularly useful in highlighting important factors in the market place, the subanalysis of products within the business and in particular in answering many of the objections to the pure growth share matrix described above.

The example portrays the market and competitive situation for five products with the consolidated position of the business at the top of the

Business	Market Size	Market Growth	Competitor shares	Ratio	Ref.
Total	3500	8.5	A28 B14 C12 D10 E8 F4 O24	2.0	B
1	1000	5.0	A45 B8 C15 D11 O21	3.0	C
5	1000	7.5	A10 B30 C17 D15 O28	0.33	B
2	750	12.5	A36 B11 C13 F18 O22	2.0	F
4	500	15.0	A16 B8 D18 E32 O26	0.5	E
3	250	2.5	A40 E40 O20	1.0	E

Figure 2.2 *Market and competitor analysis*

chart. It is an expansion of the situation shown in the growth share matrix (Figure 2.1).

Firstly the total market size is stated and products within the business below the total can be ranked in order of size. Next the forecast market growth as per the growth share matrix is given, The bars themselves represent 100% of the market and are divided in proportion with the market shares that each competitor has in the particular product. The competitors are given in the order in which they hold shares in the total consolidated market. Finally the comparative share per the portfolio management technique is given with the reference letter of the major competitor.

Working through the example the following can be seen:

(a) The market size of the businesses vary from 1000 to 250 units; this size not being proportional to the sales of company A as shown on the growth share matrix.

(b) The growth rates vary round the average 8.5% from 15% down to 2.5%, but much of company A's strength is in the slower growing markets of products 1 and 3.

(c) The bars themselves show both the strengths and weaknesses of individual competitors in different products and also the degree of fragmentation in the markets. Although company A is the overall market leader for the consolidated business, it can be seen that this is due to its strong position in the major product. In other products it has a weaker position.

(d) Competitor B is not the major competitor in any market except product 5 where it is the market leader. Also of note is the specialist competitor F in product 2.

(e) Competitors C and E do not compete against each other in any product. If one was acquired by the other, this could constitute a major threat.

(f) It can be seen that the market for products 4 and 5 are rather more fragmented than others (0 being the total of competitors with less than 4% each).

(g) The last column with the ratio gives the position the product would have on the growth share matrix comparative share column. It also shows the diversity of competitors against which this measure is made by use of the competitor reference letter. Note that competitor E is a leader in the only markets in which it competes.

As with other techniques it is always useful and illuminating to compare data over a period of time. By superimposing the bar charts for one year over those for either an earlier period or for the end of a forecast later period, it is easy to see the changes in share that have taken place or those forecast for the planning period. This use of the chart was found particularly important in Black & Decker for describing both the historical and the forecast evolution of market environments.

Full competitor profile

The bar chart (Figure 2.2) provided a good view of each competitor's strengths and weaknesses in the markets in which it competed with Black & Decker. However in many instances competitor's product ranges did not totally overlap. Companies such as AEG and Bosch with very wide business interest beyond portable electric tools were major competitors. It was therefore most important to build up a profile of the total activities of each competitor: its manufacturing policies as well as its marketing posture and also its financial strength.

Regulations on the publishing of data vary considerably around the world. A very large amount of information has to be provided for stock exchange and other requirements, for instance in Japan and the United States, and this is all readily available to the public. Whereas in Germany it is frequently very difficult to obtain any detailed financial data for companies, particularly if they are privately owned.

Nevertheless, even in countries where financial data is hard to come by, most companies do provide a certain amount of information such as company brochures to improve public relations, and of course catalogues. These, together with articles appearing in the press and other sources of information, will usually at least provide a reasonable insight into the nature of the competitors' policies and products.

This background was found to be most important when assessing competitive reaction to the company's own strategy and operational plans.

Sales growth/Share gain chart

Given that the growth share matrix was principally a method of displaying a number of businesses so that management could make strategic decisions and more easily assess alternatives, it was logical that management's response to the opportunities and challenges should also be displayed in related charts. An adaption of the sales growth/share gain chart described in Abell & Hammond's book[4] was used for portraying this in terms of sales.

Where the growth of a company's portfolio of businesses in average falls below the market growth as shown on the growth share matrix there are three alternatives by which it can achieve its growth targets. It can:

(*a*) move into new markets;
(*b*) stimulate the markets in which it participates to a higher level of growth by its own strategies;
(*c*) take market share.

The sales growth share gain chart (Figure 2.3) plots the market growth from the growth share matrix on the vertical axis and the company's projected sales growth on the horizontal axis. Thus any products plotted below the diagonal line is planned to take share and any product above the line is forecast to lose share. The vertical and horizontal lines midway through the chart are plotted at the company's sales growth target to give an indication of which products exceed this and which do not.

A comparison with the growth share matrix (Figure 2.1) shows in this example a fairly classic response to the company's portfolio, with share being maintained for products 1 and 2, share being taken by products 3 and 4 and product 5 being de-emphasized.

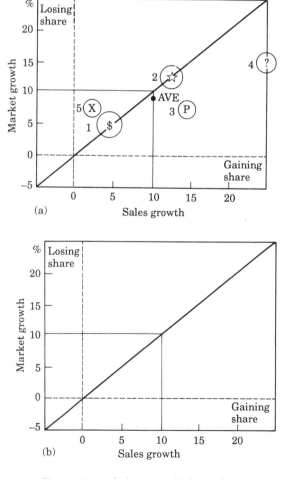

Figure 2.3 *Sales growth/share change*

The placing of product 3 on the sales gain chart is unusual in that the market growth plot on this chart is higher than that on the growth share matrix. This implies that the company, by its own efforts, intends to affect the natural growth of the market. This may be by product innovation for instance.

Whereas the circles in the growth share matrix represent the sales balance at the beginning of the planning period, those in the share gain chart represent the contribution expected at the end of the period. This gives a visual representation of the change in sales mix expected over the period.

One further adaptation of the charts is the recognition that companies may actually participate in declining markets or even have negative sales growth projections. Thus the dotted lines represent the zero growth level, giving room to plot such businesses below that point on the chart.

Profitability analysis chart
Management needs to consider not only its marketing response by way of sales growth and share changes to the environment as portrayed in the growth share matrix, but also its response in financial terms as measured by returns and profitability, and so two further charts were developed by Black & Decker to show this response. In Black & Decker Europe the ratio of income before tax (IBT) to sales was the measure most commonly used by operating management. In addition many products used common assets and a split of capital employed by product group would have required a lot of arbitrary allocation. For these reasons IBT to sales was the measure initially chosen to portray the company's financial response to its portfolio. Other companies could use return on assets or cash flows just as well. Once again the most important criteria was that the measure had to be not only meaningful but also easily recognized by operating managers.

The profitability analysis chart (Figure 2.4) plots the planned IBT to sales ratio on the horizontal axis and the growth in profitability that achievement of this ratio will require on the vertical axis. The break lines again come at the average point of the company's overall objectives in terms of profitability and growth in profits.

The chart bears some resemblance to the growth share matrix being divided into quantiles and is used in reference to it. However, the businesses will not necessarily fall in exactly the same quantiles on both charts even in ideal theoretical situations. Businesses with dominant market shares can be expected to have high profitability, and appear in the same quantiles in both charts, with those in low growth markets usually having only moderate growth in profit and those with high market growth reflected in high sales consequently having high profit growth. But for those businesses not having a dominant position careful

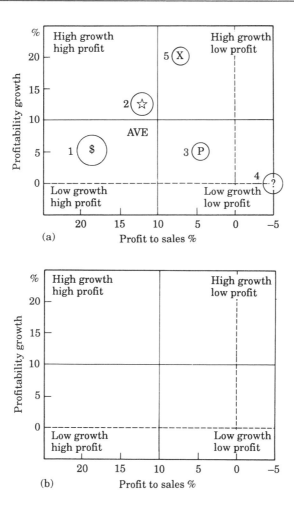

Figure 2.4 *Profitability analysis*

profit planning as well as consideration of the profit impact of the marketing strategy will be required. For instance, a 'dog' business which is to be harvested may show rapid increase in profitability although it might not achieve above average profits. On the other hand a 'question mark' business may be planned to lose money with no growth in profitability.

The size of the circles on this chart refer to the current proportion of profit contributed by each business. They can thus be compared to the current proportion of sales as represented by the circles on the growth share matrix.

Profitability growth/change chart

This chart (Figure 2.5) parallels the sales growth/share gain chart and the growth in sales is plotted on the horizontal axis, being taken from that chart. The profit growth is plotted on the vertical axis and is similarly taken from the profitability analysis chart. The result of this plotting is that any business falling below the diagonal line is planned to have a decrease in profitability during the period, whereas those above the line will have improving profitability.

The size of circles on this chart are the projected contribution to profits planned for the end of the period and thus parallel the sales contribution

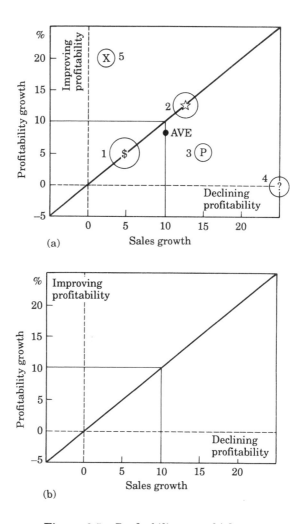

Figure 2.5   *Profitability growth/change*

shown in the sales growth chart. In the example the businesses 1 and 2 are planned to maintain profitability. Business 5 shows a rapid improvement in profitability as part of a strategy to harvest that segment, while the other products show declining profitability: business 4 to fund improvement in share and business 3 to fund a total change in the market.

By comparing the profitability growth chart with the sales growth chart it is possible to identify areas which raise questions as to the practicality of the strategic response. For instance in theory share gains can be expensive to obtain in terms of loss of profitability. Therefore for businesses plotted on the share gain chart below the diagonal line (i.e. as taking share) theory says they should also appear below the diagonal line on the profit growth chart (i.e. as suffering a decline in profitability). However again one must stress that where the charts do not conform to theory it does not mean that the strategy is wrong. It only alerts management to possible difficult areas.

The planning chart set

Having looked at the individual charts it can be seen that they are designed to be reviewed as a set. When describing the individual charts some comparisons between the business positions were described. Having all the charts as a set (Figure 2.6) the strategic responses to the portfolio can be reviewed both in aspects of sales and profits and also most importantly the differing strategic roles that each business plays in the portfolio of the total business.

The charts shown describe a theoretical situation. In practice there will almost certainly be inconsistencies in the strategies for business segments. It is the ability to see quickly those inconsistencies against a theoretic benchmark and to understand the reasons for them that made these charts useful in a practical operating environment. Although not covering 'risk' as such, the charts thus highlight areas of possible vulnerability. The size of the risk is to some extent shown by the relative size of the circles on the charts.

Looking at the charts in the theoretical example the following strategies can be seen:

1 A 'cash cow' business where the strategy is to maintain market share and profitability and keep this business as the major profit earner with well above average profitability.
2 A 'star' business where protection of share is of paramount importance if necessary at the expense of profitability but with profits still remaining above average. With the growth over the period this group also becomes a major profit contributor.

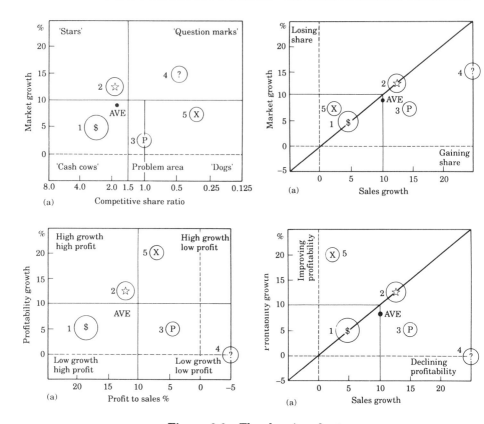

Figure 2.6   *The planning chart*

3   A 'problem' business where a specific action is planned both to change the nature of the market place and to take share. This will have a heavy impact on profits. These are planned to decline to a level of half the corporate average requirement.

4   A 'question mark' business where a rapid increase in share is required and where profits at this time are not important and losses are accepted provided they are accompanied by share gains and rapid sales growth.

5   A 'dog' business which will be de-emphasized, with share being lost and profits harvested so long as the business remains in the portfolio. Nevertheless it is recognized that the profits are likely even so to remain below average for the corporation.

This theoretic example shows a reasonable balance of the portfolio between the business segments. In practice managements have to consider not only the correct strategy for each product group, but also how to deal with imbalances within the mix of the businesses in the total group. Again the charts highlight these imbalances and give management relatively easily assimilated data from which to start to decide on their overall strategies. The average point for the total business is marked on each chart. This shows that while the markets in which the company participates do not reach its growth requirement with share gains this growth will be achieved. The share gains will require some overall loss of profitability. However the company's average profitability will remain above its required level.

Conclusion

This case study has described the implementation of portfolio management in Black & Decker Europe, the problems encountered in installing the system and how these were turned to advantage by the adaptation and extension of the original BCG growth share matrix. The major factors in the successful implementation were:

1 The premise that management was managing the company and not a firm of consultants or their theories. Although it is recognized that in many instances consultants play a valuable part in establishing planning systems.
2 The techniques and displays must be simple to understand and relevant to the business.
3 The information used had to be easily recognizable by the operating managers and be presented in such a manner as to help them in running the business and, if possible, provide an additional insight into the problems they faced.

The examples described have, in the main, assumed that the charts summarized business segment data for one company or a consolidated group. However as the system was implemented in a multinational environment it was quickly realized that the charts lent themselves equally well to displaying a number of countries' data for one business segment as they did for several businesses in one country or company.

The questions raised would have a different bias but are nonetheless important. For instance on the bar chart (Figure 2.2) if the numbers referred to countries and not product the questions might be:

(a) What if company E operating only in countries 3 and 4 was to be acquired by company C which operates only in countries 1, 2 and 5?
(b) Is competitor F using country 2 as a test market and how and when will it move to a multinational situation?

Alternatively on the planning chart set, if the circles were an analysis of various countries' performance in one product area:

(a) Why are countries 1 and 2 so successful? Can the others learn from them?

(b) Has country 3 really done a thorough job in analysing the market and competitive situation, etc?

The system has now been in operation in Black & Decker Europe for a number of years and the data that has been collected to back up the main summary charts means that a wealth of information is available on trends, competitors, products and countries. Cross references can easily be obtained by integration programmes to help the many studies and investigation made both by staff and operating managers. This data would probably not have been collected had it not been a necessary prerequisite to preparing a valid meaningful portfolio analysis.

These are some of the reasons why the project was successful and was supported by operating managers. However the final word on all techniques must be that expressed by Dr Vesper in his letter to the *Long Range Planning Journal*.[5] In it he suggests that matrix displays are an impressive tool but nothing more, they can be used for a first orientation but that real strategic planning only starts at this point. His view can certainly be supported by the experiences gained in the implementation of the planning system described in this case study.

References

1 Hedley, B (February 1977), Strategy and the business portfolio. *Long Range Planning* **10**, 9–15.
2 Hedley, B. (December, 1976), A Fundamental Approach to Strategy Development. *Long Range Planning* **9**, 2-11.
3 Abell, D., Hammond, J. (1979), *Strategic Market Planning* (Chapter 8). Engelwood Cliffs, N.J. Prentice Hall.
4 Ibid Chapter 4.
5 Vesper, Dr V.D. (June 1983), Letter to Brief Case. *Long Range Planning* **16**, 119.

3 Setting corporate objectives and operational targets for the British Airports Authority

Don Turner, Privatization Director, British Airports Authority

The BAA (British Airports Authority) owns and operates seven airports in the United Kingdom, namely Heathrow, Gatwick and Stansted in the south east, and Glasgow, Edinburgh, Aberdeen and Prestwick in Scotland. When originally formed, the BAA had four airports: the three south east airports and Prestwick in Scotland. The Authority subsequently acquired Edinburgh in 1971, followed by Aberdeen and Glasgow in 1975 (see Figure 3.1).

The BAA employed 6987 staff as at 31 December 1985 and during the financial year 1984-5 it made a current cost trading profit of £72m on a turnover of some £362m. The BAA's capital employed amounted to £925m at 31 March 1985.

In the calendar year 1985, the BAA's seven airports handled 52.9 million passengers, 614,000 air transport movements and 729,000 tonnes of cargo. The number of passengers handled through BAA airports has nearly quadrupled since its formation, from 14 million in 1966-7 to almost 53 million in 1985. The vast majority of this growth has had to be accommodated at Heathrow and Gatwick, which together handled over 46 million passengers in 1985, compared with 13.8 million in 1966-7.

Background

In order to understand how the current corporate planning process has developed within the BAA, it is important to understand how the BAA is defined and constrained by law and its relationship with its 'owner', the Government.

Figure 3.1   *BAA airports*

As a nationalized industry the Authority was bound by the 1975 Airports Authority Act which stated 'it shall be the duty of the Authority to provide at its aerodromes such services and facilities as are in its opinion necessary or desirable for their operation'. The Act further stated that 'the Authority shall have regard for the development of air transport and to efficiency, economy and safety of operation'. The written consent of the Secretary of State was required before any new airport was acquired, any existing airport closed or air traffic control or other navigational services provided by the BAA. The Government also had reserve powers in respect of landing fees, a principal source of Authority income. A series of other constraints were also imposed upon the Authority ranging from External Financing Limits set by the Government, regulation of aircraft ground noise, safety, security and a legal requirement 'to provide adequate facilities for consultation with respect to matters affecting their interest' with users of aerodromes, local authorities and with other organizations representing the interests of persons concerned with the locality in which the aerodromes are situated.

The major corporate strategy of the Authority was therefore, to a considerable extent, constrained from the outset. We cannot ask in the classical sense 'what business ought we to be in?' – we know that already.

The option of major change or diversification that is available to private sector industries does not exist in the public sector. The Authority's primary objective, as agreed with Government, is 'to respond to the present and future needs of air transport in an efficient and profitable way by operating, planning and developing its airports so that air travellers and cargo may pass through safely, swiftly and as conveniently as possible.'

Subject to all statutory duties or powers applicable to the Authority from time to time, BAA operates within the general framework of the relationship between nationalized industries and Government. The present framework dates from a major review undertaken by the previous Government and set out in its White Paper of 1978 'The Nationalized Industries' (Cmnd. 7131). That review resulted in considerable emphasis being placed upon the role of each industry's corporate plan in establishing a better relationship with the sponsoring Department. Discussion of the corporate plan with Government was to provide the opportunity for an agreed strategic framework. The White Paper was also concerned with increasing accountability to Parliament and to the public. The Government asked each industry to include in its Annual Report the following:

- the main points in its corporate plan and any Government response to them;
- the financial targets agreed with Government;
- the cash limit;
- and any general or specific Government direction.

The Annual Report should also contain a statement of how well the business was measuring up to targets and objectives agreed with Goverment and also to its own performance and service aims. Unlike industries in the private sector, the Authority is therefore required publicly to announce its targets and the main strategic issues agreed with Government.

The corporate planning process

The Authority has always had well-developed physical planning procedures due to the long lead times involved in obtaining planning permission for airport facilities, their construction and commissioning. Prior to 1976, the Corporate Plan contained little more than the budget forecasts with no qualitative discussions of policies. In 1976, in anticipation of Government requirements, a more comprehensive plan was drawn up, which has set the pattern for subsequent plans produced on an annual up-dating cycle.

In 1982, following a major re-appraisal of responsibilities and increased delegation of powers within the Authority, it was decided that the corporate planning process should be expanded to become pro-active: be a stronger stimulator of new ideas and develop further the options open to the business.

The corporate planning process described here relates to the role of the BAA as a nationalized industry. It is not aimed at privatization, which became Government policy only in June 1985.

Objectives/targets

At the start of the corporate planning cycle, the Authority has two major inputs: the objectives/targets agreed with Government, and the traffic forecasts.

The objectives, which were formalized at the Government's request in 1982, are based upon the 1975 Airports Authority Act and are a statement of the overall framework within which the Authority operates. It is not expected that the objectives will alter much over time unless the 1975 Act is amended. The targets are a set of specific, quantified goals to be achieved over a three-year period. Targets are set for the rate of return, cost reduction and manpower productivity. Given the importance of these targets to the corporate planning process, it is necessary to understand why they are set (see Appendix).

Airports are natural monopolies and true competition cannot exist between them. This can be proven by considering two vital aspects of air transport. The first is that airports are not involved at first hand in the selling of the air transport product and therefore do not have any direct control over the use of the product that they are supplying. It is the airlines who compete directly for business and the airports' role has been to provide an infrastructure which enables that competition to take place as freely as possible. The second is that the ability of existing airports to compete with each other is extremely constrained by their geography, by their capacity and by the range of services which airlines offer from them. The constraints are so severe that it is difficult to find any examples of genuine inter-airport competition as opposed to competition between airlines using different airports. It should be emphasized that this absence of true competition is not the result of airports pursuing non-competitive policies but an inevitable consequence of their role.

Furthermore, freedom of entry to the market is unachievable in terms of practicability, due to the difficulties of obtaining planning consent for airport development. Hence, for a number of reasons, it is difficult to see airports as other than monopolies.

The Government and the Authority have therefore sought to create proxies for normal competitive pressures and have agreed targets and performance aims which the Authority should achieve over a three-year period. It is these targets that are fed in at the start of the corporate planning process.

Traffic forecasts

The second major input to the start of the corporate planning process is the forecasts of passenger traffic.

The development and operation of airports is a highly capital intensive business. The BAA is currently investing around £160m per annum in new facilities, which is a high figure in relation to a turnover of £362m. The investment risk lies in the fact that airport facilities can serve no purpose other than that for which they were originally intended, nor can they be easily disposed of or moved if they are created in the wrong manner. Good forward planning, therefore, is fundamental to our business future. The planning timescale has to reflect the long lead times involved in airport development; i.e. eight–ten years for a new terminal; and at least twelve years for a new airport or a major expansion of an existing one. So our planning horizon is necessarily a distant one, and because of its distance the paths to it are infinitely variable.

It follows that long-term forecasts are more than usually important to the BAA and as a result considerable effort is expended to make them as good as possible.

Traffic is broken down by various market categories: domestic, European, intercontinental, scheduled and charter operations, business and leisure travel. In each area we attempt to explain the reasons for historic growth over a wide range of factors, from the usual economic components of income growth to sociological changes. At the same time we try and assess the likely changes in the techniques and tools of the industry.

The annual forecasts are prepared for the individual airports within the system. They then have to be translated into hourly throughputs, which become the real basis for deciding on the scale of the facilities to be provided in the future. At this stage, we can begin to test the effects of different constraints that might be applied to the developments of the airports; increasing restrictions on night operations being one example. Having identified the main factors generating demand, we can also see at this stage what benefits might be obtained if the demand pattern could be improved to eliminate excessive peaking, either by hour through the day or by day through the week; similarly where there is a pronounced imbalance of demand between airports that does not reflect the relative capacities available.

The end result is a forecast of passenger throughput, aircraft movements and cargo for each of the Authority's airports over the next five years and south east and Scottish Airports forecasts over the next fifteen years (see Figure 3.2).

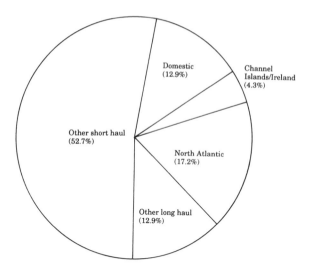

Figure 3.2.   *Analysis of traffic at south east airports by market, 1985*

The appraisal meetings

The corporate planning process begins annually in May when the Board formally agrees the objectives of the Authority, sets specific numeric profit, income and cost targets, based upon the Government targets, for the immediate future and highlights areas of the business requiring additional development within the period of the corporate plan.

The senior directors and managers meet in July at a 'Corporate Appraisal' to learn the views of the Board and to agree the overall framework and thrust of the plans to be developed. They agree the traffic forecasts outlined above, the airport targets, the main strategies, formats and the timetable.

The Business Plans

Essential as the Corporate Plan undoubtedly is to the formulation of policies and strategies, it does not in itself constitute an action programme for management. In the development of an expanded and proactive corporate planning process, two essential requirements have been kept to the fore: firstly, only those who manage the Authority's affairs are in a position to achieve the overall goals set out in the Corporate Plan; and, secondly, the planning process must recognize and support the thrust towards decentralization and increased delegation of responsibility throughout the business. The fundamental change that is now taking place in the planning process has thus stemmed from these basic considerations.

It is clear that each of the seven airports constitutes a discrete business unit, even though the units are required to work within certain overriding constraints set by the Board in its centralized role. For these discrete businesses to succeed, however, each of them must be working to its own Business Plan, formulated by its own management. These plans are essentially airport documents concerned with the operation of the airport as a business, but reflecting the overall policies and strategies of the Corporate Plan.

Within each Airport Business Plan a series of 'Appraisal Papers' are prepared for each major area of activity. These set specific objectives, give background information on current activity, provide detailed information on what is to be done over the period of the plan to achieve the stated objective and finally highlight the major risks which could undermine performance. The papers are consolidated into the Business Plan, together with the financial forecasts and an overview written by the Airport Director. The Business Plans are prepared over a four-month period and are submitted at the end of November, in time to provide an essential input to the updating of the Corporate Plan.

Budgets
Financial planning was formerly dealt with separately through the budgets for the next financial year, with forecasts for a further four years. These provided a single detailed forward projection, and as such did not test for alternative strategic options and sensitivities to changing forecasts. They showed simply the financial implications of achieving a single out-turn related to one set of assumptions. Under the revised process, the preparation of the budgets and financial forecasts takes place integrally with the writing of the Business Plans and the Corporate Plan in turn. This involves assessments of alternative traffic growths and alternative strategies for dealing with the future. It is not intended that all alternatives should be worked out in fine detail, but it is intended to reduce drastically the degree of budget detail required beyond the first year of the five-year period.

The Corporate Plan

The Corporate Plan represents the nucleus of the BAA's forward planning. It is the mechanism by which the Board sanctions the overall objectives, policies and future strategies of the Authority. As such, the Corporate Plan will continue to be updated annually, and will normally come to the BAA Board for approval in March. The Corporate Plan draws on the Airport Business Plans and expands the process to cover items which are centrally determined or have relevance to more than one airport (see Figure 3.3). The Plan sets out the overall BAA objectives and targets agreed with Government. The previous year's performance is reviewed and comments are made on significant events during the previous year which have a bearing on current and future performance. The major assumptions and constraints are set out, particularly the passenger forecasts which will be a major influence in determining future performance. Government policies, which act as a constraint upon the Authority, are considered and the major economic assumptions outlined.

The Plan also considers the options open to the Authority for catering for the growth of traffic, the facilities required, and the cost of providing them. The Plan further details the policies and strategies required to satisfy each of the objectives agreed with Government. This will include sections on safety, security, service to customers, manpower and the policies with regard to noise, land acquisition and ecology. Commercial strategy is outlined showing how the objectives can be met and the likely capital requirement needed to upgrade facilities and exploit the trading potential of airports.

The financial effects are drawn together in a detailed five-year forecast of the major items of income and expenditure, profitability and cash flow. Finally sensitivities against the base forecasts are made to determine the resilience of performance against particular alternative rates of traffic growth.

The Corporate Plan is presented to the Board for approval in March. Following approval, copies are given to the Department of Transport and are subsequently discussed between the Secretary of State and the BAA Board. These discussions are an important part of the corporate planning process, as they provide the opportunity to agree the overall strategic framework within which the Authority can then operate.

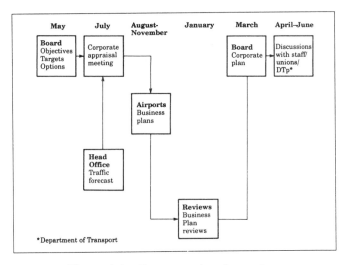

Figure 3.3   *Corporate planning cycle*

Monitoring

Most planning systems that fail do so because they become annually updated academic exercises and are not a part of the on-going management
process. An important feature of the BAA's Corporate Plan is the manner
in which the process of producing it has become inextricably interwoven
with the entire management of the business. Thus:

- The financial forecasting has become an integral part of the planning
  system and the detailed one-year budget, prepared in January, is
  derived from the plans. The plans, therefore, are the basis of any
  improvement in performance and the budgets are the financial implications of implementing the plans.
- The Appraisal Papers, contained within the Business Plans, are written
  by line management and describe what each is intending to do and
  achieve over the next few years. They, thus, become part of an on-going
  management control system.
- The targets, agreed with Government and subsequently expanded
  throughout the Authority, are incorporated into the Business Plans
  and the Appraisal Papers. These targets are monitored monthly and
  written reports provided by Directors to the Managing Director. The
  overall BAA performance against target is reported monthly via an in-
  house desk-top VDU teletext system and quarterly via a written report
  to the Board.
- Each Business Plan is formally approved and the financial and capital
  implications accepted by the Managing Director at a Review Meeting
  held soon after the Plans are submitted.

Summary

The British Airports Authority's revised corporate planning process has
therefore been developed out of procedures that have been effective in the
past, but which did not play a sufficiently positive part in the activity of
the business. The revised process now begins each year with statements
by the senior directors on the objectives, targets, assumptions, outline
strategic options and general format within which their own plans will be
written and against which they will be judged. Each Airport prepares a
Business Plan culminating in a set of five-year financial forecasts showing how targets will be met and what is required to do this. The plans are
reviewed and eventually finalized. The Corporate Plan then draws together the various strands to form the nucleus of the BAA's forward
planning and the basis of discussion with the Government in order to
create an agreed strategic framework within which the Board and the
management can make the major decisions that concern the future of the
business.

Figure 3.4

Government agreed targets

The following four targets have been agreed with the Government as a basis for the assessment of the Authority's overall performance and are set for a three year period, they are also used for internal targetting with the formulae appropriately adapted.

(1) *Rate of return on net assets*	(2) *Costs, excluding depreciation, per passenger*	(3) *Passengers per payroll hour*	(4) *Scottish Airports Break-even*
To achieve on average over a three year period a minimum annual rate of return on average net assets of 3 per cent plus one-fifth of the annual average percentage growth in terminal passengers on a cumulative basis in each successive year.	To reduce costs (at constant prices and excluding depreciation) per terminal passenger by one-half per cent per annum, plus an additional reduction equivalent to two-fifths of the percentage growth in terminal passengers over a three-year period.	To increase the number of terminal passengers per payroll hour by one-half per cent per annum plus two-fifths of the percentage growth in terminal passengers over a three year period.	To achieve a CCA break-even at the Scottish group of airports as a whole by 1985–6.

Additional targets

The following indicators are internal, are targetted on a year by year basis and constitute the goals to which the airports are aiming in the development of their business.

(5) *Duty Free and Tax Free income*	(6) *Other concession income*	(7) *Gross rental income*	(8) *Passengers per unit of employee cost*
To increase income (at constant prices) per international departing passenger from duty and tax free sales by x per cent.	To increase income (at constant prices) per passenger from trading concessions (other than duty free/tax free) by x per cent.	To increase gross rental income (at constant prices) by x per cent.	To increase the number of terminal passengers per unit of employee cost by x per cent plus a proportion of the percentage growth in terminal passengers.

(9) *Passenger complaints*	(10) *Availability of passenger sensitive mechanical equipment*		
Incidence of complaints as monitored through comment cards not to rise above the level of X per 100,000.	Availability of passenger sensitive mechanical equipment to be higher than x per cent.		

4 Assessing country risk and business potential at National Westminster Bank

David Kern, Manager and Chief Economist, Market Intelligence Department, National Westminster Bank plc

The need for risk assessment

At a practical level, the growing use of structured analyses for assessing country risks can be seen as a natural reaction to the increasingly difficult and complex problems facing those involved in international activities. Essentially, this type of systematic approach attempts to identify explicitly and to quantify the international risks arising from business operations. Since it is virtually impossible to assess all the conceivable risks one may encounter, the standard approach is to focus on a few key items which appear to be particularly relevant. The core of country risk analysis is the evaluation of factors such as political/strategic problems, structural variables (i.e. natural resources), inflation and external indebtedness, and their interaction in determining the total risk associated with a particular country. This type of evaluation can most conveniently be carried out with the aid of a formal model, and some of the techniques which may be used are described in greater detail below.

It must be stressed that the nature and magnitude of any underlying risks depend on the type of activity in which a company or a government agency may be engaged. For example, a foreign investor will be particularly concerned with the dangers of expropriation, inadequate profits or limits on their convertibility. On the other hand, an exporter's primary interest will be to assess the risk of not being paid for his goods in an acceptable currency. This chapter concentrates mainly on those risks which are of prime concern to financial institutions or to governments – above all, the risk that a particular country will be unable or unwilling to honour its commitments to service and repay the debts it has incurred.

Most conventional assessments of country risk tend, by their nature, to focus on the medium term (say, five to seven years) because their first aim is to identify problems which may arise over a period which seems relevant to international lending activities. However, when making strategic decisions, it is also important to think and plan in a longer-term framework. With this in mind, attention is focused in the final section of this article on a long-term (say, 20–25 years) view of country risk. It is particularly important to ensure that the natural wish to minimize the more immediate risks should not obscure any longer-term potential. On occasion, the existence of significant benefits over the longer term could fully justify a deliberate decision to incur any shorter-term risks associated with a particular country, and this article will attempt to provide a framework for analysing such circumstances.

Origins of the international debt problem
One must remember that, except in the very short term, even the relatively affluent, industrialized countries of North America, Western Europe and Japan cannot be regarded as risk free. The growing financial problems facing many developed countries, particularly in Europe, strongly support the view that country risk models can be employed effectively in a very wide range of circumstances. Nevertheless, the international debt problem has inevitably increased the attention given to 'developing' or less-developed countries (LDCs), and reinforced the need for a systematic approach to evaluating these countries' creditworthiness.

Since August 1982, when Mexico had to reschedule its external debts, about forty countries have been forced to restructure their debts to official creditors and banks. Some of these countries are still experiencing great problems in meeting their financial commitments. However, given the underlying international economic problems which have exacerbated the LDCs' difficulties, it is pleasing to note that genuine progress has been made since 1982 by many LDCs in restoring their external positions. This progress has helped to promote a less emotive and more balanced attitude to the whole subject of country risk. Notwithstanding recent events, it is important to remember that trading and financial links between the Western world and the LDCs will continue to expand in future, but particularly so with those developing countries which are seen to be handling the response to their problems in an effective manner.

An examination of the origins and underlying causes of the LDC debt problem will help to put into perspective the recent historical record. The underlying causes of the LDC debt problem are closely linked with the two 'oil crises' of the 1970s, firstly in 1973–4 and then in 1979–80. The factors which caused sharp rises over the past decade in the current account deficits of the non-oil LDCs, and subsequent debt service problems, have been identified by many people in recent years and can be summarized briefly as follows:

1 Over-expansionary fiscal and monetary policies over a number of years in many developing countries, aimed at sustaining high consumption and ambitious capital projects. There was an alarming and apparently inexorable growth in budget deficits in much of the developing world, from 3·5 per cent of GNP in the late 1970s to nearly 6 per cent on average in 1982 (14–18 per cent in Latin America). These deficits, which were aggravated by the sharp rise in oil prices, resulted in strong inflationary pressures, large current account shortfalls and the accumulation of substantial external debts between 1973 and 1982.

2 The worsening problems of the LDCs were exacerbated by adverse developments in the world economy after 1979; renewed upward pressure on energy prices, rising real interest rates (see Table 4.1), a severe deterioration in the terms of trade of non-oil developing countries (see Table 4.2) and finally the contraction of export opportunities as the recession of 1980–2 impacted on international trade (see Table 4.3). With export revenues falling or stagnating at a

Table 4.1 *Nominal and real interest rates, 1978–1984*

	(Per cent)						
	1978	1979	1980	1981	1982	1983	1984
United States							
Three-month Eurodollar deposit rate	8·9	12·1	14·2	16·8	13·2	9·6	10·8
Inflation (GNP deflator)	7·4	8·6	9·2	9·4	6·0	3·8	3·8
Real interest rate	1·4	3·2	4·6	6·8	6·8	5·6	6·7
Federal Republic of Germany							
Three-month money market rate	3·7	6·7	9·5	12·1	8·9	5·8	6·0
Inflation (GNP deflator)	4·2	4·0	4·5	4·2	4·8	3·2	1·8
Real interest rate	0·5	2·6	4·8	7·6	3·9	2·5	4·1
Japan							
Three-month gensaki rate	5·1	5·9	10·7	7·4	6·8	6·5	6·3
Inflation (GNP deflator)	4·6	2·6	2·8	2·7	1·7	0·7	0·5
Real interest rate	0·5	3·2	7·7	4·6	5·0	5·8	5·8

Sources: IMF, *International Financial Statistics,* Deutsche Bundesbank, *Monthly Report:* and Bank of Japan, *Economic Statistics Monthly*

Table 4.2   *Oil, gold and other commodity prices, 1979–1984*

| | (Annual averages) | | | | | |
	1979	1980	1981	1982	1983	1984
Oil ($ per barrel, Saudi-light)	17·26	28·67	32·50	33·47	29·31	28·09
Gold ($ per ounce)	306·7	607·9	459·8	375·8	422·5	361·0
Economist Dollar Index of Commodity Prices:						
Metals	94·5	100	81·1	67·1	76·2	70·6
All items	84·9	100	86·2	74·7	84·3	83·4

Sources: IMF, *Financial Times* and *Economist.*

time of rapidly increasing debt obligations, many developing countries experienced severe pressure on their debt servicing capacity
(see Table 4.4).

3 The adjustment to higher energy prices was delayed by the easy
availability of finance during the 1970s, stimulated by an intellec-
tual climate which encouraged large-scale recycling of oil exporters' surpluses to oil-importing nations. The prevailing negative
real interest rates during much of the period made borrowing rather
than saving particularly attractive. The imbalances in the external
accounts of LDCs were financed easily and on a large scale from

Table 4.3   *International growth and trade, 1978–1984*

	1978	1979	1980	1981	1982	1988	1984 (est.)
Real growth (%)							
OECD GNP	4·1	3·5	1·3	2·0	−0·4	2·5	4·9
World trade	5·5	6·5	2·0	1·0	−2·5	2·3	8·0
Exports ($ bn)							
Oil exporters	142	210	296	275	215	175	180
Non-oil LDCs	143	186	236	243	227	236	264
Terms of trade (Index 1978 = 100)							
Non-oil LDCs	100	101	97	92	89	90	92

Sources: National Institute, *Economic Review;* and IMF, *World Economic Outlook,* September (1984).

Table 4.4 *Developing countries' debt service payments and ratios 1978–1984*

	1978	1979	1980	1981	1982	1983	1984
Debt service payments ($ bn)							
Interest payments*	21·9	32·3	45·8	60·6	71·4	65·1	71·5
Amortization†	35·8	43·1	43·8	48·7	52·7	46·7	49·8
Debt service ratios‡							
Interest (%)	7·3	8·1	8·9	11·2	14·1	12·9	12·7
Amortization (%)	11·8	10·8	8·5	9·0	10·4	9·2	8·8
Total (%)	19·1	18·9	17·4	20·2	24·5	22·1	21·5

*Payments on short, medium and long-term debt.
†Payments on medium and long-term debt only.
‡Payments expressed as a percentage of total export receipts.
Source: IMF, *World Economic Outlook*, September (1984).

commercial sources (see Table 4.5), a situation welcomed by both governments and international institutions alike. The justification for this recycling process was that it seemed consistent with the maintenance of high levels of world trade and economic activity. At the same time, continuing high rates of inflation until the late 1970s eroded the real value of debt outstanding. The drawback was that creditworthiness criteria were not fully enforced and the borrowers undertook activities which were not fully justified. Moreover, the adoption of rigorous monetarist policies by industrialized countries (notably the US and the UK) from about 1978 onwards reduced global economic activity, restricted international trade, and contained inflation rates, aggravating the real burden of the external debt.

Post–1982 management of the debt problem
The international debt problem became critical in August 1982 when Mexico announced its inability to service its external debts. In the ensuing months the availability of new bank finance for developing countries, particularly in Latin America, dried up and many more countries were forced to follow suit.

In managing the problem over the past two years (1983–4), a 'case-by-case approach' has been pursued. Each country has been treated on its own merits, recognizing that each has different resources, different debt

Table 4.5   *Non-oil developing countries: financing of current account deficits. 1974–1982 cumulative totals*

	$ billion	Per cent
Current account deficits	531	90·5
Increase in official reserves	56	9·5
Total	587	100·0
Financed by:		
(a) Non-debt-creating flows (net)	172	29·3
(b) Long-term capital from official sources (net)	128	21·8
(c) Borrowing through private markets	278	47·3
Of which: banking	255	43·4
(d) Others	9	1·5

Sources: Computed from IMF, *World Economic Outlook 1984* and *International Capital Markets, Developments and Prospects, 1983.*

profiles, and different capacities to pursue appropriate adjustment policies. Given the underlying differences between the various countries involved, it is not surprising that ambitious attempts to find a 'global solution' have made no progress. Nevertheless, a number of common elements have characterized the country-by-country strategy:

1   Economic adjustments to reduce immediate borrowing requirements and provide conditions for eventual sustainable growth have been undertaken, normally in conjunction with IMF programmes. These have involved a painful contraction of imports in recent years and a period of declining 'per capita' incomes (see Table 4.6), with attendant political and social pressures.

2   Commercial banks have restructured existing loans as part of adjustment programmes agreed with the IMF, and have provided new money (some $26bn during 1983–4) to rescheduling countries.

3   The co-operation of the multilateral institutions (notably the IMF and the World Bank) has proved to be vital in holding the international financial system together.

4   The international recovery led by the US has generated a strong rise in LDC exports, particularly to the US, which ran a trade deficit of $120bn in 1984. This has provided the opportunity for Brazil, for example, to boost its dollar earnings from merchandise trade by over 16 per cent, to run a $12bn trade surplus, and to transform its

current account deficit from $16·3bn in 1982 to a surplus of $0·7bn in 1984 (see Table 4.6).

5 Finally, the steady decline in global oil prices has reduced pressure on imports for many LDCs, though creating additional problems for oil exporters such as Nigeria, Indonesia and Mexico.

A country which has achieved a very remarkable turn-round in its external finances is Mexico (see Table 4.6). In recognition of the progress achieved, the commercial banks agreed in September 1984 to a multi-year

Table 4.6 *Imports (cif), current accounts and change in 'per capita' incomes for selected LDCs, 1981–4 [$bn for imports and current account, and percentage real change for income 'per capita' (pc)*]*

		1981	1982	1983	1984
Argentina	Imports	9·4	5·3	4·5	4·5
	Current a/c	−4·7	−2·4	−2·4	−2·2
	Income pc	−7·8%	−6·3%	+0·4%	+0·4%
Brazil	Imports	24·1	21·1	16·8	15·1
	Current a/c	−11·8%	−16·3	−6·2	+0·7
	Income pc	−3·7%	−1·3%	−5·3%	+1·8%
Mexico	Imports	24·1	15·1	8·0	11·3
	Current a/c	−13·9	−4·8	5·2	4·0
	Income pc	+5·2%	−3·0%	−7·4%	+0·5%
Nigeria	Imports	20·9	15·1	8·5	8·5
	Current a/c	−5·9	−7·7	−4·7	−1·0
	Income pc	−8·4%	−5·5%	−7·5%	−3·7%
Philippines	Imports	8·5	8·3	8·0	5·8
	Current a/c	−2·3	−3·4	−2·8	−1·5
	Income pc	+1·3%	+0·2%	−2·0%	−8·5%
Venezuela	Imports	13·1	12·6	8·7	9·0
	Current a/c	4·0	4·2	3·7	4·4
	Income pc	−3·3%	−2·2%	−7·4%	−2·8%
Yugoslavia	Imports†	10·6	9·6	8·1	8·0
	Current a/c†	−1·8	−1·4	0·3	0·7
	Income pc	+0·5%	+0·1%	−1·9%	+0·5%

*Estimates.
†In convertible currency.

Source: Mainly IMF, *International Financial Statistics*.

rescheduling arrangement. Other countries which have followed success-ful adjustment programmes have since agreed similar arrangements, which are seen as an important step towards providing a more stable international environment. For individual borrowing countries, the opportunity to extend debt maturities up to the end of the century, at lower margins, is a benefit stemming from continued adherence to rigorous financial discipline. It also gives them the opportunity to re-establish their creditworthiness and qualify in due course for renewed voluntary lending from the financial markets. For banks, the advantage is that tensions in the international markets are reduced and they are given a realistic chance of receiving principal repayments, albeit over a longer period.

The future management and ultimate resolution of the debt problem clearly involve many risks. In those cases where formal IMF programmes are absent, there are serious difficulties in monitoring performance and, if necessary, imposing discipline on economic policy. In such circum-stances, the response has been for the IMF to be given a continuing role in monitoring and advising upon performance without providing it with the necessary formal authority to enforce a package. Since the IMF is an organization whose actions are strongly influenced by governments, this will reinforce the trend for the debtor/creditor relationship to be increas-ingly politicized. The difficulties in monitoring performance, and the increased politicization of the LDC debt problem, strongly underline the need for banks and other private financial institutions to pay close attention to the results of the country risk evaluations.

The structure of country risk models

The extensive literature on country risk assessment shows a very wide variety of approaches to this subject, ranging from highly complex mathematical models used by some academics to very simplified frame-works often preferred by those involved in practical business situations. In view of the enormous complexity of the economic environment, it is naturally tempting to try and incorporate all the possible factors which may be relevant, including: GNP growth, inflation, balance of payments, investments in natural resources, political and social factors, and ex-ternal indebtedness. Indeed, these are only a few of the items which could, in theory, be included. However, experience shows that it is simply not practical to try and capture the entire spectrum of possible variables in any one model.

A more sensible and fruitful approach is to analyse carefully the specific requirements of the organization undertaking the risk exercise, and focus attention on a small number of factors (say between five and ten) which appear to be particularly relevant. The variables chosen, or the specific weights attributed to them, need not be fixed. Indeed, it would seem highly desirable to re-evaluate the model regularly and adjust it gradually in line with changing circumstances. For example, it is entirely logical that, following the dramatic developments in Iran in 1979, political factors were given greater weight in any risk assessment. Whilst regular re-assessment of a risk model are both necessary and desirable, changes need not be either abrupt or very large. Indeed, if one often encounters such violent changes, it is usually a sign that the original construction of the model has not been thought out with sufficient care.

Table 4.7 gives an illustration of the various risk factors which are considered appropriate to current international conditions. This is a medium-term risk model which assumes a risk spectrum ranging from a score of zero (nil risk) to 100 (maximum risk). Each category is given a maximum level of 'possible risk' associated with the particular factor, and the figure chosen naturally reflects its perceived relative importance. The

Table 4.7   *A typical risk model: criteria and scores*

		Maximum risk score
Financial factors		50
External indebtedness		
of which:		
External debt as percentage of GNP	10	
Debt service ratio (percentage of exports)	10	
Liquidity gap ratio (percentage of exports)	10	
Reserves and balance of payments		
of which:		
Current account as percentage of GNP	10	
Import coverage	10	
Structural/economic factors		20
of which:		
Commodity reliance (percentage of exports)	5	
Economic structure and management	15	
Political/strategic factors		30
	Total	100

overall score for each country simply reflects the sum of its separate scores in each category.

Although the model is quantitative, it is important not to attribute any spurious accuracy to the results. The mechanistic features of the model, particularly the numerical value given to a country's risk rating, are simply a convenient presentational device which facilitates the communication of the results to busy operational managers within large organizations. Essentially, the approach is judgmental, with those responsible for operating the model having to make difficult choices concerning the variables to be used and their relative weights.

Table 4.8 sets the whole subject in a longer historical perspective, presenting a number of purely illustrative, medium-term models which may help the reader to appreciate how the approach to country risk assessment has developed over the past few years. The various models start from very simplified structures often used in the early 1970s. As one moves to the right, one can see how thinking on the subject has evolved in reaction to changing international circumstances. The number of variables used in the analytical framework has deliberately been kept limited so as to illustrate the potential of such models as clear and concise tools for studying complex situations, and for conveying information to those concerned with practical decision-making. Table 4.8 shows how the relative weights given to these variables have tended to alter over time, in the light of experience which has been gained and new information which has become available. The right-hand column offers some suggestions about appropriate weights when one is concerned with longer-term assessment, which is dealt with later in this article.

Individual risk factors

In its most simplified form, the model described here focuses on three main types of risk: financial (maximum risk score 50); structural/economic (maximum risk score 20); political/strategic (maximum risk score 30). This is a systematic procedure which aims at achieving a balanced result. For example, by linking 50 per cent of the overall risk to specific financial variables, an attempt is made to ensure that the results obtained reflect, to a significant extent, objective information rather than impressionistic reactions.

Financial factors (maximum risk score 50)
1 *External indebtedness* There are a number of measures of the burden of indebtedness. The most widely used are firstly, the outstanding size of the country's debt expressed as a percentage of some broad economic aggregate, and, secondly, the flow of foreign currency payments required

Table 4.8 Illustrative country risk models. Maximum percentage risk associated with various factors

Factors accounting for country risks	Historical development of short/medium-term risk models						(g)	Long-term risk/potential model
	(a)	(b)	(c)	(d)	(e)	(f)		
Financial variables								
External debt as a percentage of GNP (or as a percentage of exports)	25	—	5	10	10	10	5	
Debt service ratio	—	25	20	20	20	10	10	
Liquidity gap ratio	—	—	—	—	—	10	—	
Current account as a percentage of GNP	—	—	—	5	10	10	5	
Import coverage	25	25	20	15	10	10	5	
Structural/economic factors								In a long-term risk/potential model
Commodity reliance	30	20	20	10	10	5	15	structural and political factors relate not
Energy vulnerability	—	—	5	10	10	—	15	only to risk but also to future business
Sophistication of financial institutions	10	10	10	5	—	—	—	potential, focusing on such things as size of economy and its resources, growth in
Economic structure and management	—	—	—	—	—	15	—	total GNP or in specific industries, level of affluence (GNP per head), and other
Political/strategic factors	10	20	20	25	30	30	45	special factors (energy projects, etc.)
Total	100	100	100	100	100	100	100	100

to service a country's debt. The specific factors used in this category are:

(a) *Outstanding external debt as a percentage of GNP (maximum score 10)*   A measure of a country's overall debt burden relative to the size of its economy. It is expressed as a proportion of GNP (or sometimes exports of goods and services) because the larger the size of a particular economy, the less will be its vulnerability to a given level of external indebtedness. A debt/GNP ratio in excess of 40 per cent is usually a sign of long-term financial problems. However, a country's debt service payments are partially related to the size of its outstanding debt; the maturity structure of the debt and the rate of interest applied are also highly relevant factors.

(b) *Debt service ratio (maximum score 10)*   This is defined as the annual payments of interest and capital required to service a country's medium- and long-term external debt, expressed as a proportion of its total export earnings on goods and services. The debt service ratio (DSR) is a highly important and reliable measure of the financial burden of a country's external debt. In principle, it can be argued that countries should try to keep their DSRs below 20–25 per cent. However, prior to 1982 the ratios for many countries, particularly in Latin America, reached much higher levels. Statistical limitations of data availability make it difficult to include interest payable on short-term debt, although theoretically this might make for a better indicator.

It is interesting to note that in the early and more simplified risk models which were in use, there was a tendency to focus almost entirely on the DSR. In more recent models significant attention has also been given to outstanding debt.

(c) *Liquidity gap ratio (maximum score 10)*   This relates to expected short-term increases in external indebtedness, by focusing attention on financial requirements over the year ahead. It is in essence a forward-looking indicator, to establish a country's liquidity position for the next year. The constituent elements of cash flow which are considered are the expected current account out-turn, plus existing debt to be repaid within the next year, less an allowance for short-term euro-deposits. The net total of these three items is expressed as a percentage of export receipts from all sources. A ratio in excess of 50 per cent would signify considerable short-term financial pressures.

2 *Reserves and the Balance of Payments*   There are two criteria commonly used in this category:

(a) *The balance of payments on current account as a proportion of GNP (maximum score 10)*   In the early 1970s it was usually assumed that there was no need to focus explicitly on a country's balance of payments when assessing risks. This was because some of the risks resulting from a deficit were thought to be sufficiently reflected in other variables, particularly those relating to indebtedness. However, the experience of the past few years has demonstrated that there are some important, distinct features of a country's balance of payments position which provide guidance on a country's economic performance, the stability of its exchange rate and future trends in external indebtedness. A sustained current account deficit in excess of 7·5–10 per cent of GNP usually indicates deep-seated economic weakness.

(b) *Import coverage (maximum score 10)*   This is defined as a country's foreign exchange reserves in relation to its average monthly import bill. It is a somewhat crude statistic, measuring the number of months over which a particular country's foreign currency reserves will suffice to pay for its imports, given the totally unlikely assumption that there are no exports or other sources of finance available. Even so, 'import coverage' is a good estimate of a country's ability to withstand short-term pressures, and the financial markets focus on it as a rough, but fairly reliable, quick guide to the stability of a country's exchange rate and the strength of its external financial position. In recent years there has been a tendency to reduce somewhat the relative weight given to this variable, reflecting the greater importance now being accorded to indebtedness and to the balance of payments. This tendency is logical, but it would still seem appropriate to use import coverage as one of the important risk factors, albeit with a smaller weight than in the past. As a general rule, if reserves cover less than two months of an LDC's average imports, that country may be faced with growing short-term pressures.

Structural/Economic factors (maximum risk score 20)
Criteria under this heading focus on some important factors relating to the composition of exports and the economic structure and management of countries under assessment.
1   *Commodity Reliance as a Percentage of Export Revenue (maximum score 5)*   Excessive reliance by a country on export earnings from a narrow range of agricultural products, raw materials and/or tourism increases its exposure to sharp fluctuations in export receipts. Consequently, the foreign exchange earnings of such a country often exhibit violent movements during the economic cycle. Many LDCs are still affected by this factor, but its relative weight in most risk models has been gradually reduced as other factors have assumed greater importance. Wherever a few commodities, tourism or workers' remittances from

abroad provide more than half of export earnings, the country in question may be vulnerable.

2   *Economic Structure and Management (maximum score 15)*   This criterion evaluates the effects on a country's creditworthiness of the presence or absence of indigenous natural resources (most notably food and energy), and the quality of its economic management. A number of key factors are assessed, including inflation performance, the public sector deficit in relation to GNP, economic growth and the availability of important natural resources.

Political/Strategic factors (maximum risk score 30)
There are clearly difficulties in assessing political factors in a formal way. Nevertheless, the financial consequences of the Iranian revolution demonstrated that a political/strategic judgment, however subjectively reached, must be incorporated explicitly in any risk analysis. It should be appreciated that this risk factor is defined here quite broadly, and covers a whole range of potential problems: strategic and military vulnerability to an external threat, various forms of economic conflict and a whole variety of internal difficulties. These include regional and language differences, the country's record of stability and the ease with which succession from one administration to another has been effected.

Sources of information for medium-term assessment

There are numerous sources of information which can be used in assessing a country's political and strategic situation. These include leading domestic and international newspapers and periodicals, as well as journals specializing in regional affairs. Authoritative data for the financial indicators used in the evaluation are, however, more limited. The major sources used are as follows:

(i)   The Bank for International Settlements provides information on commercial bank lending to various countries. Data on the size of lendings are provided quarterly, and a half-yearly analysis of the maturity structure is also provided. The information from this source is reasonably up-to-date (a four to eight month delay).

(ii) The World Bank's *World Debt Tables* provide information on the public and publicly guaranteed external debt and debt service of developing countries, accompanied in an increasing number of cases by details of private debt. The information, which relates to medium- and long-term debt only, is up to two years out of date.

(iii) The OECD document *External Debt of Developing Countries* also covers medium- and long-term debt and debt service only. Military debt is excluded, which can understate the position considerably, but public and private debt is considered for all countries. As with the *World Debt Tables*, data can be up to two years out of date.

(iv) The International Monetary Fund produces monthly data of relevance to the assessment discussed in this article in *International Financial Statistics*, including information on gold and foreign exchange reserves, the balance of payments, aspects of domestic economic performance and countries' major export items.

In addition to the above sources, which have the advantage of a high degree of consistency, individual countries' Central Bank and Ministry of Finance reports can be used, as well as comments supplied to the financial press by officials.

The long-term dimension

Given the underlying uncertainties involved in country risk assessment, it is extremely difficult to pinpoint with any precision the time span over which the various factors apply. The distinction between 'shorter-term' and 'longer-term' factors raises many philosophical and practical problems, and those who are a little pedantic sometimes argue that it is impossible to know when one ends and the other begins. Nevertheless, for those involved in making practical decisions, evaluating the correct time horizon is critically important. As a rough and unscientific rule of thumb, experience suggests that it is advisable to distinguish between short/medium-term assessments, looking forward five to seven years, and longer-term evaluations which extend beyond that period. The longer the period one tries to assess, the larger the number of variables which can change and, in general, it is necessary to make longer-term assessments less mechanistic and more flexible than those where one is mainly concerned with the short/medium term. Thus, longer-term risk models should give greater weight to political trends and various structural factors (including dependence on commodities) while putting less emphasis on financial/economic factors such as external debt and the balance of payments. The illustrative nature of the figures in Table 4.8, and the need to adjust them in line with experience, cannot be emphasized too strongly. However, subject to this qualification, a reasonable 'working assumption' would be to increase the maximum risk score associated with structural/economic and political/strategic factors from some 20 and 30 respectively in a typical medium-term model such as (e) or (f), to about 30 and 45 respectively in a model which focuses on longer-term factors. There will obviously be a corresponding reduction in the maximum risk score allocated to financial factors, from some 50 in models (e) and (f), to about 25 in the suggested long-term risk model shown in column (g). Furthermore, the greater weights given to structural variables in a long-term model should not just focus on the evaluation of risks but should reflect a considered judgment about a country's longer-term potential for economic growth and development, with particular reference to the opportunities for investment, exports and marketing. In this context, it would be advisable to focus on factors such as the size of the economy, its resources and level of affluence, and the likely growth in GNP or in the specific industry with which one is concerned. Risk/potential models using numerical scores can be particularly vulnerable when one tries to project forward over long periods but, if used with caution, such models can be very helpful in providing an orderly and disciplined framework for our thinking.

Conclusions

Trying to quantify risk numerically, with reference to a small number of identifiable factors, is inevitably rather mechanistic. Some of the more subtle and complicated risks will deliberately be over-simplified in such an analysis though, from the point of view of the operational manager faced with practical problems, such simplicity may indeed be seen as an advantage. Clearly, calculating a risk score which ranges from zero (nil risk) to 100 (maximum risk) must involve some element of artificiality. Nevertheless, if the results of such an analysis are properly used, they can be an invaluable aid to those involved in making decisions. It is important to understand clearly the basic thinking underlying the mechanical approach to risk analysis, and the results must be treated with considerable care, particularly when applied to a longer-term assessment. However, there is no substitute for an orderly and structured approach to the evaluation of international risks. It provides those who, in their jobs, must make difficult decisions with a necessary analytical framework for communicating ideas in a logical and explicit manner.

5 Using issues management to deal with public issues

C. B. Arrington, Jr. and R. N. Sawaya,
Atlantic Richfield Company, Los Angeles, USA

Environment uncertainty has become a fact of life for all major business concerns in the United States. The strategic importance of factors beyond conventional economic considerations has been recognized by management. Not surprisingly, managerial innovations to address discontinuity have been developed, as extra-market, external events have impeded operations and profitability.

Like strategic planning, issues management is a constructive adaptation to discontinuity. It is not a panacea. But, as a process, issues management can inform advocacy with analysis from many disciplines, focus relations between the corporation and its publics to achieve results, and provide cost-effective public affairs functions.

Issues management may be an unfortunate misnomer. Certainly, no corporate staff function can *manage* a public issue to a corporation's desired conclusion with any regularity. An issues management process, however, can help a company to realize its business objectives by helping it anticipate and respond to changes in its external environment. Properly-conceived and executed, issues management is a *process* to organize a company's expertise to enable it to participate effectively in the shaping and resolution of public issues that critically impinge upon its operations. Issues management may be what John Dunlop had in mind when he observed that

business interests in America do not have an effective mechanism or procedure to reconcile their internal conflicting interests on a wide range of public policy issues.

Viewed within the context of corporate public affairs, the process of issues management offers a business-oriented means of conceptualizing and acting upon public policy issues. For all its professionalization over the last two decades, the public affairs function has yet to integrate itself into the business decision-making process of most corporations. Public affairs professionals often have been confined to reactive, 'fire-fighting' conduct. Issues management offers a way to integrate the anticipation of public policy issues into the corporate decision-making process.

An organized issues management process must link line and staff expertise. Its focus must be on actual business concerns; a company's effective participation in public policy making is simply never unrelated to bottom-line consequences. Issues management must embody the deliberate recognition by company decision-makers of the need for a systematic approach to public issues and to constructive participation in their resolution.

Functions

The process of issues management involves three concurrent activities: foresight, policy development and advocacy. All depend on the successful institution of an issues management process throughout the company.

Foresight

Foresight is the planning-intensive aspect of issues management in which public issue events are identified, monitored, analysed and prioritized according to their impact on business operations. Foresight is neither futurism nor forecasting; it is pragmatic, recurring judgment about external factors critical to company success.

Issues do not 'emerge' for a company mysteriously, and some esoteric methodology is not required to be intelligent about them. Issues arise and carry priority as a result of strategic business objectives, the present and prospective course of company operations. Issue identification and prioritization, therefore, occurs as much from the 'inside out' as from the 'outside in'.

In this information-intensive age, data external to a company is readily gathered through publications, information networks, consulting services and so forth. What is most difficult to obtain is an internal, consistent company viewpoint that, if successfully advocated, will align company interests with the resolution of an external issue.

An example of foresight: In December 1980, many business persons felt the election of Ronald Reagan and a Republican Senate majority augured major change in the relation between business and government. The Administration would carry out its self-proclaimed mandate to unfetter the productive private sector and enact policies that would effect economic resurgence generally. Surprising as it may seem now, this was probably the prevailing view in business circles.

Issues and Planning, the issues management group within Atlantic Richfield Company, was engaged in analysis of a different sort. Working with Corporate Planning, the group anticipated a stagnant economy in 1981, given Federal Reserve Chairman Volcker's commitment to a tight monetary policy. Furthermore, the President-elect's pledge to restrict the growth of the federal budget was taken seriously. Cuts were likely to be concentrated inevitably in the so-called social service 'controllables', in many cases, programmes that disbursed funds to the states. Many states were already in fiscal trouble, any reduction in federal funds would worsen their revenue binds. Worse yet, in the event of recession, very high countercyclical human service pressures would fall on the states.

Issues and Planning also recognized Congressional infatuation with 'supply side' tax policy. In the event legislation resembling Kemp–Roth were enacted in 1981, it would have the indirect effect, too, of reducing revenues to those states that automatically conform to federal depreciation schedules.

A state revenue crisis in 1981–2 seemed quite probable. How would state legislatures respond? They could not run deficits; they could raise taxes. Which taxes? Not property or personal income taxes – not after Proposition 13 in California and the copycat legislation it had spawned in other states. Perhaps general business taxes, though that would seem perverse in a recessionary climate. Perhaps consumption taxes on liquor, cigarettes, gasoline. What about the oil industry?

The surge in oil company revenues in 1980 had convinced the general public that petroleum profits, if not actually 'obscene', were apparently limitless. Indeed, opinion polls found 'profits' to be the principal reason why the public held oil companies in such low esteem. Issues and Planning concluded that state legislators would find belief in the 'deep pockets' of the capital-intensive petroleum industry most attractive and would adopt strategies to make oil companies their 'tax cows'.

Further analysis hypothesized a 'regulatory vacuum' that would develop if Reagan made good his pledge to deregulate administratively, especially in areas of environment, health and safety. The group judged that state regulatory activity would escalate dramatically as a result.

Overall, Issues and Planning concluded that Reagan's presidency would increase the level of state and local government intervention in the private sector. For the oil industry and Atlantic Richfield, state taxation would be the state issue to surface first.

Several actions followed from this foresight exercise. Working closely with the Corporate Tax Department, Issues and Planning developed a comprehensive company advocacy on state taxation. The group also increased its coverage of state environmental legislation. The group's directional call about state-level response to the economy and to the Reagan programme was included in the company long-range plan. The

Public Affairs Division as a whole emphasized its state and local representation.

The advantage of hindsight may make the effort just summarized seem conventional. Given its timing and prevailing attitudes within many corporations, it certainly was not.

Policy development

The routine 'heart' of issues management is reconciliation of conflicting internal interests on public policy issues of strategic importance in order to make a coherent external advocacy. Like foresight, effective policy development requires a collective, disinterested analytical act that includes a willingness to suspend belief in conventional business (or company) assumptions. Both the range of exposures and opportunities for all major business segments as well as their potential cross impacts must be identified. In a decentralized firm, brokering among divergent interests in the company is especially critical. The work done within Atlantic Richfield on reform of the Clean Air Act exemplifies this policy development process.

Most of the work on a company position anticipating Congressional reauthorization of the Act occurred during 1980. While a mature issue in some respects (the present law was passed in 1970 and substantially amended in 1977) subsequent court decisions, extensive and differing consequences of regulatory implementation for a range of company operations and several new, related issues, such as acid rain and hazardous air pollutants, made the development of a current company position necessary.

Issues and Planning initiated the process by requesting each operating unit of the company to identify, document and quantify (where possible) present and anticipated problems with the Act and its implementation. At the same time, analysis of the potential political climate for change was developed. Working from the results of these two efforts, Issues and Planning produced a comprehensive company position. A draft was then circulated to all the operating units and to other relevant corporate staffs for review and comment. Several iterations failed to resolve two key disagreements between operating units having differing concerns.

Often, such conflicts during formulation of company policy are negotiated successfully by the issues group; indeed, resolution can represent a principal contribution of the issues staff. Given the importance of the Clean Air Act, however, the issue was presented to senior management. The presentation covered major operating unit exposures and opportunities, policy analysis accomplished, the internal disagreements outstanding, key external players and their probable positions and the politics likely to prevail in 1981–2. The company's executive committee resolved the disagreements among the company's operating divisions and defined the position of the company as a whole.

Advocacy

Foresight yields what to think about; policy development how to think about it. Advocacy should yield a more constructive result: without effective advocacy, the other dimensions of issues management are irrelevant.

Action plans on major issues are usually developed within a company's public affairs division. These can take many forms and draw on an array of company resources: direct representation at the federal, state and local levels of government; coordination with other companies through trade associations; grass roots constituency building emphasizing employees, stockholders and retirees; community contacts and alliances with other interest groups; print and electronic media relations, as well as employee speaking engagements and issue advertising.

Of course, advocacy of a company position by executive management and key line personnel is also essential. Personal contact and direct correspondence with public decision-makers, speeches in appropriate public forums and media interviews, and participation in organizations devoted to public policy issues (the Business Roundtable, the Committee for Economic Development, the Western Regional Council, and so forth) all constitute channels by which executives can communicate the views of the company. Testifying at legislative hearings is deliberately reserved for line and executive management, since a plant manager or an executive of a company carry more weight with elected officials and other public decision-makers than do public affairs staff.

The advocacy of a company position must include feedback into the issues management process. The role played by company field representatives cannot be over-emphasized in this regard. In the case of the Clean Air Act, for example, the company's position was informed by a detailed political judgment as to what changes in the status quo might, in fact, be achieved. As it became evident to those in Washington representing the company's position on the Act that major changes sought by the company would not be forthcoming in 1982, a decision was made to focus on several specifics of particular concern to several operating segments in 1983. Though the overall position of the company did not change, advocacy was adjusted to political realities in Washington, in order to build support for a renewed broad-scale approach in the future.

Evaluation

Evaluating the effectiveness of the foresight, policy development and advocacy functions subsumed under issues management is inherently difficult. For while results can rarely be quantified (and when they can, often represent a successful defence of, not an addition to, company cash flow or profits), expenditures are directly quantified in annual budgets. Therefore, evaluation, properly considered, must occur on a qualitative basis, not only by executive management but also by the issues staff itself.

Executive management has to receive satisfactory answers to appropriate questions. Given the need to participate in the formulation of public policy that will affect, if not determine, the long-term business objectives of the company, is the process for doing so working effectively? Does the analysis that leads to company positions accurately capture details of present and prospective line operations? Does the overall process for developing and representing company positions avoid redundance? Are line managers and executive management sufficiently involved in position development and advocacy? Are external issues of concern sufficiently addressed by the issues management process? Are issues and their resolution taken into appropriate account in company planning?

Our experience at Atlantic Richfield provides some subjective, but realistic, benchmarks. Daily contacts with line management, under a formalized system, including iterative review of major issues and company positions, ensures comprehensive and appropriate line involvement. Issues and Planning has a formal contact with each of the nine line operating segments, and with each of the other corporate staff groups in headquarters (Tax, Legal, Finance, Employee Relations, Corporate Planning and so forth). By means of the contact network, expertise can be focused quickly on any aspect of a given issue and duplication avoided.

Lack of surprise on the part of executive and line management, as well as their personal representation of external advocacies are good indications of their involvement in the 'right' issues. Coherent, timely response that is focused on a few very important issues provides reasonable indication of efficiency.

Issues management and strategic planning

Formal liaison between the issues management group and the company planning department, particularly in the areas of long-term alternative views of the future, shorter-term planning assumptions and review of operating company plans, can help integrate public policy issues into company planning.

As depicted in Figure 5.1, strategic planning and issues management are complementary. Both are intended to help the leadership of the corporation as a whole.

Since it underlies management decisions about deployment of capital and human resources in lines of business, strategic planning is the more

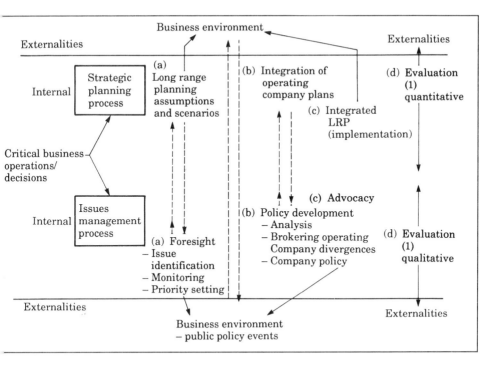

Figure 5.1 *Issues management and strategic planning*

inclusive of the two processes. Actually, the 'universe' for issues management foresight (pertinent public policy events) is a subset of the strategic planning universe: the entire business environment.

Issues management parallels and contributes to strategic planning. Issues management addresses public policy events that shape and are shaped by the total business environment. Strategic planning assumptions (calls or alternative scenarios about externalities) must include and inform foresight about public issues critical to the corporation.

Both processes must integrate the disparate views of decentralized operating entities. Strategic planning must ensure that various operating company plans are mutually consistent. Policy development in issues management must resolve differences among operating divisions on key public policy issues. In both the root meaning of strategy (leadership of an army) must be honoured; that is, a coherent hierarchy of corporate priorities must prevail. The interplay between policy development and the integration of operating company plans can be fruitful to the degree it is mutually recognized (public issues are important for business operations planning and vice-versa) and executed.

Organizationally, formal contact between the corporate planning and issues management processes at Atlantic Richfield occurs in several ways:

- The planning manager for Public Affairs in the Issues and Planning group may sit on the Strategic Planning Council, a body chaired by the head of Corporate Planning and made up of all the operating company planning managers.
- Corporate Planning, like all other corporate staff groups and all operating companies, has a formally designated contact with the Issues and Planning group.
- Issues and Planning staff sit regularly on Corporate Planning studies, where public policy considerations are important.
- The majority of Issues and Planning's formal contacts in the operating companies are part of planning staffs.
- Issues and Planning is formally involved in the designated group which develops multi-dimensional planning scenarios.
- The two corporate staff groups share the same floor at headquarters, in the belief that physical proximity is critical to effectiveness.

In both processes, of course, corporate executive management play a critical role as decision-makers. Just as implementation of the company's long-range plan fully involves all line management, so advocacies on issues involve the full array of public affairs and other company resources warranted, including the time of the CEO and his colleagues. The company's board of directors is also kept informed of the major public policy issues facing the company through regularly scheduled briefings and written reports.

Finally, both processes must be accountable. In the case of strategic planning, evaluation is primarily quantitative; in the case of issues management, primarily, though not exclusively qualitative.

Organization/Personnel

Issues management is an art, a means of deploying expertise to serve the strategies of a business enterprise in the realm of public policymaking. The personnel it requires should thus be viewed not in terms of a set of credentials (some amalgam of social science and quantitative skills) but rather in terms of a collective, critical, synthesizing *habit of thinking*.

Obviously, issues management requires strong analytical skills, not least the ability to think conceptually and to speak, write and work collectively with dexterity and precision. But, while quantitative analytical skills are valuable and necessary, they cannot substitute for incisive qualitative thought. As in any other pursuit, meaning in the realm of public policy is not data but rather the interpretation of data. Analysis of costs and benefits to a company, for example, must inform analysis of public policy issues affecting company operations. But, it cannot replace consideration of the qualitative consequences those issues may carry. Issues management is by its nature interdisciplinary and synthesis-oriented.

The analytical act appropriate to issues management also entails a counter-intuitive, or counter-conventional spirit of critical inquiry: an ability to grasp assumptions behind notions apparently disparate, sometimes frankly foreign to, the analyst's usual way of thinking; a caution about usually unexamined staples of discourse, especially when transferred from one set of issues and applied by rote to another; and, most broadly, a scepticism about apparently fundamental presuppositions.

The issue of clean air exemplifies the need for such analytical thinking. Our analysis began with an examination of conventional assumptions.

- Can air pollution control and protection of human health be approached adequately in conventional economic terms?
- Has the Clean Air Act in fact adversely affected the long-term operations of the company?
- What are the specific cases within the company of the Act's demonstrably cost-ineffective effects that do not benefit society?
- What is the issue under debate with respect to protection of human health *vis-à-vis* chronic exposure to man-made carcinogens?
- How should the company and society approach the management of unanticipated consequences of technological change?

Consideration of such questions, coupled with a thorough inventory of company operations, technical practices and business plans, resulted in a pragmatic, systems approach to a company position and its public advocacy. The necessity of effective, extra-market government regulation was endorsed. Areas of demonstrably ineffective, even counter-productive regulation and administrative practice, however, were also identified, with precise recommendations for reform. This could not have been accomplished if analysis had begun (and ended) with a simple 'How do we get government air regulators out of company operations?'

Pitfalls and other problems

Because it is susceptible to trendy packaging, issues management may be misrepresented by ostensible adherents within a corporation and misperceived by the corporate decision-makers it is designed to serve. Implemented without thought, an issue management function can become irrelevant in short order, thus contributing to a rejection of coherent participation in the public policy process. The following observations may serve as a convenient point of departure for those interested in *effective* implementation of an issues management function:

Charter
An issues management function will prove effective in direct proportion
to senior management's understanding of its utility and commitment to
its success. In particular, senior management should subscribe explicitly
to the charter of an issues management function and substantiate the
charter by full involvement in the issues management process. Issues
management will not relieve corporate decision-makers of their responsibility to participate in the public policy process; it can ensure their
participation is coherent.

Scope
Issues management is not intended to bring 'futures research' inside the
corporation, nor is it a way to institutionalize 'social responsibility'
within the corporation. It is a process to identify particular issues whose
resolution will affect the operations of a company strategically, and it can
increase the societal effectiveness of a company's interaction with its
various constituencies. Issues managers do not dictate company policy
from some imputed position of authority; they accrue authority as they
earn it; as they prioritize issues and develop policy positions according to
the strategic objectives of the company. *Operations always bound issue
agendas, and issue agendas are, therefore, always company specific.* Within
the 'issues world' specific to a company, priorities can be effectively set
according to profit (economic exposure), people (employees, customers,
etc), community (effects of company operations and decisions) and country (effects of major US policy decisions on the company). Needless to say,
such criteria will blur, merge and vary in rank as well as differ according
to short *versus* long term perspectives.

Size and make-up
Issues management functions should be started and kept small, smart and
flat. In a corporate world glutted with overlapping staff specialities, an
issues management function can early be misperceived, even by management who initially subscribe to it, as some exotic (and soon expendable)
staff fad. Or, if retained, but deployed well down the corporate staff
hierarchy, an issues management function can be quickly reduced to a
staff speciality, and, as such, subject to considerations of 'turf' and ever
narrowing job descriptions.

   In fact, the process of issues management inside a company is a species
of politics. A formally designated process for such politics demands
flexibility, direct access and a staff small enough to demonstrate *collective*
intelligence. Selection of personnel should balance 'insiders' and 'outsiders'. The initial habit of mind about, and expertise regarding, external
dimensions of some key issues may need to be imported but should always
be wedded to detailed knowledge of company operations and practices

possessed by known and trusted 'insiders'. Ideally, as an issues management function matures within a company, becoming part of its culture, a purposeful rotation of personnel through the issues unit should take place. Over time, such human resource planning would allow 'outsiders' the opportunity to assume line responsibilities and give 'insiders' (that is personnel who begin their careers in line positions) experience with a valuable managerial process.

Core functions

The fundamental responsibility of an issues management 'team', as part of the strategic process of a company, is to help exercise foresight about and collectively develop options for corporate accommodation to the discontinuities present in society. In practice, this means successful reconciliation of internal conflicting interests on public policy issues, timely education of inevitably shifting networks of expertise within the company that such issues call into being, and effective application of disciplined analysis to ensure that appropriately critical inquiry and integrated thinking are brought to bear in the consideration of issues inside the company. *All of these tend to work against the cultural grain of many corporations*, not least because the emphasis on stand-alone profit centres, or decentralization, results in strong pressure to treat issues of public policy from isolated perspectives preoccupied with short-term considerations. In fact, in a decentralized firm, successful education of line management as to the importance of public policy issues to their operations may make negotiations of conflicting interests only more difficult. In addition, it may discourage the kind of disciplined analysis that is in fact the *sine qua non* for effective company participation in the public policy process. It is precisely at this point that the strategic dimension of a company-wide issues management process must be upheld by key decision-makers in the company.

New directions

The institution of, and experience with, an issues management process raises some important questions about public affairs functions and their organization. The importance of public affairs is generally recognized: representation in Washington DC and the statehouses, grass roots political action, media and community relations, shareholder affairs, speechwriting, corporate advertising, corporate philanthropy, and so forth. Many companies expend substantial resources in these areas, organizing these functions into a corporate staff hierarchy. In times of economic contraction, however, public affairs tends to be viewed as expendable, particularly by hard-pressed line managers. This occurs despite the fact that a bad economy, by its nature, increases the probability that public policy decisions will substantially affect corporate profitability and survival.

Obviously, the understanding of public affairs by executive management determines a company's commitment to public affairs functions, economic conditions notwithstanding. Defence of a *status quo*, however, will not justify commitment. In fact, because public affairs functions are usually organized as part of a conventional corporate staff hierarchy, often at the furthest remove from line operations, understanding and commitment are probably diluted. Ideally, public affairs should be viewed as analogous to corporate planning and research and development: as a strategic process to help realize the basic objectives of a company.

Issues management can improve a company's understanding of, and commitment to, public affairs. Effective issues management is an aid to, *not* a substitute for, decision-making at line and executive management levels about public policy issues that have consequences for operations. It works more by networks than hierarchies. As such, it tends to disregard line and staff distinctions, transforming organization charts into networks of expertise, parts or all of which can be brought to bear on a given issue as warranted by analytical requirements or advocacy strategies. It also vitiates distinctions based on 'turf', by making cooperation to achieve a general goal imperative. But again, it must have the authority and involvement of executive management in order to realize its potential.

If the commitment to issues management is made and the function proves its utility, it can serve as a model for all public affairs activity by a company. In that event, the proper organizational question for public affairs becomes 'what expertise is necessary within the company in order to realize external objectives with respect to public policymaking?'. Viewed as a network of expertise, public affairs can be given an explicit issue orientation, indivisible from company business decisions, daily line operations and other legitimate 'staff' activity. In sum, issues management as a discipline can become a model for cost-effective organizational innovation.

In the early 1980s, Public Affairs at Atlantic Richfield was reorganized in an attempt to bring a selective, issue-driven *modus operandi* to all public affairs functions. As Figure 5.2 indicates, public affairs was aligned to emphasize an explicit functional orientation:

- The Foundation became responsible for targeted philanthropy.
- Constituency Relations, was made responsible for representation to selected 'third parties', such as consumer and environmental groups, labour, the academic community, and industry trade associations.
- Operations became responsible for all regional government, public and media contact, including company representation in Washington DC.

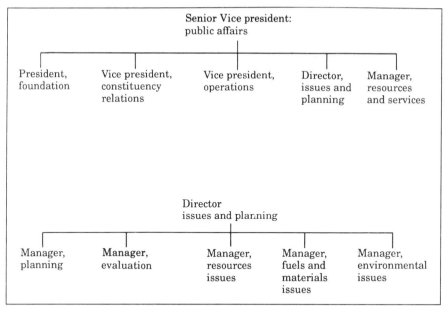

Figure 5.2 *Public affairs*

- Resources and Services was made responsible for corporate design, advertising, executive communications and publication services.
- Issues and Planning was made responsible for the issues management process and public affairs planning that includes budgetary control and evaluation of public affairs functions.

All Public Affairs activity are now keyed to the public issue objectives of the operating companies. These objectives are identified and analysed through the ongoing work of the issues managers (Resources, Fuels and Materials, and Environmental) in Issues and Planning. Broad corporate issues and integration of a coherent public affairs plan are the responsibility of the Public Affairs Planning Manager, who in turn must work with the Manager of Evaluation who is to ensure appropriate budgetary control and evaluation within Public Affairs. The success of the reorganization, of course, will depend on the close working relationship, and unanimity of purpose, of the five direct reports to the head of Public Affairs.

Conclusion

Perhaps the most fundamental requirement for effective issues analysis involves the acceptance of pluralism. A public policy issue that entails legitimate choices between conflicting values is not an anomaly in American democracy; it is, instead, intrinsic to the country's socio-political history. Issues analysis must balance the legitimate interests of a company with a consistently disinterested view of issues under consideration. This is not merely a matter of the politically possible; it is also a matter of the changing contract society makes with business. If issues management is regarded only as a tool to shape public policy to serve near-term business objectives, it will inevitably prove unsatisfactory as a legitimate function, both inside and outside the company. At its best, issues management is neither sophistic nor ideological; it is pragmatic. The habit of mind it requires and fosters may be fundamental to all decision-making that has consequences for society.

Like strategic planning, an issues management art to be practised within companies can be construed as a constructive corporate adaptation to the discontinuities of today's external business environment. Issues management may represent one way to restore critical inquiry and integrated thinking to the realm of American enterprise. In an 'age of discontinuity' adopting effective means to see things steadily and whole may represent the most fundamental challenge to American managerial practice.

Part Two

Crisis and recovery: managing radical change

Part Two   Crisis and recovery: managing radical change

Many businesses came under severe financial pressure in the period following the 1973–4 oil crisis. This was caused by the general downturn in the world economy and by increasing international competition for markets. The Japanese were starting to make serious inroads into Western markets using strategies based on new standards of product quality and reliability allied to a recognition of market needs. Suddenly customers became aware that they did not have to settle for what the manufacturer was prepared to supply: they had a wider choice!

Some companies saw their salvation in diversification. Exxon, for example, made an expensive and ultimately unsuccessful attempt to enter the 'office of the future' market. Subsequently many companies have returned to concentrate on their core markets as they have discovered they simply do not have the skills to manage other businesses. There are of course exceptions: BAT's management has continued to move away from its tobacco-based core products with considerable success. They, of course, have a strong incentive to reduce their dependency on tobacco products.

Rationalization and cutback has been the means by which many managements have attempted to restore financial viability. Carefully planned this re-establishes a stable, albeit smaller base. One of the main dangers of this strategy is that the actions taken are often too little and too late. There is a natural tendency to try to avoid unpleasant decisions, and the business gets into a downward spiral of successive cutbacks. On a more positive note, financial crisis has provided the incentive for many managements to implement radical change. The changes seen in many turnaround situations would not have been possible under normal circumstances. Too many 'sacred cows' have to be dispensed with to create radical change under usual operating conditions. The cases illustrated in this section are an interesting cross-section of the situations seen in recent years.

The first of the case studies shows how Shell Chemicals created a highly productive culture in one of their petrochemical plants through planned organizational change. The second illustrates how MFI, at one time a troubled mail-order business, achieved a dramatic turnaround by totally re-orienting its approach to the market place. The next case records how ICL fought its way back from the brink of ruin using a carefully planned series of strategic initiatives which overturned many of the previously held policies and tenets. One such initiative was an agreement with a Japanese competitor for the manufacture and supply of a main product line. The section concludes with the story of how Fiat restored firm management control and put itself into a position by which it could once again compete on equal terms as an international producer of volume cars.

6 Creating a productive organizational culture at Shell Chemicals

Ian A. Thornley, Personnel Director, Shell UK Ltd

The Carrington site near Manchester, UK, is a major manufacturing facility of Shell Chemicals UK (SCUK), producing petrochemicals from ethylene, propylene and styrene (see Figure 6.1).

In 1985 it had a turnover of about £200m, based on sales of 400,000 tonnes of petrochemicals, with a total workforce of 1150.

Figure 6.1 *The Carrington site*

The site was established in the 1940s, had grown rapidly in the 1950s and 1960s and was poised for another major expansion in the early 1970s. The cancellation of the expansion projects following the first oil price shock in the early 1970s left the site with a high overhead burden and production facilities based largely on early 1960s state-of-the-art technology. The second oil shock in 1979 found Carrington in a poor competitive position and from the period 1980–4 it made losses of £146m.

During this period Carrington undertook several phases of a rationalization programme which:

- shut down the oldest, least competitive plants and, with minor expenditure on those remaining, retained both the overall production capacity and almost all of its products portfolio;
- reduced manpower by over 57% (2700–1150) through successive voluntary severance campaigns;
- removed 'fat' within the organization and increased flexibilities within traditional employee trade groups (supervisory, foremen, process operators, maintenance craftsmen).

In 1985, with ethylene becoming available to SCUK from a new jointly owned ethylene cracker in Mossmorran, Scotland, and the expectation of continuing fierce market conditions, a reassessment of all SCUK's operations at Carrington was undertaken. The conclusion was that, to survive, the site had to reduce its fixed costs and its manpower drastically from 1150 to below 500 (see Figure 6.2).

The problem: the culture determines productivity

Carrington had had five years of continuous retrenchment and through this experience management had come to recognize that, despite reduction of the site to under half the 1980 numbers, and despite improvements in productivity, the culture had remained unchanged. This culture was felt to be a restricting force on Carrington's potential to be a winner.

An in-depth analysis of the way the site was organized convinced the Carrington management that conventional 'pruning' would only reduce manpower to about 700 and that, to achieve the reduction to 500, with the productivity improvement that this would imply, would require a change in site culture.

Equally serious, straight manpower cuts would not re-establish the confidence of senior Shell management, and the employees, of Carrington's determination not only to survive, but to become the best in an intensely competitive business. The question was, how to produce a lot more from a lot less?

The 'greenfield' Shell plants at Sarnia, Canada and Mossmorran, Scotland have manufacturing organizations and multi-skilled working

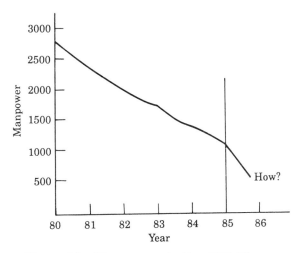

Figure 6.2   *Manpower reduction 1980–86*

practices very different from those traditionally found in the oil/petrochemical industry. The Carrington management believed these to be potentially more productive in the tasks of operating, maintaining and quality controlling the plants, and they used these examples as the start point for organization and job design changes. The simple question Carrington management asked themselves was 'How would we run the site if we were starting out all over again?'

The vision: to create a productive culture

The management was convinced that the only competitive edge that could be achieved with the Carrington asset base was through the knowledge and commitment of its people. They were also convinced that the employees wanted to contribute and become part of a successful team, and that the measure of success they were determined to champion were bottom-line financial performance and the satisfying of customer needs. The management were committed to aim for, and reward, excellence in both personal and team performance. The keys to achieving a productive environment were seen to be those of having consistency and re-enforcement of these and allied values in all facets of organization design, job design, working practices, reward systems and training/development programmes (see Figure 6.3).

The changes made: a new life for Carrington

The old organization had a six-layer structure. This was 'flattened' to four layers to improve communications and allow each job a bigger scope,

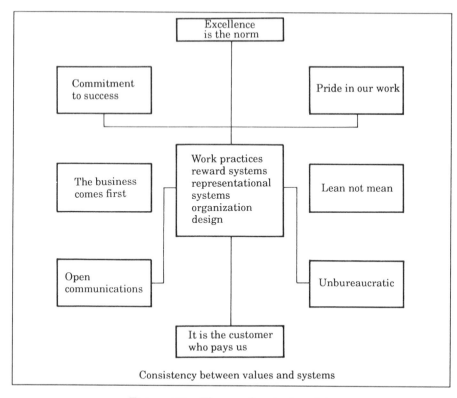

Figure 6.3   *The new Carrington vision*

with people being fully responsible for their jobs and the way they perform them.

The new Carrington is smaller and leaner with whole layers of organization removed and with those plants which could not be made profitable shut down (see Figure 6.4).

The site is changed from a functional-based organization to one based on four performance-accountable plant centres, each operated and maintained by six teams of multi-skilled *technicians* (an amalgamation of the conventional foreman, operator, craftsman positions) working a six-month cycle rotating between shifts (four months) and days (two months). While on shift they run the process operations and attend to minor maintenance as necessary. While on days *these same technicians* are largely involved only on plant maintenance. The key role of co-ordinating each team is carried out by a shift manager to whom the teams report. This manager stays with his team throughout the shifts/day cycle (see Figures 6.5 and 6.6).

Within the teams the technicians, on all occasions, do any required operating and maintenance work which they have the knowledge and

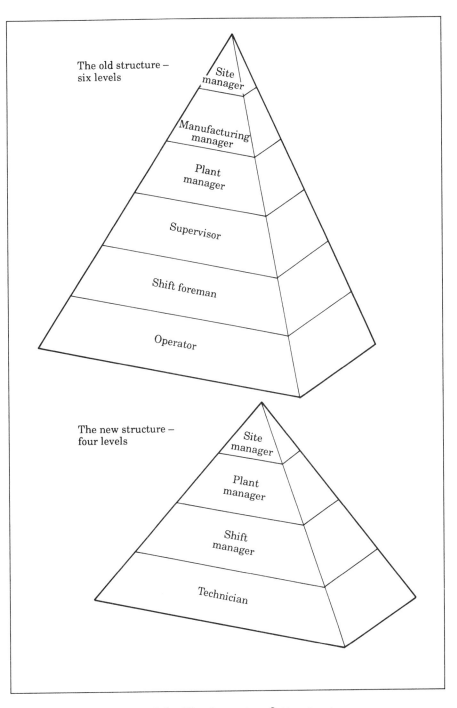

Figure 6.4   *The change to a flatter structure*

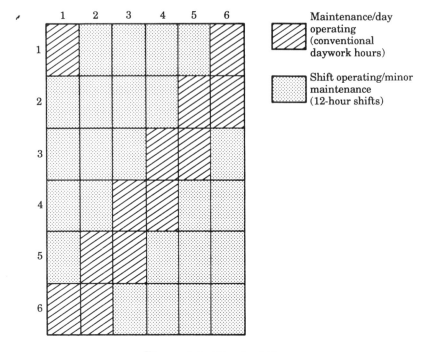

Figure 6.5 *The six shift pattern*

skills to tackle safely. There is also a small group of dedicated day technicians on each plant who carry out the most highly skilled diagnostic and specialized work.

The focus is on the main business activity and all support functions are actively questioned. The plant teams are supported by two service groups which supply essential technical and administrative backup to the four plants.

To achieve the full range of skills in the plant teams, a personal training programme is being carried out for each technician, depending on existing skills and job background (see Figure 6.7).

Divided into individual modules covering theory and practice, this training leads to qualifications against the nationally recognized standards of the City and Guilds Institute of London. These modules are in two blocks, each taking approximately six to nine months. Successful completion of each block is recognized by a salary increase (see Figure 6.8).

The new Carrington is lean but not mean. Salaries are highly competitive, reflecting the value of the jobs and the gaining of extra skills.

There is a single monthly staff status for all employees. For all technician grades there is now only one union agreement with a single set of terms and conditions. Previously there had been three separate,

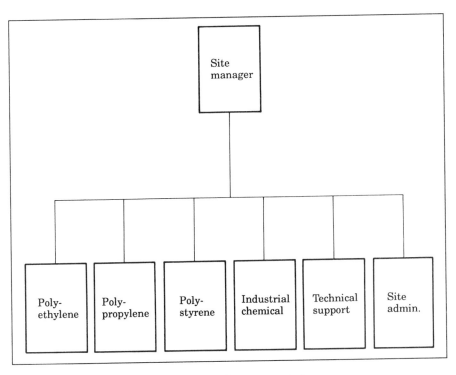

Figure 6.6   *The site manager's team*

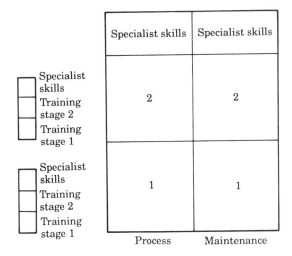

Figure 6.7   *Technician training blocks (training emphasis depends on background)*

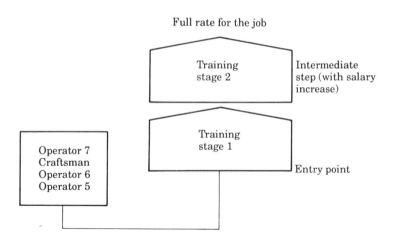

Figure 6.8 *The senior technician ladder*

demarcation-based union agreements, with distinctions between 'blue-collar' hourly paid workers and 'white collar' monthly paid staff.

The pensionable 'rate for the job' will cover a planned $37\frac{1}{2}$ hour week and some committed hours to manage unplanned absences and peak workloads.

Every employee is paid a regular monthly disturbance allowance, instead of the many incident payments that previously existed (see Figure 6.9).

Everyone in the new Carrington has the opportunity to earn an annual bonus based on their performance and contribution in the job and on the site results. Employees establish their performance targets jointly with their manager as part of the regular cycle of performance appraisal.

The change process: fair, firm and fast

The key aspects of the change process itself were:

High integrity: High resolve

There was an open bias on all information: as soon as possible, as much as possible, to as many people as possible. In the context of significant job loss there was a clear commitment to maintain the company's caring tradition via the establishment of a Redeployment Unit. In addition however there was a clear resolve on the part of the company to see the change programme through, even where this involved enforced redundancy, in the firm belief that there was no viable alternative to secure the future of the site. From the outset, and particularly with regard to the trade unions, clear limits were defined beyond which the company would

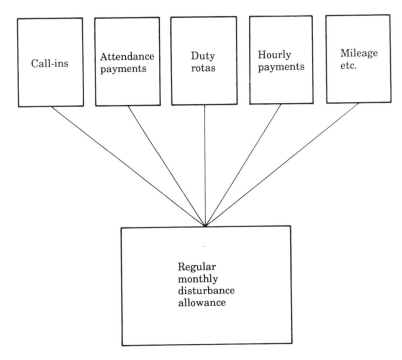

Figure 6.9   *Consolidating many incident allowances into one*

not alter its position as this could compromise the main objective of an overall culture change.

Primacy of the individual

The personal uncertainty surrounding each individual was removed at the earliest opportunity. His wishes had to be established, and then considered against the company's requirements, prior to an unequivocal statement as to whether he had or did not have a job in the new organization. This process took a maximum of four weeks. Each individual was personally counselled at least once a fortnight by his line management focal point, specially trained in counselling techniques. Throughout the communications exercise endless stress was put on the need for each employee to consider his position on the change proposals as an individual. In addition, no information was ever given to third party union bodies which had not previously been communicated via line channels to each employee.

Effective communications

The precise use of communications as a strategic management tool was essential in getting across and gaining support for a difficult message: '60

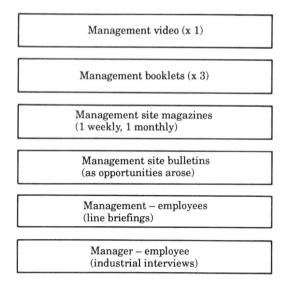

Figure 6.10   *The employee communication programme*

per cent of you must go, the others must change their demarcation-based ways of working and there must be a complete change of attitudes and site culture.' All line managers were retrained in effective 'one-to-one' communications and were regularly audited. A full-time senior management resource was allocated to the sole task of producing and co-ordinating the communications effort. Building on the revitalized solid base of the line manager/employee relationship, all modern techniques were employed, including three professionally produced handbooks on aspects of the change plan for each employee and a professionally produced video, also with a personal copy for each employee to take home and show his family (see Figure 6.10).

The simple belief which shaped Carrington's approach to communications was that, particularly in times of high uncertainty, the space between management and employees must be totally and quickly filled, otherwise, rumour and third party communications will fill the remaining vacuum.

Tight schedule
While the full implementation of all aspects of the change programme would take eighteen months, the company adopted the tightest of schedules for the formal consultation and decision-making process, involving both individual employees and third party union bodies. This schedule was published in advance and was never deviated from (see Figure 6.11). The prior informal individual consultation with employees

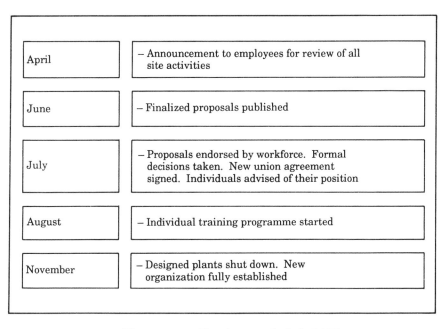

April	– Announcement to employees for review of all site activities
June	– Finalized proposals published
July	– Proposals endorsed by workforce. Formal decisions taken. New union agreement signed. Individuals advised of their position
August	– Individual training programme started
November	– Designed plants shut down. New organization fully established

Figure 6.11   *The change schedule (1985)*

on each and every detail of the change proposals meant that a momentum had already been generated such that the formal consultation phase (four weeks) was more than adequate.

Visible management leadership
Whereas the original vision for change was shared initially by a few managers, it was essential that the change programme was visibly 'owned' by all management. This process was reinforced by exclusive use of line channels to discuss every aspect of the programme. Line management were given the clear responsibility for, and were seen to manage, industrial relations without any competing influence from the personnel function. It was crucial that, to convey confidence and trust, there was a total investment of personal credibility by management as leaders in the programme.

The redeployment unit: life after Carrington

As a central feature of the high integrity and innovative emphasis of the change programme, the company set up a full-time Redeployment Unit (RDU) manned by four managers and six nominees from the trade unions. The idea itself was not new, but enhanced resources and an enhanced professionalism were applied to this important area which had previously been successfully developed by other Shell sites in the United Kingdom. The full participation of employees nominated by the site trade unions reinforced the independent and discrete role that the unit had to play. In addition to a line management focal point, each employee leaving Carrington had, therefore, an RDU 'counsellor' allocated to help him find an alternative career. The assistance offered was both intensely practical and emotionally supportive. The unit marketed itself forcefully to its 'clients' and to external employers who might be able to offer employment to Carrington's surplus workforce. A series of booklets, leaflets, handouts and a video gave the unit a profile and a credibility which was crucial to the well being of many employees faced with the certainty of imminent job loss.

Carrington now: the realization of change

The change programme, involving a 57 per cent reduction in manpower, was supported by almost the entire workforce as the best hope for the future of the site. The programme has throughout proceeded to its published tight schedule and training of the new multi-skilled technicians is (in 1988) nearing completion. Site manpower was reduced to the target level of below 500 by the end of 1986. Of the 500 staff that were laid off by the end of April 1986 some 76 per cent were helped to find alternative work outside Carrington by the Redeployment Unit, 42 per cent have also undergone some form of additional skill training which might help them find alternative work. A further 13 per cent chose not to continue working after leaving Carrington. The remainder of the surplus staff, some 200, had left the site by the end of 1986, and it is anticipated that a similar percentage of redeployment will be achieved.

The new Carrington is operating within its tight budget and the site is meeting its new profitability targets. The management believe that attitudes have really changed and that there is a new site culture, geared towards beating the competition amid the harsh realities of a highly competitive business world.

7 The turnaround at MFI: From a troubled mail-order firm to a leading furniture retailer

J. W. Seabright, Joint Managing Director, MFI Furniture Group

Even in 1972 and 1973 when mail-order houses were blooming, the board of MFI recognized that credit mail-order was a dangerous business to be in. At that time their shops were little more than clearing units for the merchandise which they had failed to sell on mail-order, but they knew that the future lay in stores retailing. They started to expand from nine shops in 1971, to twelve in 1972, and sixteen in 1973, and suddenly found that they had a totally different business. Instead of a highly centralized mail-order operation using large numbers of married ladies, full- and part-time, to open the post and send orders to suppliers, and relying on a variety of techniques to get their money, they had a widely dispersed organization requiring a high degree of management control; they had a substantial cash flow with its attendant cash management problems; they were inundated with problems caused by poor customer service and lack of spare parts; and the quality of their merchandise, although representing very good value for money, was just not up to the standard required by a retail store chain which wished to be around in five years time let alone fifty...

Early history

MFI had been set up by two friends, Noel Lister and Donald Searle, in the early 1960s to sell by mail-order a variety of merchandise including furniture. The company flourished and by the beginning of the 1970s, when people were prepared to buy anything off the pages of a newspaper if it seemed good value for money, MFI went public. The few shops it had were mainly small, in poor locations, with a strong warehouse flavour. The merchandise, although of poor quality, was very cheap. Fully-assembled furniture does not travel well by mail-order and therefore the development of flat-pack articles for assembly by the customer made excellent sense. In Europe, self-assembly furniture was beginning to sell well and rapid development was to take place over the first five years of the decade in the methods of joining pieces of chipboard simply and strongly. Only a screwdriver was needed to adjust the interlocking cams to make excellent joints. The quality of chipboard also improved and from being little more than 'veneered Weetabix' the material became highly versatile, very strong and dimensionally stable. It could be machined to extremely tight tolerances and mass production was possible; no assembly expense was incurred by the manufacturer; storage and distribution costs were far less than those for conventional fully-assembled furniture and damage was also reduced, although by no means eliminated.

In 1971 MFI went public and was the darling of the Stock Exchange in 1972. By 1973 it had lost its stripes and was down at the bottom of the performance league share. Margins were coming under considerable pressure, postal and distribution charges were rising, responses to advertising were dropping, and customers were paying more slowly or not at all. The company's response to this squeeze was to reduce prices and extend credit: which only made the situation worse.

But the shops were flourishing. The combination of stocks to take away and very good value for money was too much for the great British public to resist. The expansion programme which had started in 1972 continued; many of the new shops were profitable from the opening day and reached payback on their initial investment within three or four months. By May 1973 the company had sixteen shops (although several of them were now large enough to be called 'stores') and by May 1974 there was a total of twenty-four with another six about to open. It was a race to open stores fast enough to generate the cash flow which was needed to keep a very sick mail-order operation going.

By 1973 the Board, which had been so enthusiastic about its move into stores retailing, realized that it had a management problem of huge potential. A highly centralized mail-order company with a few shops dedicated to selling that merchandise which they could not sell off the pages of the *Sun* or the *Sunday Times* colour supplement was not the organization to control a widely dispersed retail chain. On the advice of consultants, the Board hired a number of retailers mainly from supermarkets or successful High Street chains, such as BHS, and they looked for a businessman with extensive experience of running large organizations with a high degree of management control. As a result I joined the company in August 1974.

Table 7.1 *Ten Year Record. A decade of excitement!*

					Year ended 31 May					
	1971	1972	1973	1974	1975	1976	1977	1978	1979	1980
No. of branches	9	12	16	24	33	39	52	56	64	77
Total turnover (£'000s)	6053	10505	15524	16649	15232	21149	33728	55043	87466	127344
Retail turnover (£'000s)	2554	4530	7395	9354	12508	21149	33728	55043	87446	127344
Profit pre-tax (£'000s)	912	1522	2212	813	78	1018	1862	5337	13979	16771
Sales per sq. ft (£)	N/A	N/A	N/A	N/A	32·24	43·68	50·96	68·64	88·40	97·40

By that time mail-order was in very bad shape and it was clear to me that we should have to reduce significantly our dependence on that side of the business. Noel Lister had been converted to this view at about the same time but most of the Board, particularly Donald Searle, still saw it as the sheet-anchor of the whole company. At the beginning of September 1974 the Board agreed to 'wind-down' mail-order, cut back on credit and make a major effort to recover the debt, which was standing at about £3½m. Nearly half the workforce was made redundant. This was a source of particular pain to Donald Searle who saw the mail-order side as his particular creation and its employees as demanding his special care. But there is no doubt that if this policy had not been implemented we should have 'bled to death' before the stores could save us.

My next task was to persuade Noel Lister not to shut down the mail-order side 'overnight' as I was convinced that to do so would simply mean that most of the people who owed us money would not pay. A decision to close mail-order was taken in the spring of 1975 and that side of the business was finally shut down in September of that year. More than 80 per cent of the outstanding debt was recovered.

Strengths and weaknesses

To improve standards of management generally was an immediate need but we also had to take a good hard look at the business we were in:

- We were selling furniture from stock at highly competitive prices for the customer to take away and assemble at home.

We were also selling a whole lot of other things which seemed to me to cause more problems than profit: 'disposable' golf clubs (the heads of which flew off if hit violently); plastic greenhouses which took off in high winds; personal saunas (which if they didn't suffocate you might electrocute you; rowing machines by the thousand immediately after Christmas and New Year gluttony; tents on fourteen days free approval which were often returned by happy holidaymakers as unsuitable at the end of their holiday!

We had some considerable weaknesses:

- With some outstanding exceptions, the quality of most of our furniture was very poor.
- Our customer service was non-existent.
- We had no proper spare parts provision control.
- Because of very poor packaging, the damage to our furniture in transit, in our warehouses, and by the customer on the way home was considerable.

• Control over the manufacturers was non-existent so that goods often did not meet the specifications; changes to components, finishes, assemblies, etc, would be made without proper, or any, notice.

Our shops had a very 'down-market' image with, in most cases, no passing trade.

However, what inspired everybody from the Board down was the realization that we had found a gap in the market which we could exploit. Mr and Mrs Public were not prepared to put up with expensive High Street furniture retailers who carried little or no stock, and offered waiting times of months, or even years in one notorious case. They did not want furniture which would last a lifetime, they did not want to have to wait for it and they wanted to see the same excellent value for money as they got for clothes in Marks and Spencer. I determined that we would become the Marks and Spencer of the furniture industry.

We had a record of successful advertising, we had low overheads and, as we ran down mail-order, we had cash for investment in new stores.

Organizing for the turnaround

Our most immediate problem was how we were going to re-organize the company to cater for the very different business we wanted to be in. Unfortunately there was no textbook on anyone's shelf which said 'MFI Organization, 1975–80'. We had a lot of good people, although many of them were untrained and unused to the demands of a large business. The young retailers we had brought in were beginning to make a lot of changes to the retail operation's organization and would form the nucleus of our future success.

MFI's problem was how to harness the undoubted drive and vision of the two entrepreneur founders to an efficient and flexible organization. I was convinced of the importance of the entrepreneur to the successful growth of any business. Opinions about and attitudes towards entrepreneurs tend to be as subjective as the entrepreneurs themselves. Those who have benefited from contact with them frequently extol them with an enthusiasm little short of idolatory; those who have suffered from them have little good to say. The neutral observer will acknowledge that few small businesses succeed without someone with the temperament and characteristics of an entrepreneur; but one who can adapt to the changing demands and needs of a growing organization is rare. The ability to remain successfully in the driving seat when the business is large, diverse and complex is given to very few. Nevertheless, I believe that all businesses, whatever the stage of their growth, need the challenge and the vision of the entrepreneur.

The good entrepreneur usually understands instinctively what the customer wants. He usually knows where he wants to be but often not how to get there. He has two invaluable assets: he sees solutions where others see problems and he is never satisfied! No matter how well you are doing, somebody, somewhere, is always doing better than you are: or if they aren't, they ought to be! This is possibly the most irritating and frustrating characteristic of the entrepreneur; it can be self-defeating but, on the other hand, it attacks the complacency, arrogance and self-satisfaction which are the greatest enemies of success.

The entrepreneur has a number of serious weaknesses; he rarely trusts anyone to do a job properly, in fact, many don't trust anyone at all! He is often a bad judge of men and he usually underestimates the manager. The professional manager is rarely an entrepreneur but in the really success-ful business each needs the other. It is a difficult and frequently violent marriage but without the professional manager's skills an entrepreneur's desire for his company to grow will often be frustrated; without the entrepreneur the essential vision and flair that can ensure success may be lacking. Most entrepreneurs are restless, uncompromising, uncomfortable colleagues with certain extraordinary talents. The business which aims to expand must learn how to acquire and manage those talents.

The new organization

I devised a plan which would, as far as possible, isolate the entrepreneurs from the day-to-day management of the company. The aim was to en-courage the development of a management team with everyone pulling in the same direction and to reduce, even if I could not eliminate, the entrepreneur's favourite divide and rule tactic.

I outlined the objectives of an efficient organization structure as follows:

1 To ensure that all employees, including directors, are fully aware of their responsibilities and limits of authority and know exactly what is required of them in their jobs.
2 To assist communication within the company both downwards, in the form of instruction and information, and upwards, in the form of reactions and feedback.
3 To separate the policy-making activities of the directors and the executive functions of management.

One of the difficulties I encountered was that most of my directors were really managers with board responsibilities and they were usually un-aware (particularly the entrepreneurs among them) of the different significance of their dual roles. A lot of time was therefore spent explain-ing that as directors they should be concerned with establishing policy, with deciding whether the company was going in the right direction, whether it required a change of direction: a touch on the accelerator or on the brake. A manager, on the other hand, is concerned with the day-to-day running of the company within the framework of policies laid down by the Board. Although he is bound to have views on policy and should be encouraged to criticize and suggest improvements or alterations, this is secondary to his principal job.

A management committee was set up which met monthly and comprised the heads of all the main divisions: retail operations, distribution, buying, marketing, finance and property. Noel Lister, Donald Searle and the Chairman, Arthur Southon, were not members of that committee. It was not intended to be primarily a policy-making or even a decision-making body. Its objective was to improve the understanding of each division about the activities of the others, to reduce the areas of conflict between them, and to highlight the problems either of day-to-day management or of company policy which required solutions. The divisional heads were responsible to me for the proper running of departments and the attainment of their corporate objectives. Decisions were made by them in consultation with me or, in three cases, in consultation with the other Joint Managing Director, Noel Lister. Those three areas were buying, advertising and property, where Noel had great ability and flair. He was functionally responsible for those three divisions although I was responsible for their day-to-day performance.

But the real key to the development of the MFI organization rested on four policy groups (Figure 7.1). The main one was the Retail Group which was set up to discuss the retail operations of the company and to decide on policy, new stores, advertising, margins and profitability and also to review the performance and progress of existing stores. Noel Lister, Donald Searle (until his tragic death in 1976) and the Chairman were on it and so were the directors in charge of retail operations, buying and advertising, the two senior retail managers and the personnel manager.

The other groups were the Merchandise Group, the Warehouse Group and the Chairman's Sub-Committee. All of them consisted of directors and line managers responsible for appropriate areas of the business. The last group, the Chairman's Sub-Committee, was chaired by the group chairman with the finance director and myself as members. It met only occasionally to discuss policy on personnel and training, staff relations and welfare, salary reviews, etc. We invited divisional directors and managers to attend to discuss such matters when they related to their divisions.

These groups were effectively sub-committees of the Board. The entrepreneur-founders were members and contributed trenchantly to our discussions. The first three groups met every two months and I attempted with increasing success to keep the discussions at a policy level rather than on day-to-day management topics. Some meetings were highly

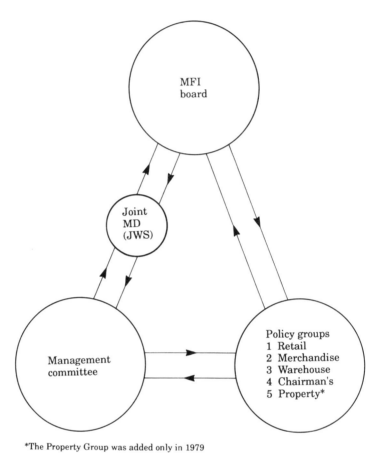

*The Property Group was added only in 1979

Figure 7.1   *MFI corporate structure*

successful, others were disasters but, if they did nothing else, they served
to underline the essential difference between direction and management.
They encouraged a broad company view rather than a narrow divisional
outlook, and they allowed the views of line managers to be heard before
important company policy decisions were made. Perhaps most important
of all they discouraged the sort of interference from the top in the day-to-
day running of the divisions which can be so destructive of morale and
damaging to an organization. The entrepreneurs were encouraged to be
constructive, their divide-and-rule tactics were limited, and the equally
destructive 'divide-the-rulers' tactics of some of the divisional managers
were blocked.

In fact the organization of MFI had three legs like a stool. Like a stool, the structure would function efficiently only if all three of the legs were in good condition. The legs were the Management Committee, the Policy Groups and the main Board. The latter was the ultimate authority for all policy decisions. When I joined the company we had an *ad hoc* Board meeting every lunchtime to discuss matters which ranged from pricing policy to the cost of paper clips. With the new organization, the Board could assume its rightful role of agreeing major policy initiatives and reviewing the progress of the Group against its main objectives.

The structure was intended to harness the creative energies of the entrepreneur to an efficient, flexible organization with the detailed management control which a fast-growing company required. It had one serious weakness: what would happen when Noel Lister and I, the two Joint Managing Directors, were in fundamental disagreement about the strategies or even the short-term tactics which the company should pursue? We were fortunate in having a Chairman, Arthur Southon, who was not only an extremely shrewd businessman but also an outstanding 'referee'. Noel Lister had known him for many years and trusted him; I had known him for a very short time but recognized his considerable ability. He would intervene (usually on request) before our disagreements had got to serious proportions, listen to both sides of the argument, take some soundings of his own and tell us his conclusions. We accepted them. Some sort of built-in-safety net of that type is essential where a company is effectively run by two people with very different skills and experience.

Training and Development

One of the most crucial problems we faced was the need to train our managers to be more than just good supervisors and to develop them fast enough to cope with the considerable retail growth we were planning. I was fortunate in having a retail operations director, Derek Hunt, who was as dedicated to good management training as I was. We spent a great deal of time, effort and money on training and I am convinced that this contributed enormously to our rapid rate of growth. In the six calendar years between 1974 and the end of 1980, retails sales increased from £9·2m and £148m. In that period we opened ninety-five stores and closed twenty. We could not have managed that sort of expansion without a massive investment in people.

Wherever possible, we 'grew our own'. There are considerable advantages in developing your own personnel; you know their strengths and weaknesses, they know your business, and people often respond surprisingly well to being given more responsibility. Nevertheless, the rate of our expansion meant that we had to recruit outside and train many people from scratch.

Merchandise selection and control

In 1974 we were overstocked with a very large range of merchandise, many items of which were slow moving or dormant. A major effort had to be made to reduce our stocks and the number of lines we carried; we had to institute a system of buying control which would limit the ability of the buyers to introduce new products while maintaining an essential element of discretion so that the entrepreneur was not hog-tied by the bureaucracy. We slashed the ranges, introduced regular reviews of all product groups and set up a system of budgetary control for buying. The controls were sometimes flouted, the restraints were not always observed but the information had the effect of enabling Noel Lister and the buying director to be far more aware of trends and developments in the market. Prior to the introduction of these controls, the most exaggerated statements about the performance of various products could be made with impunity. Once buying control became an important factor in the organization, merchandise selection and range review were highly effective.

Pricing policy

This is an area of great controversy and MFI has been at the centre of much protest about its policies. Margin control in high-volume retailing is vital and our manually-produced information was often much too late to be able to control our profits as we required. Only with the advent of the computer did we obtain the necessary rapid review of our margins which made good pricing decisions more frequent than bad! MFI was wedded to the idea of value for money and, because of its extremely close relationship with high-volume producers, we were able to buy at prices far below the average in the trade. This meant that we could undercut our competitors and still make handsome margins in many areas of our business; this, in turn, allowed us to slash prices from time to time, advertise those lines heavily and yet still make a modest profit. The MFI half-price sale and the Price-Buster promotions were developed in this way and contributed significantly to our enormous volume increases year after year. Also it meant that where we had slow-moving stock we could afford to cut prices dramatically and advertise them extensively.

Quality control

Providing high quality was a cornerstone in my strategy in developing a new image for MFI, but achieving control over quality was not an easy task. When I joined, the company had the traditional buying-dominated attitude that items would sell 'if only the staff in the shops were not so idle or incompetent'. A study was conducted to determine where our major problems lay and it revealed an appalling list of difficulties, from manufacturers changing product specifications without notice, to damage in transit and poor packaging. I set up a regular monthly meeting to review customers' complaints. Stricter control and inspection of suppliers' deliveries were instituted. Regular visits began to be made to manufacturers by MFI representatives. Untypically, MFI's heavy reliance on foreign imports in the mid-1970s began to change. It was obviously much easier to control suppliers on your doorstep than 10,000 miles away. By 1981 imports had sunk from about 60 per cent of sales to less than 30 per cent.

Customer service

Customers not only had to be convinced of the quality of our products but we had to ensure that any problems they encountered were rapidly and satisfactorily remedied. The difficulty with flat-pack furniture is that the customer is effectively buying a box of bits. There is no way of guaranteeing that the box is either complete or undamaged. Regular checks at the suppliers and in our warehouses could help to reduce complaints but never eliminate them. It was therefore essential to improve our attitude to those customers who had complaints, whether they were justified or not. We adopted, very reluctantly on the part of some of my colleagues, the Marks and Spencer's approach that all complaints were justified and some form of redress was essential. Changing the former attitude was very difficult but by 'carrot-and-stick' we achieved a considerable improvement. Inter-branch competitions with handsome prizes were insituated and every possibility was taken to ensure that customers recognized our willingness to deal speedily and satisfactorily with their complaints.

Financial resources

The lack of cash is often one of the most serious constraints on a successful turnaround, banks and suppliers want their money faster than the ailing company can pay. MFI was fortunate: our shops were profitable, credit sales were reduced and then eliminated, and our successful efforts to recover the huge mail-order debt gave us a steady supply of cash which was immediately invested in new stores. A five-year loan of £½m was raised from a merchant bank and a major supplier took up 1 million shares for £180,000.

The turnaround strategy was a success and ten years later MFI, under its dynamic young management team, still goes from strength to strength. The company dominates the retail furniture sector and has a substantial share of the flat-pack market. In April 1985 a merger was announced between MFI and Associated Dairies which set a value of over £560m on the company and created one of the largest retail groups in the UK.

We learned many lessons: probably the most important is that the kind of organization needed for a successful turnaround is one that is moulded around the people already there rather than one that is theoretical and does not take into account the staff available to implement the new strategies.

Cash availability and control are vital and until the necessary finance has been secured, whether by borrowing, selling assets or reducing debtors, no effective strategy has much chance of success.

But, most important of all, the people who will staff the new organization have to believe in the new strategy and be committed to it. As so often in business, success depends on people.

8 ICL: Crisis and swift recovery

D. C. L. Marwood, Company Secretary, ICL Ltd

ICL was born in 1968 from the merger of ICT with English Electric Computers. This completed a series of earlier mergers beginning in 1959 with the combination of the Hollerith and Powers-Samas punched card companies. It took place with the firm encouragement of the British Government and created the UK's flagship in the burgeoning world computer industry (see Figure 8.1).

New ICL product strategy resulted in the ICL 2900 Series mainframe computers, launched in the autumn of 1974. It took a number of years and heavy development costs (helped by further government cash support of £40m) to establish acceptable performance standards for the untried 2900 hardware and software. However, the basic concept of the 2900 Series was sound.

Throughout the 1970s ICL retained its independence as a designer, maker and supplier of non-IBM compatible mainframe computers, and its strategies were all based on that concept. The acquisition of Singer Business Machines in 1976 took ICL down into the small end of the mainframe market.

During the later 1970s, ICL's financial strategy was based on high revenue growth to cover its swiftly rising cost base (augmented by UK inflation) and to leave a steady profit progression. This was a high-risk strategy: the mainframe market might not grow fast enough, costs were leaping ahead and margins were being squeezed by competition.

By late 1979, ICL's major problem was how to close the widening gap between the funds needed to develop the next generation of mainframes and the funds likely to be available. The Board accepted slightly lower growth targets and management strove to increase revenue while reducing product costs.

The effort to reduce manufacturing costs led to the decision in October 1979 to close the plant at Dukinfield, Manchester, with the loss of some 900 jobs and closure costs of £7½m. This was the first of a series of major redundancy programmes.

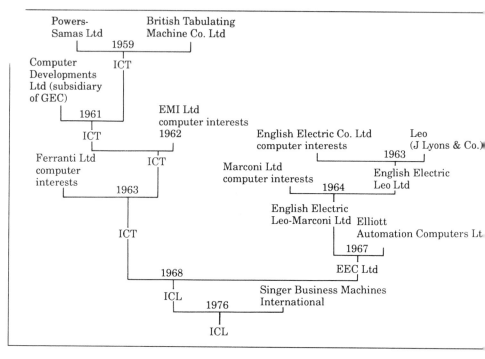

Figure 8.1 *ICI historical background*

By February 1980, there were signs that the half-year results might be worse than those achieved a year earlier. In the same month, ICL's Chairman retired upon reaching age 65. The election of his successor, a non-executive member of the Board, exhibited the classic dilemma of whether to choose a new Chairman from amongst the existing Board members or from outside.

Management began special measures to reduce overheads, such as recruitment bans. But general economic conditions were worsening and ICL's cash usage was rising fast. So it was decided to sell some of ICL's worldwide rental base to leasing companies. This short-term boost inevitably bit hard into ICL's financial sinews.

ICL's half-year results showed a 21 per cent turnover rise but only a 10 per cent profit increase. Profit was hit by the strength of sterling, greater competition, rising UK inflation and higher interest costs. The order growth was modest.

The crisis

From June 1980, there were clear signs of a sharp fall in profitability for the whole of 1979–80. There were also pressing matters to consider for the longer term. Management's draft Five-Year Plan raised a number of fundamental issues. These included a bigger development fund gap, the need to consider moving into new areas such as office automation (although strategic thinking was still based on a largely mainframe product line), and the idea of linking with a rich protector.

The Board was conscious not only of the worrying uncertainties of how ICL should shape its corporate strategy and then carry it through, but also of the immediate dangers of order shortfall and loss of profit.

By September 1980 it was clear that the 1979–80 order shortfall would be around £100m, marketing and other costs would be much too high and total cash facilities could be exhausted by the following March. The gravity of the decline had not been spotted soon enough.

The first public sign of trouble was the announcement that ICL would not proceed with its normal intake of several hundred university graduates. From a peak of 196p the ICL share price dropped sharply to 100p.

The position continued to deteriorate and the Board decided upon a second major manpower reduction involving 2500 redundancies and the closing of the large factory at Winsford, Cheshire. The Department of Industry was warned of ICL's growing need for cash cover.

The financial results announced in December showed turnover up by 15 per cent to £715m but pre-tax profit down by 46 per cent to £25m. City confidence was severely shaken, and the ICL share price plunged to 70p.

Board members again urged the need for survival action, such as seeking support from a strong outside source. Informal approaches were made to two major oil companies as possible cash-rich partners but without result. Talks with other companies on possible technical collaboration had begun in the autumn of 1980. By January 1981 negotiations had started with one of the American majors about a joint marketing arrangement.

By the end of January ICL was unable to tell whether or not it would overrun its existing cash facilities and exceed its legal borrowing powers after end-March 1981.

At the AGM on 3 February the Chairman disclosed a pre-tax loss of over £20m in 1980–1's first quarter. The full year forecast indicated a pre-tax loss as high as £50m. There were doubts whether ICL's bankers would continue support and the confidence of ICL's customers started to wane. The Board moved to a policy of seeking an outright bid or some form of joint venture which included a very substantial equity injection.

Discussions with potential partners proceeded swiftly, aided by ICL's merchant bankers. The Board pressed the Government for an immediate decision on financial support, and took legal advice about when it might have to consider whether or not ICL should cease trading (see Figure 8.2).

On 18 March, the Government and ICL's four UK bankers met with ICL and its advisers and offered a support package of £270m UK bank

• 20% growth objective continued into the recession
• High fixed cost base, mainly manpower
• Low quality of earnings; growth and costs offset by leasings; off balance sheet finance
• Erosion of margins overseas by uncompetitive Sterling exchange rates
• Margins cut and R & D expenditure demands increased by IBM price/ performance actions in 1979

• Weak, Undercapitalized, Highly Geared Balance Sheet
      Result
      • £133M Loss in 1981
      • £100M Cash Outflow

Figure 8.2 *Problems of 1980–81*

overdraft facilities to end-March 1983, of which £70m would be covered by ICL's existing floating charge to the four UK bankers (Barclays, Midland, Nat West and Citibank) and £200m would be covered by a Government guarantee. The guarantee was limited to two years because this was felt enough time to conclude a merger or other arrangement with a strong partner, which was the anticipated solution. The Government and the banks also imposed a number of conditions which were included in detailed facility and guarantee agreements.

The Government made it plain that its guarantee would not extend beyond the four UK banks. So, with unused overseas bank lines already cut off, and with the financial community's understandable nervousness, ICL walked a tightrope for months ahead to maintain its essential overseas financing facilities.

Throughout March and April, efforts continued to find a suitable longer-term partner; such a link-up would, for ICL, involve either total American acquisition or American control through product policy. Meanwhile, management strove to cut back costs and planned a third manpower reduction. But these genuine efforts were too late; the hour had struck when the Government would step in.

New management

On 8 May the Government notified the Company that, under powers in its guarantee agreement, it proposed to nominate three new ICL Directors, one to be Chairman and another Managing Director. The Government's action was supported by three major ICL shareholders, the Post Office Superannuation Fund, the Prudential and the Legal and General.

The Government had four aims:

- to ensure that its guarantee was not called;
- to maintain its own computing capability, which was very largely on ICL equipment;
- to enable that capability to be enhanced and developed;
- to maintain a substantial computer capability in the UK.

At an historic ICL Board Meeting on Sunday, 10 May, lasting $7\frac{1}{2}$ hours until early Monday morning, the Chairman and the Managing Director relinquished office. In their place came Mr Christopher Laidlaw (a Deputy Chairman of BP, with over thirty years' BP service) who was appointed full-time Chairman, and Mr Robb Wilmot (a senior executive of Texas Instruments with fifteen years' service) who became Managing Director. Mr John Gardiner (Chief Executive of the Laird Group and the Government's third nominee) joined as a non-executive director.

The aim of the new team was to stem the losses, restore confidence and ensure ICL's independent survival. So the Board at once decided to break off all partnership discussions.

The first phase: late 1981

ICL's trading position was precarious, and there was a pressing need to restore customer confidence and employee morale. The new team had to get up speed as fast as possible and to demonstrate swift, crisp decisions.

Letters from the new Chairman went to all ICL's major customers round the world, indicating the determination to succeed. A video message was distributed to all ICL employees worldwide.

The new team at once considered how best to bring the business back into balance. Employee costs were still the largest element of operating expenditure. Manpower reduction would cause high redundancy costs and would severely impact cash, but it was decided to discuss with the Government and the UK banks the manpower reduction programme under consideration by the previous management.

With ICL stuck in the crossfire between IBM and the Japanese, and with no link-up possible with IBM, it seemed sensible for ICL to try and forge a strong Japanese link. Talks with Fujitsu had started some months earlier, and now a fresh impetus was given.

Eighteen days after taking office, the Managing Director put forward, and the Board approved, the following employee cost reduction proposals:

- Manpower to be reduced by 5200 with two more plants (Bradwell Wood and Hanley) being closed.

- Temporary short-time working to be introduced at certain plants.
- A voluntary early retirement scheme to be introduced.

The Board decided to offset the adverse effect on the Group's reserves and borrowing powers by seeking shareholders' consent to:

- a relaxation of the borrowing limit under ICL's Articles, and
- an issue of up to £50m redeemable Preference shares.

At the beginning of June the Half-Year Report for 1980–1 referred to the continuing low rate of new orders, and emphasized management's primary task of restoring ICL to profitability. Part of the strategy was to seek collaborative ventures aimed at improving ICL's future products, especially collaborations aimed at providing synergy to the ICL product range and markets. The City was still not sure whether the new team would succeed, and so the ICL share price continued its downward drift, standing at 35p after the half-year results.

Restoring confidence

There was no sign of a let-up in the slump of new orders, due to the economic recession and to loss of confidence in ICL. Special efforts were mounted to reduce total inventory by £100m but the latest cash forecast showed net overdrafts increasing by over £30m.

Management felt that a worthwhile collaborative venture would help a lot in improving confidence in ICL. But to achieve such a link, ICL would have to present a reasonably hopeful profile. Thus it might be wise to seek an extension of the Government's guarantee due to expire in April 1983.

In June and July, the Chairman battled to get agreement to ICL issuing up to £50m redeemable Preference shares. These could only be placed with the banks (no one else would accept them) if they were covered by the Government's guarantee, which expired in March 1983. Never before had redeemable Preference shares been issued with less than twenty months before redemption. The next objective was that Preference shares would rank behind borrowings should ICL be wound up; but the conversion of up to £50m borrowings into equity would have a major effect on ICL's balance sheet, helping both reserves and net worth.

By the end of July, the Government and the banks had been persuaded. The change in borrowing powers and the issue of £50m Preference shares were approved at an EGM on 28 August. This enabled the Group balance sheet for the financial year to show an acceptable relationship between borrowings and shareholders' funds after providing for heavy losses and rationalization costs.

Meanwhile, the manpower reduction programme of some 5200 employees had been going ahead. The unions called a one-day strike on 8 July which was poorly supported. Management recognized that the full financial benefit of the reduction programme would not become effective until the second half of 1981–2.

Signs began of an improvement in customer confidence, with orders for June showing an increase. Great efforts were expended by senior management, from the Chairman and the Managing Director downwards, in encouraging customers to believe in ICL's future.

The Board was conscious that a restoration of confidence depended greatly upon awareness that the Government's financial support would not terminate abruptly, upon the existence of a sensible new product strategy and upon further, more permanent improvements in the Group's financial structure.

The new product strategy

The Managing Director therefore spent much time formulating a new product strategy and in exploring possible collaborative ventures. Under the new strategy ICL would supply a full, networked product line and not simply the mainframe element. Collaborative ventures would enable ICL more easily to get into new products and new markets, as well as creating a new environment for ICL's survival.

The new strategy involved a major collaboration with Fujitsu, a world leader in sophisticated computer technology. This envisaged ICL using the latest, very advanced Fujitsu technologies in its future mainframe designs. Collaboration on mainframe development would fit well with the basic strategy of supplying total networks and complete solutions, with mainframes being but one element and distributed systems and standard network application packages as other key elements. Fujitsu hoped that working with ICL would increase its volume sales. ICL would be able to reduce its development spend on mainframe technology and divert that spend to small systems development.

In September, Robb Wilmot signed heads of agreement with Fujitsu and a team was set up to settle the collaboration details. With Fujitsu at least nine months ahead of any competitor in developing CMOS gate array chips, the main area of collaboration was to be technological. The arrangement would also cover the marketing by ICL in selected territories of Fujitsu's latest IBM-compatible large M380 mainframe (which became the ICL Atlas Ten).

The Board also approved Robb Wilmot's proposal to collaborate with the MITEL Corporation of Canada in respect of electronic PABX systems. The intention was to offer PABXs as part of ICL's co-ordinated data, voice and text networked product line.

Other key areas which were the subject of top management attention during the first few months of the new regime were Company organization, space reduction, overseas controls, sales productivity in the small systems markets, better handling of inventories, improved debt collection and better business forecasting. New thinking, new attitudes and changes were swiftly introduced in all these and many other areas.

In the early autumn, management and the Board sought an operating plan for 1981–2 aimed at bringing the company back to a break-even position. The cost base was still too high, particularly in respect of manufacturing capacity. The big expense of achieving a further £25m reduction in costs could (with the need to conserve cash) only be achieved by higher revenue. Hence 1981–2's key objectives would require more revenue and using less cash. Could the Government be persuaded to extend its guarantee beyond April 1983? Would it be possible to mount a Rights Issue to ICL shareholders?

The Board was also conscious of the need to 'clean out the stable' in the year-end accounts. There would have to be a delicate balance between a heavy trading loss plus large write-offs and the maintenance of customer confidence. There was also the effect on ICL's net worth; too heavy an impact here could trigger a statutory obligation to consult shareholders.

Re-financing

In its role as ICL's largest customer, the Government was willing to help by, for example, paying cash up-front for new equipment and software. But as regards general financial support, the Government's attitude was that it had already helped ICL twice (with the original guarantee and with the issue of Preference shares) and that it was now the turn of ICL's shareholders. The Board therefore decided to sound out, on an insider basis, the three major ICL shareholders who had been involved in the management changeover.

Without a further manpower reduction, profit for 1981–2 would be little more than break-even. Financing this manpower reduction could be achieved by a Rights Issue. The three major shareholders were encouraging but their support depended on the ICL/Fujitsu deal, fundamental to ICL's mainframe strategy, being signed up.

In the five weeks from mid-November to mid-December, activity in London and Tokyo rose to a controlled crescendo. ICL and its advisers prepared the mass of documents needed for the Rights Issue. A further 2500 redundancies and the closure of the printed circuit board factory in Manchester, barely two years old, were announced. The Chairman and the Managing Director presented ICL's strategies for 1981–2 and beyond to the Government and stressed that, if the Fujitsu deal were to fail, the consequences for ICL would be grave. ICL and Fujitsu negotiating teams hammered away, for a week in London and then a week in Tokyo, at detailed terms.

These five weeks were a real 'high risks, high stakes' period. The manpower announcement committed ICL to going ahead with 2500 redundancies at an expense which the Auditors would accept in the 1980–1 accounts, thus raising the extraordinary costs of manpower reduction to more than £50m. During those five weeks ICL was exceedingly exposed to a crisis of confidence in four different, but interlocking, areas. If the Government refused to extend the guarantee beyond March 1983 (now only fifteen months away) Fujitsu would not consent to the long-term collaboration that was essential to ICL's strategy. If Fujitsu would not commit, then the three major shareholders would withdraw their support from the Rights Issue. If the Rights Issue could not be underwritten, ICL could not afford to carry out the 2500 redundancies. If the redundancies were not effected, ICL could not offer the prospect of a return to profit and the confidence of banks and customers would finally evaporate. But with the skill and dedication of all concerned the complex and ambitious plan was put into place.

The night before the Fujitsu Chairman returned to Tokyo, the Secretary of State, Patrick Jenkin, wrote to say that the Government would extend its guarantee on a tapering basis. From 1 April 1983 the guarantee would fall from £200m to £150m, from 1 April 1984 to £100m, from 1 April 1985 to £50m and would end on 31 March 1986.

Collaborative ventures

By the end of November the ICL team in Tokyo had settled all outstanding points on the detailed ICL/Fujitsu agreements, which were then initialled by both parties. The formal agreements were signed in London a week later.

While these exciting events took place, the Managing Director established four more collaborative ventures, less vital than the Fujitsu deal but important in filling out ICL's new product range. ICL obtained the right to manufacture and market the Rair computer as ICL's Personal Computer; this saved ICL at least a year in developing its own model. From the British Technology Group and Logica, ICL acquired marketing rights for the VTS 2000 word processor; this became the ICL 8800 Series. A deal with the Three Rivers Corporation enabled ICL to market and later manufacture the PER Q engineering and scientific workstation. A development agreement with Sinclair helped ICL to build various advanced Sinclair devices into its own products.

On 15 December, ICL's results for 1980–1 were released. These showed a trading loss of £55m plus extraordinary expenses of £78m, a total loss of £133m! (See Figure 8.3.) A 'cleaning of the stable' which reduced shareholders' funds to less than £72m!

At the same time came the announcement of a one-for-one Rights Issue to raise £32m. There was little choice about the terms or indeed the size,

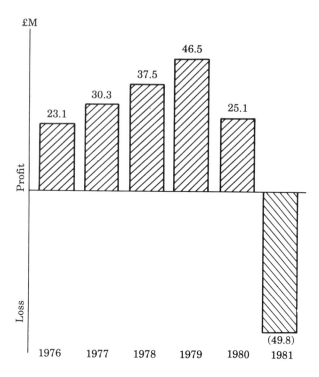

Figure 8.3 *ICL profit before tax*

since the City regarded one-for-one as very 'heavy'. ICL shares had dropped below par at the end of September and, by the time the Issue was ready, had risen to 45p. With the Chairman's statement that there would be no dividends for 1980–1 or 1981–2, a deep discount was needed to make the Issue attractive. The Issue price was therefore set at par (25p).

On 25 January the success of the Issue was announced, with acceptances of over 95 per cent. ICL had turned its first main corner back to a profitable future.

The second phase: 1982

There was still a great deal to be done. 1982 had to be a year in which ICL built vigorously on its strengthened foundations. But, with the continuing recession, ICL could not rely on any growth in the volume of its business. To maintain the growth of confidence in ICL, it would be essential to show a worthwhile trading profit for 1981–2 whilst ensuring close control over cash, the factor that had brought ICL's problems to a head in early 1981. This meant a huge task of achieving development, manufacturing and sales targets, especially in the new product lines, with simultaneous restructuring and constant, firm application of new control mechanisms.

New senior management

The quality of ICL senior management had been subject to close scrutiny and action from mid-1981 onwards. New Marketing and Finance Directors came on the main Board (the three previous Executive Directors on the main Board had left by late autumn 1981), and a series of changes were made (in line with the new organization structures), in senior management immediately below main Board level. These changes involved both the redirection of talent within ICL and the securing of talent from outside. Action was taken to find new profit-conscious country managers in ICL's major territories abroad, particularly Germany, Sweden, South Africa and North America.

ICL's 1982 pay negotiations were, on the union side, conducted in the light of the ICL pay freeze over the previous 18–24 months and the consequent desire for some catching-up. On the company's side, the aim was to keep pay costs down as much as possible. After hard bargaining, against the background of a possible dispute which could disrupt deliveries and wreck the financial recovery, there was agreement on a 5 per cent principal increase.

The efforts of all concerned brought half-year results of a pre-tax loss of £13·5m compared with a pre-tax loss of £33·9m a year previously. Turnover rose by 5 per cent, described as modest but in line with plan. Group borrowings of £132m were £57m less; this took account of the £32m from the Rights Issue, and also the £40m spent on major rationalization measures during the previous twelve months. During that period there was a net cash inflow from normal trading operations of £15m compared with the previous two years when the Group suffered heavy net cash outflows.

The removal of Computer Leasings Ltd

Another important piece of financial restructuring was announced with the results. This was the acquisition by ICL of the business of Computer Leasings Limited ('CLL'), the leasing company which since 1963 had played a key role in enabling ICL to raise money from City finance houses to finance rented equipment in the UK.

By 1982 it was clear that CLL had reached the end of its useful life. There was a continuing trend towards outright sale, and the market had moved much more towards specialized leasing packages. The removal of CLL caused an improvement of £21m to ICL's net worth, a most welcome effect, and enabled ICL to use some of its own tax losses. Moreover, criticism from the City about the volume of off-balance sheet financing, an ICL feature for many years, was no longer relevant.

In July, ICL announced a programme of collaboration with British universities, research institutions and individual research workers. Co-ordinated by the ICL University Research Council, the programme was designed to be mutually beneficial with a cross-fertilization of ideas between key technical people.

Management put forward a number of key objectives, especially those of greater productivity (helped by more capital investment), better pricing policies and improved overhead controls. The company was beginning to move out of its survival period into one of renewed profitability and renewed growth. The objectives had to be accomplished in the rapidly changing environment of the whole information technology industry. To prosper, ICL needed to be well managed and well motivated.

By the late autumn of 1982, there was still no sign of any general pick-up in business. ICL's competitors were not growing, and some were beginning to lay off employees. This climate made it all the more important for ICL to keep its costs squeezed down and flexing promptly in line with revenue. Hence management pressure on costs and on cash collection continued unabated. To help revenue, prices for ICL equipment, software, maintenance and other services were kept under constant review and increased wherever possible.

The second Rights Issue

During 1982, the ICL share price had reflected the financial market's growing confidence by climbing back to between 70 and 80p. By mid-November 1982, it was clear that the three major shareholders would support a second Rights Issue within twelve months. This was probably another financial record for a large company, but the Chairman had made it clear a year before that this further stage of financial reconstruction would be needed. Moreover, management had had an important meeting with Government and Treasury Ministers, presenting ICL's achievements so far, the challenges ahead and the plans to meet them. The ICL proposals had been well received.

In the light of this favourable climate, the Board decided to go ahead with a fresh Rights Issue and to redeem the Preference shares in four instalments. There followed three weeks of intense activity and on 6 December ICL released its 1981–2 results and announced the new Rights Issue and Preference share redemption.

The return to profit

The results showed a profit before tax of £23·7m on revenue of £710m. ICL was 'back in the black', the turnround being accomplished on the basis of

1 Hold existing customer base
2 Reduce costs to align with revenue; 10,000 manpower reduction
3 Halt cash outflow – Cut working capital (Inventories and Receivables)
4 Return to profit (Profit before Growth) – Achieved by second half 1982

5 Restructure balance sheet
     • £50M Preference Shares
     • £140M by Rights Issues

6 Improve quality of earnings and strengthen balance sheet to secure ICL against financial risk

Figure 8.4 *Management actions*

relatively static revenues in a very depressed external environment. Currency movements had again had a big, depressing effect.

The significant improvement was largely due to the cost-saving measures taken over the past two years. Headcount had gone down by 10,000, a reduction of nearly one-third. Inventories had fallen by £10m on top of the £42m reduction in the second half of 1980–1. Net worldwide borrowings at 30 September 1982 were £146m, compared with £164m a year previously. As the first priority still was to rebuild the Group's reserves, no Ordinary dividend was proposed, other than a nominal one to retain trustee status (see Figure 8.4).

Such was the improvement in City confidence in ICL that another 'heavy' issue of two shares for three was agreed possible for the new Rights Issue. This would raise £104m if a price of 60p could be secured (the market price of ICL shares then being over 80p). The issue would also be the final step in the company's capital reconstruction, and would bring net borrowings well below shareholders' funds, after adjusting for the first £20m Preference shares redemption. The remaining Preference shares would be redeemed in £10m tranches in March 1984, 1985 and 1986.

By 25 January, over 170 million new shares, almost 95 per cent, had been taken up – another City success!

Changing the organization

While these financial machinations were happening, management continued to grapple with a whole range of business issues. For example:

- Severe competition, especially in smaller products, was bringing the need for high quality hardware and software which would work first time with only rare breakdowns. There were still weaknesses to eliminate in ICL's development and manufacturing processes before achieving the right quality and reliability standards.
- The need to ram home the major cultural change in the attitudes of ICL management and staff. There was still too much complacency, lack of the profit motive and 'can't do' instead of 'can do'. As one means, Robb Wilmot instigated 'The ICL Way' with a number of key standards for managers to follow.
- Moving from custom-built to standard packages, with full business soundness in the production of these packages.
- A shift of emphasis from hardware, systems software and maintenance to total system solutions for customer needs and to the provision of specialist services. Managing change, retraining with new skills and enhancing productivity were all real challenges.
- The initiation of an 'ICL Showcase' philosophy, whereby ICL would show to customers practical examples of the total system solutions which it offered to the market.
- Re-organization of the Group's unified sales activities into five major regions, each under the charge of a Divisional Director. These were the UK and Europe, South Africa, Asia Pacific and North America. The Middle East, Central Africa, India and elsewhere abroad were placed under a sixth Director. The new structure was intended to give Group Management a better focus on all operations outside the UK and to reduce intervening layers of management.
- Strengthening ICL's internal computer facilities. Two data centres were shut and their work merged at the other two centres. Over a three-year period ICL's internal data processing capacity doubled to the level of 13 2966 systems!
- The introduction of an Executive Share Option Scheme for a limited number of top executives. This new incentive scheme augmented the very successful Save-As-You-Earn share option schemes which ICL had operated for its mainly UK employees since 1977.
- Significant improvements in Pension Fund benefits, plus further pension inceases for pensioners, all funded out of a Fund surplus of over £35m.

The battle over standards

Meanwhile, the battle to establish open system interconnection standards, fully in the public domain and with no hidden protocols, was gathering momentum. ICL's aim, strongly driven by Robb Wilmot, was to encourage both governments and companies in the industry to adopt OSI and give the user much more choice and flexibility. The OSI approach differed from that adopted by the industry giant, IBM, which had its own operating standards, not all of which were publicly available.

In February, ICL intensified its campaign to persuade British Telecom to order ICL equipment for the British Telecom network of new regional centres. This was a vital contract, for great harm to ICL's credibility would result if a foreign competitor were to win the whole of this huge British public sector order. British Telecom finally announced its decision in April 1984 to split the order, half to ICL and half to IBM.

Product improvements

Developing ICL's new DM1 and Estriel mainframes continued steadily, with Fujitsu playing a key part in providing very advanced, highly reliable chips and cubes. On the commercial and sales sides, much work had begun to plan the transition from the 2900 Series to DM1 and thence to Estriel. It would be vital to ensure that DM1 and Estriel software worked properly from the start.

The company at last began to exploit its ingenious Contents Addressable File Store ('CAFS'), first invented in the early 1970s. The price of this very fast file search facility was slashed and it was fitted as a standard feature on 2900 mainframes.

February 1983 also saw the start of a major public relations and advertising programme to improve ICL's worldwide image. The programme was drawn up in liaison with J. Walter Thompson and included a re-design of ICL's well-known identity logo.

The British government wanted to transfer its Computer-Aided Design Centre at Cambridge to the private sector. ICL, which had for some years been operating the Centre for the government on a management contract basis, decided to take a stake of up to 40 per cent in the 'privatized' Centre. By the end of March it was announced that the Centre had been sold to an ICL-led consortium. The new CAD Centre Limited aimed to develop and market CAD/CAM techniques actively in the UK. Another new venture successfully launched!

Rumours against ICL

In the early spring, ICL faced a series of adverse press and Stock Exchange rumours. The first was that the technology arrangements with Fujitsu were running up to a year late: this was quite untrue because they were running dead on time. Other adverse comment questioned the soundness of ICL's product strategy, and included a persistent rumour that Robb Wilmot was about to leave.

The effect of all this gossip was to bruise the still tender confidence held by customers and investors. This was reflected in ICL's share price which, after the second Rights Issue, had settled at around 70–75p. From August onwards, the share price slowly declined to below 60p. The company made considerable efforts to deny each rumour, but when mud is thrown some of it tends to stick.

European initiatives

In May, Sir Christopher Laidlaw and Robb Wilmot alerted the European Commission in Brussels to ICL's concern that the European industry was under threat from the interaction of four factors:

- IBM's apparent race towards a position of dominating the market.
- Signs that IBM was seeking to switch its dominance from hardware to software and standards.
- Inequity between the effect of GATT rules in the USA and EEC rules in Europe.
- The American Government's apparent intent to create a 'technology gap' between the USA and Europe.

The Commission readily accepted that there was an immediate need for a European riposte based on co-operative research helped by EEC funding, and on the pursuit of open standards and adequate training in the whole information engineering field. A similar briefing meeting was held shortly afterwards with top officials in Whitehall.

Both Britain and the EEC had launched programmes aimed at funding longer-term industrial research into information technology. The British Alvey programme involved a spend of some £300m over five years. The ESPRIT programme involved £850m over five years. ICL became an active participant in both programmes so as to be able to influence the technical direction in both the UK and continental Europe.

An important new concept in company organization emerged in mid-1983. The first of ICL's new Business Centres was established, for the retail industry. Each Business Centre encompasses the product specification, development (or acquisition), validation and marketing of those products needed to create the high-value solutions and systems required by the particular market sector. Product sales continue as the responsibility of ICL's strong, unified sales force.

At the end of May the company published its Half-Year Report for 1982–3. This disclosed a pre-tax profit of £12½m, compared with a pre-tax loss of £13½m for the previous first half. Revenue at £401m was up by 20 per cent. Part of this increase was due to currency movements and part to the absorption of CLL which, if excluded, left the revenue increase at 11 per cent.

Again there had been a swing towards outright sale, and also a significant rise in revenue from distributed systems and software. Excluding the second Rights Issue, Group borrowings at £59m had fallen by £17m, largely due to firm control on working capital.

More re-organization

Board and management continued their close watch on the performance of ICL's overseas operations. The strongest territory in terms of revenue and ordertaking was South Africa, but cost-cutting was needed to improve profitability. In Asia Pacific, overheads had yet to be brought into line with revenue. In North America, operations remained fairly fragile. In Europe, ICL Germany was steadily being restored to profitability by its able and dedicated new General Manager. ICL France, the largest European subsidiary, was the big problem, with mounting losses due to weak management actions in the past. In Africa, the market situation was changing rapidly because of political and economic conditions.

Less than half-a-dozen Atlas Ten orders had been taken when ICL decided to reallocate resources and announced that it was exploring the possibility of Amdahl taking over future responsibility for servicing ICL's Atlas Ten customers.

The worldwide IT industry was busy defining and implementing new strategies and finding new partners. ICL was no exception. Management and the Board recognized that ICL had to secure the right strategic relationship or be left out in the cold. Clearly Fujitsu would continue as a major collaborator, but discussions were held with quite a few other possible partners or collaborators. Events began to move towards at least a tactical relationship with A T & T.

In the early autumn of 1983, there was a Board-level review of the Company's product line. DM1 was to have been announced in the spring of 1984, with full production by July 1984, but sales of the current 2900 Series continued to go extremely well. It was therefore decided that to defer the public launch of DM1 would not only ensure better validation but would also maximize revenue from existing mainframe products. Ambitious sales targets for the DRS 20 Series of small distributed computers were modified in line with overall Group objectives. The review highlighted the need for better planning and management of development programmes.

Consolidation and growth

By the late summer of 1983, ICL was moving into a new phase. The rescue and survival period was over and a new period of consolidation and growth had begun. Sir Christopher Laidlaw announced that he would retire at the end of March 1984, having served a year longer than his original two-year commitment; Sir Michael Edwardes would join the Board promptly and succeed him as chairman in April 1984.

At the end of September, the Board approved the Three-Year Plan for 1983–4 and the two succeeding years. Again, the main aims were to maximize revenue from mainframe sales, to increase the proportion of small system sales, to continue the improvements in overseas profitability and to maintain firm controls on headcount, inventories, receivables and costs generally. Capital expenditure for 1983–4 was set at a high level to continue the drive for greater productivity.

In December, agreements were signed with Siemens and Compagnie des Machines Bull for the creation of a joint research institute, the European Computer-Industry Research Centre. The new Centre was set up in Munich with ownership divided equally between ICL, Bull and Siemens. Research began in January 1984 upon topics of common interest to the three partners, largely in the field of advanced information handling and knowledge processing. The Centre's formation was welcomed by the EEC and by each of the national governments concerned.

ICL's operating divisions had slowly become trained to put forward their investment proposals to a co-ordinated, standard form and to realize that no commitments could be made until each major project had received Board-level approval. The next stage came in late 1983 with the demand for quicker returns on shorter payback periods, lower cash usage, higher profitability levels and swifter cut-offs in the event of investments going wrong.

Hitting the financial targets

The results for 1982–3 were announced at the end of November, with the ICL share price standing at 61p. Pre-tax profit was £45·6m, nearly double the level for 1981–2. Turnover was up by 17 per cent to £846m; of the £125m increase, £17m was due to currency movements and £20m to revenue received from former CLL customers. The higher turnover was also influenced by the continuing industry trend toward outright sale and by a substantial rise in the sale of ICL distributed systems. Operating margins rose from 6½ to over 7 per cent of turnover, largely because of maintaining firm control on costs and better productivity (see Figure 8.5). There was also a positive cash flow on trading operations.

The picture since 1981 on worldwide net borrowings (including export credits net of cash balances) has been as follows (see Figure 8.6):

31/3/81	£189m
30/6/81	£237m
30/9/81	£164m
31/3/82	£132m

30/9/82 ....£146m
31/3/83 .... £59m
30/9/83 .... £86m
(after repayment of £20m
Preference shares)
31/3/84 .... £74m

NB: At their 1981 peak, worldwide net borrowings were £240m, plus a
further £50m of off-balance sheet financing from CLL, since absorbed into
ICL.

Shareholders' funds at 30 September 1983 stood at £232m, compared
with £114m a year earlier and £72m at the end of 1981. The two Rights
Issues contributed £116m and retained profits a further £38m.

All in all, the major financial objectives set some two-and-a-half years
previously had been accomplished. With trading conditions still difficult
and highly competitive, growth had been restored and the Group's
financial base secured.

To mark the return to a more satisfactory level of profitability, the
Board decided to resume payment of a final Ordinary dividend, re-
commending 0·7p per share. This was the first dividend (other than purely
nominal ones to maintain trustee status) since the final of 2·98p per share
(on a much lower issued share capital) announced in December 1980.

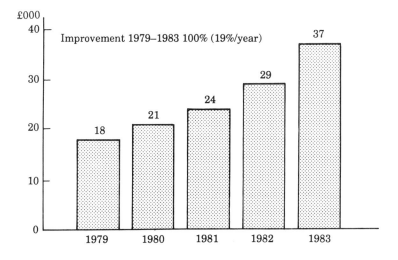

Figure 8.5   *ICL turnover per employee*

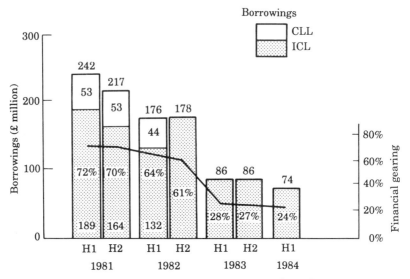

Figure 8.6 *ICL net borrowings and gearing*

More rumours

ICL's 1982–3 results were reasonably well received by the financial world, although the ICL share price dipped to 55p. But within a week ICL had suffered another of those press articles which, in what sadly seems to be the British press tradition, was a quite unwarranted and damaging blow. On 4 December the *Sunday Times* published a leading article with the banner headline 'Revealed: The Secret Fears of ICL'. The article was based on what were stated to be ICL secret documents. With all too little verification, the article set out the main contents of the documents, which alleged a range of major problems.

ICL's share price fell by 5p and some nervous customers delayed or cancelled orders. ICL management reacted very fast to stem what could have become a disastrous loss of confidence. A point-by-point refutation was circulated round the City on Monday afternoon. On Tuesday a special issue of the ICL House Journal was sent to all ICL employees. On Wednesday ICL's lawyers contacted the *Sunday Times* lawyers. On Thursday the Chairman sent a letter for publication the following Sunday. On Friday ICL management met with City stockbrokers and analysts to put the record straight.

ICL's very strong reaction was well noted, and slowly the concern began to subside.

Renewed growth

By January 1984, management were considering an extension of the ICL/Fujitsu agreement on technical collaboration. Negotiations began in February and by June both parties were able to announce an extension until the end of 1991 with an expanded collaboration scope.

The end of March saw Sir Christopher hand over the chair to Sir Michael. The Board expressed its deep gratitude to Sir Christopher for his unique services over the previous three years.

At the same Board meeting Robb Wilmot was appointed Chief Executive of the Group. Thus, with Sir Michael and Robb Wilmot steering in harmony at the helm, ICL's continued growth and success seemed assured.

With the ICL share price at 65p on 22 May, the Half-Year results to 31 March 1984 disclosed a pre-tax profit of £19·2m before exchange adjustment, a rise of £6·7m compared with the first half of 1982–3. Turnover was up by 8 per cent to £433m. European operations were profitable except for France which was still in deep trouble. Group net borrowings were down to £74m. Before the redemption of a further £10m Preference shares, the Group had generated a £22m cash inflow. The financial gearing was down to 24 per cent, a respectable level (see Figures 8.7 and 8.8).

A swift, strong recovery from the near-abyss of 1980–1! In three action-packed years, ICL had moved from survival, back into profit and then into renewed growth.

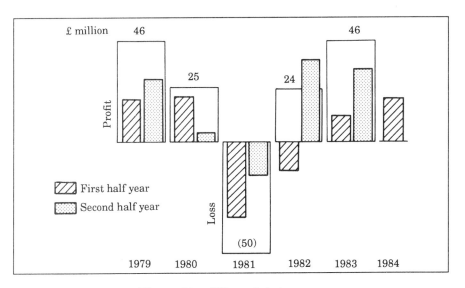

Figure 8.7 *ICL profit before tax*

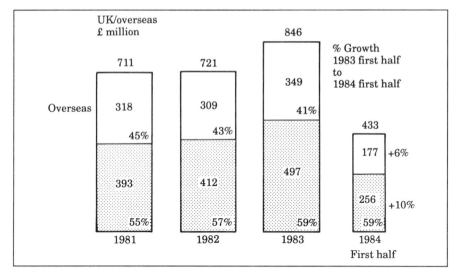

Figure 8.8   *ICL group turnover*

The STC takeover

The saga of ICL's three turbulent years would not be complete without mention of the new turn in ICL's long history which was heralded by the Standard Telephones and Cables Plc ('STC') announcement on 26 July 1984 of its bid for ICL.

The ICL Board's immediate reaction was to reject the bid as totally inadequate. Some weeks of hard negotiations followed, until on 17 August Sir Michael Edwardes wrote to shareholders with the Board's recommendation that STC's much improved offer terms should be accepted.

STC and ICL recognized the rapid convergence of computers and telecommunications and the advantages of combining the skills and resources of both to create a group strongly placed to meet the challenge of international competition and to benefit from the many growth opportunities in both markets.

The bid became unconditional on 7 September, with STC holding over 81 per cent of ICL's equity. A new and, optimistically, even more profitable ICL future had begun. Much would depend on STC's knowledge and understanding of ICL's business and on how STC, as the dominant partner and owner, would behave towards ICL in the light of that understanding.

9 Getting FIAT back on the road

Fabrizio Galimberti, Chief Economist, FIAT Group, Turin

The remarkable restructuring which has taken place in FIAT over the last five years (since 1981) illustrates two simple truths of corporate lore:

1 sometimes you have to get worse in order to get better;
2 if you market a homogeneous product in a highly competitive environment, cost-cutting is the first priority for survival.

The first truth can be properly understood only in the Italian context of the late 1970s. It is difficult, within the confines of this article, to describe how FIAT was situated in the complex array of social and political developments which marked the last decade in Italy. FIAT has been around, as a car company, since 1899. In a country where history has proceeded, by leaps and bounds, even more so than usual; in a country where institutions have convulsively changed from constitutional monarchy to fascism, to democracy; in a country where political unification is relatively recent and where real unification has still a long way to go; in a country where the priority of ideology has provided a fertile breeding ground for extremism; in such a country FIAT has always presented a clear-cut image: private enterprise, risk-taking, market priorities.

It is difficult to define FIAT as the largest private firm in Italy: there are many different criteria to define size. But certainly, from the point of view of influence, clout, weight, FIAT has always had a strong position in the social landscape.

The crisis

In the course of the 1970s both market and political developments conspired to force FIAT into a position which threatened its very survival. The oil crises had compelled a reassessment of growth prospects for the car industry, because of an income effect (the general slowdown in economic growth), and a price effect (the multiple increase in the real price of gasoline). This slowdown in growth (see Table 9.1) was super-imposed on a productive structure that was fundamentally geared to high output and high growth. All over the world the car industry was threatened with overcapacity and overmanning, but especially so in Europe where the number of producers was excessive with respect to the size of the market. Potential economies of scale were not being realized because political realities and the segmentation of European markets prevented rationalization of supply.

The adjustment process was especially delayed in FIAT: levels of productivity were lagging behind European competitors. FIAT had in fact to contend not only with the market but also with a worsening social climate. Political instability and terrorism had heightened the degree of social unrest. FIAT, because of its unique role, had become a special target for labour disputes. Wildcat strikes, absenteeism, and, in some cases, outright indiscipline and even sabotage threatened the very fabric of factory life. The physical life itself of FIAT managers was at risk, and in fact terrorist killings did occur.

A complex web of social and economic factors had thus forced FIAT against the wall. In the life of a corporation, as in the life of man, the greatest dangers often spark off the greatest courage. Things had reached such a pass that something had to give. The wounded company fought back.

23,000 layoffs

In the autumn of 1979 FIAT fired a number of workers with a record of intimidation and violence: one year later, after fruitless negotiations with labour, it announced plans for a massive layoff of workers and a massive injection of capital. The scale of the shake-out of labour which was being attempted (about 15 per cent of the labour force) was unheard of in the Italian postwar economy. And the fact that was attempted by FIAT, of all firms, was seen by trade unions and by the opposition almost as a provocation.

The opposition rightly perceived that if restructuring on such a scale was allowed, it would mark a watershed in the balance of power, it would set the tone for a new era in industrial relations. A bitter fight followed, with a long strike and a political involvement at both the municipal and the national level. FIAT could afford to wait, as stocks of unsold cars were high, and the strike allowed inventories to be cleared. But what won the fight for FIAT was not so much the capacity to weather protracted disruption: it was rather a resurgence of pride and loyalty within the walls of FIAT itself. The strike had been going on for many weeks, and the huge Mirafiori factory in Torino was heavily picketed; but one day a

Table 9.1 FIAT production

	World car production (per thousand units)							
	1970	1973	1975	1978	1980	1981	1982	1983
(A) World[1]	22370	29632	24879	31283	28989	27767	26886	29726
(B) Europe[1]	9994	11271	9133	11166	10202	9633	10053	10816
(C) FIAT S.p.A.[1]	1559	1557	1124	1246	1180	1033	1085	1170
(D) FIAT + affiliates[2](3)	1683	1701	1240	1449	1508	1275	1297	1371
(E) FIAT total[2]	2077	2245	1880	2206	2240	1864	1942	2086

[1] Cars only.
[2] Cars + small commercial vehicles.
[3] Brazilian production starts in 1976. Since 1982 Argentina excluded.

	FIAT shares of world car production							
Ratios[1]	1970	1973	1975	1978	1980	1981	1982	1983
C/B	15·6	13·8	12·3	11·1	11·6	10·7	10·8	10·8
C/A	7·0	5·3	4·5	4·0	4·0	3·7	4·0	3·9
D/A	7·5	5·7	4·9	4·6	5·2	4·6	4·8	4·6
E/A	9·3	7·6	7·6	7·0	7·7	6·7	7·2	7·0

spontaneous manifestation assembled in a city riddled by bitterness and violence. A crowd of about 40,000 people (FIAT supervisory workers, citizens, and probably also part of FIAT production workers) walked in the avenues of Torino, demanding the right to work and an end to industrial belligerence. The following day the unions and the Communist party understood that the battle had been lost, and hostilities ceased. An agreement was signed, providing for a layoff of about 23,000 workers.

Laid-off workers were still technically part of FIAT's labour force, even if their salary (to be precise, about 90 per cent of it) was paid by the state. The period of inactivity was formally temporary, but there were provisions for renewal. Apart from the technicalities, however, everybody knew that the shake-out of the labour force was permanent. Restructuring had begun. Layoffs were not linked to the weakness of the market, to a movement along the cost curve, but to a shift in the cost curve towards a different production function.

Injecting new capital

As mentioned, the layoffs were announced concurrently with a large increase in share capital. The FIAT move was to be read as the beginning of a new course, and not as a defensive posture. In one of the few multinationals which are still family-owned, the announcement of an increase in share capital translated into an assurance of continuity, into a deep confidence in the future of the company.

In its turn, the recapitalization of FIAT was directed towards an extensive re-tooling of production lines (see Table 9.2). Recapitalization was made necessary by a radical re-thinking of prospects for the car industry. Three factors were behind the change in strategy:

• The second oil crisis had just struck and already the consensus view among economic forecasters had shifted in favour of an 'energy-warranted growth path': economic growth was going to be constrained by the availability of energy. Generally, inflation seemed to have become endemic in Western economies: economic policies were going to be geared towards restriction, further dimming growth prospects.
• The car industry was faced by a double brake: not only was growth going to be slower, but car demand was not going to be leading any more. In the 1950s and in the 1960s the rate of growth of automobile demand had outstripped the general rate of growth. The convulsions of the 1970s had led the two rates to converge at a lower level. In the 1980s the demand for cars might even be lagging behind the other components of demand. Many markets had become 'mature': saturation was being approached, and the slow-moving segment of replacement demand was becoming prevalent. In addition, the increase in the relative

Table 9.2   *Fixed investment by major suppliers as a % of turnover*

	1979	1980	1981	1982	1983	1984
European producers						
FIAT Auto	5·8	4·8	4·3	9·7	7·8	8·0
Renault Regie	3·3	5·7	6·6	5·2	5·3	—
PSA	6·1	7·0	6·3	6·7	4·3	—
Volkswagen AG	4·0	6·2	5·0	6·3	5·0	—
Ford Werke	4·1	3·9	5·4	6·2	7·0	—
Ford U.K.	10·5	11·1	9·1	12·1	8·7	—
Opel	9·2	15·0	10·3	7·5	6·1	—
Vauxhall	3·9	2·9	1·6	1·1	1·4	—
Non-European producers						
GM Corp.	8·1	13·4	15·5	10·4	5·4	—
Ford Corp.	7·9	7·5	5·8	8·0	5·3	—
Nissan	4·3	5·0	6·2	6·5	3·5	—

price of energy was discouraging the use of energy-intensive consumer goods like automobiles.

• With less demand and the same number of producers, competitive pressures were bound to intensify, especially in Europe. The Japanese competition was especially threatening: the cost advantage enjoyed by Japanese producers had already allowed expansion of market shares in the US and in most LDCs, and Japanese cars were muscling in in Europe (see Tables 9.3 and 9.4).

Cutback in costs

These three factors had a clear implication: costs had to come down. With a stagnant market and high competition, survival depended on producing competitive cars at the lowest possible cost. Product innovation was and is of course essential. In 1984 the average age of FIAT models was three-and-a-half years against four-and-a-half years for the competition, reversing the situation of 1980. But sales do not depend only on the product: dealers' networks, brand loyalty, traditions, image, national feeling, determine market share together with quality and innovation. This implies a considerable degree of rigidity in market shares, both upwards and downwards. For a full-line manufacturer like FIAT, quality and product innovation are essential in order not to lose ground in the competitive stakes; but in order to make a profit it is essential to produce at costs lower than competitors!

The emphasis on cost reductions did not by itself explain the increased

Table 9.3   FIAT's market position

| | World car demand (per thousand units) | | | | | | | | |
	1970	1973	1975	1978	1980	1981	1982	1983	1984
(A) World	—	—	—	—	29157	28000	27417	29335	30250
(B) Europe[1]	7453	8754	7773	9720	9475	9258	9430	9865	9797
(C) Italy	1364	1475	1200	1382	1713	1735	1682	1582	1637
(D) USA	—	—	—	—	8973	8533	7980	9181	10390
(E) Rest of World	—	—	—	—	8996	8474	8325	8708	8910

| | FIAT market shares | | | | | | | | |
	1970	1973	1975	1978	1980	1981	1982	1983	1984
(A) World	—	—	—	—	4·5	4·8	4·7	4·5	4·4
(B) Europe[1]	15·8	14·9	12·8	12·2	12·8	13·4	13·0	12·8	13·6
(C) Italy	61·0	61·4	56·3	53·7	51·5	51·3	51·6	55·6	54·5

[1] Spain excluded.

	1970	1973	1975	1978	1980	1981	1982	1983	1984
FIAT									
own country	61·0	61·4	56·3	53·7	51·5	51·3	51·6	55·6	54·5
rest of Europe	5·5	5·4	5·6	4·9	4·0	4·4	4·4	4·4	4·9
non prod. countries[2]	9·3	9·5	9·9	8·6	6·4	6·5	6·3	6·6	6·9
Renault									
own country	31·6	30·1	33·0	34·2	40·5	38·9	39·1	35·1	31·0
rest of Europe	9·4	7·1	7·7	7·5	8·9	8·0	8·1	7·2	5·0
non prod. countries[2]	10·4	6·8	7·5	7·0	7·6	7·2	7·3	6·6	5·4
Volkswagen									
own country	26·7	25·0	24·5	30·0	30·1	30·1	29·4	28·3	28·0
rest of Europe	4·8	4·6	5·1	5·0	6·3	7·3	7·2	6·8	7·4
non prod. countries[2]	11·5	9·9	9·2	9·7	11·1	11·4	11·0	11·0	12·3
GM Europe[1]									
own country	16·4	15·6	14·6	15·8	13·8	13·4	15·6	17·0	16·4
rest of Europe	6·3	5·4	4·9	5·9	5·1	5·0	5·8	7·0	7·1
non prod. countries[2]	12·7	11·6	9·5	12·2	11·1	10·6	12·4	12·9	13·7
Ford Europe[1]									
own country	12·5	16·4	16·4	17·9	18·1	19·2	19·3	19·2	18·9
rest of Europe	5·3	5·7	5·3	7·8	6·2	7·5	7·9	7·9	8·1
non prod. countries[2]	7·9	11·1	9·9	11·7	8·8	10·3	10·2	10·0	11·6
Japanese companies									
Europe	2·4	3·5	6·1	6·3	9·9	9·6	9·5	9·7	9·6
non prod. countries[2]	7·6	11·4	15·6	16·5	26·3	26·9	26·2	26·3	22·7

[1] Spain excluded.
[2] Europe less: France, Germany, Italy, Spain, Sweden, UK.

capital investment that occurred. Textbooks say that costs could be reduced by lowering salaries, either directly or by relocating production facilities. US experience suggest that labour costs can be lowered by workers' 'give-backs', lower rates for new entrants, or other forms of salary reductions. But in Italy, and to a certain extent also in Europe, generalized 'give-backs' are unthinkable. In Europe it is more difficult to reduce wages than in North America. The degree of unionization is higher in Europe, and the protection of workers' rights is more readily assured both by public opinion and by government institutions. The downward rigidity of wages might be considered a good thing or a bad thing, according to one's philosophical preferences: but it is in any case a fact, which might be taken into account by corporate managers and planners.

If unit wages could not be significantly reduced, the only way to reduce labour costs was to decrease the number of workers. Available techniques made this possible, through modernization and automation. FIAT had already experimented with factory automation, and was, in fact, through its subsidiary COMAU, a leader in the field. In-house know-how made it possible to set an ambitious target: FIAT was to become a model car-maker, leading the way in flexible manufacturing systems applied to car production. Flexibility was another key and little known aspect in the recourse to automation: it is generally thought that robotization enhances the advantages of the assembly line, yields more mileage out of a process of mass production. But this is only one aspect of factory automation: the use of programmable robots allows repetitive operations to be switched back and forth from one model to another. An assembly line does not need to be specific to one model any more, and can in fact disgorge different cars in succession.

With respect to a more labour-intensive configuration, automation thus provides more flexibility, as well as, of course, better quality, in that human errors and tolerance limits can be greatly reduced. The issue of flexibility was especially important in view of some structural factors which were emerging in the car market. The slowdown in growth went hand-in-hand with growing instability: large swings in the car cycle made a prompt response of production necessary. Changing evolutions in different segments of the market put a premium on productive techniques that could easily switch from one model to another.

A second structural factor can be found in a more diversified demand for cars. Consumers change their tastes more frequently, as social classes and values are reshuffled. It becomes important to offer more variety, to widen the consumers' choice. In the past the number of versions was limited by the overhead relevant to each version. The advent of flexible manufacturing systems has greatly reduced this type of overhead, and has made the 'customized car' a technical possibility.

Automation

The process of automation in FIAT has proceeded relentlessly in the last five years, and is projected to continue at a fast pace (see Figure 9.1). The accompanying shake-out of labour was not limited to the initial 23,000. Table 9.5 shows that sizeable additional reductions have continued to this day: these have been obtained in a more painless way, through attrition, early retirements, and financial incentives to leave.

Automation is not limited to replacing man with robots. It starts at the drawingboard. Pieces and components are to be designed so as to be handled by robots and to be put together with maximum speed and efficiency. The most recent accomplishment by FIAT in this field is the new engine FIRE 1000 (Fully Integrated Robotized Engine). This motor has established new standards in terms of lightness, strength, consumption; it has cut down the number of parts and has been conceived together with the factory that is producing it at Termoli in the Mezzogiorno of Italy. Automation feeds back on production innovation, and the imaginative use of both yields great benefits in terms of both quality and production costs.

Concentration on key markets

The shift towards more capital and less labour was accompanied by a reconsideration of FIAT's spread in the world. Given the new priorities, cost-cutting and retrenchment, it was realized that FIAT was geographically somewhat overextended, both in terms of production and in terms of markets. A strategic revision of FIAT's presence in the different markets was initiated. As a result, the role of Europe as FIAT's 'natural' backyard

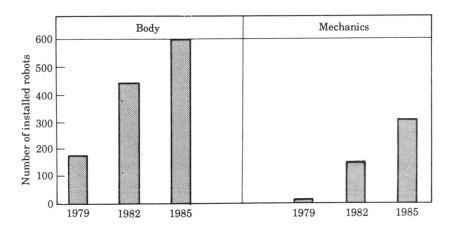

Figure 9.1 *Robotization of FIAT Auto*

Table 9.5   *Employment in the automobile industry*

	1979	1980	1981	1982	1983	1984
		(per thousand yearly averages)				
European producers						
FIAT Auto	135·2	126·5	107·4	95·1	86·6	81·4
Renault Regie	107·7	106·0	104·5	103·7	103·1	—
PSA	263·0	245·0	214·5	206·0	203·0	—
Volkswagen AG	111·9	117·1	119·4	119·5	116·7	—
Ford Werke	58·3	54·6	49·5	49·3	48·6	—
Ford UK	80·0	80·0	75·0	69·5	63·9	—
Opel	66·4	63·7	59·8	60·1	59·6	—
Vauxhall	32·7	30·7	23·8	20·5	11·5	—
Non-European producers						
GM Corp.	838·7	731·2	726·0	642·0	677·0	—
Ford Corp.	494·6	426·7	404·8	379·2	380·1	—
Nissan	56·2	56·4	57·0	58·4	59·3	—

[1] Since 1980 employees in Cassa Integrazione excluded.

was reaffirmed. A complete pull-out from the US was decided: the wisdom of such a move might be questioned, given the enormous competitive advantage which, in subsequent years, the rise of the dollar bestowed upon European producers. Even with the benefit of hindsight, however, the move appears to have been a wise one. In the US FIAT's small and medium cars were competing against Japanese producers: it was an uphill task, a risk that FIAT was not prepared to take in a moment when all the energy of the company had to be brought to bear on a structural overhaul of its car-making. The outcome of other European producers' efforts to tackle the Japanese in that market segment confirms that FIAT's pull-out was a realistic move.

More in general, FIAT's guiding principle was to ignore questions of prestige and image and to concentrate ruthlessly on costs and benefits: if a presence in a given market was not profitable, FIAT would pull out, ignoring history and traditions. In Latin America, FIAT's activities in Uruguay, Chile, Colombia and Argentina were sold out or closed. A small assembly operation in Venezuela was retained, as well as the large operation in Brazil. Brazil thus became the only major production affiliate of FIAT: an expression of confidence in the Brazilian economy and in the role of the Brazilian facilities as a possible low cost supplier to overseas markets.

The geographical rebuilding of FIAT's presence stemmed from a consideration of strengths and weaknesses in market shares. FIAT, unlike other companies, had an exceedingly strong domestic position: no other car-maker had such a dominant position in its own country (see Table 9.4). It was thus essential, for a company that was bent on restructuring, to start from home base, to strengthen the ties with its bread-and-butter business. Only after having secured again its hold on the domestic market, could FIAT rise on the stepping stone of safe headquarters and widen its horizons again. The first phase of the strategy called therefore for the sights to be lowered: for a concentration on Italy and Europe, and for a hard look at the furthest branches of FIAT's sprawling tree.

Rationalization

Four other items in FIAT's overhaul (see the overall results in Table 9.6) need to be mentioned: inventories, dealers, suppliers and finances.

While work-in-process depends on actual production, inventories of input and output can be minimized. A reorganization of production stages and stricter requirements for suppliers' deliveries has allowed FIAT to put in place its own versions of the 'just-in-time' Japanese procedures for inventory control. Inventories of finished products were lowered, year after year (from 1·6 months of sales in 1981 to 1·2 months in 1984), by a combination of methods. First of all, a frequent and timely recourse to temporary lay-offs, so as to obtain a better balance between production and demand. In addition, the financing of dealers' stocks was to be carried by the dealer. The shift in the financing burden was part of a wider effort to enhance dealers' entrepreneurship and aggressiveness. The dominant position of FIAT in Italy had transformed many dealers in 'car brokers'. New contractual arrangements changed the situation: dealerships had to become more 'sales-minded'.

The system of suppliers is a crucial determinant of a car company's performance. 'Make-or-buy' choices were revised. The number of

Table 9.6 *The turnaround in profits and productivity*

FIAT Auto – Selected indicators	1980	1981	1982	1983	1984
Profits before tax (as a share of turnover)	−1·9	−3·4	−0·9	0·8	2·2
Debt/equity ratio	2·38	1·30	0·72	0·57	0·27
Labour productivity; vehicles per employee (1980 = 100)	100·0	102·9	117·8	139·6	154·5

suppliers was reduced. Commonality of components over different models was increased. Most important of all, FIAT's considerable bargaining power was used to the full in forcing suppliers to supply at low prices, and, therefore, to reduce their costs through their own measures. The reverberation of FIAT's cost-cutting thus rippled down the whole industry: a leaner and more efficient constellation of suppliers emerged, a domino effect of industrial restructuring.

Cuts in inventories and stricter control of suppliers allowed a reduction in working capital. Capital per unit of output decreased considerably: a textbook reaction to the high cost of capital which prevailed at the time (and which, of course, still does prevail). This reduction in working capital was all the more urgent as Italian producers were relatively disadvantaged *vis-à-vis* their competitors: the real cost of capital was especially high in Italy due to the pre-emption of private savings by the huge public sector deficit. The high real interest rates are, of course, bad for borrowers and good for lenders: but a company, while generally a borrower, is also at some times a provider of funds. The centralization of finances in the holding company of the FIAT Group (of which FIAT Auto is the largest member) allowed the cost of borrowed funds to be minimized and the return on liquidity to be maximized.

Phase two

It has been said before that retrenchment and cost-cutting represents a first essential step in a strategy for survival. But of course FIAT, like all companies, does not aim simply to survive: it aims to grow and prosper. Growth and prosperity depend crucially on variables out of corporate control: the general evolution of the economies. There are, however, some variables of a 'phase-two' strategy which depend on the company. FIAT needs to widen its presence in non-Italian markets, and needs to contribute to a rationalization of supply in Europe through marketing and production agreements with other producers. It is to be hoped that the arrangements underway will confirm the emergence of FIAT as a leading car-maker for the challenges of the 1990s.

Part Three

Implementing profitable growth strategies

Part Three   Implementing profitable growth strategies

Strategies for profitable growth should form a key part of any integrated planning process, even if the organization's first priority is survival through retrenchment. The creation of a platform for profitable growth can therefore take place alongside strategic retrenchment. In many cases we have seen the processes happen consecutively. Businesses which had survived and restored some stability would then turn to examining strategies for profitable growth.

The cases start with ICI's approach, very much a board-led initiative, to developing strategies for the creation of renewed vigour in a large multinational corporation that was in danger of becoming over-bureaucratic and moribund. This strategy was based on reducing dependence on commodity businesses, expanding activities in speciality chemicals, and exploiting opportunities in new domestic and overseas markets. Other cases include Singapore Airlines' successful and novel approach to a market where it appeared that there was little room for a new entrant, and the growth strategies of International Thomson and the Thomas Cook Group.

The International Thomson history charts the development of a multinational corporation from its roots as a small UK-based business through the development of a four-phase growth strategy based partly on internal growth and partly on acquisition. It included the development of new core businesses such as holidays and travel, and directory publishing and an opportunistic move into North Sea oil and gas production.

The Thomas Cook Group has become a successful part of the Midland Bank portfolio through exploitation of its strong market reputation and excellent distribution network and a focus on its core business.

The remaining case in this section demonstrates the application of strategic planning in a 'non-commercial' organization. When the Chairman of Glaxo (India) was appointed Chairman of the World Wildlife Fund (UK) (now renamed the World Wide Fund for Nature), he immediately set about applying a strategic planning approach to fund raising and programme development, with considerable success.

10 Strategic leadership through corporate planning at ICI

Alan I. H. Pink, General Manager, Imperial Chemical Industries Ltd

'The Executive Team are the Planners.' This is a statement made whenever a member of Planning Department discusses corporate planning at ICI. It is not a disclaimer, nor is it a sign of excessive modesty: it is a statement of the fundamental philosophy which lies at the heart of both ICI's strategic planning process and the way it operates in practice.

The Chairman and the Executive Directors exert clear strategic leadership on the ICI Group. The role of Planning Department, with appropriate essential key inputs from Finance Department, is to support the executive team in its strategic role and to facilitate the strategic dialogue between the executive team and the units through whom corporate strategy must largely be implemented.

The role of the Executive Directors in strategic planning has not always been as it is today and we are, therefore, in a good position to see the advantages which flow from our current organization. Some background will help to put this in context.[1]

The challenge

ICI is large and complex. It currently makes an annual profit of over £1bn from sales in excess of £10bn, manufactures products in forty countries and sells to virtually all of the world's markets through its own sales offices in over sixty territories. It has a vast multiplicity of businesses ranging from pharmaceuticals to petrochemicals, all based on exploiting chemical, biological and related sciences and engineering. ICI is the most diverse and international of all the major world chemical companies.

The challenge is, on the one hand, to free business managers to develop individual businesses competitively and profitably whilst, on the other, directing the Group and managing the complex portfolio to achieve coherence and integration. This objective is captured succinctly by the statement 'the whole should be greater than the sum of the parts'. To this end the style of the direction and management of the Group has changed substantially over the last six years.

Changing gear

In 1980 ICI declared losses in two quarters, and reluctantly cut its dividend for the first time since the 1930s. The exceptional drop in performance was due to a combination of factors: world recession following the oil shocks of the 1970s, particular weakness in the UK economy, high domestic inflation and an overvalued currency supported by oil, which was penal to a major exporter like ICI. The difficult situation in the external economic environment was exacerbated by the fact that ICI, in the late 1970s, had invested heavily for further growth, particularly in plastics and petrochemicals. This growth did not materialize and in the early 1980s capacity surpluses worldwide caused intense competitive pressure and a resultant squeeze on profit margins.

In the short term massive restructuring took place across the chemical industry in Europe, but the particular circumstances of the United Kingdom meant that ICI had to improve its cost base more rapidly than its competitors. Manpower in the UK was reduced by almost 30 per cent in five years and many older production units were closed. The intended capacity *expansions* of the late 1970s became effective modern low cost *replacement* plants. As a result, and helped by a range of portfolio exchanges, ICI was put into a strong competitive position and was poised to benefit from the improving economic conditions in the second half of the 1980s.

These moves were urgent and successful, albeit painful, reactions to a profits crisis. In addition a major reassessment of both the short-term performance objectives and the long-term strategy of the ICI Group was also clearly necessary. Part of the recovery plan called for a reappraisal of the role of the Executive Directors in planning for, directing and managing the company. The financial budgeting and monitoring processes were also completely restructured and formed a key part of the overall new approach.

One major change was to delegate profit and operating responsibility for business units clearly and unambiguously to the level of management immediately below the main Board. This left a smaller team of Executive Directors (reduced from fourteen to now only eight) free to concentrate on Group financial performance and corporate direction as a whole, without having personal profit accountability for the individual parts of the company worldwide. Executive Directors thus ceased to be advocates for particular spheres of influence and started working as a more closely-knit team to develop a shared vision for the ICI Group. They became better placed to determine where to take ICI as a whole and to decide objectively about the allocation of resources to the individual units in a way which best meets the corporate aims.

The problems faced by ICI in the early 1980s have already been defined broadly. They led to an urgent need to:

- Increase profit
- Improve profitability
- Achieve consistent improvement in performance.

This had to be done against the background of key issues faced by the chemical industry:

- Lower growth
- Overcapacity in commodity chemicals
- Greater competitive pressures
- More rapid change/more uncertainty

and particular issues faced by ICI:

- Overdependence on the slow-growing UK economy
- Collapse of UK customer base
- For historical reasons, major involvement in the sectors with most overcapacity
- Overvaluation of sterling
- Poor relative labour productivity.

The broad strategy was set, therefore, to achieve two major thrusts. These were to improve *competitiveness*, in terms both of costs and of the ability to add value, and to *change Group shape* in respect of both products and territorial spread.

In the case of products, the aim was to move the balance away from the cyclicality and competitive vulnerability of commodity chemicals, particularly where these were exposed to foreign currency fluctuations, towards differentiated, high value-added, effect (speciality) chemicals. In the basic chemicals businesses in Europe the thrust was to achieve the maximum cost efficiencies of scale and concentration, whilst also adding value in the product chain in differentiated sectors of the market. The businesses to be emphasized included Pharmaceuticals, Agrochemicals, Seeds, Advanced Materials, Electronics, Polyurethanes, Films, Explosives, Colours and Speciality Chemicals. All of these were judged to have good growth prospects and potential for further development.

In the case of territories the emphasis was to increase business outside the slow-growing UK market towards the higher growth United States,

	1982	1986
Return on chemical sales (%)	5	10·5
Return on assets (%)	7	19
Earnings per share (pence 1986)	29	92

Figure 10.1   *ICI performance*

Japan, and selected less developed countries, especially on the Pacific Rim.

ICI thus embarked upon a major and strategic problem-solving phase in which existing businesses had a key part to play alongside central initiatives directed at macro-restructuring, generation of new businesses and achievement of targeted acquisitions. The last five years have seen the major problems largely solved, and the need today is to build successfully on the solid base which has been established. Figures 10.1–10.3 illustrate in different ways the considerable changes achieved in the ICI Group between 1982 and 1986. The overall objective now is to move forward aggressively and to achieve sustained growth in earnings through time.

Against this objective the broad strategic thrusts on competitiveness and Group shape are still relevant. They are required now, less in the sense of urgent problem-solving, but more to encourage a continuous evolution of appropriate competitive strategies for existing businesses and for developing new vehicles to bring ICI's core innovative skills to an ever-changing market. Blended together and applied to a mix of old and new, they are the means of sustaining the momentum of growth, renewal

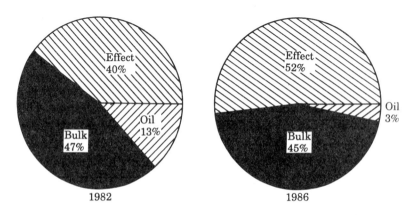

Figure 10.2   *Product shape*

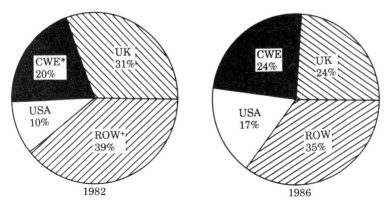

*CWE = Continental Western Europe
+ROW = Rest of the World

Figure 10.3 *Chemical sales: territorial distribution*

and more growth, through time. This strategic intent will be achieved only if the processes throughout the ICI Group enable and encourage good decision-taking by the level appropriate to the decision.

The strategic process

The strategic processes introduced in the early 1980s have been developed and refined to achieve a tightly integrated strategic planning and financial budgeting process which aims:

- to give the Executive Team the ability to steer the Group;
- to retain the necessary financial control at the ICI centre;
- to delegate as much as possible responsibility and freedom of action to Chief Executives of operating units.

The need is to ensure that individual businesses and territories are following strategies which are consistent with Group strategy and that the implementation is broadly following the intended path on the required timescale. This means that at the heart of the process is the agreement by the Executive Team of a strategy for a unit, followed by subsequent monitoring of financial and strategic performance within the context of the agreed strategy.

At any time each unit has an agreed strategy to which it must work. There is no fixed pattern for a fundamental review of strategy, but a review will be called for if, from the perspective of the Executive Team, the strategy is clearly becoming untenable or if the Chief Executive Officer (CEO) of the unit believes he must offer different options.

- Strategy paper and background review documents produced by businesses in consultation with planning and other Millbank Functions
- Papers circulated by Business Director with covering letter highlighting key issues. Single brief prepared by Corporate Functions
- Presentation by CEO to Executive Team
- Initial feedback after discussion by Executive Team; Minutes issued by Secretary's Department
- Summary of Issues, preferred strategy and milestones prepared by Planning Department and Business
- Strategy summary amd milestones submitted for main Board approval

Figure 10.4 *Business strategy review: the process in practice*

The strategy review is carried out against a common economic background using central assumptions. It must provide an assessment of the range of strategic options available to the unit over a ten-year planning horizon (and for some business units a longer view is also appropriate), and should evaluate these against the background of ICI Group strategic aims.

When a preferred strategy is agreed it provides a framework in which the CEO can operate and it commits ICI Group resources in principle to the strategy. It also establishes definitive 'milestones' against which to measure progress of implementation of the strategy.

Figure 10.4 summarizes the process in practice. The 'milestones' cover a ten-year period, being more detailed and precise in the early years and less so later on. They are a mixture of quantitative and qualitative critical factors which provide reference points for the annual evaluation of budgets. They also act through time as key-markers against which to test whether performance is meeting requirements or significantly and persistently falling short, indicating the need for strategy to be reappraised.

At any time the add-up of the business strategies indicates what the ICI Group as a whole will achieve if the businesses are successful in the execution of their strategies. The add-up may or may not match the aspirations that the Executive Team have for the ICI Group to achieve sustained growth of earnings and to be strongly competitive in its performance. In order to test this the Executive Team divorces itself from day-to-day activities and retreats, at least once a year, for two days to Hever Castle in Kent to reflect on both Group strategy and its implementation.

During these discussions corporate objectives are reviewed and the totality of business projections is tested for credibility, adjusted as appropriate, and the resulting overall forecast performance is compared against the corporate objectives. The total resources required to fund existing strategies are reviewed against available resources and the impact through time on company financial ratios is assessed. In other words the strategy loop is closed and the Executive Team tests whether the totality is credible, acceptable and can be financed. It also identifies the need for additional initiatives which may be either offensive or defensive.

Also during these Hever discussions, the business portfolio is reviewed to judge its strength, to identify problems and to seek ways to eradicate weaknesses. The deployment of the company's resources across the portfolio is assessed critically to ensure that the strong and profitable businesses are being adequately funded for maximum growth and that the poorer businesses are receiving minimum cash until their future is clear.

To help the process a simple broad, four-way categorization of businesses is used. The categories are:

Strong,

Ongoing/Cash-generating,

Problem

and

New.

Figure 10.5 shows the characteristics and objectives for businesses in each sector. For the businesses in the ICI portfolio we have found this essentially qualitative approach to be more appropriate than such techniques as the Boston Consultancy Group Growth/Share matrix or the Shell Directional Policy matrix. The factors incorporated on the axes of those matrices, relating to industry sector prospects and our own competitive position within the industry, receive considerable attention. However, the process by which the Executive Team assesses the appropriate categorization for individual businesses, and then moves on from there to approve a specific strategy, embraces a wider range of relevant judgement factors, including the Group corporate goals and objectives.

This approach is a particular example of a strongly fulfilled general determination that techniques should be kept in perspective as tools and should not become potential substitutes for applying business experience and judgement. Further, in line with this general thesis, the business categorization is not a mechanical, fixed classification. It is a dynamic process with businesses moving between categories if this is justified by a strategy review.

A problem business, for example, which can develop a convincing and financially rewarding strategy to turn itself around, within a reasonable period, into a good cash business or perhaps eventually into a strong business, will get reasonable support through its time of crisis. There are some outstanding cases of successful turnarounds, probably best exempli-

ONGOING/CASH	STRONG
Profitable cash generator but with no major growth prospects	*Strong and growing profit contributor based on good competitive position in growing good quality market*
—Run for long-term cash, increasing contribution by improving profits through limited selective investment directed at increasing efficiency of existing operations in preference to expansion	—Stimulate innovation and invest to sustain profitable growth and to increase total size of this sector
PROBLEM	NEW
Inadequate profitability and cash generation —Turn around, divest or close down	*New business with the potential of being 'strong' but meanwhile relatively high cash requirement with relatively high risk* —Nurture; then select and invest sufficient resources and management attention in chosen business to develop 'strong' positions

Figure 10.5 *Selectivity overview: characterization and objectives*

fied by ICI's Polyurethanes business and its Fibres business. The corporate use of this selectivity quadrant is broad and units are encouraged to apply the same kind of categorization to their sub-portfolios. Many do and some elaborate the four categories into sub-groupings to define more accurately the strategic issues facing the businesses.

The categorization is simple, but the Executive Team finds it has provided it with a clearer overview of the portfolio and enabled it to arrive more quickly at decisions to encourage Chief Executives to divest poorly performing businesses with little recovery potential or, at the very least to limit resources until prospects improve. Similarly the Executive Team can ensure it is channelling sufficient resources into strong businesses and that enough 'patient' money is being devoted to the long-term development of new businesses without unduly straining current Group profitability.

The Executive Team believe they are now better placed to manage the diverse portfolio effectively, to direct resources towards making the maximum contribution to sustained growth of earnings and also to assess objectively management performance. The use of the categorization model down the organization is contributing to an upgrading of strategic thinking throughout the Group. It is helping the management to focus more consciously on the need to be selective in their use of resources and to apply strategically differentiated criteria in their business decisions. The quality of the strategic debate around the Group is sharper and is still improving against a heightened appreciation of the corporate direction.

Corporate strategy *does* make the difference

The iteration between the review of the whole Group strategy at Hever and the review of individual strategies with CEOs, coupled with the launching of central strategic initiatives aimed at improving the performance of the whole, provides the process for ensuring that, in spite of its diversity and complexity, the ICI Group moves forward coherently and proactively under positive strategic direction.

There are always critical decisions to be taken on the relative importance to be given to strategic and financial control of individual businesses. Some companies go unequivocally for one or the other. The ICI Executive seeks to balance the two so that, in difficult times, financial targets are met as closely as possible whilst key strategic initiatives are preserved. This is a very appropriate, but difficult, style of management which requires a considerable understanding by the Executive Team of the individual business issues and of the strategic parameters which are key to the future competitive success of the business. As will be seen later, Planning Department has a role in highlighting key issues relevant to any debate with strategic implications. This does not set a restrictive agenda, and additions are made by the Executive Team or by the responsible CEO, but it is expected to provide the core focus for the dialogue.

This role, together with the Department's formal and informal involvement in the total strategy process, will be seen to be at the heart of the contribution made by Corporate Planning at ICI towards the pursuit of corporate strategy. To quote Michael Porter, 'Corporate Strategy is what makes the whole add up to more than the sum of its business unit parts',[2] and it is one of the factors which will ensure that ICI's future performance exceeds that of a diversified conglomerate.

The budget process

Each year the Executive Team, as a group, assisted primarily by Finance Department and also with input from Planning, reviews the budgets of all the main units for the next three years with each CEO in what is known colloquially as 'hell fortnight'. This is the key instrument of financial control and the agreed budget becomes a contract between the Executive Team and the Chief Executive of the unit.

At the budget review the Executive Team tests briefly whether the unit is proceeding along its agreed strategic path and whether the milestones are being passed. This provides an essential interlinking between the strategy process and the budget process (see Figure 10.6). The performance of a CEO against his agreed profit and cash budgets is subsequently monitored quarterly to ensure business performance is on target. If it is not, the CEO must take corrective action or persuade the Executive Team that dispensation is justified. It is under these circumstances that the debate will centre on whether to continue to incur costs on following longer term strategic goals.

Once a CEO has a budget agreed in the context of an established strategy, the approval of capital investment subsequently falls naturally into the overall process, as illustrated in Figure 10.6.

Where the cost of a planned project or acquisition falls within the sanction authority delegated to a CEO, he can approve it provided he will still meet his profit and cash budgets. Where the cost exceeds his delegated authority, the CEO presents for consideration by the Executive Team a short paper outlining the case and the way the proposal fits the approved business strategy and the agreed budgets. Unless there are

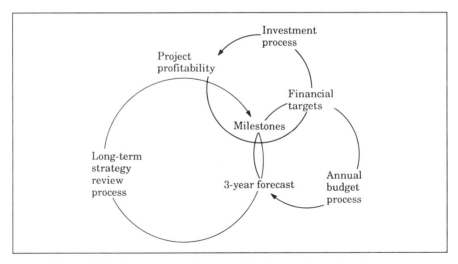

Figure 10.6   *Interaction of strategy, budget and investment processes*

exceptional reasons for believing the business has moved off course, there is no recycling of the strategic issues. The debate with the CEO, which is usually quite short, focuses on the market, technical and financial aspects of the proposal. The purpose is to establish whether the project is robust and of a quality which justifies the commitment of the requested capital. This is the final step in ensuring that financial resources are put to fully beneficial use consistent with the Group meeting its profitability targets.

The result: integrated and interactive

Overall this adds up to a tightly-knit process for corporate planning, business strategic planning, financial budgeting and strategic/financial control. As with all things it is capable of further improvement and refinement, but we believe that the broad pattern gives the necessary insights and stimulates the right debate between the Executive Team and those running individual businesses. The major interaction is between these, but Planning Department, along with Finance Department, have a key constructive and facilitating role to play and it is worth describing in some detail what this is.

Role of Corporate Planning Department

The key elements of the role of Corporate Planning Department can be summarized as follows:

- Provocation and catalysis of Executive Team strategic thinking, identifying Group strategic issues and possible new initiatives.
- Management and development of the strategic planning process.
- Acting as custodian of the Group strategy, proposing options on Group objectives and milestones for achievement.
- Provision of strategic framework for discussion between Executive team and business and territorial units.
- Provision of worldwide economic assumptions for planning and budgeting, and continuous assessment of the implications of economic trends on Group strategy.
- Assisting units to put strategy proposals in corporate context.
- Assisting Executive Team in highlighting key issues for debate in units' strategy or project proposals.
- Assisting units in recording strategy summaries and developing appropriate milestones.
- Assisting Executive Team in assessing units' budgets for progress against strategic objectives and achievement of milestones.
- Early identification of problems for the Group and its customers.

- Monitoring competitors and interpreting their strategies.
- Seeking out opportunities for the Group and ways to exploit them.
- Assessment of strategic relevance and value of potential acquisition targets.
- Making proposals for resolution of business-related organizational issues.
- Supporting the Executive Team in presenting and explaining Group strategy inside and outside the Group.
- Acting as a forceful advocate of strategic planning throughout the Group.

This role involves working for the Executive Team on one hand, with implications of a critique of the units' performance, whilst on the other hand working with the units themselves. This is a difficult dual role and can be carried out only by planners who are respected for their views and for the practical contribution they can make to thinking at both levels, whilst most importantly being, and being seen to be, honest. On many occasions a planner prematurely receives information, which used inappropriately would be unhelpful to the unit. The whole department recognizes that they would not get a second opportunity to break this trust.

The Executive Team helps to guard the impartiality of Planning Department. The principle that briefs, which are written for the Executive Team about a unit's proposal, are also discussed with and received by the unit, helps to keep the process 'open'.

Three or four longer-term scenarios are considered by the Executive Team each year and they select the scenario to be used for planning purposes. The other scenarios are used to set the boundaries of upside and downside on the forecasts and to assist in judging whether the balance of probability lies above or below the planning assumptions. The scenarios are kept updated and are used as background for all strategy and budget projections.

A macro-economic model of the Group is maintained which gives the ability to test the effect of different economic growth rates and varying exchange rates on financial performance. The economic work is given a long-term dimension by a 'Futures' capability which projects social and technical trends. The purpose is to raise the Group's eyes above current horizons to try to spot trends and even discontinuities in markets and technology and to encourage use of this insight in identifying threats to existing business and also new opportunities of high potential.

Planning is a department with a graduate strength of twenty, divided into two mainstreams: a Planning Group and an Economics and External Studies Group. The former works largely internally on the corporate and business strategies, and the latter is mostly involved with assessing the external environment. These skills must be integrated and information about the economic environment, the health of customer industries, competitor performance and major strategic thrusts of competitors is brought to bear on both ICI corporate strategy and the evaluation of individual business options. For many tasks, mixed discipline teams of people from across the department are formed to provide the strongest possible blend of skills.

To assist integration within the Planning Department and also with other departments (principally Finance and the Acquisitions Team), a unified data base of internal and external data has been generated. Manipulation and clear display of these data is critical to their value in improving decision-taking. To this end a third group of Planning Department has been established to manage Information Technology (IT) in the ICI corporate headquarters.

The IT skills are developing very rapidly and a suite of models and displays is being created which will transform the capability to test interactively various options and events. Such a system needs to be tightly managed, but provides a powerful new tool in support of strategic thinking and dimensions to communication.

Planning in a nutshell

The description of ICI's planning and budgeting processes and of the role of Corporate Planning has covered many of the key characteristics of the way the company operates. It may be helpful to summarize these operational characteristics and add one or two more:

- An Executive Team with a strong strategic planning role
- A concise and precise statement of agreed strategies for units, with achievement milestones
- Short-term profit and cash budgets for units set using the strategic milestones to provide a linkage with their long-term strategies
- Close working between Corporate Planning Department and Finance Department
- A simple, flexible, action-orientated, portfolio management tool
- A quantitative vision of the Group ten years ahead with assessment of availability and allocation of resources
- A process for setting corporate objectives and milestones and for identifying potential shortcomings in the corporate achievement
- Strategic identification and justification for acquisitions
- Understanding of both customer industries and trends in society to provide early warning of changes or even discontinuities in ICI businesses
- Interpretation of competitor strategies

- Identification of territorial shifts and opportunities
- Ensuring changes in business shape are reflected by changes in employee skills and organizational structures
- Strategies for maintaining excellence in innovative skills central to competitive success in present and future business.

A corporate planning process with characteristics as diverse as these presents a challenging role to Planning Department to keep the various threads appropriately connected. The disparate issues must be sufficiently related to allow individual decisions, whilst at the same time they must be sufficiently separate to allow discrete decisions without over complicated debate on each and every subject. Planning Department, therefore, has a major role in ordering and allocating priority to issues and in helping to sort wood from trees.

Overall this adds up to a job which is difficult, challenging and hectic, but which is also stimulating and exciting for all concerned. A staff role, yes, but one which is involved, proactive and above all *additive*.

References

1   Turner, Graham (1984), ICI becomes proactive, *Long Range Planning*, **17** (6), 12–16
2   Porter, Michael (1987), From competitive advantage to corporate strategy, *Harvard Business Review*, **65** (3), 43–59.

11 Successful strategies: The story of Singapore Airlines

Karmjit Singh, Company Planning Manager, Singapore Airlines Limited

Singapore Airlines (SIA) is the national air carrier of the island-state of Singapore. SIA's roots can be traced back to early 1947 when a twin-engined Airspeed Consul under the Malayan Airways insignia first started scheduled services between Singapore, Kuala Lumpur, Ipoh and Penang.

By 1955, international services were added using DC3s to Jakarta, Medan, Palembang, Saigon, Bangkok, North Borneo, Sarawak, Rangoon and Brunei. The airline underwent several fleet changes whilst additional destinations were added.

In 1963 it was renamed Malaysian Airways. In 1966, the governments of Malaysia and Singapore acquired joint majority control of the airline and in 1967 it was again renamed, this time to MSA (Malaysia–Singapore Airlines). MSA started to expand beyond the region with a chartered B707 operating to Sydney in the same year.

SIA was born on 1 October 1972 when MSA ceased operations and SIA took to the skies as Singapore's own national airline. The 'new' airline retained the B707s and B737s and continued to serve the entire international network formerly served by MSA. Today, SIA has grown to be among the top ten international air carriers in the world. Its production of 18,801 million RPKs (revenue passenger kilometres) in 1982 puts SIA ahead of such well-known names as Qantas and Swissair and just behind Lufthansa and Air Canada (see Figure 11.1).

Over the past ten years (up to 1984), total revenue has grown from S$389m to S$2,621m or more than six times (see Figure 11.2). Staff strength, however, has grown at a slower rate from 4906 ten years ago to 10,655 (see Figure 11.3).

SIA's fleet today comprises seventeen B747s, eight A300s and two

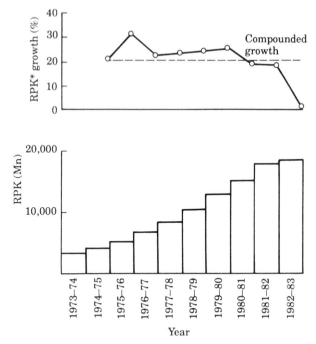

*RPK = Revenue passenger kilometres

Figure 11.1 *RPKs and growth rate*

B727s. The average age of this fleet is less than three years old (as at October 1983), making it one of the most modern of any major airline.

SIA has also shown a decent profit in every year of its operations since 1972 (see Figure 11.4).

Reasons for SIA's success

What, one may ask, accounts for the enviable success of an air carrier from a tiny developing island-state half the size of Los Angeles with a population of only 2.5 million inhabitants and ill-endowed with natural resources other than its people?

Both external and internal factors have played equal and complementary roles in accounting for SIA's prosperity.

External factors
Singapore straddles the Equator and is strategically located at the crossroads of one of the world's busiest sea and air routes. More importantly the airline's homebase is increasingly becoming the hub of the

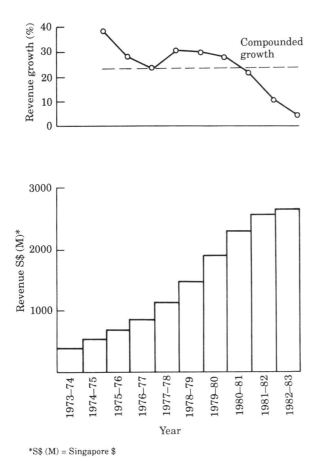

Figure 11.2 *Revenue growth*

ASEAN hinterland with its thriving economies. It is also centrally located in the fastest growing region in the world: the Intra-Orient-Pacific Basin.

Hard work and pragmatic government policies have turned Singapore into a modern and efficient metropolis, making it the most prosperous country in Asia after Japan. Its free enterprise ideology has attracted many Fortune 500 companies to set up regional headquarters in Singapore. Singapore today is the second largest port after Rotterdam and has the third largest oil-refining centre in the world after Rotterdam and Houston.

Liberal visa rules, good hotels and infrastructure and the promotion of Singapore as a shopping paradise have also helped to attract visitors by

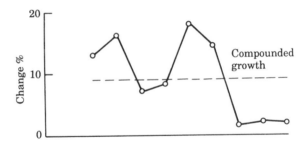

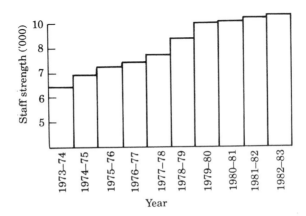

Figure 11.3   *Staff strength*

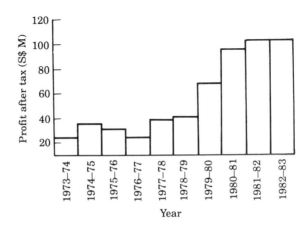

Figure 11.4   *Profit after tax*

the thousands. Singapore now handles the largest number of foreign visitors among the Asian countries including Japan and Hong Kong.

The Government also welcomes airlines from all over the globe to land at Singapore either as a terminating or transit point. To entice more of them to do so, airport and ancillary activities are constantly upgraded. Consequently, SIA was able to take advantage of reciprocal traffic rights to expand. (Its current network extends to twenty-seven countries spread over four continents.) Now, more than thirty scheduled international airlines call at Singapore in addition to numerous non-scheduled operators.

Internal factors
Skilful expoitation of the opportunities created by the Government was the key to SIA's success. In order to gain a better insight into the airline's ability to exploit its strategic location, and other advantages, we must return briefly to its inception stage.

Though almost wholly government-owned, the airline does not receive any subsidies (which is taboo for all government-owned industries in Singapore). SIA is run along purely commercial lines (i.e. to make a reasonable profit for its shareholders). The airline is taxed like any other business and pays dividends yearly to its shareholders. SIA even has to pay fees to the Government in return for guarantees that may be required by some banks on loans for aircraft purchases. The airline is constantly reminded that Singapore can exist without an airline since it is already well connected by air to all corners of the globe. Thus SIA fully recognizes its fate should it not make good in the marketplace.

Fleet re-equipment decisions

SIA started with only five B707s and five B737s. To this were added four more B707s in 1972. After careful evaluation, the fledgling carrier decided to take a quantum leap into the jumbo league by ordering two B747s for delivery in 1973. This was not a hasty decision. Detailed studies had shown that this aircraft had the lowest unit-operating cost. This was the first of many bold fleet re-equipment decisions.

Thereafter the airline started to grow rapidly. More B747s were acquired in 1974, 1975, 1976 and 1977 as SIA's route network expanded to more European cities. Passenger response to the new aircraft and the inflight service was encouraging. In 1976 orders were also placed for three B727s. This order was then expanded to six in early 1977. These aircraft were needed to strengthen SIA's regional services and to replace the older B737s and B707s.

In late 1977 two more advanced versions of the B747 and five DC10s were ordered to service the TransPacific services.

In 1978 SIA shocked the world by announcing the then largest commercial aeroplane order ever placed, valued at US$900m for thirteen B747s and another six B727s. A few months later two more DC10s were ordered from McDonnell Douglas.

In 1979, it ordered six airbuses with options for a further six. Another huge order worth US$1·6bn was placed in December 1981 comprising eight B747-300s with the stretched upper deck and eight more A300s. May 1983 saw yet another large order of aircraft: six more B747-300s plus six A310s and four B757s. Technologically obsolete and fuel inefficient aircraft were meanwhile retired.

By April 1988 SIA's fleet consisted of the following:

  9   B747–200B
 14   B747–300SUD
  6   A310
  4   B757

What was the justification for all these purchases? Firstly, SIA was able to exploit its traffic rights through skilful marketing. This, in turn, helped to stimulate traffic, enabling the airline to expand at a rate of about 25 per cent a year in the 1970s.

Secondly, to support SIA's high service standards, the airline decided to invest in the latest technology. It has since been part of SIA's strategy to maintain a youthful fleet with the lowest operating costs. The two fuel crises in 1973 and 1979 vindicated these 'bold' decisions, since the new aircraft proved to be an excellent hedge against fly-away inflation.

Thirdly, the major purchases were made at the bottom of the business cycle; best deals were therefore struck. With the carefully phased-out delivery of these aircraft, SIA could take advantage of any upturn in the economic cycle when demand for additional capacity was strong.

Service

From the start SIA understood that superior service, especially the standard of in-flight service was paramount in order to establish itself. To provide a service 'that even other airlines talk about' became the unofficial motto for SIA's employees, beginning with its cabin staff. According to Fortune magazine 'the combination of gentleness and efficiency helps the airlines lure customers from competitors on routes that now span half the globe.' The unceasing pursuit of excellence continues in the air as well as on the ground.

SIA's passenger load factors have been consistently above 70 per cent for the greater part of the past ten years (see Table 11.1). Accolades from the trade and customers too have borne out SIA's belief that a superior

Table 11.1   *Load factors by year (%)*

	Passenger load factor	Overall load factor
1973/4	71	63
1974/5	67	60
1975/6	68	64
1976/7	71	66
1977/8	74	68
1978/9	73	70
1979/80	74	71
1980/1	72	69
1981/2	75	72
1982/3	73	69

quality of service is paramount under conditions of open competition where carrier's network, frequency and capacity are generally equal.

While the in-flight service has been highly visible, the airline has also spared no expense to raise its standards on the ground. Ground services are reviewed continually to match the standard of service provided in the air. With the passenger foremost in mind, SIA has invested millions of dollars in computers to link its reservations network worldwide to provide instant access on schedules and seat availability.

Owing to its high in-flight standards and charming cabin crew, SIA has managed to capture the mystic of the Orient in its 'Singapore Girl' advertising theme. The 'aura' created by the Balmain-clad girls has made the stylized yellow bird logo of SIA instantly recognizable everywhere. Advertising recall of SIA advertisements is generally one of the highest wherever polled. This evergreen theme has also won some of the most prestigious awards in the advertising industry including the 1983 Clio award for the best International Television and Cinema category. SIA has also won Clio awards for the best television commercial (1975) and best overall print campaign (in 1976 and 1977).

Human resources

Because Singapore lacked natural resources it has had to rely on its human resources to upgrade itself. Recognizing this, investment in human resources has been one of the cardinal facets of SIA's game plan.

During the recruitment phase, the best available personnel are sought. The new recruits are exposed to various departments and on-the-job training. High priority is given to staff training and development in diverse forms, both in-house and out-house, locally and overseas. Total expenditure in this area of staff development and training ranges between US$15m and US$20m annually.

This huge investment has been well spent. For example, its engineering staff can do almost all the maintenance on the latest generation of aircraft and engines. Hitherto, a greater part of the maintenance was contracted out-house at higher cost.

As mentioned earlier, innovation and creative ideas are highly regarded and rewarded. Staff are continuously encouraged to send in ideas which save costs, increase revenue or productivity or upgrade service. Numerous ideas have been recognized, rewarded and implemented. Not long ago S$50,000 was awarded for an idea which saved the company about S$1·5m a year on fuel. It is through such schemes that employees are encouraged to give of their best.

Innovations

The innovative spirit also gave the travelling public the first slumberettes on B747 upper decks, jackpot machines to relieve boredom and Round-the-World fares. SIA also became the first airline, apart from British Airways and Air France, to operate the Concorde which cut travelling time, between London and Singapore, to nine-and-a-half hours. This not only fulfilled SIA's goal to provide total service to the public but also enhanced SIA's reputation and image in the industry.

Behind the service standards lies the corporate philosophy supporting it. Among the attributes ingrained into employees are teamwork and the pursuit of excellence. The smallest possible units are created to carry out required tasks. Authority is delegated down to the lowest level consistent with accountability and efficiency. Decentralized decision-making enables fast reaction from the man-on-the-spot and especially the sales staff in the field. Executives are encouraged to progress to 'problem-solving' and on to opportunity-finding. Training and retraining remains the unwavering object of the company.

Productivity

Productivity is SIA's catchword in its drive for excellence. Staff recognize that survival in today's harsh competitive environment rests on raising their own productivity. With assurances from management that retrenchment is not the objective in seeking productivity gains, employees have been forthcoming with suggestions of improvements. SIA's employee productivity measured against the number of CTKs produced, ranks amongst the highest in the airline league (see Figure 11.5).

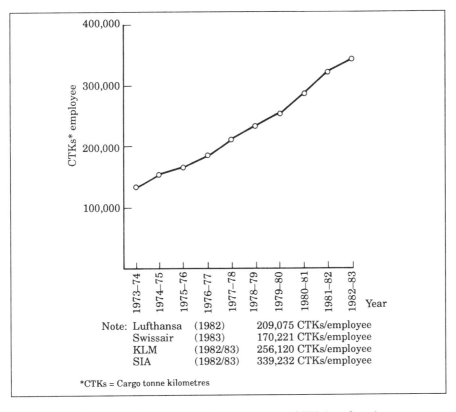

Figure 11.5 *Productivity comparison (CTKs/employee)*

SIA intrinsically believes in being slim and trim. Staff recruitment is tightly controlled and is closely related to capacity growth rates. Staff made surplus through technology are either retrained or redeployed or induced to leave through generous redundancy schemes.

Industrial relations

Because of the huge investment in human resources it is not surprising that management and unions try to co-exist for the good of the airline. Most industrial relations problems are solved amicably.

The cordial management–union atmosphere enables management to concentrate on its task of running the airline instead of being preoccupied with 'public relations battles against criticisms and fighting for support of government and unions'.

Quality of management

Of all the major and well-established airlines in the world, SIA has one of the youngest management teams. The average manager is in his late thirties with executive directors only three to four years older.

The young and dynamic team has been able to react quickly and decisively in decision-making. Luckily for SIA the Government does not interfere in day-to-day affairs and quick decisions can be made and actions taken.

Financial conservatism

Management also believes in prudent financial management. New aircraft, for example, are depreciated over ten years. This policy of accelerated depreciation reflects the rapid and continuing increase in the cost of new aircraft. Start-up costs of aircraft are also written off fairly quickly. This has enabled SIA to finance a huge portion of its aircraft and other capital expenditure from self-generated funds. Because of SIA's credit standing, it has been able to tap the market for funds at the finest rates.

The role of corporate planning

When SIA was expanding at double digit growth rates the company Planning Department was preoccupied mainly with fleet planning. Over the last two years (1982–4), with both capacity and traffic growth showing modest growth, the company Planning Department became actively involved in identifying and establishing corporate objectives and corporate goals. To support the accomplishment of corporate goals, the Company Planning Department acted as a facilitator and catalyst and got the Divisions to establish their respective Divisional goals. Consequently the smallest department in the company was functionally linked in one way or another to the broader corporate objectives and corporate goals. In this way staff at various levels were motivated to do their best since the goals were well defined and measurable. The company Planning Department monitored the progress of the goals, monthly, on behalf of management.

More importantly, in the realm of strategy formulation, the company Planning Department consolidated the 'environmental and resource analysis' inputs from all the departments and prepared an 'issue analysis'. Essentially this 'issue analysis' provided the kernel for management response and strategic thought and eventual functional strategy development. Implementation was, of course, decentralized.

Strategic issues for the future

The company, historically, experienced capacity growth rates close to 20 per cent per annum. This was possible thanks to the systematic exercise of attractive traffic rights. Most of the relatively attractive traffic rights have now been used up. Meanwhile the global economic recession has served to heighten protectionist sentiments in several airline quarters. The prognosis is that we have to live with modest to low capacity growth rates in the future.

Strategically, we are now preoccupied with issues such as how to maintain profitability in the face of slow growth and rising costs. Also, in a low growth regime, how do you keep improving productivity continuously? There are other issues; and these feature prominently in the search for suitable strategies.

Conclusion

Through sheer hard work, innovation, bold and pragmatic decisions and huge investment in the staff, SIA has grown from its humble origins to serve thirty-six cities in twenty-seven countries. Its strategy is quite simple. It believes in giving the customer a quality service at a competitive price while earning a small return. This has been made possible by the high investment in the most up-to-date equipment and facilities and in staff training and development.

In short, SIA's success is founded on the prudent practice of sound and well-tried business fundamentals rather than any earth-shattering or new corporate strategies.

12 Implementing corporate strategy: The story of International Thomson

Gordon C. Brunton, President, International Thomson Organization Ltd

Twenty-five years ago, International Thomson Organization* was a small, Britain-based national and regional newspaper publisher and operated a commercial television franchise. Today it is a Toronto-based corporation with worldwide interests in information and publishing, holidays and travel, and oil and gas. Annual sales approach $2.5 billion. Growth has involved several strategic changes in emphasis and direction. How did these come about and what lessons can be learned from them?

In the early 1960s, with its narrow interests in newspapers and commercial television, the company was potentially vulnerable on three counts:

- Commercial television in Britain operated under government franchise. After an uncertain start, it became highly profitable and that brought the danger that the Government would want to take a larger slice.
- A disproportionately high share of the company's revenue came from advertising, rendering it particularly vulnerable to the vagaries of the economic cycle.
- There was also a clear danger of legislation to control the ownership of media, and that would inhibit the company from growing in its traditional areas of interest. In 1965, severe constraints on the acquisition of newspapers were imposed by new anti-trust legislation.

With these problems ahead, it was necessary to chart a new course for International Thomson. It was, however, with relatively limited financial resources that the company embarked upon a programme of diversification.

It is possible to identify four main phases to this diversification which spanned approximately the last twenty years:

---

*Prior to 1978, the company was known as the Thomson Organisation: for simplicity, International Thomson is used throughout.

- The first phase, about 1961 to 1965, was a move into related areas of information and publishing.
- The second phase, 1965 to 1971, was concerned with the creation of two new profit centres. One was in a totally unrelated business, holidays and travel, and the other in the closely related business of directory publishing.
- The third phase, 1971 to 1977, was the opportunistic move into oil and gas production offshore in the North Sea.
- The fourth phase is the current programme of development in the United States. The aim is to concentrate on information and publishing markets. Other interests in the United States involve travel and oil and gas.

Phase one

The objective of the first phase was to spread some of the risk from consumer advertising, the company's major source of revenue, onto industrial and business advertising. A related objective was to create new publishing centres that were not dependent upon advertising at all. In a series of acquisitions, Thomson moved into three areas:

- Educational and trade book publishing;
- Information technology; and
- Consumer, professional, and business journal publishing.

During this five-year period, International Thomson became the second largest trade, technical, and business publisher in Britain and the largest in Australia and South Africa.

The company also launched several new publications, including two women's monthly magazines distributed only through supermarkets. At the same time, the newspaper business was being actively developed with the launch of new titles and supplements.

By 1965, a substantial new profit centre had been created. However, its growth and size were not sufficient to protect the company against the vulnerability of its television profits which were imminently threatened by new licences, levies and taxes, and by anti-trust considerations.

It was urgent to plan the next phase of diversification despite the fact that the first phase was incomplete and still needed substantial resources in terms of people and money.

Phase two

The second phase of the company's diversification plan was based on three major factors:

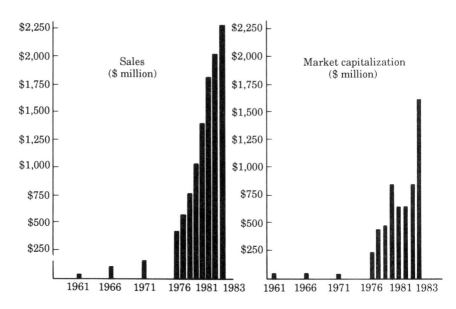

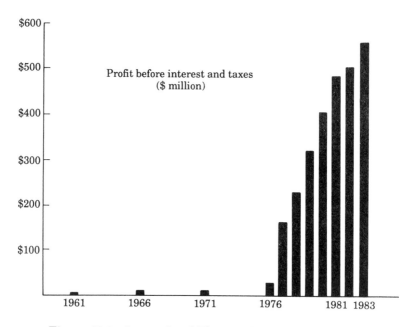

Figure 12.1   *International Thomson: historical performance*

- International Thomson's main attribute was as a market-oriented company with experience in selling to final consumers.
- The company's experience with the introduction of commercial television to Britain had shown that what works in North America tends to work in Britain, though it may take longer.
- The company had a cadre of entrepreneurial managers who were well trained, imaginative, and versatile.

With limited financial resources, International Thomson's objectives were twofold:

- To create quickly a significant new profit centre at a relatively low cost; and
- To lay the foundation for a major new profit centre of the future where the development costs would not be excessive in the initial stages.

A new profit centre

Deciding where to create the new profit centre took several months of intensive study. The criteria included:

- Relatively low initial investment;
- An area that did not require too much technical know-how; this almost certainly meant a service industry;
- Substantial growth potential;
- An area where Thomson's skills, particularly in marketing, could contribute;
- An operation with a different cash-flow cycle from that of the newspapers. (The newspapers' cash-flow was poor in the early part of the year and relatively good at the end of the year.)
- A business that could use the company's newspapers and magazines to deliver messages to consumers at a low cost.

International Thomson decided that the package vacation business was a good prospect for these reasons:

- It was a relatively young industry in which a few entrepreneurs had foreseen opportunity. But, in many cases, these entrepreneurs did not have the necessary resources to develop it.
- It was clear in the mid-1960s in Britain that vacations for the working population were going to be both significantly longer and more frequent, and that growing prosperity would give people higher discretionary income for leisure spending.
- With the advent of the new generation of jet aircraft, air transport was going to become cheaper, faster, and more efficient.

- The media, particularly television, were awakening the population's aspirations for travel abroad.
- The British climate has always been unpredictable. If the opportunity were available to vacation in the Mediterranean sun at low cost, it seemed a proposition that many people were likely to find attractive.

Once the decision to enter this market had been made, the strategy was implemented quickly. Three existing package tour companies and a small airline were bought for well under $3 million. In 1964, none of these had succeeded in making a profit. But in 1966, the first full year of operation under International Thomson, these new acquisitions achieved a trading profit of almost $3 million. They continued to operate profitably for some years. Then, as often happens in new growing markets, the competition became intense. There was a bitter fight for market share: margins were pared to the bone; and standards were inevitably reduced. In the early 1970s the industry suffered the inevitable convulsion, with many major bankruptcies and failures. Thomson Travel survived as the largest operator with double the market share of its closest competitor. Profits then turned around very quickly and increased rapidly in the second half of the decade and into the 1980s. In 1983, pretax profit was in excess of $60 million on sales of $620 million. In fact, the travel business met most of the criteria that had been set:

- The initial investment was relatively low.
- It achieved significant profits almost immediately.
- It has been shown to have substantial growth potential.
- Most of its senior executives were recruited from our traditional publishing businesses.
- It significantly corrected the seasonal imbalance in the company's cash flow. Vacationers pay in advance in the early part of the year, and the bulk of the bills are settled many months later.
- There is a clear synergy with other Thomson businesses, particularly the ability to advertise vacations in the newspapers and magazines.

Thomson's entry into travel was researched from scratch. Development in this area was based upon management's own judgment rather than on an approach from outsiders. This is a story of the development of an industry with very rapid early growth and good profitability. This was followed by intense competition and very low profits. Then the industry matured and showed excellent profit levels.

The longer-term project

The longer-term project was the introduction of *Yellow Pages* into Britain. The *Yellow Pages* was a concept imported from the United States where for over seventy years this business information service has been available to telephone subscribers and users. It has become essential to users and extremely profitable for both the telephone companies and the advertising contractors. In Britain, the company that had had the contract for selling advertising for the Post Office telephone directories for over twenty years had hardly exploited the opportunity at all. They had achieved total sales of less than $1 million.

Thomson studied the performance and publishing methods of similar directories in other parts of the world. When the contract came up for renewal, Thomson won it. The company then persuaded the Post Office that there should be a *Yellow Pages* directory for all sixty-four regions. Reuben H. Donnelley joined Thomson first as consultants and then as partners.

This enterprise was an example of applying the selling and marketing skills developed in Thomson's newspapers to a completely new area. Eventually, International Thomson built the directories into the third largest advertising medium in Britain after television and the press.

By the time International Thomson surrendered the contract in 1980, the total advertising revenue paid to the Post Office was over $400 million. Commissions paid to Thomson *Yellow Pages* were some $150 million, with total profits of $50 million.

The lessons learned were important:

- Initial research was based on Post Office projections which exaggerated the rate of growth of telephone connections. This was a key factor in directory usage, and Thomson underestimated the length of time it would take the conservative British public to accept this new concept. In fact, it took seven or eight years to reach viability. But International Thomson persevered because it believed the idea to be conceptually right and because it was sure it had the skills and expertise, with Reuben H. Donnelley, to make the idea succeed.
- International Thomson learned the constraints and difficulties of working in a commercial venture: first with the Post Office as a government department and then with British Telecom as a publicly owned utility. The major constraint was the difficulty of communication. That is, understanding and agreeing on objectives between a commercial enterprise and a government department or public service corporation.
- Another lesson learned was that it is dangerous to have a major investment and profit centre dependent upon decisions and policies over which the company has little or no control. The experience also confirmed the dangers of businesses based upon franchises over which the company has no ultimate control.

Some of the problems encountered were:

- All printing had to be undertaken by a government agency on a non-competitive basis, and modern printing technology was not available largely because of labour union resistance.

- Pricing policies were extremely sensitive to the pressures of the government of the day and were often determined by political rather than commercial considerations.
- A key factor to success was swift and efficient directory distribution to ensure the greatest exposure and longest life. This was rarely attained because it was largely dependent on the enthusiasm, the efficiency, and the resources of local telephone managers which varied across the country.
- *Yellow Pages* was continually caught up in the industrial relations problems both in the Post Office and with the government printer. As a result, during the fifteen years that International Thomson held the contract, the full annual publication programme of sixty-four directories was rarely achieved, and this had severe repercussions on the profit performance.

When the contract came up for its third renewal in 1980, the Post Office decided to split the franchise among three companies. Although Thomson was one of the companies, it felt the areas allocated to it offered insufficient development potential. International Thomson made a major decision not to accept the contract terms and to start a new directory operation of its own (*Thomson Local Directories*) in competition with *Yellow Pages*. This became a joint venture with Dun & Bradstreet.

Phase three

The next major diversification move came in 1971. At that time, some 80 per cent of Thomson's profit was coming from newspapers and other information and publishing activities. The remaining 20 per cent came from travel and some other interests. Only a very small interest in Scottish Television remained. This paid a modest dividend compared with ten years earlier when it had accounted for half of Thomson's total profit.

Phase three, International Thomson's move into natural resources, was totally opportunistic and has had the most profound impact on the size and nature of the company.

In early 1971, the company was approached by a consortium consisting of Occidental Petroleum, Getty Oil and Allied Chemical Corporation. Before applying for licences to drill for oil and gas under the North Sea, they needed a British partner in order to comply with government conditions.

International Thomson was offered a 20 per cent stake. The immediate reaction was lukewarm because the company had no knowledge of or experience in the oil and gas business. It decided, however, to undertake a quick but careful evaluation before making its decision.

What were the factors that the company considered in that evaluation?

- Thomson established from expert sources that the licence areas open for application in the North Sea were highly promising.
- It was indicated that despite the depth of water, current technology could be adapted to do the job, though the risks would be considerable.
- The company established that its potential partners were a well-balanced group. The chances of the consortium being allocated 'good' blocks were likely to be enhanced by International Thomson's participation because of its strong Scottish connections.
- It was clear at an early stage of discussions that the consortium would badly need a British partner with an understanding of political sensitivities in Whitehall and Scotland and who knew its way around the 'corridors of power'. The conclusion drawn was that International Thomson could play a meaningful role in the consortium, even though the other members dwarfed it in terms of financial strength and ability to take risks.
- Thomson's share of the cost of carrying through the exploration programme required by a reasonable allocation of blocks was likely to be $5 million (approximately $20 million at today's prices).
- It was generally considered that the chances were 10:1 against a discovery on any block. However, the very crude models Thomson management was able to construct indicated that a medium-sized discovery gave a very good return. And on a big discovery, the rewards could be very high indeed. The conclusion was that to risk $5 million was not unreasonable when set against the rewards that success could bring.

The decision was made to join the consortium subject to three conditions:

- International Thomson's investment would be limited to $5 million;
- The company maintained the right to withdraw at any time; and
- The $5 million investment would not come from the company funds, but from the Thomson Family (the family who founded the organization). The reason was that the company's balance sheet was extremely stretched because commitments to other parts of the Group were considerable. The company could not responsibly allocate $5 million to a very high-risk venture. International Thomson would accept management responsibility and run the project. In return, it would have an option to acquire at cost 90 per cent of any oil or gas discovered at any time.

The consortium was formed and it was subsequently allocated six blocks. Oil was found in the third area drilled, and it proved to be a field with over 800 million barrels of recoverable oil. This field, which has become known as the Piper Field, is not the largest in the North Sea, but it has proved to be one of the most profitable. In a second field, Claymore, 400 million barrels of recoverable oil were discovered.

The initial Thomson Family investment of $5 million eventually resulted in a financing requirement of over $500 million to pay for the 20 per cent share of two production platforms and an on-shore oil terminal. There was no way that borrowing of this magnitude could be supported by either the Thomson Family or the balance sheet of International Thomson.

The company developed a new method of financing. In essence, the money was raised so that the bulk of the risk was passed to the lenders in exchange for a royalty. The rate of repayment was geared to the rate of production, with no claim on the existing assets of either the Family or the company. In other words, the oil reserves were used as collateral with the banks taking the risk that the consortium could recover them.

These oil discoveries totally transformed the Group in terms of opportunities and resources: Group trading profit in 1977 was almost $190 million compared with less than $20 million in 1971. Although oil was not yet part of the public company, it accounted for 70 per cent of total Group profit. Information and publishing were reduced to approximately 25 per cent of the profit and travel to only 5 per cent.

This brought with it a new set of problems. It had totally unbalanced the Group. While the company was going to enjoy substantial cash flows, the fact remained that oil was a finite and depletable asset. Although International Thomson would continue to explore, it would have been unrealistic to plan on the basis of further major discoveries. The company had to look to a future in which a period (perhaps ten years) of high oil earnings would be followed by one of very sharp decline. The task was to convert this finite asset into permanent longer-term earnings. It was essential to develop a new strategy and a new plan to deal with this situation. This process was started in 1976: before any oil profits had accrued. It was a classic strategic planning exercise covering objectives, strengths and weaknesses, the external environment, strategies, and finally the organizational implications.

This task was undertaken over a six-month period by a committee consisting of senior directors working with a team of managers and specialists. An outside moderator from one of Britain's leading business schools was appointed.

The development policy guidelines were determined. One consideration was that much growth potential existed in several of the company's existing British businesses. The first priority was to allocate sufficient financial resources to enable them to develop within their own management capabilities. These businesses, however, suffered from three major constraints:

- Volatility in advertising-based publishing and, to a lesser extent, in travel.
- Almost exclusive dependence on the British economy, which accounted for only 5 per cent of total Organization for Economic Cooperation and Development (OECD) output and which had performed relatively poorly for many years; and
- Relatively high market penetration in some sectors of the business with a consequent threat from anti-trust legislation.

Consequently, there was a need to develop new businesses with high quality earnings. The goal was to compensate for:

- The weaknesses in International Thomson's existing business mix;
- Excessive dependence on Britain; and
- The progressive decline in production from the Piper and Claymore Fields as reserves were depleted.

International Thomson decided to seek majority rather than minority equity positions so that it could manage businesses rather than adopt the passive role of investors. It rules out the concept of functioning as an investment holding company.

International Thomson also decided it would concentrate on its existing skills and strengths and on product areas where it already had expertise. There was likely to be more than sufficient opportunity in information technology (including publishing), travel, and natural resources (three growth sectors) to absorb all available funds. Although several interests in London urged the company to regard itself as an oil company and invest the bulk of the North Sea revenues in further exploration around the world, it rejected this concept for two reasons: it did not have the technical skills even though given time they could be developed; and, more important, it could see far better opportunities in other areas, opportunities that were both immediate and long-term.

International Thomson determined its main thrust would be in information technology. The insatiable global demand for information provides one of the major commercial opportunities of our time. Thomson Organization would continue to be a major publisher in the traditional areas of newspapers, magazines, and books, but it would increasingly embrace the possibilities provided by the new media: on-line and micro-computers, cassettes, disks, and cable.

Thomson Organization defined the market sectors in which it was primarily interested as:

- Carefully selected sections of educational and reference publishing;
- The professions, particularly medical, legal, taxation, accounting, and banking;

- Publishing for growth sectors such as telecommunications, electronics, computers, and the emerging technologies.

Information publishing and services in these sectors satisfied certain criteria Thomson had set:

- *Stability* This involves a product area that is not necessarily risk free but in which the risks are substantially within the control of management. To a major degree, the product area should not be susceptible to economic cycles.
- *Speciality products* These are products that are essential to their consumers. The products have long life cycles and are not prone to changes in fashion. Users are generally buying these products as agents of a business which pays the bill.
- *Growth potential* After an initial period of heavy investment, International Thomson seeks strong growth and above-average rates of return.

As for the direction of its development geographically, the company sought:

- *Politically stable countries* It had had some unfortunate experiences during the 1960s and 1970s in the developing economies of Africa, the Middle East, and the Far East with nationalization and indigenization.
- *Economies of reasonable size* International Thomson did not wish to dissipate its energies over a large number of countries.
- *Developed economies* The chosen market sectors determined that the growth possibilities would be in highly developed service economies.

Broadening the geographical spread of its business required that International Thomson have the freedom to invest abroad. This involved a change in the structure of the company which took place in 1978. The public company based in Britain had always been ultimately controlled by Thomson Family trust companies in Canada, and this factor was recognized by the creation of a new public company domiciled in Canada to embrace the old public company and the oil interests which up to this time were part of a British Thomson Family company. This gave International Thomson the freedom to invest funds anywhere in the world.

That has been and remains International Thomson's basic strategy. The company recognizes, of course, that policies will evolve as circumstances change and that these policies should be subject to annual review.

Phase four

After comprehensive consideration, International Thomson identified the United States as its prime target and immediate priority, recognizing that eventually it might want to widen its international scope to include other developed economies. The principal reason for choosing the United States was its massive specialized information market. The value of the chosen market sectors in 1983 was approximately $13 billion, and the level of concentration allows scope for new, strong entrants. Information-based publishing tends to be a fragmented market and is changing rapidly.

The company's approach has been to buy key bases in its chosen areas and develop them creatively within its guidelines. Much of the development cost is written off as incurred. This is preferable to buying mature, goodwill-intense businesses and in the long run produces better returns.

In six years, the company has invested approximately $400 million in the acquisition of US information publishing businesses and on their subsequent development of new products. The company has over 4,500 employees; sales in 1983 were over $425 million; and the company is growing quickly. Given that it could not be planned precisely, International Thomson's market profile is a surprisingly good one. It is particularly strong in health care which is a very big market in the US. It is also strong in law and tax banking and accounting and college publishing, particularly in the mathematical sciences. There are also smaller but key bases in computer science, consumer electronics and cable.

While the main thrust has been in information and publishing, the company has established bases in two other product areas: travel and oil and gas. For travel, conditions are quite different in the United States from those in Britain. In the United States, there is not a single homogeneous market as in Britain, but a series of separate markets. This means it is necessary to establish offices in a number of locations. It has taken five years to reach viability, but now that this has been accomplished the potential is considerable.

In oil and gas, the company first looked for an acquisition, but at that time (1977–8) acquisitions were overpriced. So the company set up from scratch by recruiting an experienced and established executive in the oil business. While International Thomson will never be an oil major, there is considerable opportunity for relatively small companies. To date the company has committed approximately $150 million in acquiring production and it expects a good return on the investment. It has recently established a base in Canada along similar lines.

The full impact on profits of the implementation of International Thomson's strategy has been adversely influenced by the severe recession in British publishing. The company is only now beginning to recover from it. In 1983, the trading profit contribution of the information and publishing sector at around 27 per cent was only slightly higher than in 1977. International Thomson's US publishing operations are flourishing, and their contribution is already significant and growing strongly.

By 1988 (the end of its current five-year plan) Thomson expects information and publishing, within a substantially increased total, to account for perhaps 60 per cent of trading profits. Travel's share increased substantially to 17 per cent in 1983. With a turnaround in the US operation and the expansion in Britain. Thomson expects it to reach perhaps 20 per cent by 1988. The planned share of oil and gas is expected to decline from 56 per cent in 1983 to perhaps only 20 per cent in 1988.

By the end of the period, therefore, information and publishing will be making the major contribution, and Thomson will have succeeded in converting the relatively low-quality profits from oil and gas into high-quality profit streams from its other businesses. The marginal tax rate on a barrel of North Sea oil is some 90 per cent. By substituting for these highly taxed profits, profits bearing a more normal tax rate, International Thomson's net earnings will benefit greatly. Thomson expects the United States to account for some 50 per cent of total profits by 1988.

Lessons learned

That then is a fairly comprehensive history of the growth of International Thomson. What lessons have we learned; what conclusions can we draw; and what management style have we adopted to enable us to run this diverse business?

First, it should be emphasized that, with the benefit of hindsight, one has to be careful not to exaggerate the degree to which everything was planned. As far as the first phase was concerned (this was long before the days of formal corporate planning systems) it is fair to say that the company only had a broad strategy. It had a clear idea of the areas of publishing it wanted to enter, but the company certainly did not have a detailed diversification plan. It struck out in a large number of directions. This would not be the approach today. Phase two was much more carefully planned. Phase three was, of course, totally opportunistic. For Phase four, planning had been rigorous. The company was clear about its objectives; it developed a strategy and an implementation plan and has pursued it with determination. Up to a point, International Thomson has been constrained by what is available, but the company has approached a considerable number of potential partners on a friendly basis rather than waiting for them to come to it. There have been cases where the first reaction was negative, but persistence brought subsequent success.

The need for senior managers to think strategically about their businesses and to plan their futures cannot be emphasized too strongly. But this must not be allowed to stifle entrepreneurial flair. Flexibility is essential because opportunism is superimposed on planning. Success comes from creating opportunities, not from looking for problems to solve.

I would not want to give the impression that everything was plain sailing or went according to plan. Along the way, the company went through several difficult periods, which required a reassessment of its strategy and a re-examination of its soundness. For example, with *Yellow Pages*, the company found shortly after signing the contract with the British Post Office that it had locked itself in for ten years. The company had made its move based on false assumptions and it had little prospect of profitability for a considerable number of years. International Thomson persevered because it confirmed that the concept was right and that it would be extremely profitable eventually.

In 1974, the travel industry was approaching a state of virtual collapse. International Thomson had to re-examine the whole question of its involvement. At one stage there was a substantial majority view on the executive board that Thomson should either withdraw or strictly limit its involvement by finding a partner or partners. However, we asked ourselves whether anything fundamental had changed. We re-examined the reasons why we went into the business in the first place to determine whether our basic thinking was still valid. We reached the conclusion that it was. The market was still there and the company had the marketing skills to exploit it as well as the financial strength to see it through.

In the North Sea, there was a time when the project seemed almost too big for International Thomson to handle. In 1971, it did not have the financial resources to commit $5 million to exploration; yet less than five years later it needed to raise $500 million to pay for its share of the capital expenditure. Obviously, the company examined whether it should sell its stake. It would have been irresponsible not to look into the possibility. But the company had the necessary financial expertise and a very good relationship with the banking fraternity, and this combination brought a solution.

And, of course, there have been changes of direction and even failures. The most publicized was the withdrawal from national newspaper publishing with the sale of *The Times* of London and *The Sunday Times*. This was a major strategic decision. After a long struggle, International Thomson was unable to get the print unions to agree to the introduction of modern technology on terms it believed to be essential to make the papers efficient. International Thomson finally came to the conclusion that these papers could not be made consistently profitable under its ownership and that they would continue to be a serious cash drain on the rest of the business. So in 1981 they were sold.

While we have to put this down as a failure, it has had the advantage of releasing management resources for the development of more profitable ventures. In addition, it has caused the company to look perhaps more rigorously at the performance of all its operating divisions.

Rather than viewing divestment as a last resort when all else has failed, Thomson views divestment of unprofitable interests or interests that no longer fit into its overall strategy as a management option.

Strategic planning and management style

It is absolutely fundamental that any planning system take into account what might be termed the 'culture of a company', rather than try to impose a style to which managers have to conform. I have a strong belief that planning is a line function. Planning is a little like religion: It's a way of life, not something to turn to now and again when the mood takes you. Planning is not something that line managers can leave to 'professionals.' All International Thomson senior managers now understand that unless they demonstrate their ability to think strategically, their future career potential will be limited accordingly.

This commitment to thinking strategically must come from the top. I review the company's objectives and broad strategy personally and communicate them directly to senior management. I regard this as an essential part of every chief executive's function.

13 Strategic planning for the World Wildlife Fund

George J. Medley, Director World Wildlife Fund, UK

The national organization of the World Wildlife Fund operating in the United Kingdom (WWF UK) (now known as the World Wide Fund for Nature), is a 'not for profit' organization registered as a charity. It was founded in 1961 with the object of promoting education and research on the conservation of world fauna and flora, water, soils and other natural resources. In its early years, it developed like the majority of 'not for profit' organizations using relatively low-paid staff who had a concern for the charity's objectives. By 1973 gross income had risen to around £750,000 per annum and it stayed in this region for the next five years.

In 1977 a new Chairman of Trustees, Sir Arthur Norman, was appointed who was, himself, chairman of a major British corporation. He identified the necessity of bringing in sound business management to develop the charity and when the previous Chief Executive Officer (CEO) left in April 1977, he searched for a senior executive who had already demonstrated a sound and successful business career. I took up appointment as CEO of WWF UK on 1 January 1978, arriving to a relatively demoralized staff who had been without direct leadership for nine months.

Preparing for change

The first task was to identify, from the existing staff of seventy, those who would fit in with a sound business approach compared to those who were working because of their interest and dedication to conservation. Whilst there was a need for good conservationists in the project departments, those in the fundraising areas needed to be capable of taking a wholly professional and sound business approach to their work. A structural reorganization took place in September 1978 and coincided with the introduction of strategic planning based on a 'management by objectives' (MBO) process developed by me in my previous assignment as CEO of the subsidiary of a large multi-national. This was the first time that WWF UK had taken a hard look at its operations and it turned out to be a most revealing exercise.

The management team consisting of the heads of each of the organization's departments of Promotions, Membership. Regional, Information, Education, Finance and Administration under the chairmanship of the director, met for the strategic planning exercises for two days at the end of September 1978.

To help with these exercises we were very fortunate to have the late Ron Felstead, a member of the Urwick Orr Partnership, who had been a considerable assistance to me in introducing MBO in my previous assignment. Ron's quiet, clear, concise and informative control of the discussions played a very substantial part in converting a somewhat sceptical management team to a realization that strategic planning was not only an essential to success but also a major annual therapy and a forum at which matters which, for the rest of the year, were difficult to address, could be brought out into the open.

Deciding on the purpose

The first essential was deciding the purpose of WWF UK. The purpose is the reference point which makes possible the formulation of clear and realistic objectives. Prior to the strategic planning exercise the general view was that WWF UK was a conservation organization. After some considerable discussion however, it was recognized that in fact WWF UK was a fund-raising business, but that it also had as its purpose the proper spending of the funds raised. In 1978 the team decided that the purpose was 'to raise the maximum funds possible from UK sources and to ensure that the funds are used wisely for the benefit of conservation of the natural environment and renewable natural resources with emphasis on endangered species and habitats'.

Key areas

Having decided the purpose, attention was then turned to the result-influencing areas of the organization, specific areas in which success would contribute significantly to improve results or areas in which failure would have an adverse impact on results. The team were asked to give free range to their thinking and a list of some sixty possible areas emerged on the blackboard. Further analysis of these showed that many of them were in fact overlapping or similar and a final list of nine was chosen.

It is interesting to see that these nine can be matched to the more usual designations found when this process is followed in industry. 'Marketing' is the same word. 'Public Awareness' and 'Fund Status' relate to customer and shareholder perceptions of a business. 'Innovation' is the same concept as research and development and, most importantly, 'Net Funds' is the same as profitability. (The full list is shown in Figure 13.1.)

Each key area was then taken in turn and subjected to a strengths, weaknesses, opportunities and threats exercise. This systematic review identified the internal strengths and weaknesses of the organization and examined the external environment to identify the opportunities that might be available and the threats that might exist.

The marketing strengths of WWF UK in 1978 were seen largely to be its emotive and visually appealing message, its 'panda' logo and the uniqueness of its work. It was weak in its lack of a large donor base, its poor record on innovation and its lack of marketing penetration.

The rising awareness of the need to conserve the Earth's natural resources, the size of the market-place and the general increase in disposable income, all presented opportunities to be tapped. On the other hand, competing charities were also growing and some legislation proposals threatened certain freedoms to fundraising in specific areas, notably national lotteries.

In the key area of fund status, WWF UK's international connections and scientific authority were seen as strengths; offset by the weakness that the organization was not itself active in conservation work, nor was it campaigning.

A major effort to devise and publicize a strategy for world conservation was to be carried out in the near future by WWF's international scientific sister organization, the International Union for the Conservation of Nature and Natural Resources (IUCN) with the financial backing of WWF and the United Nations Environmental Programme (UNEP) and

---

1 Marketing
2 Public awareness
3 Fund status
4 Quality of application
5 Use of personal resources
6 Use of financial and physical resources
7 Administrative control
8 Innovation
9 Net funds

Figure 13.1 *WWF UK key areas, 1978*

STRENGTHS

Image
Logo
Charity
Emotive appeal
Visual appeal
Achievements
Communications
Schools Lecture Service
Flexible
Technical support
Diverse
In fashion
Cost : Income Ratio
Recognition of need
Awareness of market research
Unique
Caravan

OPPORTUNITIES

£700m given to charity in 1977
Schools
Legislation
Better positioning
Current events
Economic climate
Untapped sources
Growing awareness of conservation importance

WEAKNESSES

Image
Small membership
Poor lists
Communications
Inadequate intermediaries
Transience of fashion
Reference to Cost:Income Ratio
Conservatism
Inadequacy of follow-through
Lack of innovation
Lack of physical resources
Scientific inflexibility
Inadequate market penetration
No active conservation
No audio-visual equipment
Photographic resources

THREATS

Competition
Legislation
Economic climate

Figure 13.2 *SWOT analysis: key area – marketing*

this was seen as a major opportunity to improve further the public perception of WWF UK. A concomitant threat was the Government's lack of interest in the environment and its reluctance to enhance existing legislation in this field.

The full lists of strengths, weaknesses, opportunities and threats in the areas of marketing and fund status are shown in Figures 13.2 and 13.3.

STRENGTHS	WEAKNESSES
Achievements	Non-controversial
Clear aims and programmes	Snob charity
Non-political	No active conservation
Practical	Lush literature
Affiliate of largest most effective conservation organization	Trading company
Scientific authority	
1001	
Elitism	
Good financial standing	
Management	
OPPORTUNITIES	THREATS
World conservation strategy	Possible defeat by Government on major conservation issue
Lack of conservation legislation	Adverse publicity
Confused conservation ethics	
Global 2000	

Figure 13.3 *SWOT analysis key area – fund status*

Agreeing strategies

At this point in the exercise, comprehensive answers to questions such as: Where are we now? What do we think will happen in the future? and Where do we want to go? had been determined.

It was now necessary to devise guidelines (termed strategies) which would be developed for all future actions: 'strategy' is a guide for action. Clearly the marketing strategies concentrated on improving those areas of fundraising that were perceived to be weaknesses. Thus the first strategy was to increase membership and the second to increase the number and yield effectiveness of WWF's volunteer supporter groups around the country. Business would be concentrated on through effective commercial promotions and licensing the 'panda' trade mark and increased efforts would be made to raise income from business and charitable trusts. As the donor list had been identified as a major weakness, significant efforts would be made to build these lists. At that time, the cleaned list yielded 12,000 members together with a further 25,000 trading customers. The full strategies in the key area of marketing are shown in Figure 13.4.

1 We will increase our membership and improve services to members.
2 We will increase the number and yield effectiveness of supporters' groups.
3 We will undertake a research programme to ascertain the best marketing opportunities in schools and will then increase fund-raising in this sector.
4 We will increase the yield effectiveness of commercial promotions and licensing.
5 We will liaise closely with WWF International to improve the yield effectiveness in the United Kingdom of international promotions.
6 We will make a concerted effort to increase substantially our income from business and charitable trusts.
7 We will improve the profitability of our trading operations and will search for new ways of increasing income from trading opportunities.
8 We will ensure that we are able to take advantage of special opportunities for raising funds.
9 We will build our lists in order to maximize fundraising.
10 We will seek to further improve and widen our market image.
11 We will build up active key contacts in show business, commerce and conservation, and programme them centrally.
12 We will ensure that we have adequate and effective audio-visual equipment.
13 We will ensure that we use the caravan to the greatest advantage.
14 We will ensure that WWF photographic material is made more readily available for fundraising purposes.
15 We will encourage donations in covenant form.
16 We will increase our share of the legacy market.

Figure 13.4 *Strategies: key area – marketing*

This exercise covering all the nine key areas took two days, at the end of which WWF UK had a document setting out its clear objectives for the immediate and medium-term future.

The last key area ('net funds') equates to a corporation's profitability. The achievement of the net funds objectives would show the progress of the organization. Net fund objectives were therefore agreed by the management team for the coming three years.

Action plans

The next part of the process was to devise the actions needed to achieve the strategies. Each department was asked to take each of the strategies and write down the actions they proposed in the coming year to fulfil the strategy. Clearly a number of strategies were not applicable to all departments whereas others had impact across all departments. The final action plans from each department were amalgamated into a single document and this became the working forward plans for WWF UK.

Budgeting to meet objectives

At the end of this strategic planning exercise, written documentation existed to show what WWF UK was hoping to achieve in all the key areas and how each department was going to take action to fulfil these strategies. At this stage, however, there were no financial figures determined. The second part of the planning process involved the compilation of departmental budgets designed to achieve the strategies. Each department produced both income and expenditure budgets for the coming year and forecasts for the next two years. The departmental budgets were then consolidated to produce the budget for WWF UK. It was a surprise to most members of the management team that when the departmental budgets were amalgamated the overall net fund projected for the budget year was extremely close to the objective net fund set in September as the final stage in the strategic planning exercise. This came as no surprise to me because in my experience in the subsidiary of a major multi-national, the management team setting itself objectives with considerable 'stretch' produced budgets which met those objectives, and more importantly produced results which came within a very few percentage points of achieving the budgets.

The setting of objectives in a strategic planning process and the compiling of budgets to achieve those objectives, are of no use without adequate factual information to show progress and achievement. WWF UK's financial management was strengthened and systems set up to provide quarterly reporting by department against budget. At the end of each quarter departmental performance was assessed and where necessary corrective action was taken, although the disciplines of budget and assessment of performance against budget led very rapidly to excellent control of expenditure.

The strategic planning exercises have been carried out each year in WWF UK and it is interesting to see how the process has evolved. The basic structure has remained unchanged but, over the years, a number of key areas have been identified and a number dropped. For example, regional activities became important but when the problems within the regional area were resolved, that area no longer merited the microscopic examination of the planning process. It is also interesting to look at three measures of success and to see how the planning process has helped in the achievement of these successes.

Measures of success

Net funds is the best measure of success. Net funds remained static
between 1972 and 1977 at £400,000–£600,000. After the introduction of
strategic planning in 1978, net funds grew steadily although there was a
slight decline in 1983 due to an unexpected and unexplainable drop of
significant proportions in income from legacies that year. The upward
trend was resumed in 1984 and the last two years have been exceptional.
Figure 13.5 shows the growth of net funds from 1972 to 1986.

Productivity in WWF UK is measured in terms of both gross and net
income per employee. Staff numbers at seventy remained fairly constant
from 1972 through to 1980, but since then marginal increases occurred so
staff numbers at the end of 1986 were eighty-five. With the growth in net
funds by a factor of some eight times, it is clear that productivity will
have increased substantially, as is shown in Figure 13.6.

At each annual strategic planning meeting net funds are projected
forwards for the next budget year and the two following forecast years.
Plotting each year's projections produces a matrix and adding to that
matrix the actual achieved for each year gives an interesting diagram
showing the fluctuations in objectives year-on-year set by the management team compared to actual achievement.

In the first three years, 1978–80, actuals were remarkably close to
projections, but in the following period there were considerable shortfalls

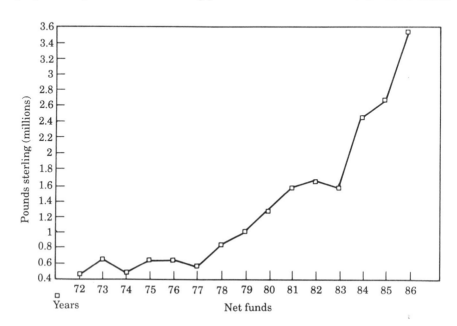

Figure 13.5   *WWF UK net funds*

Figure 13.6   *WWF UK income per employee – productivity*

against projections which have been corrected in the last two years. Actuals now appear to be running ahead of projections which perhaps indicates that inadequate 'stretch' is being placed in the objectives, even though growth in the last two years has been considerable. (See Figure 13.7.)

One other measure of success is the growth in the size of the donor list. At the end of 1986, WWF UK had 110,000 members and a donor list of 450,000 names. This compares with the 12,000 and 25,000 in 1978.

The purpose of the organization has changed little and for comparison Figure 13.8 shows the 1978 purpose and underneath the 1986 purpose. Figure 13.9 shows the 1978 key areas alongside the 1986 key areas.

Conclusion

When strategic planning was first suggested for WWF UK there was a considerable degree of scepticism coupled with a willingness to try a new business method which might bring good results for the organization. After the first year it became clear to the whole management team that the exercise was invaluable, giving an opportunity for the whole team to participate in the forward planning resulting in a feeling of commitment by the whole team to the objectives that had been agreed after full and open discussion. This commitment seemed to transfer itself to other staff

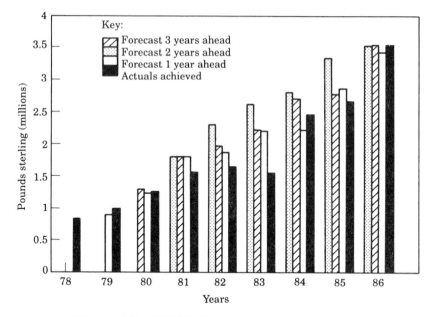

Figure 13.7   *WWF UK forecast net funds vs actuals*

members, giving the whole organization a sense of purpose and of drive which, coupled with team work, produced the outstanding results that the organization has achieved. It is now inconceivable to think of WWF UK working without an annual strategic planning exercise, developing clear strategies in key areas with action plans to achieve those strategies. The success of this method of management by objectives must be seen in the light of WWF UK's performance in the last few years.

1978
'To raise the maximum funds possible from UK sources and to ensure that the funds are used wisely for the benefit of conservation of renewable natural resources, with emphasis on endangered species and habitats.'

1986
'To raise the maximum net funds possible from UK sources and to ensure that these funds are used wisely for the benefit of conservation of renewable natural resources, in accordance with the principles of the world conservation strategy.'

Figure 13.8   *Statements of purpose compared*

	1978		*1986*	*Key areas*
1	Marketing	1	Fund-raising	
2	Public awareness	2	Reputation	
3	Fund status	3	Implementation of World Conservation Strategy	
4	Quality of application	4	Use of personnel and physical resources	
5	Use of personnel resources	5	Communications	
6	Use of financial and physical resources	6	Education	
7	Administrative control	7	Management	
8	Innovation	8	Lists	
9	Net funds	9	Leverage	
		10	Net funds	

Figure 13.9 *A comparison of key areas*

14 Strategic planning in the Thomas Cook Group

Adrian H. T. Davies, Director, Group Planning and Business Development, Thomas Cook Group Ltd

One of the greatest difficulties in writing about Thomas Cook is to distinguish between reality and the powerful legend which surrounds the name of the company. The expression 'Cook's tour' has become a generic term in the same way that Hoover has passed into the English language and Frigidaire into the French. Thomas Cook himself was the personal tour operator for royalty, and for a host of famous names, and yet the business which bears his name is today largely a retailer selling air tickets, packaged tours and travel money to millions of people as well as major international companies each year.

The business started in Leicester in 1841, initially to promote temperance by organizing outings for groups, largely of working people. It developed quickly due both to the need for relief from the harshness of daily work in Victorian England and to the possibilities for cheap travel afforded by the burgeoning railways. Once the business had been firmly established in the United Kingdom, Thomas Cook turned his attentions to Europe and, not only made established destinations like Paris available to a wider clientele, but created new markets such as Switzerland. Well before the end of the nineteenth century, Thomas Cook and his energetic son, John Mason Cook, had opened up the Egyptian market and had established businesses in the USA and elsewhere. These ventures were largely managed by the Cooks themselves, who still found time to act as tour managers with many of their itinerant groups. Increasing fame, and a growing reputation for quality, led to the appointment of Thomas Cook as travel agent for many of Europe's royalty, and even brought about the establishment of a special department to handle the business of the numerous and wealthy Indian princes.

Travel was stimulated not just by the harshness of much of Victorian life but by the needs of empire. Thomas Cook was involved in many aspects of this form of travel, not least the organization and execution of the travel arrangements for the relief of Khartoum by General Kitchener. Thomas Cook was not just a tour operator by that time but actually built and managed a fleet of river steamers on the Nile and later owned a hotel on the Isle of Wight and a holiday camp at Prestatyn.

The main thrust of growth was, however, in the opening of retail travel shops in major world markets. These shops not only sold the company's tours, tickets for steamers and rail journeys and hotel accommodation, but became involved in travel money. Well before the end of the last century Thomas Cook invented the 'circular note', a form of promissory note valid for payment in Sterling for local currency paid to the holder. This was the precursor of the travellers cheque, which was first issued in 1892, and which has now become a major part of Thomas Cook's business.

After the death of Thomas and John Mason Cook, the business had no committed leadership and was sold to its European associate, Compagnie Generale des Wagons-Lits, in 1929. Under the control of Wagons-Lits the business did not have its previous scope for development. In 1941, following the conquest of Europe by Hitler, Thomas Cook was taken by the Custodian for Enemy Property and placed under the control of Transport Holdings.

Thomas Cook remained nationalized until 1972 when the Conservative government invited tenders to purchase the business. Several consortia were formed and the successful bid was made by Midland Bank, with minority support from Trust Houses Forte and the Automobile Association.

But in 1977 the Midland Bank purchased the minority shareholding of Trust Houses Forte and the Automobile Association and became sole owner. Since then the business has been thoroughly reorganized and substantially recapitalized. A new and more professional management team has been formed and a number of marginal businesses, like freight forwarding, have been divested. Part of the reorganization process involved moving the Group headquarters from Berkeley Street in London to Peterborough, which enabled the management and support functions to be grouped in one location and to expand to meet the growth of the business. Berkeley Street remains the London headquarters of the Group and offers the facilities of the world's largest travel centre.

Following the reorganization of the core of the business, Thomas Cook has been active in the last five years in expanding its business.* A new corporate image has been introduced throughout the organization and the number of travel shops has increased from less than 600 to over 1000 worldwide, including those of Thomas Cook's associate, Wagon-Lits.

The travellers cheque and foreign money businesses have expanded rapidly and now have a worldwide dimension. The tour operating, business travel, group travel and inbound travel businesses have also developed strongly so that Thomas Cook is now the largest travel agency business in the world.

*Figures 14.1 and 14.2 show the situation of the business in 1979 and Figures 14.3 and 14.4 the present range of products.

1 Largest travel agency network in the world – Over 1000 outlets in 145 countries, handling 10 million persons a year.

2 Fourth largest issuer of travellers cheques in the world – Sales nearly £2 billion.

3 Substantial tour operator, particularly in UK – over 150,000 passengers a year.

4 Large foreign exchange operation – wholesale and retail. Sales over £500 million (after eliminations).

Revenue Analysis:		
— Retail Travel	49%
— Wholesale Travel	7%
— Travellers Cheques	29%
— Retail Foreign Exchange	12%
— Wholesale Foreign Money	3%
	100%

Figure 14.1 *Basic facts about Thomas Cook*

Total sales	:	£2·6 billion
Revenue	:	£80·5 million
Pretax profit	:	£10·1 million
Employees	:	6875 worldwide

Figure 14.2 *Thomas Cook group, 1979*

Planning problems in the travel industry

Herman Kahn has predicted that, by the year 2000, the travel and tourist industry will be the largest in the world. This seems at first sight to be incredible, compared with the size of the worldwide oil or motor industries, but reflects the diverse and amorphous nature of the travel industry, ranging from the provision of transport to the supply of the smallest services, like porterage. This diversity opens the door to identifying the

Figure 14.3   *The diversity of the travel industry*

Figure 14.4   *The diversity of the travel industry*

---

1 Diversity of the travel industry
 — What are the boundaries of the travel industry?
 — What choice does the customer want?
 — What assistance does the customer need?

2 Intangibility of travel product
 — How can the product be specified?
 — What is the customer's perception of the product?
 — What is the trade-off of quality and price?

3 Variability of customer requirements
 — How is the market segmented?
 — Which customers are we seeking to service?

4 Changeability of public taste
 — What factors affect the taste of our target customers?
 — How susceptible is our market segment to fashion?
 — Should we pioneer or follow fashion?

5 Narrowness of operating margins
 — Need for strong control of systems, policies and finance
 — Local flexibility to meet threats/opportunities

6 High volume of transactions
 — Need for effective systems
 — Speed of communications
 — Productivity

Figure 14.5 *Planning problems in the travel industry*

main planning problems in the travel industry, which may be summarized as follows (see Figure 14.5):

1 The diversity of the industry
2 The intangibility of the 'travel product'
3 The variability of customer requirements
4 The changeability of public taste
5 The narrowness of operating margins
6 The high volume of transactions

1 The diversity of the industry
The diversity of the travel industry may be gauged from consideration of a relatively simple business trip. It might involve car parking at London

Airport, a flight to Paris, ground transport to the centre of the city, a hotel, some restaurants, perhaps car hire to visit a town outside Paris, some taxi trips, evening entertainment, duty free purchases at the airport and insurance of life and baggage. Travellers cheques and foreign money would be needed, and perhaps a voucher for the hotel. This list has grown quickly, without any consideration of incidental items like porters and bookstalls, and begins to show the diversity and complexity of the industry.

The ability of travellers to cope with this situation depends on co-ordination. Either the traveller will organize the whole operation himself if he has the time, the information and the relevant experience, or he will need some outside assistance. This is the role which the travel agent is uniquely equipped to fill, in that he can offer the widest choice without prejudice and provide the judgment needed to arrive at a practical solution to travel problems. For example, the travel agent can eliminate confusion in the traveller's mind who, when wishing to select a package holiday, is faced with a vast array of tour operators' programmes.

2   The intangibility of the 'Travel Product'

Most engineering products can be described in clear specifications and subjected to precise performance standards. Travel products are more difficult to perceive: are people buying transport, or an experience involving transport, or are they buying a status symbol involving transport, etc? The merchandizing of the product depends on a clear answer to such questions and such clear answers are rarely forthcoming. Because the content of the product is imprecise, it follows that it is difficult to produce a meaningful specification, let alone a British Standard specification! Judgment in respect of travel is almost purely subjective: no two travellers will have the same opinion of a tour in which they have both participated and their public opinions may differ significantly from private comments. The perception of quality will differ before and after a tour, since expectations usually differ from experience (and not necessarily in a negative sense).

The intangibility of travel products leads to many false comparisons in the industry and the failure of customers to perceive differences in product content (e.g. transfers to/from the airport, the availability of resident couriers, etc). The difficulty of specifying the product in advance of consumption means that the ony real guide to quality is the size and consistency of repeat business. This is a factor which is closely monitored in Thomas Cook and we recently had the pleasure of giving a free US holiday to a lady who has bought 99 holidays from Thomas Cook over the past fifty odd years!

3 The variability of customers' requirements

In the same way that no two travellers will react in the same manner to a tour, it is impossible to produce travel products to suit the needs of everybody. The first requirement in planning for the travel industry is to develop a very detailed segmentation of the market in order to establish specific target groups. This segmentation has to be multi-dimensional (economic grouping, age, sex, residential area, main interests, etc) in order to be meaningful. The motivation of the customer is a key, but very elusive factor, in this process. Thomas Cook spends considerable time and effort in establishing client motivation and changes in social behaviour and sees the need to place increasing emphasis in this direction in the future.

4 The changeability of public taste

The effort of segmentation described above is complicated by the changeability of customers' tastes and needs. While there is an underlying pattern of customer requirement which can be discerned, the exact details will change as quixotically as fashion. Travel is indeed partly a fashion product; even businessmen will wish to try Concorde or experience a new hotel which has an interesting review in the papers! Travel fashion is created in many ways, some of which can be foreseen, like the growth of travel to the East, the development of the US holiday market, and some more difficult to predict, like the development of the holiday market in Gambia. Much of fashion is set by a 'trendy set', for instance the French Riviera last century and the Algarve in the 1960s. When the fashion changes, the result can be disastrous for the area concerned and for those who have invested in hotels and other tourist facilities.

Anticipating the vagaries of fashion and, more positively, helping to create or develop trends in fashion, is a key factor in travel industry planning and an area where greater sophistication will be needed as investment values increase and public taste becomes more and more volatile.

5 The narrowness of operating margins

The average margin earned by travel agencies is some 8–10 per cent of sales, depending on the mix of travel business. The margin on travellers cheques is only one per cent and that on foreign currency is also low. This means that the profitability of a travel agency business depends on strict control of costs. The cash flow implications are also important. Holiday travel is normally a cash business and can contribute to cash flow; business travel is usually sold on credit and in some circumstances creates a negative cash flow.

Lack of financial control was one of the weaknesses of Thomas Cook before the reorganization, but action has been taken to install the policies, systems and procedures needed to rectify this. A strong Audit and Security function now exists which is essential in a business dealing in large quantities of money. The narrowness of operating margins, especially in the money business, make it essential that management is quickly reactive. This quality is developed by job experience and by training, but is needed to ensure that any tendency for the business to become bureaucratic is resisted. Speed of response is essential for survival in markets where, in some instances, ticket prices may vary several times each week and where organized crime is constantly probing for weaknesses.

6 The high volume of transactions

Thomas Cook deals with over ten million people each year and, in addition, handles millions of casual enquiries and ticket validations. During the peak summer months, Thomas Cook handles nearly one million paid travellers cheques daily through the clearing system and issues, and subsequently pays, up to two million vouchers per annum for hotel accommodation, excursions and other overseas services. Every year twenty million sheets of information are printed for use in the business, ranging from updates to the extensive manuals used in branches to daily rates of exchange for the foreign currencies in which the Group deals.

This high volume of transactions and large requirement for information makes the existence of effective paper-handling systems mandatory. Speed and accuracy are at a premium and increasing emphasis is being placed on contingency planning as the business becomes increasingly highly geared to meet the growing volume of transactions and information flow. The pressure lies not only in the handling of paper but also in the volume of telephone calls and telexes handled daily. Strict control and a constant drive for productivity are essential in order to cope with this growing mass of activity on a profitable basis.

Planning in Thomas Cook Group

Until Midland Bank took control of Thomas Cook in 1972, there were only rudimentary accounts in the Group and no systematic attempt to budget its operations. An immediate priority was to establish an effective finance function and the first planning activities of the Group were centred in this area. In 1978 it was decided to strengthen the planning function:

(a) by having it report to the Chief Executive, and
(b) by increasing emphasis on strategy in the preparation of plans.

Within the last two years substantial progress has been made, although there remains a large amount of work to be done before the contribution of planning to the Group's results can be considered satisfactory.

Annual cycle
The annual planning cycle of Thomas Cook is geared to that of its parent, Midland Bank Group, although Thomas Cook operates with a considerable degree of autonomy. The cycle is shown diagrammatically in Figures 14.6 and 14.7.

The cycle begins with emphasis on the strategic dimension of planning. An estimate of the profit targets for the five years of the new cycle is made in order to establish the broad framework into which the planning operation will fall. The first main stage in the cycle is, however, the Group Strategic Conference.

	Planning	Review
January	Establishment of outline targets for the new cycle	
March	Group Strategic Conference	First review of Key Actions
April		Strategic Review
May	Group Planning Conference	
May/June	Regional/National Planning Conferences	Second review of Key Actions
June/July	Local draft plans, computer-assisted planning	
August	Draft plans reviewed at Centre	
August/September	Plans finalized, consolidated and submitted to Board	Third review of Key Actions
October	Group Plan submitted to Midland Bank	

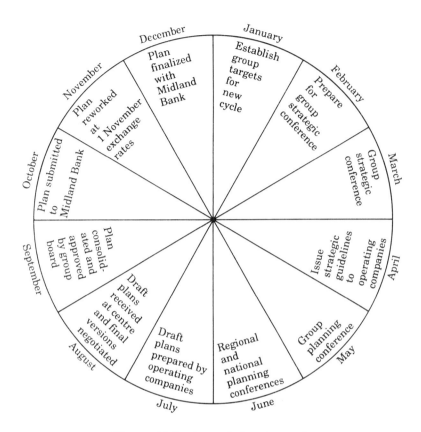

Figure 14.6 *Annual planning cycle*

Group Strategic Conference This conference involves members of the Group Board and certain selected executives and is held over a 24-hour period in an isolated location. The objective of the conference is to take a medium- to long-term view of the Group's activities and the economic, political and competitive situation which is expected to condition them. No specific limit is set to the time-horizon of discussions, but the deliberations are subject to an agenda and guided by position papers issued prior to the conference. Unconventional ideas are encouraged and are discussed frankly and constructively.

From the conference a scenario for the new planning cycle is distilled and the Group's objectives and strategies are tested against the scenario. A briefing is sent to operating companies, detailing the scenario, and the planning framework which reflects the targets for profit and market share which it is expected will be each business's contribution to the total Plan. The main Group objectives are confirmed or modified and the major

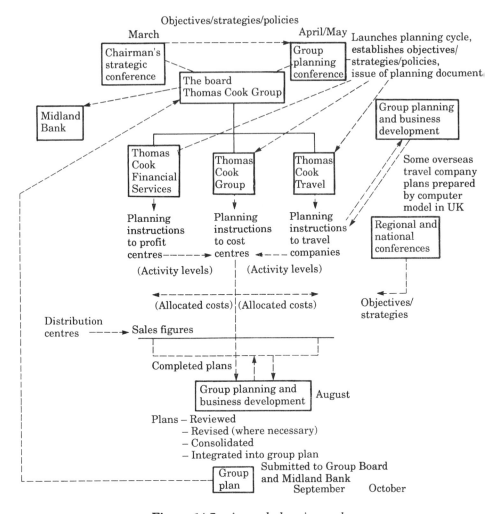

Figure 14.7 *Annual planning cycle*

strategies are restated together with any changes which the scenario makes necessary.

Strategic Review Following the conference, a strategic review takes place which is a re-assessment of the objectives and strategies of the previous Plan, completed six months previously. This reflects the output of the conference and acts as an early warning to Midland Bank of any significant changes in strategic direction.

Group Planning Conference This conference opens the cycle for Group operating companies. Having received a briefing after the Group Strategic Conference, operating company managers are expected to arrive at the conference with their objectives, strategies and Key Action programme in draft form. This ensures that they have thought about their business strategically immediately prior to the conference and that the development of the planning cycle and the detailed numbers in the Operating Plan flow from that strategic re-assessment.

The conference is concerned to achieve the following objects:

- to 'set the scene' for the new cycle;
- to debate a number of key issues (usually in working parties);
- to confirm the strategic direction of the Group and its constituents;
- to launch the detailed programme for the new cycle.

The Planning Process The planning process is guided in detail by a planning manual, which is issued to all operating company managers, and which gives specific instructions on the use of the forms required by the Centre on every aspect of preparing a plan.

The Thomas Cook Plan is prepared over a five year period, with the first year being planned in full detail and produced as an Operating Plan (or budget in its numerical implications) and the subsequent four years being prepared as a Strategic Plan with only a broad framework of numbers. Both plans are mainly orientated towards the provision of strategies and Key Action programmes. These Key Action programmes are the heart of a Thomas Cook Plan and are detailed proposals for the achievement of specific actions which are essential to make the operating strategy successful. Details of the Key Action Programme are shown in Figure 14.8 and a typical example in Figure 14.9.

Each operating company will have its own approach to completing the planning process and importance is attached to results, not methodology. Many will have their own planning conferences, or regional conferences may be held where appropriate, while others will complete the cycle by individual discussion down the line. Many of the smaller companies do not have computers suitable for planning and their draft plans are produced from coded input on a computer model at the Centre. This process reduces the clerical drudgery of planning and allows more time for strategic assessment before generating numbers and for multiple revisions afterwards, where necessary.

Plans are generated from the bottom upwards, so that individual branches of a travel company or distribution centres of the travellers cheque business, will create the basic input into the Plan. There were previously some attempts to plan without involving the 'front line' parts of the business; these often produced elegant results but suffered from lack of up-to-date realism and failed to achieve commitment from the managers on whose performance the whole Plan depended.

1 *Objective*
The programme is intended to develop in detail the main strategies
to be pursued during the plan period, so that they can be effectively
and appropriately executed

2 *Content*
The Key Action programme contains the main strategic actions needed
to achieve the plan results, detailing:

2.1 Definition and justification of the Key Action
2.2 Objectives to be achieved through the Key Action
2.3 Tactics to be pursued in achieving these objectives
2.4 Specific Programme of Action
— What to do?
— Who is to do it?
— By when will it be completed?
2.5 Effect on Business:
— What specific benefit(s) will be achieved in measurable terms?

3 *Review*
The Key Action Programmes of all Group and Subsidiary/Associate
Company Plans are reviewed:

3.1 Quarterly for the Annual Operating Plan
3.2 Six-monthly For the Strategic Plan (four years)
The Reviews are communicated to operating management and a
Summary Report is made to the Chief Executive's Committee

4 *Effect*
The use of the programme and review procedure ensures:
4.1 That action is taken in time to achieve planned results
4.2 That plans are prepared with a results-orientated emphasis

Figure 14.8 *Key action programme*

Finalization of plans The finalization of plans is an iterative process
involving the preparation of multiple drafts within the operating company and the negotiation of the agreed draft with Group Management at
the Centre. The process of review at the Centre is critical since it involves
not only an assessment of the merits of the individual plan, but also a
measurement of the plan's contribution to the total profits target, as
established at the beginning of the cycle in January.

Within Thomas Cook the emphasis still lies predominantly on 'bottom up' planning. Targets have been set at the Centre in terms of optimizing the present business rather than in terms of a Group target to which the present business may make only a partial contribution. This has been done intentionally in order to concentrate on improving the performance of existing operations before diversifying into new activities.

When approved by Group Management, plan figures are consolidated by computer, both uninflated (as submitted) and inflated at local rates of inflation for each element of revenue and cost.

The resultant numbers are then subjected to sensitivity analysis, particularly in respect of changes in sales, revenue and costs. Sensitivity analysis is not only carried out on the Group Plan but also on operating company plans and is of particular importance at times where travel has held up well in the face of recession but where a sudden break in confidence could have a damaging effect on a business with a high break-even point and limited elasticity of costs.

The input plans include detailed cash-flow projections, since the travel business is very sensitive to cash-flow, particularly where business travel, which is often sold on limited credit, is a significant part of turnover. These are also examined in depth and subjected to sensitivity analysis in certain critical cases. The Group Plan does not emphasize the cash-flow element but concentrates on the projection of balance sheets and sources/application of funds statements over the five year cycle. At Group level the final concern is with free capital rather than with cash-flow, provided that the cash-flow of operating companies is individually satisfactory. Free capital is, of course, the proportion of net assets which is readily realizable as cash.

The final Group Plan is presented to the Board for approval at the end of September and comprises the following main sections:

1 Role and enduring objectives of the Group
2 Business and financial objectives for the cycle
3 Financial targets for the cycle
4 Economic and political assumptions and forecasts
5 Major market and technical factors affecting the business
6 Key development areas:
     strategies
     key actions
7 Resources:
     capital expenditure
     personnel
8 Financial statements:
     profit and loss account
     overview of financial Plan
     sensitivity analysis

Company/Operation: Australia

Authorised by:
Date:
Worksheet No:

Operating Plan

Key Action No.	Key Action and Planned Financial Result	Responsibility	Date Implementation Planned	Date of Implementation Actual	Disposition or Status of Key Action and Achieved Financial Result
10-FY80	DEFINITION To Improve Representation in New Zealand, Europe and Fiji by Installing TC Australia Inbound Competence. Our Association with Silver Fern in New Zealand will be Terminating and the Plan is to set up an Inbound Division Under the Control of TC Auckland. Additional Representative Effort will be Researched in West Germany in Conjunction with the Frankfurt Office of TC. In Fiji, if we are to Hold Japanese Business, we Must Improve our Operating Effectiveness for Movements Entering that Territory Under our Control OBJECTIVE To Underwrite the Planned Level of Performance by an Extension of Representation and Operational Efficiency STRATEGY Install an Inbound Division in New Zealand				
10.1					

10.1.1	Select and Train a Manager and Staff	General Manager Inbound	1.11.79	15.12.79	The Managerial Duties were Combined with the Present Manager of Wholesale. Staff were Recruited and Trained and it is Operating Very Effectively
10.1.2	Promote New Arrangements in Overseas Markets	General Manager Inbound	1.11.79		The New Arrangements were Very Well Promoted Overseas and a Major Portion of the Japanese Market is Now Being Handled by the Office in New Zealand
10.2	Research the Viability of Opening a Sales Office in West Germany in Conjunction with TC Frankfurt	General Manager Inbound	1.1.80		Research was Conducted into the Viability of Opening a Sales Office in West Germany in Conjunction with TC Frankfurt. It was Determined that at this Time it was not a Viable Proposition and a Consultancy Firm, PROMO Tourism was Retained to Keep a Watching Brief on the Market
10.3	Examine the Effect of Establishing Operational Representation in Fiji	General Manager	1.1.80	1.7.80	The Effects of Establishing an Operational Representation in Fiji were Studied and it was Determined that with the Introduction of Direct Flights from Japan, this could be a Very Viable Office. It was Opened on 1 July 1980

FINANCIAL EFFECT
A Large Share of the Traffic to Fiji and New Zealand has been Captured by the 2 New Offices Established in FY80. The Financial Results for New Zealand are Found in Their Review of Key Action No. 8 FY80 and the Results for Fiji are Expected to be Near the Breakeven Point by the End of the Financial Year.

Figure 14.9 *Key action performance review*

key financial ratios
deflated profit statement
operating company pre-tax profits
operating company pre-tax profit targets
balance sheets
sources and application of funds
9   Market analyses and traffic forecasts

Increasing emphasis is now being placed on market analyses and on forecasts of air traffic, oil prices and other key determinants. The strategic element of the Plan is also expanding both because of the changes affecting the travel industry (deregulation of air fares, oil prices, etc) and the merger of Thomas Cook's travellers cheque business with the new European Travellers Cheque movement, and because of the growing battle for a share of the relatively profitable travel market at a time when so many other businesses have gone to the wall or have no growth prospects.

Strategic planning
Strategic planning is of crucial importance to Thomas Cook because of the company's extensive international commitment and because of the dynamic state of the travel market. The development of strategy takes place through the following media:

(a)   the Group Strategic Conference;
(b)   the meetings of the Group Board;
(c)   the meetings of the Chief Executive's Committee;
(d)   the Group Planning Conference;
(e)   regional and national planning conferences;
(f)   sectional conferences (business travel, travellers cheques, etc);
(g)   meetings of operating company boards;
(h)   management meetings in operating companies.

In this manner strategic thinking is generated at all levels of the Group and each operating company is encouraged to develop its own strategies within the framework of Group strategy. Commitment to strategic thinking has not been easy to achieve at all levels but support from the top, combined with growing confidence that the Group knows where it is going, is strengthening motivation to plan strategically.

Operating Plans
Operating Plans were originally prepared with a budgetary purpose and still form the basis for management reporting each month. These plans are produced with a detailed analysis of sales, revenues and costs and with emphasis placed on a number of key ratios:

(a) gross revenue: sales (needed to monitor the mix of business);
(b) contribution: revenue (the basic measure for branches and operating departments);
(c) payroll costs: revenue (the basic measures of productivity);
(d) pre-tax profit: revenue (the basic measure of operating company results);
(e) pre-tax profit: shareholders' funds (the basic measure for Group results).

The strategic content of Operating Plans has increased considerably in the last two years, reflecting improved ability to produce speedily accurate budgetary data, and the growing grasp which managers at all levels are getting of their business. Many of these managers are new to the business and the high turnover of staff inherent in the travel industry has made continuity difficult to achieve until recently.

Reviews

Reviews are playing an increasingly important role in the planning process, because:

(a) They impose a discipline on management to meet its Plan commitments.
(b) They allow flexibility to meet changing circumstances (where justified).
(c) They provide continuity in the development of plans.

The reviews in Thomas Cook are linked into the planning cycle as shown above under 'Annual Cycle', and the quarterly reviews of key actions are timed to coincide with quarterly forecasts of the results of the current year. This acts as a direct stimulus to the prompt achievement of Key Action programmes!

The Strategic Review is intended to ensure that major strategies are examined in mid-cycle and modified where necessary. Changes are rarely fundamental but a shift in priorities can occur, due to the fast-changing pattern of the travel industry.

The Key Actions included in strategic plans are reviewed twice yearly, the first review being the start of the build up to the Strategic Review and the second providing the detailed input into the new Strategic Plan.

New developments

The main priorities for planning in the Thomas Cook Group have been in establishing control of the business following denationalization and in achieving a stable pattern of profitability. These objectives having been substantially achieved, it is now intended to place emphasis on optimizing existing Group businesses and helping to ensure that the new European Travellers Cheque movement is a success.

As a result of this change in emphasis, the immediate new developments are seen to be:

- the further development of branch and departmental planning;
- the further development of productivity planning;
- the further development of manpower planning;
- the development of marketing planning;
- new refinements in targeting;
- planning by passenger numbers.

Branch and departmental planning

Branch planning already takes place in most parts of the business, and operating departments produce their input to the plans of their companies. In most cases, however, these plans remain orientated towards budgetary needs and do not have sufficient strategic content to act as meaningful guides for their authors throughout the operating year.

Action has already been taken in a number of countries to train and motivate branch managers to write business plans and the results are beginning to be seen in their overall performance. This process of taking planning to the 'grass roots' still needs further effort, and work needs to be done to bring departmental managers to plan with a view to achieving specific objectives rather than just produce budgets. This is particularly important for overhead departments which need to test rigorously and honestly their relevance to the operations which they service.

Once the basic elements of the business are fully involved in planning, results should be more controllable, since there will be greater commitment to the overall Group objectives.

Productivity planning

Thomas Cook's business relies heavily on manpower and, at a time when the average price of air tickets is declining, it is essential to achieve productivity savings to protect profitability. Productivity has been planned and controlled to date largely by reference to the Productivity Ratio (see 'Operating Plans' above) which has enabled productivity gains to be monitored effectively in the past.

Emphasis will now switch to achieving productivity gains by increased training of staff at all levels and by the increased use of automation. The main savings to be achieved by automation will lie in the use of Viewdata information terminals and automated booking and billing terminals in branches, although substantially higher volumes of business will also be handled at the Centre, without equivalent staff recruitment, by greater automation of operations and accounts functions.

Planning will switch its emphasis from the control of productivity to the active search for productivity gains, especially in overhead areas, in order to meet the twin challenge of growth in transactions and lower unit values of sales.

Manpower planning

The need to restructure the business from 1972 onwards has accelerated the development of the personnel function in Thomas Cook and has established the basis for further progress. The planning of head-count at the present time has been taken from a numerical exercise to control by individual position and by named incumbent. A strict control exists on temporary staff and overtime worked.

Further development in this area is seen in terms of forward projections in detail of the specific staff grades needed in each territory, so that recruitment and training can be planned to meet those requirements. At senior level, management succession plans will be developed; these have not been possible in the last few years due to the rapid growth of the business and frequent organization changes which this growth has required.

Marketing planning

Thomas Cook Plans to date have been geared to the immediate needs of the business and have been expressed in a framework largely derived from Midland Bank. It is now intended to develop further the planning facets which have not been sufficiently structured to meet the needs of Thomas Cook Group. One of these is marketing planning.

This will require increased analysis of:

(a) customers' real and potential needs;
(b) segmentation of market by customer type (economic grouping, age, etc);
(c) product design and specification (product life cycle);
(d) competition;
(e) product distribution;
(f) pricing (where applicable);
(g) promotion (advertising, sales promotion, public relations, sponsorship, etc).

Targeting

The essential features of targets are that they should be meaningful and that they should be acceptable to those responsible for striving to achieve them. Setting targets in the travel business is made difficult by a lack of reliable market information and by the variety of special circumstances in different markets. The targets currently used by Thomas Cook are imperfect for these very reasons and work is in hand to achieve more meaningful targets which will probably be related to return on funds.

Passenger numbers

As a retailer, Thomas Cook has not felt the need to plan other than in money terms and this measurement is the planning medium used by Midland Bank. Thomas Cook's wholesale functions, in particular tour operations, are planned in terms of passenger numbers, because this is the common denominator for contracting and for operational control. All principals in the travel industry plan and manage on the basis of units of sale (passenger/kilometres, bed/nights, etc) and this measure avoids any confusion arising from inflation or mix of business.

The need to improve the Group's knowledge of the market and to see clearly movements in volume terms, market share, etc mean that planning will be done by passenger numbers for retail purposes as well as for the wholesale business. This is important as it will also identify volumes for accounting and automation functions. The increasing use of EDP systems for booking and accounting purposes will make the capture of passenger data from booking slips relatively simple and will add a new dimension to the planning and control of the business.

In addition to these developments, planning at Thomas Cook has a number of other areas for future action. These include:

Business development This function is handled by the line but Group Planning provides a resource to assist in this area and is also involved in advising Group Management of potential acquisitions and diversification opportunities.

Allocation of resources At present plans are largely generated by operating companies and fitted into a Group framework. Work is planned to examine the marginal return on incremental investment in certain markets, bearing in mind local operating conditions and risk, management capacity and the strategic needs of the Group.

Strategic management This concept is believed to be of value in order to increase concentration on strategic issues. At present operating management is heavily committed to tactical issues in a business which has traditionally operated on a short horizon. It is believed that future success will depend on the dual optic which strategic management provides, enabling operations management to optimize short-term results while, in parallel, strategic management plans and develops the future shape of the business.

It will be seen that Thomas Cook is not yet very sophisticated in its planning. However, Thomas Cook's view is that sophistication is not the ultimate achievement. Planning has to serve the needs of the business and as the business grows and becomes more volatile and capital intensive, so planning must change to meet these needs.

The threats and opportunities of the next twenty years: inflation, oil prices, local wars, the battle for market share between airlines, the growing trends to changes in distribution and the quickening pace of change in travel fashion, all make for the certainty that the travel industry will become much more complicated as it grows to pre-eminence. In the same way that the 'seven sisters' and the major chemical groups emerged from the wreckage of hundreds of less skilful competitors some fifty years ago, the future leaders of the travel industry will be those with a clear sense of mission, high standards of service and the ability to exert the greatest possible control over their environment.

Reference

Peters, Thomas, J. and Waterman, Robert H., *In Search of Excellence*. New York: Harper and Row, 1982.

Part Four

Transforming company cultures and achieving excellence

Part Four   Transforming company cultures and achieving excellence

In many ways the process of transformation of company cultures is a combination of Parts One and Three: it is a turnaround without the crisis element (and hence is usually more difficult to achieve) and it is a route to achieving profitable growth through a change in staff attitudes and company culture.

The transformation process is therefore aimed at achieving new attitudes and performance standards in the short-term through widespread education. Books such as *In Search of Excellence* have identified the kinds of organization structures, management styles and staff attitudes necessary to develop and maintain 'a competitive edge'. The cultural change is seen in quality programmes. Quality circles, zero defects, total quality, and 'getting things right first time' are terms which are typically used in manufacturing firms. Customer service and customer care programmes provide a similar impetus in retail and service businesses.

In practice implementation has met with mixed success. It is extremely difficult to change entrenched ideas and attitudes where there is no immediate financial threat. The features common in successful transformations are:

- A new emphasis on and investment in staff training.
- An ability to communicate objectives, strategies, plans and programmes in simple operational terms.
- A direct management style using face-to-face communication with all levels of staff (i.e. not allowing unions to be the means of communication): 'Management-by-walking-around'.
- A pre-occupation with improving efficiency and effectiveness and a new awareness through techniques such as Competitive Benchmarking of the performance standards required to remain competitive.
- A reflection of political trends in strong leadership (as opposed to 'consensus' management) and pro-active rather than reactive attitudes to social issues. Therefore businesses are responding positively to issues such as health and safety at work, urban redevelopment, professional and product liability, ethnic minorities and so on.
- Encouragement of entrepreneurship and innovation through 'ideas

programmes', development of venture teams, recognition of 'product champions' and similar approaches.

- Professional rather than amateur management on the basis of payment by results through bonuses, share options and the like.

The cases reflect these features in various ways. The Bridgestone case presents a classic and dramatic example of corporate transformation based on *the Japanese model*. The Philips and Xerox cases demonstrate corporate responses to the threats posed by Japanese and other Far East competition in the consumer and business equipment markets. This type of threat will be even more likely to arise in the post-1992 market place as more pan-European businesses develop.

Strategic transformations in the rapidly changing service and retail markets are illustrated by the Scandinavian Airlines and Woolworths cases, and these are followed by a case based on a confectionery business, Trebor. Trebor is a medium-size business which has been employing a positive approach to communication and employee involvement in order to put the company in a sound position to deal with the increasing rate of change in the market place.

The final case in this part illustrates how SEGAS developed and implemented an *information systems strategy* aimed at providing better levels of customer service, increased cost effectiveness, and good management information. The introduction of information technology has played a key part in the successful development of many modern service industries. Good systems allow close central control of distributed operations without the need for an extensive layer of middle management as intermediaries.

15 Achieving Japanese productivity and quality levels at a US plant

Kazuo Ishikure, President and Chief Executive Officer, Bridgestone, USA

On 10 January 1983, Bridgestone Corporation of Japan (see Figure 15.1) bought a tyre plant in Tennessee, as well as inheriting both its active and laid-off work-forces, from an American tyre manufacturer. For the sake of convenience, this American tyre company will be referred to as Company 'A'.

Bridgestone Corporation, founded by Shojiro Ishibashi in 1931, is Japan's leading tyre manufacturer, having approximately 50 per cent of the market.
It is also the third largest in the world with marketing activities in more than 100 countries world-wide.

A.   Annual Sales: approximately $6bn

B.   Twelve plants in Japan

C.   Seven overseas plants including Australia, Indonesia, Thailand, Taiwan and the United States (Tennessee)

Although the name 'Bridgestone' sounds like a British or American company, it is a Japanese company. The founder Ishibashi christened the company with an inverted English translation of his own family name: *Ishi* means Stone and *Bashi* means Bridge.

Figure 15.1   *Outline of Bridgestone Corporation in 1987*

The plant, located in a city just outside Nashville called La Vergne, was completed by Company A in 1973 for the production of truck and bus radial tyres (TBR). From 1978–82, Company A pulled resources away from Research and Development and capital investment in TBR due to the high cost of operation. Between March and May 1982, two-thirds of the work-force was laid off, and between June and September 1982, the plant was shut down for two weeks a month. In consequence productivity, product quality, and employee morale all suffered.

In February 1982, Company A announced that the plant would either be sold to a prospective buyer or it would be closed. When the deal was consummated between Bridgestone and Company A in January 1983, a spokesman for Company A made an announcement stating, 'We would have had to make investments of over $100m to stay competitive in the radial truck tyre market. Our analysts figured we could invest that money elsewhere at a much higher return.'

We compared the Tennessee plant in the first half of 1983 with a similar plant in Japan. The results showed that the productivity level of the Tennessee plant was less than one-third that of the Japanese plant. Also, the percentage of defective tyres produced in the Tennessee plant was far higher than in Japan as was the frequency of machine failure.

Quality: the top priority

Bridgestone bought the plant at the price of $52m. We started production from the evening the deal was signed, since we had agreed on the continued production of TBR with the Company A brand as one of the conditions of purchasing the plant. In order to continue production the plant's organizational structure went unchanged and within this structure we placed the administrative office. When I inspected this plant my first thought was that we would have to maintain mass production to utilize the large plant and make a profit. We researched the problem of the low operating rate of 700 tyres per day and we came to the conclusion that it resulted from mediocre quality reputation. Field interviews were carried out by an outside market researcher and the results also supported this view.

The researcher visited 73 fleets, 103 tyre dealers and retreaders and twelve truck makers, carrying out 'image research' on TBR tyres by brand. The results did not rank the tyres made by Company A very highly. The report also concluded that image data were heavily influenced by the quality and performance of the company's radial tyres. We were positive that an increase in sales would result from the production of a high quality tyre. We set a goal to reach within four years whereby, through improving quality, we would produce and sell *four times* the number of tyres being manufactured and sold at the time of acquisition.

The underlying policy of our company was 'quality is top priority' and the president's policy was:

- To produce tyres of the highest quality (to produce the best radial truck tyres in the United States)
- The tyres should be equal or better in quality than those made by Bridgestone in Japan.

The plant's slogan was: 'Quality today will result in quantity tomorrow'.

Good housekeeping: the first step

When Bridgestone bought this plant, we felt it had not been properly maintained. Wastepaper, cigarettes, paper cups, bolts, nuts, nails, wood chips and so on lay scattered on the floor. Employees in the plant believed that cleaning up after the workers was the job of the janitors. We said that 'a clean workplace is everybody's responsibility'. We displayed actual samples of defective tyres containing foreign materials and pictures of the defective tyres in a showcase near the dining hall. We also posted the amount of money lost due to foreign materials in tyres on the previous day and in the previous month. A sample notice might have read 'A loss of a $X was due to foreign materials'. Also, we held section-by-section cleanliness contests. As a result, the plant became clean. High quality products cannot be produced in a dirty workplace. They are the result of 'good housekeeping', the first step towards effective quality control.

The '4M' approach

We used the '4M' approach in order to produce the highest quality tyres. '4M' stands for Machine, Material, Method and Manpower.

On machines, we changed or improved about 530 items in the first two years. This was achieved by following detailed plans. The two goals we wanted to achieve through updating the equipment were:

(a) to improve the quality of the product, and
(b) to decrease the workers' load.

Our attitude toward machine maintenance also changed, from 'ex post facto maintenance' (repairing a machine once it is broken) to 'preventative maintenance'.

As for materials, we used only brands which had been approved by Bridgestone's technical centre in Japan and made severe tests at the Tennessee plant before sending samples to the technical centre. Company A inspected all incoming raw materials and when they came across defective material, it was exchanged for good material. Bridgestone introduced the concept of quality control in the purchasing of raw materials.

Since good, consistent manufacturing process control leads to high quality products, we visited the plants of our raw material suppliers and checked their quality assurance policies, manufacturing control and so on, and set guidelines for each supplier concerning the inspection of incoming raw materials.

Even if we inspect incoming raw materials very strictly, a practice which takes many man-hours, we cannot prevent the inclusion of substandard raw materials, so the institution of quality control methods at the material source brought an increase in productivity.

Company A's method of producing tyres were changed to Bridgestone's methods. Of course, we had a lot of trouble in achieving these changes. Machines, equipment and most materials were different from the ones we used in Japan, yet the test tyres were produced to the same specifications. Finished tyres, and their components, contained subtle differences when compared with the tyres made in Japan; so the desired level of quality could not be achieved, despite the fact that the tyres met the same specifications as those made in Japan. The number of test tyres increased and we had to increase the in-company tests. Meetings between Japanese advisers and American managers were held day and night in an effort to come up with effective counter-measures. After clearing many obstacles, we got test results which showed that the quality of the product made in Tennessee was equal to that which was achieved in Japan. The abrasion resistance of the product that Bridgestone made in Tennessee was superior to that which had been made by Company A by 30 per cent. *These results were achieved in the year following the buy-out.*

Manpower proved to be the most difficult problem. The improvement of machines, materials and methods was not enough to produce high quality tyres. It was also essential to instil the concept of quality in the minds of all employees. To achieve this we had to alter past behaviour patterns. 'Change and innovation' was necessary. We adopted the policies of TQC (total-quality-control) and MBO (management-by-objective) as the tools of management. We chose TQC and MBO as operating philosophies because they originated in America and so it is easier for Americans to understand them.

The division between blue-collar and white-collar workers

There was a wide communication gap between non-union members (salaried workers) and union members (hourly workers). Immediately after Bridgestone bought the plant, the union representatives came to my room and told me that they thought some of the salaried workers were not good for the company. 'We want you to discharge some of the managers, foremen and supervisors,' they said. On the other hand, some of the managers, foremen and supervisors criticized the union members for being lazy. In order to bridge the gap between salaried workers and hourly workers, we emphasized that we were all members of the same family. Some changes were made. For example:

(a) We relocated some staff desks to the plant office.
(b) When staff worked in the plant they were asked to work without ties. It seemed that a tie was viewed as a sort of status symbol.
(c) We abolished reserved areas in the parking lot for some managers.
(d) We discontinued a friendship party to which only the managers and their families had been allowed to attend. Instead we presented *all* the employees with Christmas presents bought with the money budgeted for the party.

In order to improve labour–management relations and human relations in general, we asked a consulting company to conduct an opinion poll among the employees in October 1983 and had a management seminar to discuss the results of this poll. We spent an entire weekend at a hotel in the suburbs of the city of Nashville. There were thirty-six participants, including five Japanese. We divided them into five groups of about seven people each and they discussed questions which had been assigned to their respective groups. The discussions became so intense that time was forgotten and some groups continued until 3 a.m. We found through these discussions that human relations had been unsatisfactory in the past and mutual distrust had increased within the plant. We concluded that the problem which confronted us was how to establish good human relations, that is, *'mutual trust'*.

Each group offered suggestions for the solution of these difficult problems. We discussed these and drew conclusions on each item. Top management then discussed these conclusions and decided upon measures to solve the problems. We divided the employees into over thirty groups, explained the measures to be taken, and began to implement some of them immediately. In 1984, all managers above the rank of supervisor and union officials were given a one-day training course on the improvement of human relations with the consulting company's help. The trainees were divided into five groups and the training was conducted for eight hours a day. It was done once a month for an entire year.

Interviews with the President
The president held one-hour interviews with all managers who were above the rank of foreman and asked them about the company's problems, their personal difficulties and concerns, their suggestions for improving their workplace and so on. Three men, two Vice Presidents (one Japanese

and one American) and I interviewed at the first meeting. Because there were three interviewers and only one respondent, we felt that there was some reluctance on the part of the respondents to disclose their true feelings. Therefore, I conducted the interviews on a one-to-one basis from then on. As for the supervisors, I did not have time to interview them on an individual basis so I interviewed them in groups of four or five. For two years, 1984 and 1985, I interviewed all men ranking above supervisor twice and asked for their opinions and proposals, many of which became useful for the improvement of plant management.

Training

At the time of putting TQC into operation, we trained all the managers, foremen and supervisors as well as all the clerical staff, including secretaries. The main training activities in 1983 and 1984 are shown in Figure 15.2. One thing we found out through the TQC training was that some of the supervisors and clerks were not very good at mathematics. Therefore we added the 'elementary mathematics course' to the training menu.

The study trip to Japan

'Seeing is believing. At any rate just go and see,' we said.

We sent the first study group of division managers to Japan in April 1983 and continued to send plant staff above the rank of department manager and union executives for study trips of approximately two weeks through 1984. As 'seeing is believing', we expected them to notice and learn about the Japanese plant's cleanliness, productivity, discipline, and

Subjects	Participants	Note
Guidelines of TQC	All employees	Using the brochure *Guide to TQC* which was drawn up by the company
QC basic	Managers, foremen, supervisors	Studying the 'seven tools of analysis'
QC intermediate	Managers	Lecture by a local university's professor
IE basic	Foremen, supervisors	

Figure 15.2 *Menu of training in TQC*

Company A's method	Bridgestone method
1 No thought concerning acceptance for the next process.	1 Next process is the customer: 'The Customer is king'.
2 Main QA activity is performed by staff departments.	2 QA activity is performed by line departments with support from staff.
3 Analysis of QA problems from EDP information.	3 Analysis based on facts from actual process or product.
4 When defects occurred, emphasis was placed on 'accept' or 'reject'.	4 Main emphasis on product problems detection/disposition/prevention.
5 QA/QC education mainly for technical staff.	5 QA/QC education for all including line supervisors and workers.
6 Standardization done mainly by the corporation.	6 Standardization done in the plant with input from all members.

Figure 15.3 *Comparison of two management systems: plant manager's findings*

TQC activities. This is why we sent them to Japan. We thought that a one-way explanation from the Japanese side was not enough. Also, in order to adapt the newly acquired knowledge to the Tennessee plant, we also let the Japanese adviser, who worked at the Tennessee plant, go along. A plant manager, who had also been a plant manager in his Company A days, participated in the first study trip and reported on the management systems of both Company A and Bridgestone upon his return to America. The content of his report is summarized in Figure 15.3.

Impressions of work methods and labour–management relations were also reported by the others participating in the trips. Their impressions are described in Figure 15.4.

TQC management: the key points

We would like to explain two of the points which we emphasized in TQC management.

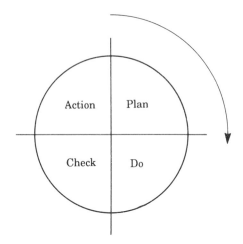

Figure 15.4   P-D-C-A

P-D-C-A

'P-D-C-A' became part of the daily work routine. 'P-D-C-A' (also called the Shewhart cycle) means Plan-Do-Check-Action. Under the previous employer, the management had been in charge of 'planning', the workers had been in charge of 'doing', the supervisors had been in charge of 'checking', and the workers had also been in charge of 'action'. However, P-D-C-A has to be practised by all line members otherwise the improvement efforts will not be successful. Therefore, we asked all employees to adopt P-D-C-A and to practise it in their daily routines.

Genba, Genbutsu

So far, decisions had been made based on written reports and not on actual situations. The staff members who had private rooms were called 'engineers' and the people under the engineers were known as 'technicians'. Based on data which had been collected by these two groups of employees, many meetings were held by the managers in the plant manager's private room. The subjects reported in the meeting were almost always the same. Consequently, anything not to do with these particular subjects was not considered during these meetings, even if it was important. There was a tendency to deal with everything in the private room which was far away from where things actually occurred, the production place (genba). In order to make plans based on actual working situations, we emphasized the importance of *genba, genbutsu*. An explanation of *genba, genbutsu* is given in Figure 15.6.

An oral explanation of *genba, genbutsu* was not sufficient, therefore we carried out on-the-job training repeatedly and persistently in order to

United States	Japan
People do not care what goes on in other departments. All jobs are compartmentalized (each manager has his own little area of responsibility).	More co-operation and communications between (a) staff and line (b) departments.
If an objective is not achieved, people are afraid they may 'Catch Hell'. Some people are afraid they may even lose their jobs.	Tend to set very tight and aggressive objectives. Never seem to be satisfied with the current status.
QC circles won't work in the United States because money saved goes to the company and not to the individual.	Team work approach Group activities Working together

Figure 15.5 *Comparison of two management systems (impressions expressed by American employees after visiting Japanese plants)*

teach the employees its real meaning. Also, since we wanted them to keep *genba, genbutsu* in their minds, we added 'see' and 'think' before P-D-C-A thus our policy became '*See-Think-Plan-Do-Check-Action*'. Nowadays, all employees use the Japanese words *genba* and *genbutsu* as they are part of their daily lives. Furthermore, they all understand the meaning of these two words quite thoroughly.

Genba means 'To go and see the place where the problem is occurring'

Genbutsu means 'To observe the material or product with defects itself'

Usually a manager can get reports or information from his subordinates in his office. But sometimes this information is not sufficient to understand fully the scope of the problem. The actual site where the mistake took place and the materials involved is where the information stays. The old proverb says 'Seeing is believing'; in other words 'seeing gives us more than 100 times the information that hearing gives'.

Figure 15.6 *The meaning of* Genba *and* Genbutsu

Mistakes and misproduction

When we bought the plant, it was a rare occurrence when a mistake or problem was reported to us. Mistakes included the usage of wrong raw materials, improper labelling, incorrect shipments from the warehouses, the inclusion of sub-standard products and so on. In February 1983, there were only two reports concerning mistakes or misproduction. This did not mean that errors had not occurred. Within the plant, the employees had not been totally open with the management for fear of being reprimanded over their mistakes.

However, from the point of quality assurance (QA), it was a serious mistake when inferior products were shipped to the customer. In addition, we could not solve the plant's problems under such circumstances. *Whether a mistake is trivial or not it must be reported without exception.* So, we encouraged the employees to report problems openly. We rewarded the people who did so with small gifts such as a ball-point pen. Through this type of encouragement, employees recognized that they would not be penalized by the supervisors even if they made mistakes. As a result, reports about misproduction increased rapidly. There were approximately thirty such reports a month in the last few months of 1983. Various kinds of mistakes were disclosed and we decided that our next step would be to establish a 'misproduction counter-measure committee'. This board consisted of employees who had made mistakes in the past, their co-workers, and the supervisors who were supposed to supervise them. We let the committee look into the real causes of mistakes and ways to prevent them from happening again. When we held a meeting to explain 'misproduction' to all employees we used the chart shown in Figure 15.8.

Also, we taught them that the customers, referred to at the end of Figure 15.8, meant not only the users of Bridgestone tyres but also the workers who worked at the next manufacturing process in the plant. The phrase that we repeatedly emphasized was *do not send defective components to the next step*. We also emphasized the necessity of *highly visible standards* as the method for preventing the recurrence of misproduction. This method's goal is to make it easy to distinguish different materials and their standards by using different colours and shapes. Figure 15.7 shows an example of the devices which we used to avoid errors.

The QC circle

Before we created QC circles, we completed various kinds of TQC training.

Reports which had been written by members of the first inspection trip to Japan stated 'QC won't work in the USA.' Therefore, we participated in the International Association of Quality Control in 1984. We wanted to let our people study how other American companies handled QC activ-

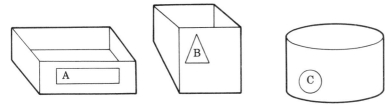

Use storage containers of different shapes and sizes

Figure 15.7 *An example of devices to avoid mistakes*

ities and also let them see how widely accepted the practice was. We also used a consulting company to educate the QC instructors. Of course, participation in the QC circles is not compulsory but voluntary.

The number of QC circles gradually increased so we held meetings to present the TQC's activities three times in 1984. In the summer of 1984, the best QC circle, which had been chosen from among all the circles, participated in the 'all Bridgestone QC circle meeting' in Japan as a representative of the Tennessee plant. Ever since, we have sent our best circle to participate in this meeting each year. Participating in the meeting has become a good incentive for all QC circle members.

Management-by-Objectives

The company's fiscal year is the same as the calendar year. Every year the President makes his preliminary policy statement in the middle of November and then allows plenty of time for several executives to examine it. After that, the President proposes it to the executive committee as a theme of discussion aimed at drawing up a final presidential policy statement.

---

1 Bridgestone encourages the reporting of all errors in production.

2 If we are aware of problems they can be solved by:
   (*a*) discovering the real causes;
   (*b*) implementing counter-measures to prevent similar mistakes.

3 Bridgestone encourages negative information and constructive criticism from customers.

Figure 15.8 *'Learn from mistakes'*

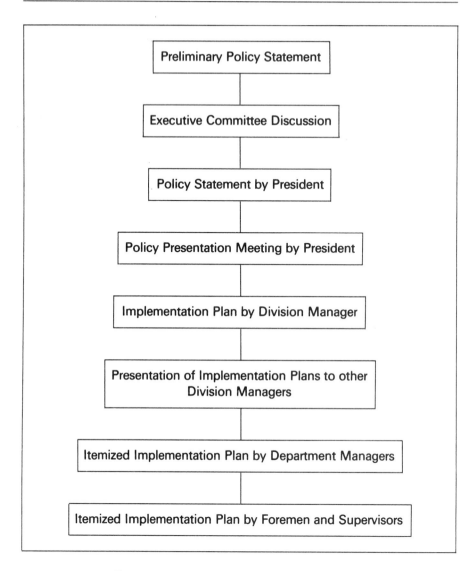

Figure 15.9   *Process of 'Management by Policy'*

The meeting is held annually at the end of December with staff above the rank of department manager attending. Then we distribute the policy statement, including many graphs, to all managers. Each graph indicates the following year's monthly budget and last year's results. The purpose is to explain the attainment of the target and to stress the importance of continuous improvement.

A policy statement which lists the budget or objectives, is usually under ten pages, but the graphs and charts may occupy more than forty or fifty pages, since there is a potential for misunderstanding if only written words are used for the explanation.

Our aim was that the policy file should be understood by everyone and the discussions should be based on a common understanding. We encouraged the staff to bring the file to their daily meetings. Each division manager drew up an implementation plan according to the President's policy statement. Department managers, who work under division managers, developed the items in detail, and drew up an itemized implementation plan. Figure 15.9 illustrates this process.

When we held the policy presentation meetings, we divided the employees into groups of forty to fifty people so that we could explain to them in person the circumstances of the company, next year's budget, our future plans, and our goals, and provide the opportunity for questions and answers. We held the meetings after working hours so as not to interfere with production. In addition, we met with the union staff individually and explained the policy over lunch, where we could have constructive discussions in a relaxed atmosphere.

The results

As a result of our efforts we achieved the following:

1 *Quality* The quality of the tyres improved remarkably and reached the level of Bridgestone tyres made in Japan. We were praised in surveys conducted by industry periodicals as making *the best TBR tyre in the business*. Our TBR tyres have been named as the best for the past three years.

2 *Rehiring* By the middle of 1985 we had recalled all the union employees who had been laid-off. When the last member was recalled, I called the union and commented on this achievement. The summary of what I said is as follows: '*Increases in recruitment and productivity go together*. We have proved it.'

3 *Safety* Safety levels have also risen and our company received the '*Most Improved*' award from the US Rubber Manufacturers Association in 1985. We also received it in 1986.

4 *Improvement of performance* Our achievements for the years 1983–5 are as follows, in comparison to Company A:

- Production volume: about tripled
- Productivity: about double
- Percentage of defective tyres: about half
- Energy efficiency: about a 40 per cent improvement

As a result of these improvements, we made a profit in the latter part of our third year of ownership. It was a while coming. In December 1985, I held a party to celebrate our going into the black. On that day I invited all employees and their families to the cruise boat *General Jackson* which floats on the Cumberland River. Incidentally, the river flows through Nashville City. Here is an extract from my speech on that occasion.

Welcome aboard the *General Jackson*. Our plant has come a long way. Through your fine efforts and just plain hard work, Bridgestone's first US manufacturing operation is now showing a monthly profit. For this, I would like you to join me in a round of applause. Not for me, but for you, and for every person sitting next to you. Because it was a team effort, everyone contributed. Not only the employees, but also their family members who accepted that their husbands or wives had to be away from home often on overtime work assignments. Therefore, I applaud you, employees and families, and the Bridgestone plant in La Vergne, Tennessee. As I stand here today, I notice *we are in the same boat*. Both with Bridgestone and with *General Jackson*. This is most symbolic ...

I had often used the phrase 'we are in the same boat' during my tenure at the Tennessee plant. When I repeated it while standing on board the *General Jackson*, everyone burst out laughing and applauding. Since that time I have always used that phrase, 'we are in the same boat', at policy presentation meetings.

16 The quest for quality at Philips

Kees van Ham and Roger Williams, Philips
International and Erasmus University Rotterdam

The need for total quality

In order to understand the major changes currently taking place in organizations in their quest for quality, it is necessary to look at how the Western business environment has changed since World War II. Over the last few decades markets have become far more difficult to satisfy. Perhaps this is most clear in the consumer goods area. In this field the situation in the late 1940s was one of shortages. Customers had been starved of goods during the period of hostilities and thus could be relatively easily satisfied. The result was that the determinants of commercial success became price and availability in the market place, and the production function formed the pushing power. There was virtually no international competition and sales forces were often merely order-takers.

However, industrial capacity built up rapidly and national tariff barriers were slowly dismantled. As a result the first signs of market saturation appeared. Consumers started to become more critical as the shelves began to fill up. At the same time changes in distribution patterns led to the number of buying points in many markets being drastically reduced with the consequent swinging of influence towards the retailer. At about the same time, consumer organizations began to use the mass media effectively in order to inform the public about competing products quality, reliability and price performance.

Manufacturers, in this new climate, had to become more concerned with customer desires. More attention had to be paid to marketing and to information about product characteristics, instructions for use and service facilities. The production function was no longer the driving force and organizations became much more market driven.

The continuing battle for low prices led to the movement of business to

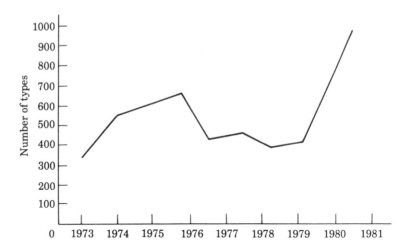

Figure 16.1   *Television sets: increase in product range*

cheap labour areas and insistence on economies of scale. Throughout the 1960s and 1970s this trend towards increasing customer power continued steadily. Not only price but also product quality and reliability became essential. Those companies which could not meet these demands were shaken out of the business. Markets became global, facilitated by lower tariff barriers and cheaper transport and this, in turn, was followed by a globalization of product development and manufacturing. In the fight for competitive advantage, providing maximum choice for the customer became a favoured weapon. The situation now is that new products are appearing more and more frequently and product life cycles are shrinking rapidly.

In addition, the options available to customers, have developed dramatically. For example the number of different types of television sets produced by Philips trebled in under ten years (Figure 16.1).

Markets now demand top performance not just in terms of price and quality but also in terms of innovation and variety in product range. New product development times have had to be drastically reduced and manufacturing flexibility increased. Initially the introduction of new technology in development, production and marketing was often seen as the possible cure for all these woes by manufacturers, but soon it became clear that this, of itself, was not enough. Such major changes in the busines environment necessitated important adjustments not only in technology but also in management styles, organizational structures and social systems.

New corporate capabilities

Although we have taken as our example the changes in the business environment of consumer goods, similar increases in customer demands have been occurring in a wide variety of markets both in the industrial and service areas. The systems and ways of working which were successful in the 'production push' period, when customers were hungry for goods, are no longer fit to cope with for ever upward spiralling demands for product variety, reliability and quality.

Many long-established and previously highly successful practices had to be changed (Table 16.1).

Management has realized that it has to take a clear lead in directing the organization in the quest for quality of performance. It is the people in the organization that make the vital difference. And to move into new patterns of working, management has to express and practise the new values which it believes will lead to the development of new capabilities.

Table 16.1   *The evolution of effective approaches to quality improvement*

Was effective	Current
• Partial improvement approach per business function	• Interrelated improvement approach per business process
• Quality improvement efforts concentrate on production	• Quality improvements efforts throughout all areas of the business
• Quality: responsibility of specialist function	• Quality: responsibility of line management
• Improvement mainly through experts	• Improvement through involving all employees
• Inspection to correct mistakes made	• Prevention designed into product service and process
• Complex control systems	• Stimulation of self-regulation
• Standardized repetitive tasks	• Experiments with enlarged individual responsibility
• Suppliers chosen on basis of narrow range of criteria	• Suppliers chosen on basis of wide range of criteria
• Contract based relationship with many suppliers	• Co-makership agreements with selected suppliers

Changing company cultures unfortunately cannot be learned only from books. There are no standard techniques for overall application. The procedure manuals have still to be written. The process has to start at the top and work its way slowly and thoroughly right down through the organization. This process takes time, dedication and persistence.

Company-wide quality improvement at Philips

Philips is a large, diverse and complex company. It operates within many different national environments with a great variety of product/market combinations and thus a great diversity of customer circumstances (Table 16.2).

During the late 1970s and early 1980s awareness was growing that new initiatives would have to be taken in order to keep the company up amongst the world leaders. From the late 1970s onwards more and more information became available from internal change projects which were enabling differing parts of the organization to adjust successfully to the new business environment. In addition, information about approaches taken in other organizations and careful competitive analysis clarified the picture still further (Table 16.3).

In 1983 these internal and external signals were brought together by the Board of Management, and resulted in a policy statement issued by the President in October 1983. He stated that: 'The quality of products and services is of the utmost importance for the continuity of our company', and continued: 'The Board of Management has decided to give vigorous direction to a company-wide approach to quality improvement.' He went on to outline the major elements of the new quality policy. This

Table 16.2 *Some facts about Philips (1985)*

Sales: US Dollars	24 billion	
Fields of activity:	(as a percentage of total turnover)	
	Lighting	12·4%
	Consumer electronics	26·3%
	Domestic appliances	10·3%
	Professional products and systems	27·8%
	Components	18·1%
	Miscellaneous	5·1%
Employees:	345,000	
National organizations in approximately sixty countries 420 factories throughout the world		

A case: the birth of a new business group

In the early 1980s one of Philips' Business Groups was facing major problems. Many of their products were outdated and market share was declining. There was talk of removing some of the business to other units and as a result, morale amongst the employees was poor.

In 1982 a major change process was started. Structural measures were taken to shape the Business Group into a more self-contained organization encompassing ownership of all necessary functions. Markets were thoroughly investigated, the necessary financial investments were made and development of new products started. Despite this new approach there remained a high degree of scepticism amongst many of the employees. The whole culture of the organization had to be seen to change, and to help this process, employees were kept fully informed every fortnight on production, sales, market movements and competitive developments. Then management formed groups from the next two hierarchical levels to assist them in developing business plans. Next, at a meeting attended by everyone, all were asked to say what their major problems were with working in the Group. From this list the 'top ten most important' problems were identified. And during the next six months priority was given to ensuring their solution. By this means trust in management and staff was revived.

At the same time as these changes were being implemented, a structured total improvement plan was developed. This plan addressed basic issues like quality, reliability and flexibility, and was discussed with all employees. Their suggestions were then incorporated and put into action. As a result a wide variety of operational improvements covering work stations, routing, lay-out, procedures and organization of the work flow were achieved.

Within two years product quality has increased such that customer complaints have become almost non-existent. And today, each and every complaint is addressed with top priority throughout the organization. Production through-put time and thus 'response to market' time has been reduced from six weeks to a few days, and the production area is now capable of producing any sales order within a few weeks.

As a result, efficiency has been improved and customers have regained confidence in the products. Prices have been reduced, market share has risen and the Group has become profitable once more. The original goals of the change programme were to improve quality, reliability and flexibility. The result was increased efficiency and thus the opportunity both to lower prices and yet to increase profits, and hence to ensure continuity, which is the ultimate objective of any improvement activity.

Table 16.3 *Characteristics of the new road to success*

- The drive for absolute customer satisfaction.
- The need for management to take full responsibility in leading the quality improvement movement.
- The need for the integration of functional capabilites in a total approach with clearly set priorities.
- The need for involvement of all employees, functions and suppliers.

statement was sent to all senior executives of the company who were shortly afterwards invited to attend seminars where the message was further elaborated and discussed. During the seminars the Board of Management asked all senior executives to communicate the message to their own organizations and to personally start a change process along the lines indicated.

The approach

In such a complex company careful consideration had to be given to the question of how far the new approach should be centrally prescribed in a standard format or how much freedom should be allowed for local initiative and adaptation. It was decided that all units should start from the corporate policy statement issued in October 1983 and from the basic principles discussed during the seminars (see Table 16.4).

Existing management reporting systems would be used to monitor progress and to give new impulses where needed. However, within these boundary conditions, local management was free to develop its own approach, using local resources as far as possible. The whole company thus entered an era of intensive 'learning by experimentation'. To foster local initiatives a central resource team was set up to provide support through consultancy and information dissemination and to help encourage the growth of networks of managers and specialists. The creation of such networks, it was hoped, would intensify and accelerate the exchange of local experience and knowledge.

Five main activities

In all approaches five main activities involved in bringing about change have been utilized (Figure 16.2).

It is possible to start the process with any of the five activities, depending on the specific circumstances and wishes of the units concerned, and thence to proceed in any order, but eventually all five activities have to be worked through; because only then will all facets of the change process have been covered. Only then will the changes be really embedded in the organization.

All these five activities must be worked through within the organization level after level, in a vertically linked process. Corporate improvement policy must be split down into policies for specific product divisions and national organizations, and these must be further translated into improvement policies for particular business groups and then finally for each individual operational unit. Activities at any one level must dovetail into the levels both above and below.

Table 16.4 *Company-wide quality improvement principles*

1 Customer satisfaction
A perfect interface must be achieved between company performance and customer needs in all aspects that customers consider to be important.

2 Leadership
Quality improvement is primarily a task and responsibility of management as a whole.

3 Total involvement
There must be total involvement of all employees at all levels and in all functions. Equally important is the complete involvement of all suppliers of goods and services.

4 Integrated approach
Integration must be achieved between functions and between levels. Traditional organizational barriers must be removed.

5 Systematic approach
A systematic approach must start with a clearly defined business strategy which is then translated into an improvement policy, objectives and priorities. These must be followed by detailed planning, implementation and monitoring of progress.

6 Defect prevention
Defects must be prevented from occurring. Performance must be the result of built-in capabilities.

7 Continuous improvement
The approach should not have the character of a campaign or a project. Excellence can only be achieved by continuously investing in improvement, step-by-step, year after year.

8 Maximum quality
Long-term objectives must be set which reflect the will to strive for excellence. The path towards excellence must be marked by challenging but achievable and acceptable targets.

9 Education and training
Widespread attention will be given to education and training. A new work culture can only be realized if all people are more than ever prepared to make their contribution.

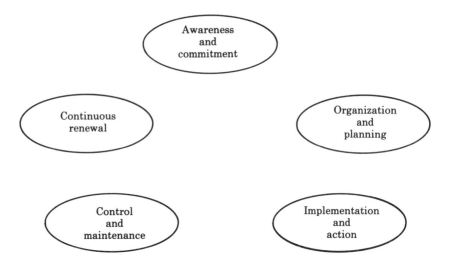

Figure 16.2   *The five main activities involved in bringing about change*

Results

Once a year a major evaluation is carried out for the Board of Management of the progress which has been achieved. Two-and-a-half years after the official start, (that is, in 1986) results are promising. Significant performance improvements have already been achieved, some of which, of course, are the results of initiatives taken well before October 1983. improvement policies for particular business groups and then finally for including through-put times, service respond times, system reliability, accounting reporting dates, stock levels, product call-rate, accuracy of files and documents and reachability (see Table 16.5).

Essentials for a learning process

This is only the start of a long-term learning programme. There are three essentials for a successful organizational learning process. The learning must be seen to be legitimate, possible to achieve, and worth achieving. All three are built into the programme.

The issue of legitimacy has been achieved by choosing, from the beginning, a top-down strategy and making it quite clear that management at all levels regarded Company-Wide Quality Improvement as a top priority matter. Secondly, through holding up examples of successful programmes in comparative organizations, both within and outside Philips, it is emphasized how it is possible for any unit, in any situation, to start improving their quality performance. To this end many different forms of communication are used, ranging from laser-vision to a common

Table 16.5   *Some examples of results*

Typical measures	Typical improvements		
	1983	1984	1985
Development through-put time	18 months	18 months	15 months
Out-going defect level	3%	2%	0·2%
Number of approved suppliers	0	0	10
Change-over time in production	1 hour	1 hour	5 min
Stock level (as % of turnover)	15 days	9 days	6 days
Fall off rate	25%	20%	9%
% Errors in invoicing	6%	4·3%	2·3%

*In a credit control area the percentage of overdues as % of total debt decreased from 23% in 1981 via 16% in 1983 to 13% in 1985.

*The Q-factor indicating the absence of defects in the operational process of a computer centre increased in one year from 92% to the targeted value of 98%.

*Implementation of a CWQI-programme in a Commercial Department decreased sales costs within two years by nearly 30%.

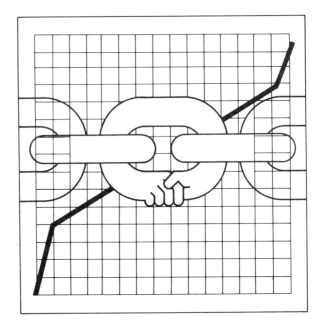

Figure 16.3 *The company-wide quality improvement logo*

logo and newsletters, from video tapes to internal discussion forums or informal get-togethers.

It is hardly necessary, in a well-run organization, to point out that quality improvement is worth achieving. However, in addition to this natural desire to succeed, through the introduction of a Philips Quality Award system, management teams are given something extra at which to aim. Competition to show excellence, compared to one's peers, is highly motivating. Such quality awards not only provide a little extra spice to normal day-to-day working, but they also make clear the standard towards which to aim and give clear unambiguous feedback to all involved of their progress (see Figure 16.3).

Evaluation and Conclusion

In the past years awareness of the need for quality improvement and knowledge on how to manage improvement programmes has been communicated through over 250 awareness and commitment seminars to well over 15,000 managers. By now structured programmes are running in more than 150 organizational units, together employing more than 60,000 people. These unit not only include production facilities but also sales groups, supporting functions and administrative departments. In evaluating what has been learnt to date the following conclusions can be drawn:

- The top-down cascade model has proven to be successful in spreading awareness and commitment. It is not a once-and-for all-input by top management. Rather it requires their continued attention at regular intervals in order to maintain momentum, especially if there are to be clear and lasting changes in company values.
- Management ownership of the programme is a basic condition for success. Best results are achieved in those places where managers lead improvement programmes from personal conviction. One of the worst things which may happen is a manager delegating responsibility for the programme to a specialist.
- Involvement of all organization members is crucial if improvement is ever to become a routine part of everyday life, but this is not easy to achieve. It must come from personal example and commitment. For example, if involvement is forced upon supervisory management, it may well become a mere window-dressing exercise and thus fail and be difficult to repair.
- There must be consistency between what management says and what management does. People will not believe in the importance of new values unles their application is demonstrated by the hierarchy.
- Small-scale improvement is relatively easy to achieve. Merely focusing management's attention on this area will achieve a few percentage points improvement. On the other hand breakthroughs in performance can only be realized by breakthroughs in traditional habits. These take time, dedication and persistence and can lead to frustration. Some of our organizations are disappointed that, even after two years, break-throughs are not yet in sight. This necessitates continuous en-couragement by management. Perseverence can also be helped by the knowledge that other, eventually successful, breakthroughs have also often taken so long.
- Market performance evidence seems to be the only argument which convinces managers to spend time and energy on a total quality programme. If this evidence is lacking or if it is not hard enough, organizations may go through the motions, but will not take the difficult decisions needed for breakthrough.
- There is indeed no standard way, no recipe which guarantees success. Many quality improvement packages are available for the market. Philips has by now experience with most of them. The conclusion is that such programmes can help in starting up the change process, but units then have to be able to 'personalize' the package in some way and to develop their own skills and resources, if they are to maintain the momentum.

Company-Wide Quality Improvement is a programme of strategic sig-nificance. It helps management to build up the capabilities needed to obtain an improved position in the market place.

17 Changing the corporate culture of Rank Xerox

Paul Chapman, Director of Business Management Systems, Rank Xerox (UK) Ltd

When David O'Brien joined Rank Xerox (UK) Ltd as Managing Director in early 1986, his major strategic objective was to exploit the technological opportunities offered by the company's office equipment range of products, particularly its multi-function workstations and Xerox network services, by becoming a key player in the emerging office systems market. While this market offered enormous potential growth it was (as yet) not dominated by any single supplier.

For many years Xerox Corporation had been able to develop concepts and products at the leading edge of technology through its world famous Palo Alto Research Centre (PARC) – in fact Xerox researchers had developed many techniques to support the use of technology in the office, ranging from Ethernet local area network and document management architecture through to WIMP technology (windows, icons, mouse, pull-down menus) and the working desktop view concept; but had never really commercially exploited these products and ideas.

O'Brien analysed the challenge facing him into two main areas, the first concerned the company's strategy (see Figure 17.1) and its marketing, and the second its organization and management processes.

Strategic/Marketing challenge

The historic strategy, organization and culture of Rank Xerox had evolved to optimize the selling of 'copiers' as stand-alone boxes. The copier/duplicator products which had made the name Rank Xerox famous, represented a 'replacement' market, and one which had been aggressively attacked by Japanese competitors. Such a market did not offer Rank Xerox the prospects for growth latent in the office systems market-place. Most marketing actions were, in spite of quality improvement and a good record of product innovation, tactical and reflected the

INFORMATION TECHNOLOGY STATUS

Many executives today do not believe they have gained the full value of their investment in Information Technology despite the growing awareness of the strategic value of information.

OFFICE AUTOMATION vs OFFICE SYSTEMS

Office automation has applied technology to the automation of discrete activities.

Office systems applies technology to the support of overall processes in the office.

THE TRUE OFFICE ENVIRONMENT

requires support for both unstructured and structured activities involving
Office Systems Technology
as well as
Data Processing Technology

Office Systems Technology can only be effective if it is built on an architecture designed to support the true office environment.

Figure 17.1 *Rank Xerox's view of office systems*

intense competition:

- Aggressive pricing
- Selling features and price
- 'Box' selling
- Cost reduction programmes
- Product focus

To help achieve Xerox/Rank Xerox's world-wide corporate revenue and profit growth target, David O'Brien's task was to develop the office systems revenues of Rank Xerox (UK) to a half of total revenue within four years. O'Brien's previous experience in the systems business told him that an entirely different set of skills, marketing programmes and strategic objectives would be needed to succeed in the office systems market, in particular:

- Account management
- Selling solutions
- Executive awareness, and
- Customer focus

The development of this approach and the associated skills could also have a positive effect in the more 'traditional' areas of the business, particularly as the technologies of the copier/duplicator and office systems market-places began to merge: facsimile on the net, electronic reprographics etc.

Organizational/Infrastructure

Until Japan Inc's entry into the market, Rank Xerox had had the lion's share of the copier/duplicator market although it faced, and continues to face, tough competition from other technologies (e.g. offset printing at the 'top end' of its product range). IBM, Kodak and others, had begun to play in specific market areas as the Xerox patents expired, but without denting Xerox's share to any great extent; and its structure and culture reflected that position. Strong, functional directors with a clearly demarcated territory, geared to consolidation of the company's (and their) position, internally focused with large staff groups concentrating on internal issues.

The company's systems and processes were geared to 'box selling' and were functionally owned. With the new strategic business dimension of office systems being added, these systems and processes needed a fundamental review to cope with a highly competitive business environment, in which resource efficiency and competitive edge are paramount, with the added complexity of the integrated systems product range (see Figure 17.2).

The classic approach to this situation would have been to replace the executive directors whose experience had been predominantly in the copier/duplicator market-place with tried and tested executives experienced in the systems business, in order to drive the company towards achievement of its enlarged strategic objectives. However, there was a large ($300m turnover) copier/duplicator business to run. The company continued to innovate to retain product leadership in its copier/duplicator core business and the returns from this 'traditional' business would need to fund the investments needed to succeed in the office systems market.

O'Brien therefore adopted a different approach. He retained intact the Executive Board with all of the 'operational' functions still in place:

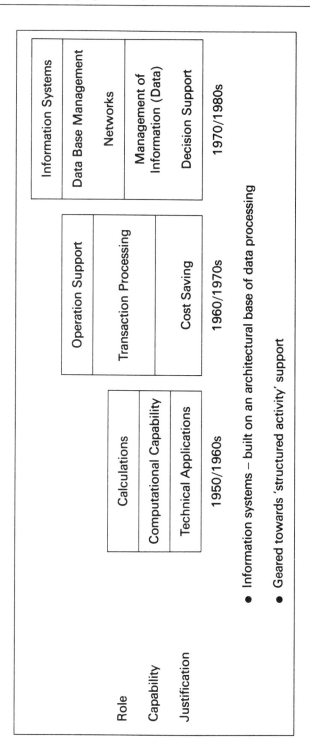

Figure 17.2 *The impact of information technology 1950s–1980s*

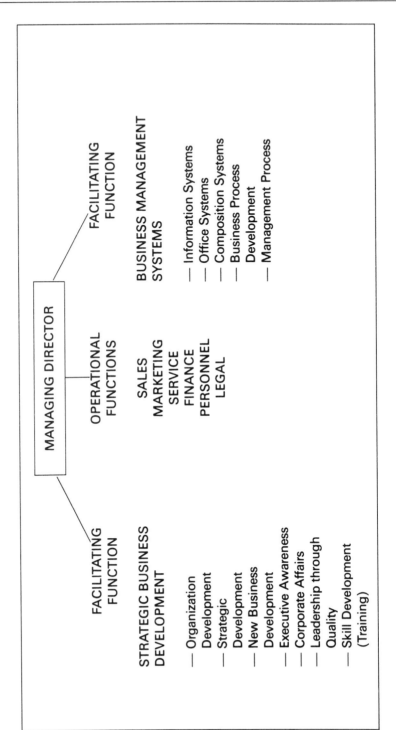

MANAGING DIRECTOR

FACILITATING
FUNCTION

STRATEGIC BUSINESS
DEVELOPMENT

— Organization
    Development
— Strategic
    Development
— New Business
    Development
— Executive Awareness
— Corporate Affairs
— Leadership through
    Quality
— Skill Development
    (Training)

OPERATIONAL
FUNCTIONS

SALES
MARKETING
SERVICE
FINANCE
PERSONNEL
LEGAL

FACILITATING
FUNCTION

BUSINESS MANAGEMENT
SYSTEMS

— Information Systems
— Office Systems
— Composition Systems
— Business Process
    Development
— Management Process

Figure 17.3　*The new board arrangement*

sales, marketing, finance, service, personnel and legal, and he appointed two new directors as 'facilitators':

- Director, Strategic Business Development, to facilitate the changes required from a strategic and marketing viewpoint
- Director, Business Management Systems, to facilitate the changes required from an organization and infrastructure point of view.

The organization of the new board is shown in Figure 17.3.

Having put the broad organization in place, the next key step was to develop the 'vehicle' to deliver the strategy. One jewel which shone through the mist of issues was the company's own Leadership Through Quality Programme.

The Leadership Through Quality Programme was an initiative that had been started by David Kearns, CEO of Xerox Corporation. Kearns had recognized that much of the entrepreneurial spirit which had led to the spectacular growth in the Corporation in the 1960s and 1970s was becoming stifled by the growth of a cumbersome, bureaucratic, internally focused organization as the company 'matured'.

The inspiration for the programme, in common with a number of programmes introduced in the 1980s by Xerox to underpin its successful fight to regain market share from the Japanese competition, was Fuji Xerox a 50:50 joint venture between Rank Xerox Ltd and Fuji Photo Film Company of Japan (see Figure 17.4).

Therein lay the problem. The Xerox definition of quality was 'conforming to customer requirements', and the Leadership Through Quality Process was clearly focused on identifying who the customer was (internal or external), determining his requirements, and then developing plans

---

- **Unique Joint Venture:** Xerox, Rank Xerox, Fuji Xerox, Modi Xerox

- **Total Revenues:** ca £6bn + Office Systems, £2bn Rank Xerox

- **Employs:** 125,000 world-wide, 26,000 Europe, 8,000 UK

- **Business:** Office Systems, Document Management Focus

- **Investments in R & D:** £500m pa
  Human Interface   — Workstations
  Communications   — Networks/Electronic Printing
  AI   — Understanding

Figure 17.4 *Xerox Corporation: key facts*

to satisfy those requirements. This was very much an 'oriental' approach to business problems, and in many ways clashed with the traditional 'occidental' managerial approach which was based on establishing objectives and achieving them via action plans.

A good illustration of the 'clash of cultures' is a story relating to Ray MacDonald, CEO of the Burroughs Corporation whose autocratic approach to his employees extended to his relationships with customers and suppliers. Visiting Tokyo to review a joint venture Burroughs had established in Japan to market its products, MacDonald was convinced that the executive offices were on the fourth floor, as were his own offices back in Detroit. Having informed the lift operator of his destination, his Japanese hosts, not wishing to disagree with the 'customer', suggested 'Fourth floor very good, but fifth floor may be better.'

The implementation of the Leadership Through Quality Programme in Rank Xerox (UK), with its emphasis on the customer, had led to some severe organizational strains. The statement 'I am the customer, satisfy me' threw many of the traditional problem-solving processes into total confusion and led to substantial resources being dedicated to satisfying non-essential requirements.

Clearly what the process needed to be effective was a framework in which to operate. During his time as Sales and Marketing Director at Burroughs, O'Brien had introduced a process called Business Development Planning, used successfully by his account teams, sometimes with customers, to determine the key strategies and objectives within an account. Facilitated by an external consultancy, Cambridge Associates, he introduced a similar process, but one tailored to the distinct requirements of the new situation in Rank Xerox, and developed a comprehensive approach to implementing an integrated management process.

Although the actual processes used in the Business Development Planning approach and Leadership Through Quality were very similar, their focus was entirely different. Taking each methodology at the appropriate 'organizational responsibility' level, he was able to implement a comprehensive and fully integrated planning approach. The step between Business Development Planning and Leadership Through Quality, the Business Systems Requirements Review, used the same methodology as Business Development Planning but focused on rules (policies, procedures, and guidelines), systems requirements, management processes and resources required to deliver the objectives defined from the Business Development Planning Output (see Figure 17.5).

Throughout the whole process, the emphasis was on teamwork. At the root of all the methodologies now incorporated under the banner of 'Leadership Through Quality' was the emphasis on true consensus and team commitment, on a cross-functional basis. Although initially decisions seem to take longer within this kind of process (and indeed the

LEVEL OF RESPONSIBILITY WITHIN THE ORGANIZATION	DEFINITION OF ROLE	METHODOLOGY	OUTPUTS
Direction	What are we going to do?	Business Development Planning	• Mission • Strategy Responsibilities
Function Management	What do we need to do it?	Business Systems Requirements	• Management Process • Systems and Rules • Resources
Operational Management	How are we going to do it?	Leadership Through Quality	• Quality Improvement Projects • Operational Improvements • Team Commitment
Operations	Doing it	Teamwork	

Figure 17.5 *The Business Systems Requirements Review*

whole process outlined above took many months, with senior management locked at close quarters, often for week-long sessions) this is only due to the initial investment required in training and understanding. As the functional barriers break down and individuals see the process as a 'natural' way to conduct their business, decision-taking speeds up and the *quality* of the decisions shines through.

This methodology and philosophy can best be illustrated with some examples of results. Quite obviously, the major effects of such an approach are long term, but already (in 1988) the organization is beginning to see the benefits.

From the Business Development Planning sessions, roles and responsibilities and objectives were established for every function, duplication and conflicts resolved, and a management process developed which cut down the number of senior executive monthly management meetings from eleven to three core meetings.

From the Business Systems Requirements Review, which involved more than seventy senior managers for week-long sessions, over 1200 major defects in information, policies, guidelines, etc were identified and a strategy developed and approved which would benefit the profit line by over six times the investment required ($5m) over three years.

The Leadership Through Quality process is used now in many areas as a way of life. Over 3000 people (out of a total of 4500) have been fully trained in the process and by mid-1988 every employee will have been trained. The process is being used to solve many hundreds of problems large and small: from how to use the Company couriers more cost effectively to how to improve profitability on office systems – and every project has a payback!

Just one final illustration of how decision-taking speeds up once people are familiar with the processes and philosophy. When I joined the company in August 1986 as Director, Business Management Systems, one of the first major problems I confronted was the state of the order processing systems. The IS function had produced outline specifications for a new system and I was told that the operational functions had stated it was to take 240 weeks to agree the specifications! By using the Business Development Planning Process, with a cross-functional team of eight people, the specifications were agreed in four days and design of the system started the next day.

With a clearly defined methodology and management philosophy in place, the planning process could easily be developed (see Figure 17.6).

The new methodology was still resource intensive, however, and the next step was to look at how technology might be applied to the process, both to use internally and to articulate to customers and prospective customers how they could apply the philosophy, methodology and technology.

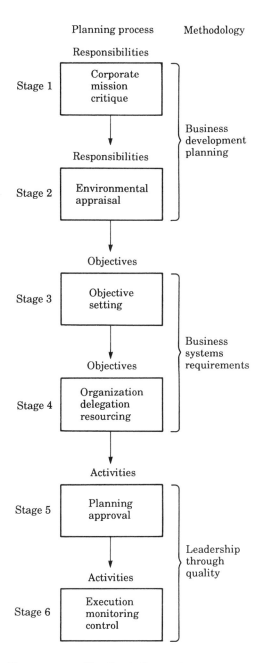

Figure 17.6   *The Rank Xerox planning process*

The basic elements of any management process are:

- ACQUIRE (acquire information)
- UNDERSTAND (build understanding)
- COMMUNICATE (communicate conclusions).

The understanding process is an iterative and interactive exercise of exchanging views, opinions and thoughts. Through the technological developments in the 1960s and 1970s most companies had acquired some level of capability in acquiring information via basic information systems, and some level of capability in communicating via networks and publishing systems. However, this is not where the majority of management cost and resource is expended. Case studies have shown that 20 per cent of the cost is in acquiring, and a similar percentage in communicating, leaving 60 per cent of the costs in the understanding area.

Clearly, therefore, this is where technology could achieve the maximum cost benefit. Also, the *understanding* element of management is the key differentiator between companies; it is the area where management adds value to the business.

Even within the process of understanding, the three basic elements – acquire, understand and communicate – can be found, but this time dealing with thoughts, not data. Office systems technology is ideally suited to this part of the process with its ability to handle unstructured processes, data and information, and to communicate the resulting conclusions through publishing or composition systems.

Within the Rank Xerox range of products, there were all the elements to create the necessary office systems technology, via multi-function workstations, the integration capabilities via networking and the communication devices via laser printers, fax etc.

The value that management adds to the business is its ability to facilitate understanding, the processing of thoughts, not just facts and conclusions. By developing and implementing an integrated team management philosophy and by supporting this with Rank Xerox's own office systems technology, O'Brien has been able within eighteen months to make the UK arm of Rank Xerox the shining star in the Xerox world. Revenue is up 20 per cent year-on-year (the first time since the 'glory' days of the 1960s and early 1970s) and management profits have more than doubled.

In the process, he has begun to fulfil his major strategic objective, to exploit the opportunities in the office systems market by demonstrating the power that the right technology can have in turning a business around. This has already resulted in some major successes: for example a 200+ workstation network ordered from Logica, the systems house, the largest network order for Xerox ever outside of the United States; and an order for £3.2m worth of electronics printers from Lloyds Bank, in direct competition with IBM.

The opportunities for business and organization development offered by this approach to the application of office systems technology supported by a full Leadership Through Quality philosophy of management possibly herald the start of the next stage of the 'technological' revolution.

18 Creating a new organization and culture at Scandinavian Airlines

Olle Stiwenius, Senior Consultant, SAS Management Consultants, Sweden

The dramatic turnaround of SAS probably owes more to changes in people and organization than to anything else. There is no doubt that the changes in profitability are exciting. However, once we have carefully studied the annual reports, they are merely historic facts. The major transformation was from a production-oriented airline to a market-oriented service company. The management of SAS realized they had to become customer-oriented, simply to start working as a service company. One of our directors pointed out that 'the battle for the air will have to be fought on the ground'. The change has also emphasized the role of the manager in corporate renewal and the adoption of an explicit business philosophy in order to gain commitment and involvement.

'Something had happened out there'

For a long time SAS had lived in a steadily growing market very much protected by the international airline agreements. The business was managed to profitability by generally economizing and reciprocally dividing the markets.

As the market grew 'automatically' we were simply taking orders. Profitability was reached by keeping down costs and protecting our investments in aeroplanes and other assets. And we did very good business, focusing on technical improvements and selling our aircraft, very successfully (Figure 18.1).

Unfortunately, the more we cut costs the more we cut back our service and consequently lost market share. We got into a kind of vicious circle (Figure 18.2).

Then many things changed: increased fuel prices, rising costs, price

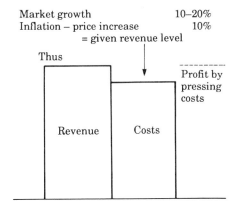

Figure 18.1   *We could calculate profitability*

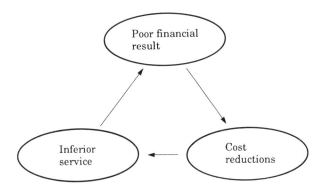

Figure 18.2   *The vicious circle*

wars, dwindling demand and liberalization of air-transport competition. SAS lost money at the rate of £7000 per hour (Figure 18.3). It became apparent that a competitive market called for an entirely new corporate philosophy, and our deteriorating service was having disastrous consequences.

Now, an airline business can adapt to any level of market-share, but cannot live on with a falling trend. So we had to make a quick pull-up and to work together on becoming the world's best service airline. To master the accelerating deficits, caused by the vicious circle, we had to act and act fast (Figure 18.4).

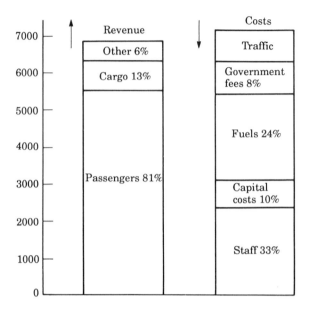

Figure 18.3   *Revenues and costs 1980–1*

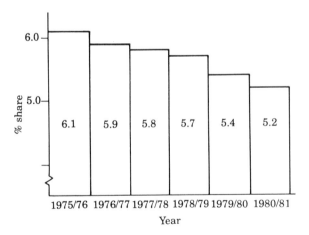

Figure 18.4   *SAS market share*

Influence on organizational culture

The aim was to adapt to the market preferences. This meant that we had to become attractive to our passengers by meeting their demands. Because the only ones who are willing to pay our cost next year are the satisfied customers of today.

As our President pointed out:

We can have as many beautiful aircraft as we like and still not survive if we don't have passengers who would rather fly SAS than our competitors.

This also meant that we had to look upon our costs as a potential basis for income and to generate income by market-orientation.

Obviously the staff closest to the market tend to notice market-changes first, but our organization was not arranged to pick up the signals fast enough. Thus we might have been a bit late in adapting to the new environment.

The major reason for our former slowness was unquestionably that we had put too many restrictions on the behaviour of our front line employees, who account for roughly 50 per cent of our personnel. Living by the detailed rules and regulations did not allow our 'front soldiers' to give the service our customers demanded.

Who is in the best situation to adapt to the market's needs? Who has the most frequent contacts? Who is able to initiate better service and who knows the market's need the best? The Front Line of course!

With our 'Front line personnel' we already had all the knowledge we always tried to buy in market surveys. So we 'classified' all other human resources as 'support troops' or 'support functions', who are supposed to look upon the 'Front Line' as their primary customer.

These basic circumstances called for a reorganization in order to achieve the greatest possible market contact and the greatest possible delegation of responsibility and authority to the 'Front Line'.

In fact, no instructions or regulations whatsoever, could possibly 'direct' our annual 40–100 million individual passenger contacts to create customer satisfaction. It called for an entirely new view on 'the customer in focus' (Figure 18.5).

Towards a new corporate philosophy

The SAS turnaround had to be directed towards the reality that the only thing that counts in a service company is a satisfied customer.

Our company's philosophy and its organizational structure were based on the same prevailing ideas as industrial society. It was created to satisfy growing market needs by effective use of production resources (i.e. primarily managing investing capital) to keep installations profitable.

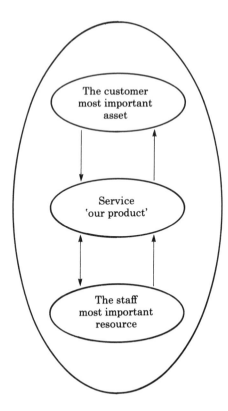

Figure 18.5   *SAS concept*

Many corporate reorganizations during the 1970s tried to bring about profitability by planning from their own production resources out to the market (Why don't they buy our super-product?) All business education aimed at handling cost-cutting programmes, and the salesman's job was just to sell what the company produced.

SAS also fell into that trap. Specialist functions and specialists were created for every conceivable task; functional organizations were supposed to look after the assets, but instead they tended to preserve the investments already made. And manuals were produced abundantly with the aim of making us produce even more efficiently. The bitter truth however was that we were putting more and more restrictions on our employees' methods of working (Figure 18.6).

This belief in one 'right' course of action worked very well for a long time. But looking around in the world of uncertain income SAS management realized we had to start with the market, not with our resources. Product development and planning called for reversing our strategic approach.

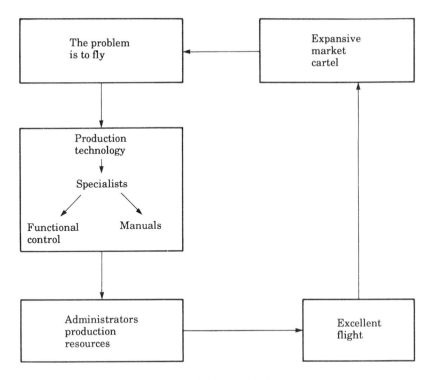

Figure 18.6 *Old SAS*

As the growth in sales slowed down we started to look upon market development as our major challenge (Figure 18.7).

Our strategic decision thus became, firstly, an offensive directed towards market-segments we singled out. And, secondly, we marshalled our resources to the needs of those markets, that is strengthening the 'Front Line'. Our corporate philosophy was reformulated thus:

In a stagnating market, where competitive forces are set free, a company can achieve profitability only by adjusting and aggressively investing to meet customer needs better than the competition.

SAS enters the 'Virtuous Circle'

One of the basic facts in business is that a deficit will arise if costs are higher than revenues. So to reverse the situation, you either have to reduce the costs or increase your income. SAS decided to do both at the same time.

Our strategy meant that we had to bring our resources into line with

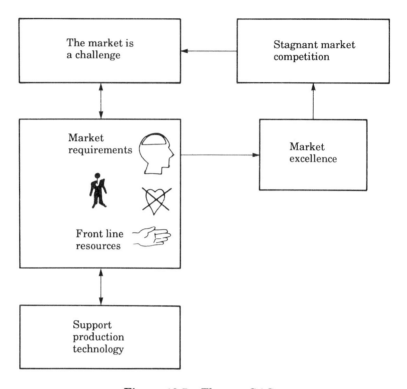

Figure 18.7   *The new SAS*

their revenue-making potential. In other words simply cutting costs across the board would not be the solution to meet customer needs. Our President gave an expressive illustration of this, pointing out that:

... you have to set a car moving before you apply the brakes. Otherwise no other change may occur but the obvious risk that you may step through the floor and damage the car.

In practice we worked hard on helping our staff to understand what they should expect. The entire change process was supported by clear and simple information (brochures, videotapes, debates, inhouse magazines, etc) on our course of action. The introductory information on our new strategies was published in a brochure called *'Let's get in there and fight'*.

This communication produced an increase in motivation, like all understanding does, and this was further reinforced by 'service-training'.

Our third basis for the virtuous circle was an extensive management training programme to increase the organization's ability to act according to our new philosophy.

In short we created consciousness, knowledge and desire to change to the new approach.

Organizational structure and service management

We had to adjust our organization to the fact that income is created by offering the customers those products they are prepared to pay for. (Basics in a market-orientated organization as opposed to a technology- and production-orientated one.) Clearly, market segmentation is nothing new. On the contrary, it seems so evident that many industries have overlooked it in their struggle for production efficiency.

In the case of SAS we created the 'businessman's airline', in which we offered the business traveller a product to suit their needs.

Now, what about the costs? Certainly we focused on those as well, but we decentralized the initiative to managers closer to the market than our head office. And this is where the service concept is so important.

Costs are largely incurred in the 'delivery system' of a company's structure: primarily in the human resources. We realized we had to improve our performance in these areas, to the concept of service, where you engage yourself in solving the customer's problems.

So we moved staff from the back office to more needed functions closer to the customer/passenger, to provide peripheral service (booking, checking, waiting, comfort, attentiveness, etc) in the front line 'delivery-system' and we trained them for the new tasks.

We are now organized in relatively small, result-oriented and independent functions. We have discarded the old military organization where hierarchies tend to disrupt the communication patterns, thus delaying vital decisions close to the customer/passenger (Figure 18.8).

Strengthened market-organization

The new SAS organization is adjusted to market-demand and based on widespread delegation. It could be viewed as a wheel, in which the customer/passenger constitutes the hub.

This kind of structure encourages the customer-orientation and flexibility. It opens up possibilities for competent personnel to develop quickly and take responsibility for results without direct supervision. The organizational form also emphasizes communication, co-operation and co-ordination. And it is supported by a very ambitious programme of personnel and management development.

The significance of SAS 'cultural patterns'

A corporate culture is the pattern of habits, goals, concepts, ideas and behaviour that are found within a company. It is strongly influenced by

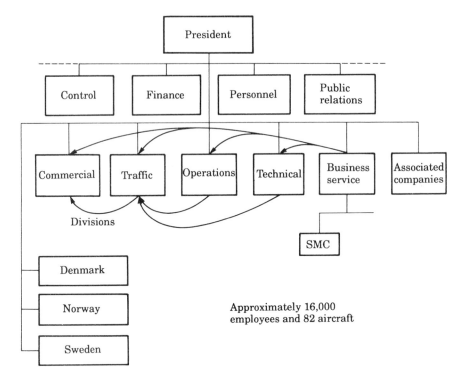

Figure 18.8 *SAS organizations*

the formulas which management develops to the benefit of the company. In a successful enterprise the culture reflects the market situation. It develops differently in a situation of growth than in a stagnating market.

Thus, the corporate culture should harmonize with the commercial environment. When this changes, the culture has to change as well, if the company is to survive.

This change took place and is still taking place in SAS. In fact our organizational market-orientation meant a new 'corporate culture'. We believe that in order to maintain SAS as an excellent service company we have to have the same basic values shared among all our staff. We are convinced that a satisfied customer continues to fly SAS rather than simply to fly, and is therefore the result of a market investment. Our values also suppose that customers want to be treated as individuals: they want personal service, to feel at home and to be taken care of by SAS.

We have described this culture by concluding that 'SAS lives with its customers' and 'a satisfied customer is our only real asset'. We also try to treat our own staff as individuals. We have created a culture where our customer is in the centre and creates opportunities for individual initiative and commitment that invests in market segments and 'backs winners'.

Open attitudes

A major transformation calls for radical structural and cultural changes. And changing an obsolete success formula, deeply embedded in the minds of key company personnel, also calls for strong action. Probably, before meaningful changes can be carried through, it is imperative to demonstrate dramatically that the former, well-proven formulas are no longer valid.

The SAS way of doing this has been to provide generous and open information to create new attitudes towards the customer and to colleagues. For example, the consequences of market orientation had to be clearly formulated and communicated. The new SAS philosophy states that 'change is a condition for survival and thus provides security'. So we focused very much on our view that the only way to survive is through a continuous process of change in people and organization.

We also made it our responsibility to give information fast, and to back it up with concrete initiatives. As we openly declared that 'our staff is our foremost resource' we made it our policy that 'Everyone is responsible for making sure that we have satisfied customers' and 'Seek the information you need so that you can assume your responsibility'.

When something goes wrong...

There are always reasons when things go wrong. But we made it acceptable to risk mistakes. One of our most important messages from management was that 'Mistakes can be corrected, but lost time can never be regained.' So we had to allow our staff to make decisions so that the customer's needs were satisfied immediately. The normal procedure would be *not* to refer the matter to a superior, who primarily has a supporting function and the responsibility to develop the quality of staff.

In the 'new SAS' the philosophy is instead to allow oneself a few misses now and then by testing new ideas instead of spending excessive time to be absolutely certain that the decision will be a complete success.

When things go wrong, information must immediately be given, internally and externally, explaining what has gone wrong. The reasons why the problem occurred and the current position must be clearly formulated. The opposite, to emphasize uncertainty by total silence, will only result in confusion, scepticism and irritation. This is the core of SAS's new, open attitude.

New supervision and leadership

To focus so much on the employee requires supervision and leadership to support those who provide the customer-service. It also requires that product planning and the product itself are arranged so that the contact between personnel and passengers is positive.

All the components work upon each other, thus enabling every employee to provide a service to the individual customer/passenger, which creates positive feelings: the 'Moment of Truth' for SAS.

New goals and strategies

To support the individual in his decisions, our philosophy includes providing goals and strategies that are so easy to understand that all staff can help according to their abilities. The framework, set by management, has to allow our departments to change operations on the basis of market demand instead of keeping to detailed internal requirements. Thus, during the change process we have lived with roughly only one goal:

To create such a profit by 1990 that we can favourably finance the need for new aircraft by then.

And we regard all costs as potential resources for the market. Even our own support functions have defined their 'internal markets', because services produced internally have 'buyers', who can define their need, volume, quality, etc just like other purchasers (Figure 18.9).

Our main strategy is to develop 'The business traveller's airline', and as many resources as possible were directed towards this task. We also produced complementary strategies like marginal-, concentration,-, trading- and transformation-strategies. Of these none was allowed to influence our 'main strategy'. Thus everybody was focused on serving our business travellers in all situations.

The change

The most important feature of our transition was maybe the strategy of speed. The organizational restructuring was carried through in approximately five months. It was probably our 'crisis-awareness' that triggered the start. Everyone came to understand that our heavy deficits called for something to be done. Thus all of the staff wanted to change things (Figure 18.10).

Also, the direction of change was carefully communicated. At an early stage we gathered around the slogan: 'Let's get in there and fight', which clearly pointed out our strategy. It was formulated in a booklet sent to

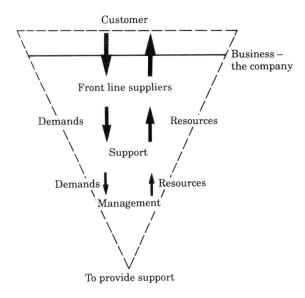

Figure 18.9   *What is the purpose of the 'organization'?*

each employee's home which outlined SAS's goals, philosophy and course of development.

Popularly it was referred to as 'Carlzon's Little Red Book' and it was very helpful for working out decentralized strategies and change-programmes, which were achieved within two months.

One of the most interesting messages our President presented was 'to become one per cent better in a hundred details rather than 100 per cent better in one detail'. The change was heavily supported with an extensive information plan, internally, to help the staff to understand what was happening and to encourage them to participate in changing their way of working.

Creation of credibility

To build up a belief in communication, a detailed programme of activities was worked out and carried through.

To realize our business strategies we invested $20m in 150 projects to become more customer-orientated, like 'business-traveller's airline, Euroclass and First business class'. This orientation towards market potential involved most of our staff in work to create 'a new SAS' instead of becoming too problem-oriented.

Simultaneously we carried through a comprehensive management development programme for approximately 2000 'key-persons' among

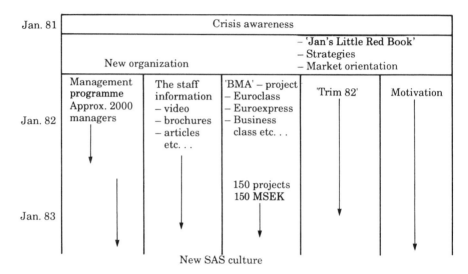

Figure 18.10   *Plan of activities for the SAS change*

upper and middle management. And in addition we offered all our 10,000 front line staff a two-day course in 'Personal Service through personal development'. There is no doubt that this programme brought about a remarkable change in attitudes among our employees.

Emphasis on training

The reason for the SAS success is that we were able, through training and combined information efforts, to create a new, creative and market-sensitive 'climate'. Our organization with very open channels of communication has become more venture sure through this intensive programme of spreading our philosophy.

The basic programme has now been completed by bringing more middle managers, supervisors and foremen into training. As everything is aimed at changing our 'corporate culture' the subjects have included strategy finance and service management.

Market-value analysis

A vital element in the change process was to relate resources to needs. This was carried through in the form of a decentralized value/activity-analysis, performed by each new division.

By holding a serious discussion between internal service functions (support-functions) and the receivers of this support (mainly Front Line personnel) we were able to define our 'over-capacity', that is services nobody was prepared to pay for. As a consequence these resources were transferred to other activities, where a shortage of resources could be found. This strengthened the Front Line organization by offering better service to our 'key-staff', meeting our customers in numerous 'moments of truth'.

New management role

This also means that a completely new management role has been recognized in SAS, that is the task of maintaining the continued development of our 'Corporate Culture', where will-power, energy and ability to push through a new policy might be decisive for success or failure (Figure 18.11).

It requires a business-oriented and participative leadership to imbue a team-spirit and to revitalize personnel attitudes. Thus management must be supportive and inspirational, setting goals and guidelines and delegating operational responsibility in a strong and clear manner.

In addition there is a strong emphasis on being result-orientated, where

Figure 18.11   *New roles of management*

it is the result which is assessed and judged rather than the course of action that led up to the result.

In this result-orientated organization, department heads are expected to be businessmen rather than administrators, to cause action instead of reaction and to give information rather than instructions.

In other words the new leadership in SAS means that a manager's primary responsibility is to develop the quality of his or her staff.

The future

We are pretty sure that our markets will undergo substantial changes in the future and that these changes will occur very swiftly. We also recognize that it is frequently difficult for existing management to review an earlier market-situation and radically question, re-orientate or reject former activities. Therefore we will probably be faced with the continuous re-organization of our business in order to formulate new demands, new goals, a new management philosophy and new strategies to achieve these goals.

We must also be prepared to draw up new internal management systems to change our company's culture and revise the modes of thinking among 'key personnel'.

Such changes are already taking place. We are now organizing for a 'Total travel and service concept' in order to adapt to new market requirements, and the change process goes on, or rather a new one is already emerging.

So, now that we have been successful in making a quick pull-up, we are building for the 1990s.

Leadership

No doubt the turnaround of SAS has been greatly inspired by the new type of leadership that Jan Carlzon represents. Some key characteristics could be noted:

- SAS staff at an early stage were made aware of the clear vision of the future that our President held: his ideas about probable changes in the market-situation.
- He believes in the individual's ability to take on greater responsibilities given the opportunities. This is of course a supportive management philosophy, executed by Mr Carlzon and many others which clearly challenges people to be more adventurous and entrepreneurial.
- He has communicated with great skill during the entire change. In a very simple and understandable manner our weak and strong points have been described. And through visual communication our staff has been encouraged to handle the business in an unorthodox way.

- Knowledge is also vital to carry through major changes. As Mr Carlzon had experience of managing a successful domestic airline (and other travel businesses) he could act very confidently and this gave other people confidence in carrying out his decisions.

Changing the corporate image

The actual change in SAS service was quickly noticed by our passengers and aroused much interest from the media. Also our image as 'the businessman's airline' was projected in a number of brochures and advertisments, distributed to our customers and to our own staff. The distribution was based on the idea that 'you should not inform your customers better than your own employees'.

The presentation of the company's image is so vital in a change process that SAS management decided to change the firm's 'brand image'. We changed our logotype, colours and uniforms and completely redesigned our aircraft and office interiors. Not only did this signal an important change in the eyes of customers and employees, it was also intended to prolong the economic lifetime of our assets.

We chose 'punctuality' for special attention as a central part of our image. For an airline employee 'punctuality' is the one thing everyone can easily do something about. Our President put up a TV monitor in his office so at any time of the day or night he could check our punctuality. And he had this particular priority projected to customers and employees. Thus we could all see how important 'punctuality' was to the new SAS.

The role of project teams

SAS management believes in the effectiveness of project teams in solving specific problems and consciously uses them in the change process. The best example is probably the goal 'to become the most punctual airline in Europe'. A project team was asked what it would cost SAS to reach that goal. After a short time a comprehensive report was presented. Management, however, was primarily interested in the cost: estimated at some million Swedish kronor. They decided that 'punctuality' was worth that amount, and they gave the project an immediate 'go-ahead'.

In less than three months SAS was the most punctual airline in Europe, and our President summarized the situation in these words:

We became Europe's most punctual airline. It didn't cost millions. It cost a fraction of the estimate, and we don't know how the money was spent.

If the project team had been given detailed instructions on how to make the airline more punctual, it would probably have spent the millions to find out they could not carry out the task.

It is this freedom of action which now guides all our project teams at SAS.

19 Woolworth's drive for excellence

Don Rose, Personnel Director, Woolworths plc

In November 1982, when the Paternoster consortium of City financiers acquired F. W. Woolworth from the American parent company, the retail giant was regarded as the 'sick man' of British retailing. It suffered from a poor image with the City, its suppliers and the British public.

The new management team identified key problems which were substantiated both by research and performance figures. Woolworths had:

- Become a 'store of last resort' with an unacceptably low average spend per shopping trip.
- An outmoded concept of retailing.
- Over 1000 stores, many either too small in growth centres or too large in declining centres.
- Some 8000 suppliers providing inferior quality merchandise.
- No recognition as a serious retailer with good management, either by the business community or the media.
- Over 30,000 demotivated staff who had become the benchmark for poor service.

The new management decided on a rescue mission which was launched in March 1986 under the banner 'Operation Focus'. It was to involve:

- The disposal of low-profit sites with the least potential.
- The identification and development of new, more appropriate sites and the rationalization of existing store sizes where appropriate.
- A multi-million pound refurbishment programme: by the end of 1987, 160 stores had been totally refurbished (some 2·3 million square feet of selling space) and the remainder re-merchandised.
- The creation of a new trading concept focusing on five areas of strengths, in order to reposition the chain as a specialist in key areas.
- A reduction in the number of suppliers to just over 1000.
- A significant reorganization and culture change through a specially-designed, multi-million pound staff training and development programme.

The new management recognized that a highly efficient and motivated staff would play a key role in this rescue mission. Indeed, innovations in the battle for High Street sales had reached a stage where quality of service was now very often the only advantage one retailer could offer over another. Accordingly, the change was towards customer service and satisfaction.

Attitudes of staff and store management

The attitudes of staff are best summarized by the results of an attitude survey which achieved an 85 per cent response:

- Managers were not communicating with staff.
- Staff were frightened to express their views openly because they were afraid of the likely reaction.
- Sales staff were afraid of customers. They had been hired to man tills and fill shelves and had little confidence if asked to operate outside these parameters.
- Staff lacked pride.
- Managers regarded themselves as managers of systems, procedures, stock and property: people were there to be directed, manipulated and disciplined.

Overall, Woolworth's management style was authoritarian and driven by fear. Staff were told to get on with a job and not to ask questions.

As a result, sales staff became cynical. They believed their jobs were dull and humdrum. This was, not surprisingly, increasingly apparent to customers.

Attitudes of line and personnel management

A similar study was carried out among line and personnel managers to determine what they perceived as the major contribution the personnel function could make to organizational effectiveness.

Line managers identified three areas where the personnel function could better satisfy their needs. These were:

(*a*) Recruitment and selection
(*b*) Training and development
(*c*) General support and guidance

Line managers saw customer care and positive company results as the basis of personnel management excellence. Attitudes had to be changed within the personnel department if it was to better serve the needs of the business.

The personnel structure

Traditionally, Woolworths recruited via Job Centres. Recruitment interviews lasted about ten minutes. Induction took twenty minutes. Training consisted of on-the-job learning.

Until 1985 there had been no board-level responsibility for personnel at Woolworths. The Personnel Controller reported to the Store Operations Director. Regional Personnel Managers (RPMs) reported to, and were paid by, Regional Managers – resulting in the RPM taking on the role of 'bag carrier' for the Regional Manager. Area Personnel Officers reported to District Managers at the next level down.

The problems which existed can be summarized as follows:

- The personnel function was shackled to line management, and therefore unable to set and maintain its own standards.
- Recruitment and training procedures were inadequate.
- Serious attitude problems existed at store management level.
- Personnel management itself needed to be re-educated.

Adopting a new philosophy

As a result of surveys, Woolworths redefined the aims of its personnel strategy. 'People Serving People' was adopted as the phrase to summarize the company's new staff and customer care philosophy. This would be achieved by demonstrating the importance of:

1 Concern for the customer: creating a friendly environment in stores which makes customers feel welcome so that they will continue to shop at Woolworths.
2 Concern for staff: recognizing the role of the sales assistant as the most important member of the team because this is the vital point of contact with customers.
3 Concern for the community: a commitment to prove that Woolworths has an important role to play in local communities.

Reorganizing the personnel structure

Following the appointment of a new Personnel Director in 1985, control of the personnel function was moved from the hands of line managers to the Regional Personnel Managers who now reported direct to the Personnel Director.

Area Personnel Officers reporting to Regional Personnel Managers were renamed Area Personnel and Training Officers (APTOs) with specific responsibility for personnel *standards*.

To improve the level of service to each store, additional APTOs were recruited and existing APTOs retrained. Each was made responsible for 12 stores and committed to visiting each store every seven days.

It is indicative of Woolworths' commitment to APTOs and their new role that training of the 100 prospective APTOs, from initial planning to its completion, took only four months.

Finally, the areas of responsibility for APTOs were succinctly and memorably defined by the mnemonic RITA – Recruitment, Induction, Training and Advice.

Reorganizing the management structure

With the implementation of Operation Focus, Woolworths needed to reorganize its management structure at store level.

Merchandise in the stores was rationalized and concentrated into five key departments or 'Focus Areas', and the basic unit of management was defined as the merchandise team: one per focus area and each headed by a Section Manager.

The existence of both Assistant Store Managers and Staff Managers mitigated against the Store Managers' ability to be truly responsible for the management of store staff. Woolworths phased out these two roles with the result that section managers now have a 'real' job: resulting in a more simplified structure and more clearly defined roles.

The new structure put more emphasis on personal responsibility, more scope for the development of teams and freer, more open, communication.

As each store is refurbished in line with Operation Focus, a team goes in to give special training in the new responsibilities and modes of behaviour. Staff are also issued with smart new uniforms to replace the old overalls.

The overall result has been a new understanding by each staff member of the importance of his or her role in the future success of the chain. Staff have a renewed sense of pride in their jobs and an evident confidence in dealing with customers.

Manager training

Research identified the fact that managers were essentially bureaucrats: managing systems, stock and procedure. Therefore, if the new store structure was to work, and if Woolworths was to fulfil the primary aim of serving customers, it had to effect a fundamental shift in the attitudes and behaviour of managers.

Woolworths sent a clear signal across the company: management means doing things right, but leadership means doing the right things.

The physical manifestation of this is a three-year tailormade management training programme at Henley Management College for all Woolworths' 1200 managers, including Store and Head Office Managers, emphasizing:

(a) Leadership and the Team
(b) Leadership and the Customer
(c) Leadership and the Business

The course, which is residential, is business-driven and designed specifically to build managers' leadership skills.

Under the strategic banner, 'Working and Winning Together', Store and Section Managers are taught how to conduct team meetings and to encourage two-way communication. Consultation via elected representatives at each level is a key part of the process.

A new approach to recruitment and induction

In response to research conducted with line managers, recruitment and induction of store staff are now given a high priority. Woolworths provides the appropriate facilities and trained interviewers to conduct all recruitment interviews, as well as using high-profile advertising in the community to attract applicants.

Store and Section Managers are responsible for recruitment and, as 'licensed' interviewers, are trained in the art of interviewing and selection.

Successful candidates spend their first day away from the store, participating in the induction programme which involves:

(a) A welcome to Woolworths and explantion of the chain's trading philosophy and high street positioning; and
(b) An explanation of the importance of good customer service, the sales assistant's role and the support which sales assistants will receive from other functions within the organization.

Woolworths has also produced its own induction magazine, *The Woolworths Scene*, which is given to all new recruits prior to joining. It is presented in a bright, readable format and outlines not only the 'dos and don'ts' of sales assistant work, but also gives tips on make-up, presentation, diet, how the company is organized, and what it is like to work in a store.

The Excellence Programme

This was introduced in July 1987, designed to motivate and reward: offering rewards to staff in recognition of their achievements and progress towards standards of personal and team 'excellence'.

The programme divides up as follows:
Section One: Skills and Behaviour
E: Induction: welcomes new recruits to Woolworths and demonstrates that working for the company is both enjoyable and rewarding.

X: Feelings: designed to help staff feel good about themselves, behave positively to customers and colleagues, and hence improve the shopping environment.
C: Till Skills: covers the different ways in which a customer can pay for goods, how to operate the till, and how to order goods.
E: Secondary Selling: encourages staff to work towards additional sales through better, more thoughtful customer contact.
Section Two: Merchandise Knowledge
This consists of training programmes designed to cover all merchandise areas: teaching staff how to handle individual ranges correctly and looking at the special types of display used for each merchandise areas.
L: Entertainment
L: Gifts and Sweets
E: Kids
N: Looks
C: Kitchen
E: Home and Garden
   As staff pass each test they are awarded letters. When they get to *EXCEL* they get a cash award. When staff finish Section Two of the training programme they receive additional cash bonuses and complete the *EXCELLENCE* badge.
   After one year, staff are re-tested to ensure continuity of the programme; failure in any area could result in the loss of a letter.

Results

The results of the Excellence Programme were:
   Greater satisfaction with service amongst Woolworth's 9·5 million customers per week. This was shown by in-depth research before and after the implementation of the training programme.
   Reduced number of customer complaints, which are logged weekly: in one year there has been a reduction of 21 per cent on the same period the previous year.
   Pre- and post-opening research for the refurbished store in Leicester revealed that:

● Staff were found to be readily available, friendly, polite, willing and helpful whenever requests were made of them.
● Consequently, customers felt that the level of service was superior to that which had been provided in the past.
● Staff uniforms were considered by customers as both modern and attractive.

   Recognition outside the company of Woolworth's staff training developments: major organizations such as Laing Homes and Harrods have been so impressed that they have asked Woolworths for advice on tailoring similar schemes for themselves.

30,000 motivated staff who have all helped Woolworths achieve greater profits: since the introduction of Operation Focus, pre-tax profit for Woolworths has risen to £45m in 1987–8 from a loss of £5m in 1984–5.

Sales per square foot have increased by an average of 15 per cent.

Increased sales in stores where the training has been carried out. For example staff in the recently refurbished Southport store have the highest number of *EXCELLENCE* stars of any of the Woolworths stores and sales have risen by 16 per cent.

20 From organization development to corporate development at Trebor

Arthur Chapman, Personnel Director, Trebor Ltd., Essex UK

This paper is about development in one particular company over a period of about eleven years, from 1972 to 1983. It is a case study of strategic development that began with an organization development project which led to the emergence of a new corporate development function. So it is *not* about corporate planning, which demonstrates how to get to known destinations; whereas 'corporate development', as the term is used here, has to do with asking questions about destinations. 'Organization development' refers to the framework of concepts and skills which is used in an enterprise to improve its processes (commercial, technical and social) in a deliberate and systematic way.

The paper starts, in the next section, with an overview of the company's planning and development activities during the whole period, to give a broad picture. Some of the key features are then enlarged in more or less chronological order in successive sections. At the end, some of the main issues, old and new, are identified.

Background

Trebor is a £200m, privately-owned family business manufacturing sugar confectionery and wholesaling sweets and chocolate, tobacco and related products in the UK; and also making and distributing sweets around the world in a string of scattered, mainly small, overseas operations.

Although it began in Forest Gate, East London as long ago as 1907, it emerged fully from its first 'pioneer' phase only in the late 1960s, as two brothers took over the running of the business from their strongly entrepreneurial father. He left his stamp of benevolent paternalism on the company marked by concern for people as individuals and relative absence of status distinction. As the organization moved into a 'differentiated' phase more scientific approach and a full panoply of specialisms replaced the instinctive, speedy responsiveness of the earlier period.

It was natural, as part of this change, to turn to consultants for help. Not so typical was the use of behavioural science to clarify the connection between managers' behaviour and commercial results. From 1973 onwards this took the form of collaboration with the UK offshoot of a Dutch consultancy group, NPI, now known in the UK as Transform.

By this time also, the company had acquired a planning department and produced its first five-year plan. But this lost credibility because not even short-range forecasts of sales could be reliably made. In the mid-1970s long-term planning, with a three-year horizon, was re-introduced. It was little more reliable than its predecessor as the Group Chairman pointed out at a senior manager's conference, with a devastating comparison between forecasts and outcomes over several years.

Within the past two years, corporate planning has been concerned with the careful definition of company strategy and its subsequent dissemination. This has provided, apart from the excellent discipline of thinking through the issues, a direction for the business: a framework for action which is now focused through a number of long-term planning projects which concentrate on the main thrusts of the strategy.

Also in the past three years, some significant restructuring of the company has been carried out which led, in 1981, to the setting up of a Corporate Development Unit charged with the task of identifying and developing new, long-term profit opportunities; and, in 1983–4, to developing into four businesses.

The story is to some degree about an issue which is still being faced: How to balance attention to the pressing concerns of today's business with care for the long-term development of the company, commercially, technically and socially?

Picture of the future

At the outset of the OD project in 1973, the Executive Board produced a document called *Our Picture of the Future*. Since it has become fashionable recently to talk about the need for vision in business, it is worth reproducing (see Figure 20.1).

This document was issued and discussed around the company. Then, at a two-day conference, heads of functions listed the major issues facing the company. They then selected two which offered potential for learning as well as benefit from a satisfactory outcome. One was a severe labour turnover problem on a major site and the other the difficulty a new service division was having in participating fully in the decision-making processes of its line department clients.

KEYNOTE: Our primary aim is the healthy development of the organization basing this firmly on a concern for people and a belief that corporate excellence is absolutely compatible with developing people as far as they can go and want to go.

PEOPLE: We see this concern for the development of people as follows:
- A recognition of everyone's contribution;
- A wide and deep involvement in decision-making;
- A higher earning work group with improving conditions of employment;
- Providing the kind of working environment in which constructive personal development can take place throughout a career;
- Building integrated and committed working groups;
- Maintaining a balance between specialization and integration;
- Providing protection from hostile elements in the environment and connecting with supportive elements.

EXCELLENCE: We would like 'Our' company to be trying to excel in a number of ways:
- Profitable, in the top 20 per cent of the food industry;
- Productive, bigger in sales and output, but the same in numbers and flexible and simple in structure;
- Effective, helpful and economic in our dealings with customers, suppliers and staff;
- Up-to-date but realistic in regard to the market, technology, products and business methods;
- Able to be open with people inside the company about policies, behaviour and attitudes and to gain respect for them externally;
- Consistent in our policies.

Figure 20.1 *'Our Picture of the Future'*

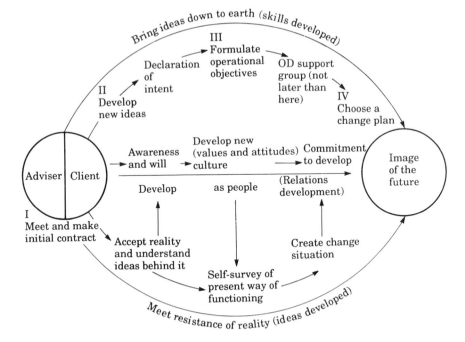

Figure 20.2   *A model for development organization*

At the same time, a Steering Committee of directors and senior managers was set up to support the new projects and to register and disseminate what was learned from them. We were starting out on a process which, somewhat later, was pictured to us as a development model (see Figure 20.2).

Diffusion

After a year in which much progress was achieved on both projects, and the Steering Committee had begun to realize that its role was counselling not directive, a need was felt to move on to a new phase. This was to be a phase in which new concepts, a new 'language' and even a new culture could be shared amongst a much wider group of managers. The vehicle for this was a one-week residential management course in which all the levels of management and supervision were deliberately mixed. The content was an amalgam of systematic problem-solving techniques and group process work with supporting lectures and skill-development exercises. At the outset a group of about twelve people, five of them directors, drawn mainly from line management, were selected and trained as trainers. This immediately provided a very powerful support group for the whole project (this has since become the pattern for many training courses).

At the end of the main series of courses, a further meeting of heads of functions took stock of OD work and selected five projects for the next phase of work (review meetings of this kind, held every two years or so, have become regular events). Several of these followed up needs that emerged during the management courses; for example, for team development seminars and for supervisory training.

Strategic awareness

The most significant development project selected at that meeting, however, was the building of a new factory. It had already become clear that production capacity would have to be extended and upgraded. The significance of making it a development project was that it became an opportunity to apply, in a greenfield situation, all the lessons learned in three years of OD activity. There were longer-term financial consequences, too, especially since the project was conceived in a boom but born during a recession. Nevertheless, everything about the project was seen as an opportunity for further, conscious development, in fields as disparate, for example, as the process for selecting an architect and applying the concept of autonomous work groups. The factory is now up and running at a high level of efficiency; it has just been awarded one of the RIBA 1983 awards for architectural merit; and the Medical Research Council surveys have recorded one of the highest levels of job satisfaction it has ever encountered on the shop floor.

In hindsight this can be seen as an exercise in taking a long-term view, with all the pitfalls as well as the opportunities entailed (the forecast need for more production capacity was wrong!).

While this project was under way the executive board put itself through a self-critique on company strategy, using an approach suggested by Igor Ansoff. This enabled the top management group to work together through an assessment at the match between the present and prospective environment and the company behaviour; and then to audit its internal capability to make any shift in behaviour that might be necessary. At least as important as the outcome of such an exercise is the increased level of awareness of strategic issues that it produces. Figure 20.3 describes the process which was used.

Crisis

1980 brought a severe recession in the confectionery market, especially in sugar confectionery which has lost an average 3 per cent by volume of each of the last four years. This was matched in the company by

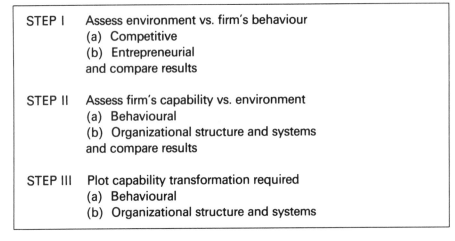

STEP I	Assess environment vs. firm's behaviour (a) Competitive (b) Entrepreneurial and compare results
STEP II	Assess firm's capability vs. environment (a) Behavioural (b) Organizational structure and systems and compare results
STEP III	Plot capability transformation required (a) Behavioural (b) Organizational structure and systems

Figure 20.3 *Auditing the Company's capacity to respond to its environment*

contraction in numbers and a factory closure. In addition, a difficult top management change had to be made. Restructuring, so often a substitute for genuine and necessary change, had been held back for some years but now was felt to be timely. Amongst a list of criteria used to review alternatives was 'a place for development in the top team'; and so a small corporate development unit was set up and added to the personnel director's area of responsibility, alongside organization development. Its primary role was to help identify and develop longer-term future profit opportunities. The direction of the other changes in structure made in 1981 was towards the closer integration of activities around the core business.

Rooting development in the organization

By this time senior managers were beginning to feel that we had lost our way somewhat in OD. Disquiet was expressed about the separation of this sort of activity from the 'real' business. To an extent, the problem of how to reconnect activities back into the business, from which they had been separated so that they can be given proper attention and resourcing, is an occupational hazard of all development work. The people working in the new corporate development unit were very conscious of this and made a special effort to avoid separation. At the beginning a wide group of managers was consulted both about development opportunities they could see and about how to avoid lack of ownership of development work.

There followed a stage of intensive staff work which led to a board review of possible futures for the market; an analysis of opportunities and barriers; the development of options and assessment criteria; all of which produced a clear picture of the path for future business development and the selection of three initial projects. Because the development strategy was an incremental one of building out from our existing business, all three of the projects touched closely on existing spheres of responsibility. Indeed, one of them was already under way in an operating division. After some initial hesitation about the degree of involvement that the new Corporate Development Unit 'ought to have', the line people were left to get on with it. A second project required new work to be done, but in an area where an existing department felt it had a claim.

Timely initiatives by two managers, below the top, rescued the project. The OD habit of carrying out a careful review of work done ensured that learning points were carried forward. In the third area a short-lived project group activity plus support for the initiatives of line managers gave the work considerable impetus.

Conclusions

How to connect development work with managers' everyday activities is a recurrent theme of this paper, whether 'development' is in the area of OD or of business development. We are currently considering how to emphasize each manager's responsibility for development in his own area, by including it in performance appraisals. To some extent it was accidental that OD and corporate development became connected in one person's area of responsibility, but there was some serendipity in it. As Ansoff points out, strengthening the capability of the organization is every bit as important as searching for opportunities in the market place: both are needed; neither alone is enough.

The latest chapter in the story included the deliberate ending of the OD Steering Committee, as the executive group takes over responsibility for its work; and a sharp change of course on structure, with the devolution of the Company into four profit centres. The purpose of these changes is to increase the scope for initiative and develop the climate in which it will flourish.

So what has been achieved by the process of organization and corporate development described here? The three projects referred to above have all been successful and are now contributing to profitability, albeit as yet in a minor way. Perhaps it is even more noteworthy that they are completely owned by the line managers in whose areas they operate – even to the point where it is forgotten that they were ever designated 'corporate development' projects. Nevertheless, three years on from the establishment of a corporate development function, the Company is only just beginning to face up to the question of how to make a fundamental response to the long-term decline of our basic market. The steps we are now taking to move into other markets with better profit potential will not produce a significant contribution to profits for about three years. Is six years a reasonable time to produce a radical shift in the business posture of a company? Only time will tell!

21 A management strategy for information processing: the Segas case

A. C. Collins, Director of Corporate Planning and Management Services, South Eastern Gas.

The environmental circumstances of any two organizations, albeit in the same business sector, may be entirely different and thus require substantially different approaches to the implementation of office systems. It should, therefore, be borne in mind when examining what has worked well for Segas (South Eastern Gas) that those same approaches may not be entirely appropriate, or indeed work well for other organizations. Some of the environmental factors which influence these considerations are:

1 *Business priorities* There may be many more critical issues to be tackled within the company or group before office automation. Structural re-organization, improvement of cash flow, radical changes to office procedures, changing the direction of the business, etc, may rank above the introduction of major office automation activity. It is important to know *when* is the 'right' time to launch into the type of project Segas is currently engaged in.

2 *Industrial relations* Over the previous five years, there have been a number of notable failures in the office antomation projects as a result of inadequate industrial relations preparations. In some organizations, even to raise the subject with trade unions would be like waving a red rag at a bull. Hence, a careful appraisal of the IR implications at the outset is important.

3 *Management awareness* In some organizations the general awareness of senior and middle management is limited at best to the broad (and frequently inadequate) views presented on TV, and at worst to the belief that it is all a new fad and if ignored it will go away. One has, therefore, to consider to what extent management need to be educated and how best this can be achieved.

4   *Fragmentation of responsibility* Some companies have different parts
    of the organization with responsibility for the various elements of
    what has become (or is becoming) an integrated system for inform-
    ation handling. Large scale computing applications may be the
    responsibility of the Finance Directorate, office services may be the
    responsibility of the Company Secretary or Administration Direc-
    torate, telephone services may be fragmented, and organization and
    methods may be part of a small specialist Management Services
    Department.

    As a consequence of such fragmentation each component service
    may pursue separate 'strategies' without necessarily interfacing
    effectively. Where this happens, the wider issues of 'Information
    Processing' will be lost, and the office automation concepts, which
    will require five to ten years to optimize, will not be achievable
    without radical and expensive changes of direction.

    In my opinion, it is important in every organization moving
    towards office automation to have one person (whom I normally
    designate the Information Strategist) to establish an overall app-
    roach to this complex task. An alternative is to have a liaison
    committee of the various interests responsible to one person able to
    make the necessary decisions and resolve areas of contention.

5   *User involvement* It has become customary in most organizations for
    the end-users to play a leading role in co-operative development of
    large scale computer systems. In some companies, however, systems
    may still be developed, keeping users at a defined distance. It is
    important in moving into the office automation field that strong co-
    operative projects are undertaken with the end-users fully involved
    from the outset.

In presenting our experience, I will adopt the following structure:

1   The background and strategy adopted during our developments
    between 1975 and 1982
2   A description of the current situation
3   Some examination as to whether the overall approach has paid off
4   The basic difference between IT and conventional data processing
5   Some key factors in achieving success in this field

Background to Information Technology developments in Segas

Segas is one of twelve Regions of British Gas Corporation (at the time of
writing) the nationalized gas industry serving England, Scotland and
Wales. British Gas Corporation is the largest integrated gas industry in
the world and is fully vertically integrated, covering:

Exploration
Transmission and storage of gas
Distribution of gas
Retail of gas appliances
After-sales service of appliances
Research and development

Even though Segas is a regional division of the main Corporation, it is in its own right a major business. It serves almost two million customers (the majority of whom are domestic customers), employs 10,200, and has a turnover of approximately £550m. The geographic area is 3300 square miles south of the Thames covering Kent, Sussex, Surrey and those parts of inner London south of the Thames.

The growth of computing in Segas since 1975 has been dramatic as shown by the increase in use of VDUs throughout the region (Figure 21.1). These VDUs are operated on-line from the central computing installation based at Croydon, where there has been a corresponding increase in central computing power (Figure 21.2). This network is operated via a combination of dedicated telephone lines, and microwave radio connecting approximately sixty offices (as shown in Figure 21.3).

Figure 21.4 illustrates the relative computing power used by the twelve Regions and headquarters of British Gas Corporation. It can be seen that Segas has the largest central computer installation, together with the largest VDU network (Figure 21.5), but this does not equate to the largest expenditure per customer.

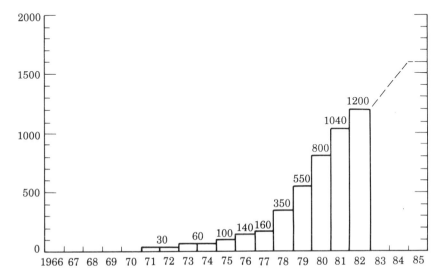

Figure 21.1 *Segas VDU population (number of terminals installed)*

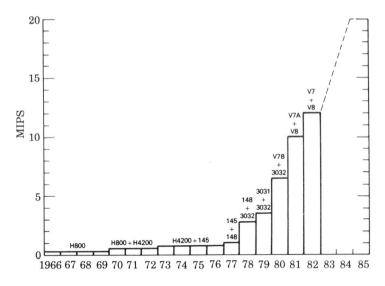

Figure 21.2 *Segas CPU power (millions of instructions per second)*

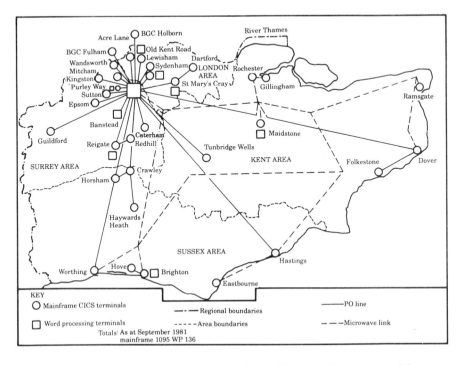

Figure 21.3 *Map of computer terminals at administration centres of Segas*

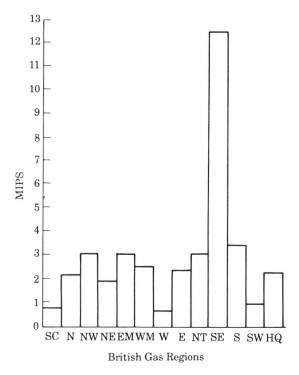

Figure 21.4 *CPU power*

As is customary in most organizations, the foundation for Information Technology in Segas was the application of data processing using mainframe computers, with a major emphasis being placed upon on-line computing. The next phase was the introduction of text processing, and the third was the development of an integrated network of text and data processing workstations.

The development will continue over the next five to seven years (from 1983) with the following emphases:

(a) Connection of personal computers and other management workstations to the network.

(b) Introduction of facsimile/image storage and transmission throughout the network.

(c) Addition of value-added services at low marginal cost to enhance the services provided.

(d) Merging, where economic and desirable, the voice network with the data/text/image processing network.

However, let us first examine the developments undertaken between 1975 and 1982 achieved via a three-phase strategy.

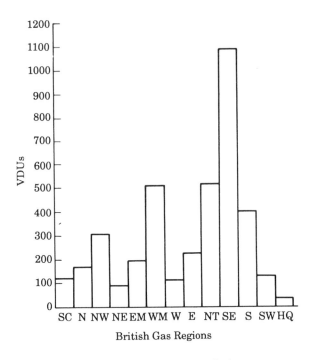

Figure 21.5 *VDU population*

(a) *1975–6: Resolution of system deficiencies* The initial phase consisted of conversion from Honeywell to IBM technology, making sure that the critical systems were secured against machine failure, and bringing in-house considerable activity carried out on bureaux. This was accompanied by a major programme of education for management and a major recruitment programme.

(b) *1976–8: Laying the initial foundation* The second phase involved an intensive programme of new developments of both major DP applications to satisfy the initial requirements of the various functions, and systematic development of a series of interactive models. A number of large models were translated from the ADP Bureau to operate under VM/CMS. In 1976, the first trials of word processing were undertaken using ATMS.

By the end of 1978, most of the fundamental building blocks were in position and it was then appropriate to carry out a major review of our forward strategy. To do so, we used the IBM methodology, Business Systems Planning. The primary objective of BSP is to provide an information system plan that supports the business short- and long-term information need and should be integral with business plans. It is carried out as a top-down exercise, and in the case of Segas was chaired by the Deputy Chairman. One of the issues identified was the need to develop a major system for handling text which would interface with the data processing system.

In 1976, the first developments of word processing were undertaken using the IBM product, Advanced Text Management Systems (ATMS). This system appeared to offer several distinct advantages at the time, namely:

(i) A text processing system which could be available to any of the terminals operating on the CICS network.

(ii) The cost of the software was relatively low and it used standard data processing terminals which were also relatively cheap.

(iii) It interfaced with STAIRS, a major product for information retrieval, which was seen to offer distinct advantages.

However, within three months of introducing the facility, certain inadequacies were identified, as explained later.

(c) *1978–Present date (1983): Major implementation* During the last four years, the major issues of data processing strategy have been to continue the educational efforts for all levels of management, staff and trade unions. We have completed the second phase of the BSP exercise and introduced a hierarchy of modelling for management. Logical data analysis and other techniques have been introduced and a database team has been set up. A significant increase in new systems has also occurred.

The Business Systems Planning Study undertaken in Segas during 1978–9 was one of the most important strategic steps taken for Information Technology within the Region.

Another important element in the co-ordination of the development of Information Technology has been the creation of the Business Systems Committee. This meets quarterly under the chairmanship of the Deputy Chairman and covers the full spectrum of developments in this field including business models developed by Operational Research, data processing, word processing, telecommunications, and long-range development projects. It has representatives from each of the major functions and specialist sub-groups maintain a co-ordinating role in key project areas. The objectives of the committee are to provide a clear direction for forward developments, and to ensure that the full spectrum of Information Technology is covered with uniform attention.

This committee also ensures that cross functional co-ordination exists and that priorities can be allocated on a regional basis to developments in each field. The functional representatives are chosen as senior representatives of their departments having a detailed knowledge of the developments being undertaken for their respective functions.

The Business Systems Committee is responsible to the Regional Management Committee, which at intervals of approximately six months discusses in detail issues of a strategic nature relating to Information Technology. This approach was adopted as a replacement for the previous Computer Policy Committee which dealt with large scale, data processing systems. As the associated technologies have developed, it was important that the inter-relationship of the various elements of IT could be taken into account on a cross-functional basis. This approach should prove to be sufficiently flexible to cope with the rapid change in technology over the next few years, and to ensure that the Region obtains maximum benefits from it.

Definition of the IT philosophy

From the outset of our developments of word processing, we had adopted the concept of a common network to serve both word and data processing. Because we wanted harmony between the two, it was essential that we drew up criteria which would allow us to select equipment to fulfill our objectives and at the same time guide us through the plethora of new equipment which was blossoming on to the market at that time. To do this we established ten criteria which we wanted word processing equipment to fulfill.

The decision had been made in 1973 to replace the Honeywell computer with IBM technology, and that general philosophy has been pursued over the intervening years. However, plug-compatible equipment has been used in place of IBM equipment to obtain benefits from the price/performance differences of the various manufacturers. Although Amdahl mainframe computers, Memorex disk drives, Documentation printers and Harris VDUs are the basis of our network, the basic operating principles are those of IBM. Since 1977 the Systems Network Architecture (SNA) of IBM has been the basic framework for developing our network concepts.

As a consequence of adopting SNA, and in order to have a shared network for data and word processing, it necessarily followed that any equipment we would add to the network would have to adhere to these principles. After we had established the ten criteria for selecting word processing equipment, we established a general philosophy which can be summarized as follows:

1 To provide one network for all information needs, including data, text, voice and graphics.
2 To provide a single network to meet the needs of all levels of management and operations throughout the Region.
3 To provide a system which will allow for organizational change without creating major problems either for the organization or in a redevelopment of systems.
4 To provide a system which will allow for information to effectively support business decisions at all levels.

It is clear from the above statements, that we were planning for more than just bringing together word and data processing. We wished to include the provision of adequate modelling facilities to meet the needs of management. As technology develops we want to include voice communications, and handle image and graphics on the same network.

Choice of office technology equipment
The objectives for introducing office technology were:

(a) To improve the productivity of typists.
(b) To improve the handling of information.
(c) To provide facilities which would enable management to be more effective.
(d) To enable office operations to be more efficient and cost effective.

In 1976 the scope for introducing word processing at Regional headquarters was examined by Productivity Services. A survey of typing activity by all categories of typing staff was carried out to determine the relative volumes of each form of typed output (i.e. memos, formatted tables, reports etc). From this, the immediate areas for introducing word processing could be identified, together with some indication of the benefits in terms of cash savings.

Wherever possible the existing office practice was modified before introducing word processing. However, the use of large grouped typing resources in 'typing pools' was not favoured. The sharing of local resources in smaller groups to provide more effective and flexible support to local management was preferred.

In view of the smaller groupings of individuals it was not generally cost effective to provide a dedicated work station for a single individual. The survey showed that typing activity generally constituted less than 30 per cent of the total duties of the majority of those support staff who were involved in typing. It was, therefore, considered to be more effective to provide word processing resources which were shared by a number of individuals in a common office. There were, however, a number of exceptions to this general rule.

From the outset it was the intention to provide word processing as part of an integrated network also handling data. As a consequence, the IBM product, Advanced Text Management System (ATMS) was chosen as the most appropriate facility. It should be borne in mind that in 1975–6 word processing was just becoming recognized as a major growth area and during the ensuing two year period more than sixty different models of stand-alone or shared-logic word processors emerged on the market. However, at this time there were relatively few products available for consideration and the IBM ATMS software, which could be mounted on a mainframe, appeared very attractive both in terms of cost and flexibility since it could be operated from a terminal which could be a conventional IBM VDU.

Within three months of introducing the facility certain inadequacies were identified, namely:

(a) The cumbersome operations for the average typist to handle text.
(b) The inadequate communicating magnetic card typewriter (CMCT) printer which operated at very slow speeds.
(c) The problems of having support for various aspects of the product from the Office Products and Data Processing Divisions of IBM.

Sufficient interest had, however, been stimulated in word processing within Segas to warrant the introduction of a limited number of stand-alone word processors as alternatives to ATMS. The latter was retained for specific activities associated with the preparation of large catalogues, the updating of the Region's telephone directory and for maintaining the system documentation within Computer Services using the mainframe computer. Indeed over the ensuing five years approximately twenty-eight ATMS workstations were used in this context.

AES was initially chosen as a stand-alone word processor since it was claimed that communication to IBM mainframes had been achieved. In the event, this proved to be teletype mode whereas we wished to have full 3270 VDU mode communications.

The rate of development of further word processing facilities over the period 1976–8 was relatively slow as negotiations proceeded with the trade unions and a limited number of trials were agreed at various locations at Regional headquarters. Procedures were developed in conjunction with the trade unions for ensuring that they were kept fully informed of developments and that, subject to satisfactory trials being completed, agreement could be reached on the introduction of word processing.

In 1978 the IBM 3730 shared logic facility was introduced into Management Services Department on a trial basis. This system consisted of eight VDUs and three Qume printers. The system proved to be cumbersome and unreliable and after a year's trial was abandoned. At the same time a number of other products were benchmarked including Lexitron, ICL 7700, Phillips 5002, Jacquard and the Wang 10a systems. Of these, the Wang stand-alone word processor met our requirements most closely and three units were introduced at that stage.

In 1979, agreement was reached with the trade unions regarding a modular training programme for typists/secretaries similar to that we had previously negotiated for the introduction of data processing systems for clerical staff. As a result we were prepared to introduce larger scale facilities, initially at Regional headquarters. Remembering the principles to which we were endeavouring to work, selection criteria had been established for this phase.

In effect we were looking for user-friendly facilities, compatibility with IBM software, extendable functions to provide more than just word processing, utilities which would allow the development of small administration systems and some measure of a hierarchy of hardware. We were particularly conscious that the range of sizes of offices throughout Segas was very wide. We did not, therefore, want to be tied to a system which would only permit us to deal with the larger offices cost effectively. Ideally we would wish to have single work-stations in small offices where there might be only one or two typists, and a range of shared-logic facilities in the larger offices where justified. As part of this ideal scenario we wanted to interface the word processing system with our data processing network, where that was proven to be necessary. We wanted to have the potential of inter-connecting any equipment used in order to be able to introduce electronic mail in due course.

Not unexpectedly few suppliers were able to meet these requirements, and it eventually narrowed down to IBM or Wang as potential suppliers. Our experience with the then current range of IBM facilities in this particular area had not developed as fruitfully as we had hoped. Wang, therefore, with the combination of OIS and VS systems, appeared to offer a very close match to the specification we had drawn up. However, having had several previous disappointing experiences with other vendors' equipment, we asked for a specific demonstration of certain features before we committed ourselves to purchase.

The Wang menu-driven word processing screens were already well known to the organization as a result of our experience with stand-alone Wang facilities. We, therefore, asked for a working demonstration of two factors:

(a) Communications of a Wang VS computer at their Richmond office to our mainframe, so that one of our staff with the appropriate security codes could access data processing files from a remote location.

(b) A demonstration of the utilities available both under DP and WP mode which would permit the rapid development of small administration systems.

Wang, working in conjunction with our staff, were given two weeks in which to achieve the connection to our mainframe and a non-DP member of Management Services Department was given a three-day project to develop a small administration process with assistance from Wang staff. Both features were successfully demonstrated and there was a strong commitment from the Region's Management Committee when these facilities were demonstrated to them. As a consequence, Wang equipment was chosen as the basis for development of the integrated DP/WP functions we wished to introduce into Segas.

Although I have been critical of IBM's early products in this field, such as ATMS and the 3730 system, it is true to say that there have been marked improvements in recent years. Not only has the hardware/software developed apace, but the IBM organizational problems which many of the customers faced have been overcome, and Office Products and Data Processing are now welded into a single entity providing a good service.

I do not wish to give the impression that we are firmly welded to Wang or any other supplier. Our approach has been to use the IBM 'architecture' as a standard, but to purchase equipment and software from any plug-compatible supplier where we can obtain cost-effective services without posing problems of network compatibility. As a consequence, we have Amdahl mainframes, Wang WP/VS computers, Documentation line printers, Harris VDUs and remote printers, Memorex and IBM disc storage, IBM 3680 point-of-sale retail equipment, etc, and a host of plug-compatible software.

The essence of our approach is to have a firm technological philosophy on to which we can graft a variety of cost-effective services without being *indefinitely* tied to a single supplier.

The current network

Figure 21.6 illustrates the central facility of Wang computers as it was in April 1982. A network of sixty-four work-stations is now connected to two Wang VS computers, a 0·5 Mb VS80 and a 2 MB VS100 respectively. In addition, Wang OIS units are used at two district locations and Wangwriters are located in small offices at a number of locations in the Region.

The Wang computers used at Regional headquarters have Cobol, Basic, Assembler and Procedure compilers. They provide a combination of both word and data processing together with the Wang electronic mail system 'Mailway'. The system is linked to the Amdahl computers which provide the major teleprocessing facilities for the Region. This provides access

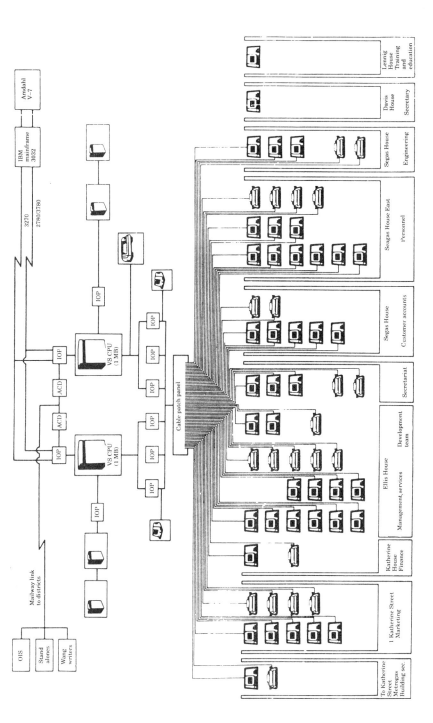

Figure 21.6 *Segas integrated information system, Wang computers regional headquarters*

from any of the Wang terminals connected to the VS machines in standard IBM emulations (3270, 2780 and 3780).

The central Wang facility at our headquarters currently provides 1200 megabytes of hard disk storage which is equivalent to storing 240,000 documents of A4 size. The remote Wang OIS units and a Wang VS80, which is installed in a district office, is connected via a dial-up service to the headquarters Wang installation.

At present there are approximately 1400 VDU 'terminals' of one form or another in use. There are 6000 office workers throughout the Region including managerial and professional staff. We have, therefore, close to one in four of Segas' office workers using a terminal. The majority of these terminals are connected to the network, and it is our firm intention to provide 'connectivity' for those which are currently stand-alone machines. The composition of the terminals used is:

(a) Data processing terminals: 1100 CICS Sytem.
(b) 'Scientific/Engineering' terminals: 150 VM/CMS System.
(c) Word processing terminals: 100 Wang.
(d) Personal computers: 80 Apple II and IBM PCs.

Our objective is to be able to 'network' a range of services so that each level of the organization can obtain access to services which will reduce costs and improve operational effectivenes. It is, therefore, important that we ensure that methods are available for connecting each element of the service to the various work-stations requiring them. We need, as a consequence, to be able to connect the 'scientific', data processing, word processing, personal computers, image input/output devices, printers and storage devices in a harmonious manner. This is achieved by ensuring that any equipment used must have the capability of connecting via IBM network principles.

At present, Apple II micro-computers are connected in a number of instances to the network via protocol converters enabling them to operate as if they were IBM 3270 VDUs. The Wang facilities are integrated via the central VS installation as part of the data network.

Connection, via Amdahl developed software, between the data processing (CICS) network and the scientific/engineering interactive network (VM/CMS) has been achieved. At the same time, the 150 terminals on the scientific network can gain access to the data processing network via standard IBM software.

Most current data/word processing networks used by companies are predominently operated by clerical and typing staff. Relatively few professional/managerial staff have ready access to terminals dedicated to them and the management information available is generally derived as batch reports. This is certainly true of the Segas operation. The current network handles the basic 'transactions' of the Region's day-to-day operations. It does not, at present, give truly adequate support to professional/managerial staff except in a few specific and isolated areas.

This situation also applies to the vast majority of computer-based systems used throughout the world with the exception of a relatively small number of specifically designed systems. It has arisen because of the clearly defined cost effectiveness of applying computer technology to deal with mundane, repetitive tasks such as those which constitute the basic transactions of most organizations.

Recent technological advances in software development, network concepts and hardware are now opening new horizons for the application of Information Technology to serve middle and senior management in many organizations. Examples are the application of Prestel and other View-data systems, the use of digital voice exchange facilities, electronic mail and message handling, facsimile transmission and other techniques of this type.

It is interesting to note that the major demand for personal computers in most organizations including Segas, is not for routine use by clerical staff, but as a personal aid to professional/managerial staff. Relatively few of the people using personal computers actually develop into proficient programmers, but more often use pre-packaged software such as Visicalc and Visiplot-Trend. This suggests that given the right facilities, many managers might adapt to the use of computer facilities. The key issue is to ensure that the *right* facilities are provided within the framework of a systematic philosophy which can maximize the benefits of the technology for the overall organization.

What then, are the facilities required to support professional/ managerial staff in order to increase their effectiveness?

It has become clear as we have developed our current systems that at the transaction-handling level, the vast majority of terminals will be 'single function'. By that I mean that unless the job content of a Customer Service Assistant is changed, the terminal used will for greater than 90 per cent of the time be attached to the CRESSY system (a major on-line customer service system used in Segas), or a closely related system. It will not need to be a typing station or have access to planning models or computer graphics. It may, however, need to provide some general utilities for local administration.

Equally, a word processing work-station in one of our district offices may occasionally need to be linked to a network for two reasons:

(*a*) To despatch or receive mail
(*b*) To access data resident on the mainframes or somewhere else in the network.

In providing the facilities to date we have allowed for this to be developed over the next five years.

Considering the facilities that would need to be provided for professional/managerial staff, two factors need to be addressed:

(a) What type of facilities (Hardware/Software) would best serve the various levels of management, recognizing that the job functions are less repetitive and more creative?

(b) To be able to identify productivity improvements and quantitative benefits which will assist both the design of the system and give a firm basis for justification in future years.

Some consideration has already been given to the types of facility which will be required and which we would intend to tailor in any 'management network' that we would provide.

Does it pay?

Some basic financial performance statistics will illustrate the pay-back we have achieved in Segas. It was clear at the outset (1975–6) that major investments would have to be made in terms of both capital and development manpower to achieve the required objectives of the Region. The intention of building large integrated systems to cover the major transactional operations also had implications in terms of development lead and equally important in terms of implementation timescales.

Large systems such as the Segas on-line customer service system required more than 100 man years of development effort, and required more than 800 staff to be trained in twenty-two districts. The implementation from pilot stage took between two and three years. The system also required about one year to become a 'settled-in' aspect of office operations.

It was, therefore, inherent in the approach taken that major investments would be made over a period without immediate or short term pay-back. The systematic foundations laid, however, were seen as providing the means for more rapid development later with faster pay-backs.

It is required that all systems developed are assessed at an early stage to determine the costs and benefits associated with the expenditure. Projects are expected to achieve a New Present Value at 10 per cent over five years as a general investment criterion.

Figures 21.7, 21.8 and 21.9 illustrate the growth in systems between 1975, 1982 and the forecast for 1985.

At the end of 1982, approximately 80 per cent of the basic data used by the Region was handled by computer and by 1985, approximately 95 per cent will be computerized.

The profile of total expenditure and benefits are illustrated in Figure 21.10, expressed in terms of September 1982 prices for the period 1976

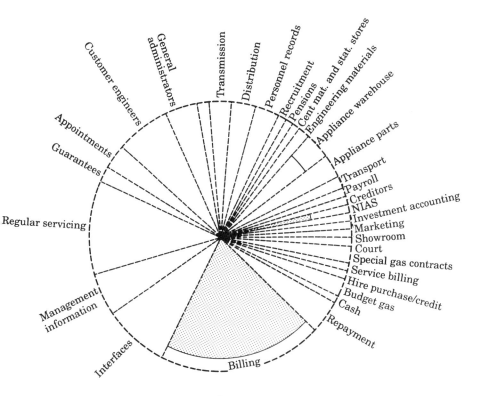

Figure 21.7 *South Eastern 1975*

through to 1988. Although the benefits appear to flatten out beyond 1985, this is purely illusory. Had snapshots been taken in 1979 and 1981 they would have shown a similar fall-off after three years (i.e. 1982 and 1984). This is simply due to the perceived time-horizon of current systems development.

Of far greater importance are the actual benefits achieved today as a consequence of past developments. Equally important is whether these benefits match the forecast benefits at the stage where major resources are committed. In general, projects have yielded either in line with or better than the forecast at the outset.

Rigorous post-investment appraisal is applied to all projects to date, no projects have shown a net present cost against a forecast net present value.

The Region employs a £9m capital investment, taking into account depreciation of computer capital in terms of linear depreciation over five years. To review the overall performance in financial terms it is, there-

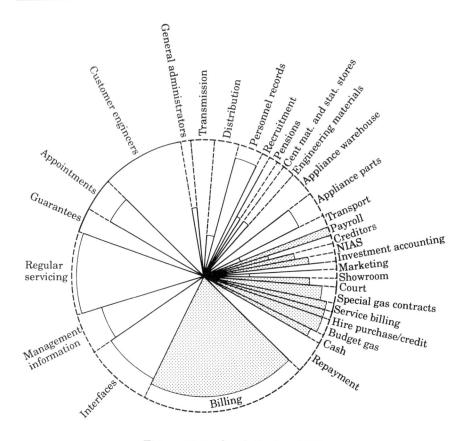

Figure 21.8   *South Eastern 1982*

fore, worth noting the following:

Capital employed	£9m
Annual Capital Expenditure	approx. £2m per annum
Investment in systems (cost)	£11m
Investment in systems (manpower)	700 man years
Annual Revenue Expenditure (1982/1983)	£6.2m

The tangible benefits of introducing Information Technology in Segas to date derive from three basic areas:

(*a*) Avoiding recruiting extra people to deal with additional workload.

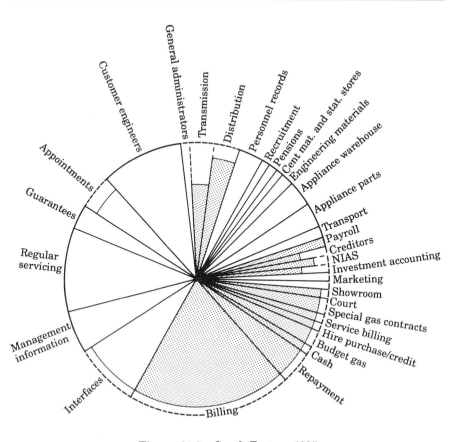

Figure 21.9 *South Eastern 1985*

(b) Decreasing the staff employed to handle the current workload.
(c) Improving the cash flow to the Region (i.e. by reducing bad debt, incurring less interest charges, speeding cash handling etc).

As a general measure (a) and (b) consitute 67 per cent of the benefits achieved to date and (c) constitutes the remainder.

During 1982–3, the benefits of systems installed moved into profit, writing-off capital expenditure in the year in which it occurred. The profile of *net* benefits are successively £2·58m, £5·06m and £7·7m for the period 1982–3 through to 1984–5. The average capital employed will remain at about £9m, allowing for depreciation.

The successive returns on capital employed are, therefore:

1982–3	28%
1983–4	56%
1984–5	86%

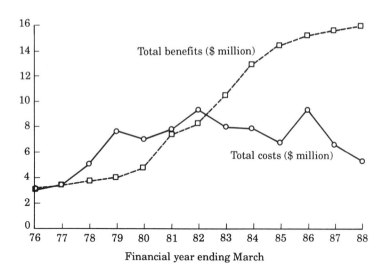

Figure 21.10   *Annual costs and benefits at September 1982 prices*

In physical terms, the contribution of Information Technology at the transaction level of the organization is clearly demonstrable. The profit per computing employees used in Segas during 1982–3 was £9000 profit per employee.

The overall aggregated return expressed in terms of conventional discounted cash-flow, taking into account capital and revenue expendi-

Table 21.1   *Revenue Costs (1982–3)*

	£m	£m
Staff related costs		
Development	1·2 (20%)	
Operations and others	1·6 (25%)	
Total staff costs		2·8 (45%)
Hardware (Rentals)		2·9 (46%)
Stationery and other costs		0·5 (9%)
Total revenue costs		6·2 (100%)

tures over the period 1975–6, 1986–7 yields a Net Present Value of £13·5m at 10 per cent.

The distribution of Revenue Costs are detailed in Table 21.1.

As a general index of computing expenditure, regional and industry expenditure is compared with published data for large organizations in the USA. Segas, typical of other Regions, spends 1·4 per cent of turnover on computing. A survey of large US companies in 1982 showed an average of 1·3 per cent of turnover spent on computing.

It can, therefore, be concluded that by current standards, Segas spends about the same as major US companies as a fraction of turnover. It can also be said that developments to date have been highly profitable, giving a good contribution on capital and computing staff employed.

In terms of long-run returns on investment, the developments to date and those proposed also yield a good return by any reasonable standards.

How does IT differ from DP?

The general development of Information Technology stems from the introduction of microchip technology, which has led to the convergence in recent years of what had previously been distinctly separate technologies, namely computing, telecommunications and office machinery. This overall convergence has led to a new field requiring new technical skills, strategic tools and implementation techniques.

There are a number of significant factors which have to be taken into account when considering the wider field of Information Technology when compared with traditional Data Processing.

There are a number of similarities, namely:

(a) Both approaches require a 'systems approach' in terms of identifying the overall strategic direction, the detailed structural requirements, etc.

(b) Both IT and DP require, ideally, systematic justification in terms of costs and benefits against agreed investment criteria pertinent to your organization.

(c) Both systems have a blend of technologies: in both cases the microchip plays a major role, and presents, therefore, many similarities in terms of design, application and implementation skills.

(d) Project management is a key issue in both areas, since in each case discrete projects, with programmed phasings, can be identified. The management of IT developments requires very similar project management techniques throughout the entire process of design, development and implementation to conventional data processing.

There are also major differences in implementing IT when compared with conventional DP:

(a) Data processing is very structured in its approach and lends itself, therefore, to strategic planning techniques such as Business Systems Planning. IT, on the other hand, incorporates speech storage/transmission, text and image handling facilities etc. It is, therefore, much less structured, and conventional strategic planning methodologies used for DP that do not work well in this field.

In general, many of the planning methods used are 'bottom-up' approaches based on detailed measurement of current operations, and provide estimates of time saving per category of office worker. The broad application of IT can, however, radically change the whole work process and influence organization structure. New methodologies need, therefore, to be introduced which involve a combination of strategic objective setting, analysis of organizational development with and without IT, and a quantitative evaluation of the forecast benefits. A number of companies, including Segas, are involved in developing such concepts.

(b) There is a very strong 'behavioural' element involved in IT. Wang have recognized this factor as being extremely important and refer to it as one of the basic six technologies involved. Because IT tends to be all-pervasive, it influences many of the normal tasks of the office. The way in which people work is, therefore, very important. Experience to date shows that greater attention has to be paid to the design, user friendliness and implementation tactics used in IT projects than in DP.

(c) In general, the acceptability of and the impact on the business of DP systems are relatively easy to predict. This is not always true for IT. It is difficult to forecast, for example, the extent to which an administration system providing diary management, electronic mail and other facilities will be readily accepted by the organization and the estimated benefits achieved.

(d) IT tends to use facilities developed as packaged software and hardware to a greater degree than in conventional DP projects, where major software development programmes have to be undertaken. In addition, a variety of external services, such as Viewdata or Prestel, may play a significant part in these developments. This has the advantage of more rapid implementation that in conventional DP, but there is also less capability to tailor the facilities in many instances to the organization.

(e) Techniques have been evolved for the measurement of the use of time by various categories of staff. However, it is much more difficult to produce traditional cost justifications for IT, since, in many instances, justifications are made in terms of time saving for professional and managerial staff. Unless these savings result in additional business or major staff reductions as a result of reorganization, the benefits are difficult to represent in traditional accounting terms.

(*f*) In Segas we have carried out a number of trials involving diary records held on the computer and the use of electronic mail and messaging systems. Two lessons were learned in the process:

   (*i*) It is necessary to connect natural 'peer groups', that is to say groups of people who communicate regularly between each other. These groups have to agree between them that certain essential information will be communicated only via electronic mail on a regular basis. The scope of coverage has then to be gradually increased as the trial progresses.

   (*ii*) A large enough group of people need to be involved to maintain a momentum for the trial. In the case of Segas, we have found that a group of six to eight individuals was too small, and we believe that for an organization such as ours about thirty to forty people need to be connected on the network and need to have clearly set objectives throughout the project. This concept can be referred to as having a critical mass for successful implementation.

(*g*) As a general rule, data processing systems serve the basic clerical operations of an organization and are designed to cope with repetitive tasks. Whilst there is some degree of inter-action between the operator and the system, the degree of inter-activity in IT systems tends to be higher, and the sysems may be more flexible and responsive to the user. Utilities, such as Visicalc, is a good example where the individual creates a working system, either as simple or as complex as his or her work requires. In effect, there is a greater degree of personal inter-action between the user and the system.

(*h*) IT projects tend to be introduced not only to serve typing and clerical staff, but also professional and managerial workers. The projects, therefore, tend to be more visible in the organization than traditional DP systems. It is, therefore, easier for a sceptic, particularly if he or she is a senior member of the organization to be able to capitalize on any shortcomings experienced. Care has to be taken, therefore, in the selection of the managers and staff involved to maximize the prospect of success.

There have been one or two notable cases where organizations have attempted to introduce IT too quickly into the higher echelons of the organization without careful prototyping and previous pilot trials to guide them. In general, such approaches are more likely to lead to failure than to success.

(*i*)   Many of the devices used in IT are simpler and easier to use than
        the VDU. This, in some cases, makes training and implementation
        easier and faster. However, at present there are relatively few
        substitutes for the screen and Qwerty keyboard we all know, fear
        and hate. Many managers express the view that they will be
        unlikely to operate a conventional keyboard. This may well be true
        for some of us of the older generation, but more and more school
        children and university entrants are having to come to terms with
        modern technology of this type, and it will not always remain so.

Key factors for success

The rapid introduction of extensive computer facilities throughout Segas
has posed a number of challenges in the management of the change
process. A number of factors can be identified which have assisted in this
process:

Top level support
Throughout the seven-year period there has been a steady commitment
from the Chairman and the Regional Management Committee to the
philosophy of reducing costs by the use of advanced technology. Had
there not been this commitment much of the work attempted would have
been fruitless. Each member of the Regional Management Committee has
had an important role to play in the many aspects of successfully
introducing Information Technology to the degree achieved today.

A clear and consistent strategy
The stage-by-stage development of the system and the use of Business
Systems Planning techniques has considerably assisted everyone involved in the process including trade unions and staff in having a clear
understanding of the direction the Region is moving in. Regular reviews
by the Business Systems and Regional Management Committees ensures
that the direction is maintained and priorities are clearly established at
every phase.

Education
A consistent and high level of effort has been put into educating management, staff and trade union representatives throughout the entire programme to date. Typically five courses each year are held for middle
management on the principles of managing with computers and approximately 300 managers have already been trained in this way. Regular
presentations and seminars are laid on for the Regional Management
Committee on major strategic issues, such as Database, new technological developments and new announcements from relevant manufacturers.
    Information Technology has been a central focus at the various Par-

ticipation Conferences held throughout the Region over the past three years. Occasional presentations on topics of particular interest are also relayed to staff via the internal communications facilities using video.

In 1980 a two-week technology fair was held at Regional headquarters and approximately 3500 staff from all parts of the Region had the opportunity of seeing the full spectrum of information technology in use throughout the Region.

A regular educational programme was established for members of the Regional Councils including visits to IBM to demonstrate the use of the technology we are currently implementing.

This whole programme has been extremely beneficial in changing the culture of the organization and focusing attention on a major change process, which has been in progress over the last seven years.

Good development teams
It has been essential to recruit and maintain teams of high calibre specialists within Management Services. This has sometimes proven difficult, when salaries in the private sector have been able to move more rapidly than in the gas industry and at a time when there has been a high demand throughout the country for good quality specialists of this kind. We have, however, been particularly lucky in recruiting key specialist managers, having high reputations in their respective disciplines and these, in turn, have been able to recruit and hold strong teams around them.

As can be expected in a function such as Management Services the majority of the work is project orientated, and of a highly specialized nature. The major resource employed is skilled manpower. To achieve the best results these teams need to be well motivated and this is generally achieved by a relatively informal style of management throughout the department and by allowing teams a high degree of freedom in their approach to work providing that the Region's standards for developments are maintained and the principles of project control are adhered to.

Organization for Information Technology
Some companies have different parts of the organization with responsibility for the various elements of what is becoming an integrated system for information handling. Large-scale computing applications may be the responsibility of the Finance Directorate, office services may be the responsibility of the Company Secretary or Administration Directorate, telephone services may be fragmented and Organization and Methods may be part of a small specialist Management Services Department.

As a consequence of such fragmentation each component service may pursue separate 'strategies' without necessarily interfacing effectively. Where this happens, the wider issues of 'Information Processing' will be lost and the office automation concepts which will require five to ten years to optimize will not be achievable without radical and expensive changes of direction.

It is important in every organization moving towards office automation to have one person (whom I normally designate the Information Strategist) to establish an overall approach to this complex task. An alternative is to have a liaison committee of the various interests reponsible to one person able to make the necessary decisions and resolve areas of contention.

In Segas the introduction of word processing has been handled by a joint team comprising Productivity and Computer Services with a Project Controller responsible to the two managers of these disciplines. This has ensured that a balance of experience from O & M and DP is brought to bear so that office practice and network considerations are balanced.

The role of the Business Systems Committee also assists in ensuring that telecommunications issues are taken into account in the wider considerations of an IT strategy.

Industrial relations

Good industrial relations are of paramount importance if large-scale Information Technology changes are to be introduced. This has been achieved in Segas where shop floor participation has been operating for approximately five years. The discussion of IT issues with staff and trade unions plays a very important role in gaining acceptance of the objectives and achieving a smooth introduction of the technology.

Human factors

Above all it has to be borne in mind by all concerned with managing the change process that the most valuable resources we use in the organization are the people who will use the technology. If we lose sight of this fact and design systems which are cumbersome or de-humanize the job involved, the technology will rapidly be rejected. Careful attention needs to be paid to the requirements of the job and equipment/systems carefully tailored.

A typical example of this was the design of the system to handle cashiering in showrooms using the IBM 3680 retail equipment. The first system introduced was slower than conventional equipment and produced some problems in follow-up by Customer Accounts Department after transactions had been posted. By careful re-design, the system halved the time for a cashier in a showroom to receive a payment and issue a receipt and made much less work for Customer Accounting. Attention had to be paid to the views of the operators to ensure that the system was successful.

These then are some of the factors which materially assist the successful implementation of large scale Information Technology.

Part Five

Responding to deregulation and privatization

Part Five   Responding to deregulation and privatization

In the 1960s and early 1970s government policies in Western Europe and the USA were frequently antagonistic to business, with an emphasis on social policies and business regulation. When Ronald Reagan became President of the USA he summed up the situation in the phrase: 'Government is not the solution, it is the problem'.

Since then there has been 'less government' in both the US and Europe. In Britain, the Government's insistence on privatization, the commercialization of services in the public sector (e.g. through sub-contracting and competitive tender) and the creation of a 'property-owning, shareholding democracy' has provided many new opportunities for business, particularly in the service sector. Industries such as management services and consultancy, catering, waste management, telecommunications, road transport and private health have all benefitted from this policy. The slimming down of companies has also led to a demand for outside services as headquarters and overhead functions been cut back or eliminated.

This section starts with a case showing how a strategic opportunity was exploited by a new telecommunications company, GTE Sprint Communications, as American Telephone and Telegraph (ATT) was deregulated in the USA. This is followed by two further cases featuring the Trustee Savings Bank and the National Freight Consortium both of which have been 'privatized', the former as a share issue, the latter as an employee buy-out in which 80% of the employees own shares.

22 Competing with AT & T

Kathleen Reichert Smith, Vice President, GTE Sprint Communications Corporation

The dramatic structural changes occurring within the telecommunications industry have been widely publicized. It is exciting to watch the metamorphosis of an entire industry; and it is intensely challenging, demanding and occasionally disconcerting to be a *participant* in such a process.

Telecommunications restructuring is a story of evolution and continuing development. Various major forces have created trends; several key events have caused discontinuities. All have contributed to the restructuring and unfolding competitive environment that is still (1985) in the midst of significant change.

It is hard to think of another contemporary industry or market which has evolved so quickly from a classic monopoly structure, through an environment of emerging competition and regulatory protection, to a position now moving toward *de-regulation* and free-market competition.

Changes in the voice telecommunications industry

What caused the emergence of competition, which, in turn, drove the restructuring of the industry? The development of competition was primarily the result of three major forces:

1 regulatory changes,
2 technology, and
3 the marketplace.

The strategic responses and planning systems of companies like GTE Sprint have developed around the opportunities and constraints resulting from each of these forces. To effectively analyse a competitor's strategic position, one must be able to evaluate its capability to exploit the advantages and to avoid the pitfalls presented by these three industry forces.

Regulatory changes have been the most visible, and perhaps the predominant force in the restructuring of voice telecommunications, regulation focuses on the Federal Communications Commission (FCC), which was established as a separate government agency by the Communications Act of 1934, to act as a surrogate for competition and to represent the 'public interest'. Simultaneously, the Bell System had the responsibility and privilege of being the sole provider of long-distance voice telecommunications. This charter continued Bell's monopoly status until the landmark FCC policy changes of the late 1960s and early 1970s.

A critical, 1974 FCC decision granted permission for companies, such as MCI and GTE Sprint (then known as Southern Pacific Communications Company), to begin selling private line services in competiton with Bell. Thus, the door had been slightly opened to competition. The second, and even more significant decision occurred in 1978, when the new 'alternative carriers' were allowed to enter the much larger and more lucrative *switched voice services market*. This multi-billion dollar market offered the opportunity for the new long-distance carriers to thrive.

It is important to recognize that one of the strategic assumptions made by new competitors was that regulators would recognize the constraints placed on the 'alternative carriers' during the early battle with the 'goliath' Bell System. Indeed, the FCC has retained the role as primary decision-maker on issues of critical importance to the industry. Likewise, their initial decisions providing cost protection to 'young' competitors while holding up the price umbrella of the traditional Bell System services has allowed some flexibility for the new competitors.

Technology is the second major factor which triggered development of competition in the telecommunications industry. The two technological forces at work were:

(a) the convergence of data processing and telecommunications technologies, and
(b) the advances in current technologies, such as microwave radio and satellite.

The convergence of data processing and telecommunications technology blurred the lines which had previously allowed the industry to be divided into either monopolistic voice services or competitive data services. Also, 'basic' voice services were considered to be rate-regulated, monopoly areas, while 'enhanced' voice services were considered to be competitive. As technologies of switching and data processing merged, they acted as major motivating factors in the 'divestiture'. Essentially, the Bell System divested its operating companies and terminated its local/long-distance telecommunications monopoly in exchange for permission to enter data processing markets; along with this, they presumably took a calculated risk that eventual regulatory changes would allow them to compete freely in the long-distance voice arena.

Advances in telecommunications technology have contributed significantly to long-distance voice competition. Historically, coaxial cable was generally believed to be an essential backbone component of any reliable, nationwide network. SPRINT's (and MCI's) initial nationwide networks, *solely* dependent on analogue microwave radio, proved that there was a viable alternative network technology available. More recently, companies have used satellite as the sole technology to create acceptable quality networks. A gradual dispelling of the assumption that coaxial cable was a necessary network component, and the development of alternative technologies, provided a basis for market entry.

The third major force which contributed to the development of competition occurred in *the market itself*. It is obvious from the success of the alternative carriers that there existed a latent demand for 'discount-priced' long-distance services. Initially, the discount price was a function of lower quality, due to the inferior type of inter-connection which the local telephone companies provided to the new, alternative carriers. However, the response to 'discount services' is evidence of the potential for a second-tier market in long-distance.

The new competitors had a strategic opportunity to meet and stimulate this demand because they initially had a cost advantage over Bell relative to local inter-connection. The industry cost/price structure which had developed over decades of regulation allowed the alternative carriers to underprice Bell and still achieve the financial performance necessary to attract growth capital.

A historical look at SPRINT

GTE Sprint has evolved along with the long-distance voice telecommunications industry. The company's strategic position has developed, over a compressed period of time, from that of an entrepreneurial start-up company to that of a major billion-dollar corporation.

The company's initial strategic response to the restructuring environment was to *seize* a potential *opportunity*. Presented with a highly uncertain but potentially profitable business in telecommunications, members of the Southern Pacific Railroad Company began to offer the excess capacity along Southern Pacific's rights-of-way through the southwest. Southern Pacific Communications Company (SPCC) was created as a subsidiary organization, separate from the railroad, to exploit this opportunity. This name remained with the company until its acquisition in 1983 by GTE Corporation, at which time it became GTE Sprint. The initial intention was to sell a private-line service (a distance-sensitive, leased circuit service to business customers on a regional basis). During this start-up period the uncertainties surrounding regulatory policy, consumer demand, and Bell System co-operation threatened the new company's very existence.

The company's initial development was characterized externally by its concern for achieving regulatory approval in order to offer a service alternative to Bell, and internally by its focus on building a nationwide network. With favourable regulatory support, in 1976, after the purchase of several regional microwave companies, GTE Sprint became the first 'alternative carrier' with a nationwide network – and an even more inter-growth period ensued.

As the network was becoming established management began to focus their attention on the marketplace. With the opening of competition in the switched services market by the FCC decision in 1978, SPRINT seized the opportunity to develop a range of services which could compete with Bell's MTS* and WATS† offerings, and the company growth substantially accelerated.

Initially, SPRINT focused its competitive effort on the business sector. The services developed were labelled 'SPRINT', and offered as economical alternatives to Bell; they were potentially appealing to any commercial user of long-distance services. In 1981, the company began marketing its switched service to residential users and the results were impressive. There was a dramatic increase in both revenues and numbers of customers.

The implicit mission of the company was to *attract customers away* from the Bell System by offering discounted long-distance service. MCI was the only other company offering a comparable range of services, but Bell remained the target of management's competitive and strategic action. This mission, later documented, remained the strategic directive of the company until the major event of divestiture changed the competitive environment, and thus required a new orientation.

The development of strategic planning

During the company's early, entrepreneurial stage, strategic planning did not exist on any formal or overt basis. GTE Sprint's initial development was primarily dependent on the vision and motivation of the company's first President, Mr Gus Grant.

Decision-making at this time was controlled by the President and his directives merely executed by subordinate managers. Direction could be altered instantaneously to take advantage of opportunities to purchase switching equipment, to offer services to a new customer, or to re-direct the company approach to the FCC on a key issue.

This approach worked for SPRINT during the time that issues facing the company were less complex, due to both the size of the organization and the straightforward nature of competitive actions. During this period, planning, as it existed, related almost entirely to budgeting. The horizon of outlook was typically one year, and most 'plans' were not documented.

As the company's position solidified and SPRINT moved into a period of high growth, planning began to emerge on a *technical* basis. Leading this phase of development was the Engineering Department whose responsibility, as the developers of the network, required the production of a five-year, documented, construction plan. As with many technology-based companies, the engineering function led the entire company, more as a result of their functional responsibility than by intent.

Planning was not integrated on a corporate basis and departmental planning was primarily short-range, informal and usually not documented. It met the management and functional needs of the company during this period of rapid growth because the programmes of departments other than Engineering followed the lead of the network-building effort. Very little effort was directed toward market estimating and forecasting or toward analysis of market needs and desires. It would take some time before the company could become a market-driven organization.

Although engineering plans were well developed at this point, external factors, such as regulatory and competitive threats or opportunities, which are a critical part of strategic planning, were not yet overtly addressed. Decisions which dealt with these issues were usually made on an *ad hoc* basis, through informal discussion between two or more senior managers.

Senior functional managers had gained substantial autonomy in making and implementing decisions. SPRINT's planning culture has been affected both positively and negatively by this condition. Flexibility, operational control, and rapid programme implementation were resulting benefits; but inter-departmental efforts were not always well coordinated. The existence of independent departmental control influenced the company's organizational structure, which is a classic, functional hierarchy. This functional alignment is substantially different from GTE Sprint's key competitor, MCI, which has organized itself along business lines.

By 1980, it was recognized that SPRINT was evolving into a major corporation, and that a leadership change was required to make this transition. When Southern Pacific hired Dale F. Pilz (previously President of Kaiser Steel) to lead the company, programmes were implemented to strengthen the internal structure and operation of the company. It was readily apparent to Mr Pilz that a more formal, structured planning effort was necessary.

A 'planning audit' was undertaken by me to determine what level of planning existed in the various departments, and to survey managers on their attitudes toward planning. This was done in order to evaluate reaction to a formal structure and to set the stage for its introduction. It was clear from the audit that some rudimentary systems were in place and should be incorporated into the development of any formal strategic planning effort. Also, there was a strong desire expressed by most senior managers for more clearly communicated and integrated plans. In reality, formal planning met with some resistance as senior managers became involved and recognized that they had to relinquish a certain level of autonomy. Mr Pilz initiated the first corporate-wide strategic planning process at GTE Sprint in 1981, in an effort to raise management to a level of sophistication necessary to handle the transition to 'corporate status'.

In its initial strategic planning, SPRINT used a system developed by SRI (Stanford Research Institute). This approach had major strengths in the areas of environmental assessment and creativity in developing alternative strategies. The emphasis on external assessment was expressed via 'scenario development' which addressed the wide range of uncontrollable factors. The focus on developing creative alternatives was particularly useful because the volatile long-distance environment required innovative approaches. The SRI methodology stimulated discussion and encouraged the development of a dynamic planning process.

One major outcome from the formation of a strategic planning function has been particularly beneficial. It was the development of a *mechanism* by which management could reach *consensus* on overall corporate *direction*: a means was provided for open discussion and the review of alternative views for the assessment of the environment, and for the resolution of conflicts. The first jointly agreed strategies provided for improved integration, and a sense of pride and direction for the company. This was critical to a company which was facing phenomenal growth and a volatile series of regulatory and competitive actions. Despite the improved interaction and exchange at the senior management level, there were some difficulties in 'translating' the corporate strategic decisions into actual programmes to be implemented at the department level. Likewise, strategic plans had yet to be linked to annual budgets.

A second area of accomplishment was in the development of the capability to focus on external issues: the uncontrollable factors which have tremendous impact on results. Open recognition of existing threats and opportunities was a critical development. Particularly important were the competitive analyses which influenced key decisions by senior management. The shift of top management focus to competitive issues resulted in a stronger team commitment. The team approach allowed senior managers the opportunity to make strategic choices, and at the same time lead their departments in implementing plans based on their functional needs and perspectives.

The SRI approach to strategic planning continued to be utilized through the first year-and-a-half of the corporate planning effort and it was instrumental in setting the stage and creating the discipline and exchange needed for an effective long-term corporate planning effort. It essentially concluded when SPRINT was purchased by GTE Corporation in the summer of 1983. Following the acquisition, SPRINT adopted the GTE approach to corporate planning. The GTE approach emphasizes competitive analysis, focuses on pragmatic issues and actions, and stresses strategic implementation.

The post-divestiture environment

Bell System's 'divestiture' was a catalyst of revolutionary proportions that has propelled the telecommunications industry into an almost totally new environment. The event of divestiture was somewhat anticipated; however, the speed and intensity of its impact on the already-evolving competitive structure was not expected. Prior to divestiture, competition developed along relatively predictable lines. The divestiture of the Bell System's operating telephone companies brought an abrupt change – a discontinuity – to the evolving industry structure. From the point of divestiture, the existing monopoly in local and long-distance service ended. A new set of 'rules' and interactions was set in motion: an entirely new industry orientation had begun and a new phase of competitive evolution began with it.

The new orientation in long-distance voice competition resulted from two major 'consequences' of divestiture. The first outcome was a basic change in the previously unfriendly relationship between alternative long-distance carriers and the local Bell operating companies. Prior to divestiture, a unique situation existed. The Bell operating companies were both the *sole source suppliers* of local inter-connection facilities to the long-distance carriers *and* their *chief competitors* as part of the Bell System. Divestiture *eliminated* this competitive posture through the disassociation of local operating companies from Bell.

Second, there was a jolting *realignment* of the industry *cost structure*. With the operating companies divested, the division of revenues/ settlements arrangement which had existed (and had become more complicated) for decades between local and long-distance services terminated. In order to continue to support or 'subsidize' low local rates, all long-distance carriers now had to pay access charges to local companies for inter-connection. The post-divestiture access charge plan requires equal payment by all carriers for equal quality inter-connection. Over time, the plan allows alternative carriers to phase in the premium quality of inter-connection, used by AT & T. Before divestiture, alternative carriers' costs of inter-connection were lower than Bell's (as was their *quality* of inter-connection) giving the new competitors a cost advantage and price differential. The FCC access charge decision results in a *common* cost structure for AT & T Communications (the new AT & T long-distance subsidiary, roughly equivalent to the earlier Bell System Long Lines division) and the new carriers over time. Thus, with the movement toward a common cost structure and extremely *unequal* market positions, a new dynamic is developing.

This dynamic reflects itself most significantly in pricing strategy since, prior to divestiture, *price* was the basis of competition. As costs converge, prices converge and the alternative long-distance carriers must determine a way to differentiate their services on attributes *other* than price. The 'discount' alternative to AT & T is being effectively eliminated.

It must be noted that, along with increased local access costs, are improvements in the type of inter-connection provided to alternative carriers by local companies. Because of this factor, not only are the costs and pricing of alternative carriers moving closer to those at AT & T, but the *services* themselves are moving toward *parity*.

These two key results of divestiture, a new and improved supplier relationship with the local operating companies and realignment of competitive cost structures, are the driving forces of the current phase of industry restructuring. To understand their impact and the new evolutionary phase, which began in early 1984, once again the same factors of regulation, technology and market place are the significant areas to trend and monitor the performance of various competitors.

The three major factors stated above are *all* undergoing profound change as a result of the AT & T divestiture of 1 January 1984. The changing position and policies of the FCC in dealing with regulation are of particular significance. Initially, the FCC acted to support the development of competition, but there has been a shift away from this posture. As the alternative long-distance carriers have grown, the FCC has begun to assume a new role as *manager of deregulation*, by stepping away from 'competitive support' and attempting to allow the market place to control the dynamics among competitors. This recent attitude has presented a tremendous challenge to 'alternative carriers' whose industry position is massively out of balance with AT & T Communications' *93 per cent market share*. The FCC appears to be encouraging a free-market, deregulated environment. This may be a desirable goal, but to competitors whose relative share is so small, there is still a need for some regulation and overseeing which will allow the market for alternative long-distance to mature, and thus create a more 'level playing field'.

In reviewing the latest trends in technology, it is important to recognize the potential benefits of new technologies in terms of their cost efficiency *and* their importance to the capability to offer enhanced services, not only in voice, but in messaging, teleconferencing, and so on. The effective use of technologies, such as fibre optics, combined with efficient technology mix, could give a competitor a major cost advantage.

The market place must also be reviewed from a perspective of reorient-ation. Buying patterns among businesses must change from a single vendor to multi-vendor environment. Their willingness and capability to deal with *choice* in long-distance communications is critical. Also, with-out the Bell System to depend on, businesses are likely to be required to increase their internal knowledge and resources to deal with the manage-ment of systems and costs. As a corollary to this, the carriers must prepare to deal more extensively with customer service issues in order to retain customers. The consumer or residential market is experiencing a similar reorientation. Substantial confusion exists regarding complex rates and 'choice' between long-distance carriers; it will take some time before the new competitive market becomes accepted by the average telephone user.

One of the most exciting market-related reorientation forces is pre-subscription, which requires all business and residential users to desig-nate a *primary* long-distance carrier. This event is so unique and new that there is no data or experience on which to make marketing decisions. Pre-subscription is tied to an 'equal access' (or improved inter-connection arrangement) schedule under surveillance of the FCC which will take approximately three years to 'roll-out' in all major areas of the US. As the FCC decision stands now, individuals or businesses not designating a primary carrier will automatically go to AT & T.

The post-divestiture strategy

GTE Sprint, already established as the third largest long-distance voice carrier, is well-placed to succeed in the new environment. The company historically responds well to a changing environment by recognizing issues and seizing opportunities. It is young enough to be flexible and progressive, and the strategic planning process set in place has become accepted. Continuity of capital investment, which had been difficult under Southern Pacific, has now improved after the GTE acquisition. Equally important is that GTE has allowed SPRINT latitude in establish-ing its own identity, direction and potential. The company is presently developing a comprehensive strategy to optimize its resources and strengths in the post-divestiture environment.

One of the major thrusts of this strategy is to enhance and develop the network, expanding capacity in both existing and new areas. Digital technologies are being rapidly installed in order to provide the highest quality possible, as well as to increase cost efficiencies and provide the capability to offer new services. By increasing its use of fibre optics, digital radio and satellite, the company plans to have a virtually *all digital network* within several years. Large, more sophisticated digital switches are currently being put into service at a rapid rate as part of this effort.

Another major thrust is to *gain market share* rapidly. Capital investment for 1984 was budgeted at $800m in order to expand capacity substantially. In addition, 'New SPRINT' was introduced in January: offering added value and such features as simplified rate schedules, no monthly service charges, volume discounts and 24-hour service to any location in the domestic United States including Hawaii, Alaska, Puerto Rico and the Virgin Islands. Like AT & T, a customer can call anywhere, anytime using SPRINT. A 24-hour customer service was recently introduced to answer questions or give assistance to customers placing calls on the GTE Sprint network.

An extensive programme is underway to take advantage of the pre-subscription opportunity. This effort extends over the three-year period of 'equal access' conversion required of the local Bell operating companies. GTE Sprint's management believes it can capitalize on pre-subscription to significantly increase market share.

Attention is being focused on creating a basis for competition on attributes other than price. Management is taking measures to differentiate its service from that of its competitors and to develop a brand identity in the minds of its present and potential customers.

In addition to its basic marketing and technology thrusts, GTE Sprint is continuing to plan for the future. New products, such as sophisticated messaging, data services, video conferencing and others are being considered and developed. The company will be expanding to serve international markets, beginning with a service to Canada, and possibly several other foreign countries by the year-end, as part of its developing effort to provide its customers an excellent alternative to AT & T.

New developments in planning

The management team recognizes that effective strategic planning plays a pivotal role in determining the future of the company, as it does with every major contender in the telcommunications industry. The emphasis on competitive analysis continues as a major focus, especially as GTE Sprint enters a more competitive and dynamic environment and issues of 'relative position' become more compelling. Strategic planning is evolving to meet the needs of management in assessing external factors and implementing tracking critical, strategic programmes.

The company is attempting, under the direction of GTE Corporate management, to further integrate strategic planning into the day-to-day management process. This new planning philosophy and process centres around senior management's identification of a small number of controllable factors which must be successfully managed in order to succeed.

This small set of 'Critical Success Factors', and their associated implementation programmes are closely tracked. This methodology avoids the problem of conventional strategic planning where one overall strategic document is produced on an annual basis, making it very difficult to use as an ongoing operational tool.

As part of this planning and management system, critical strategic assumptions are also briefly stated and constantly tracked for changes in the external environment which require strategy reassessment. This provides management with frequent looks at developing trends, and provides a particular benefit in industries like GTE Sprint's because the system corresponds to the highly volatile environment; surveillance is continuous rather than periodic, and frequently reported to management.

In summary, management recognizes the need for strategic planning to become an easily-used tool in the total management process rather than a separate function to be dealt with on a periodic basis. The company's planning is currently focused on the issues most important for competitive success. The emphasis is on less extensive documentation and more limited analysis responsive to the changing external conditions. The company is attempting to achieve a balance between formal documentation and effective communication and implementation by line management.

Conclusion

GTE Sprint has developed from a tiny company to a major force in long-distance telecommunications. During that evolution, which resulted from the opportunities available in a changing industry, GTE Sprint has adapted and evolved, improving its management and planning systems.

As the still new post-divestiture environment unfolds and new trends and developments become visible, GTE Sprint intends to be a significant part of the competitive inter-action. The timing of key events in deregulation and technological development will be critical, but equally critical is the company's ability to anticipate, plan and respond to this new phase of industry restructuring. The evolution of our planning and management systems will play a key role in support of the company's capability to seize opportunities and to succeed. We believe we have the right elements in place to carry GTE Sprint forward into the future.

23 The transformation of the Trustee Savings Banks

I. Marshall, TSB Group Central Executive, London, UK

The Trustee Savings Banks have their origins in the industrial revolution of the early nineteenth century. A certain Reverend Henry Duncan opened the first savings bank in Ruthwell, Dumfriesshire in 1810. His motives, like those who followed him were:

- to provide a haven for the savings of the poor;
- to encourage self-sufficiency by the promotion of thrift;
- to alleviate the hardship caused by seasonal employment and fluctuating commodity prices.

At the time there was no one else to look after the savings of the poor and so savings banks proved very popular and spread rapidly. By the middle of the nineteenth century the number of individual banks had risen to over 600. Over the years the banks tended to merge into larger units as their business grew in size and complexity. However, even in the early 1970s tiny banks still existed. In 1973 at the time of the *Page Report* there were still seventy-three banks with 1549 branch offices.

Throughout this 160-year period from 1810 to 1970 TSB remained dedicated to serving personal customers. The banks were essentially vehicles for personal savings. They boasted strong local identities and close links with the community. However, from the 1960s the traditional savings bank movement was beginning to change in response to changing customer needs. For example, in 1965 the savings banks for the first time introduced cheque accounts; and in 1967 the Group formed its own unit trust company.

However, TSB was still restricted in what services it could offer. The banks could not give loans to their customers and were restricted in the way funds could be invested. It was at this critical stage in 1973 that the Page Committee, set up by the Government to review the whole area of National Savings, reported its findings. In brief, the Committee recommended that TSB be freed from government control and allowed to develop its service range: to become a third force in banking.

The major strengths of the movement at the time of Page were:

- a large, loyal customer base;
- a national network throughout the UK;
- a dedicated staff;
- one of the most sophisticated banking computer systems in Europe.

The Group's principal weaknesses stemmed from previous government restrictions. In brief, these were:

- a restricted service range: TSB had a few basic money transmission and savings services and carried out no lending;
- a lack of any commercial business: TSB was solely dependent on the personal mass market;
- a network which was skewed towards the Midlands and North and had limited coverage in Southern England;
- a mismatched balance sheet with negligible reserves;
- a fragmented structure with seventy-three independent savings banks.

TSB in transition 1976–84

Following the publication of the *Page Report*, the banks took a major step in reducing their number from seventy-three to nineteen in the space of one year. This group of nineteen independent banks under a central co-ordinating authority, the TSB Central Board, formed the basic Group structure during the next eight years. Within the framework, TSB management undertook a series of fundamental changes. The aim was to move TSB from being a savings institution with few services and heavily dependent on the government to a leading financial services group which was both profitable and independent.

The Group's broad strategy in the years 1976–84 can be summarized under the following headings:

1 Service range;
2 Staff;
3 Retail network and technology;
4 Profitability and balance sheet management.

Service range
The area of development most visible to the public has been that of customer services. During the eight years up to 1985, TSB has moved from a group of savings banks offering one or two basic deposit services to a fully-fledged financial services group offering a wide range of personal

and commercial services. The principal developments can be summarized as follows:

Money transmission services The TSBs had traditionally catered for the customer who requested a simple interest-bearing deposit facility. Increasingly, those people needed to use money transmission services. The Group had introduced the cheque account in 1965 and at the beginning of 1976 there were approximately 750,000 cheque account holders. By the end of 1984 this figure had grown to over 3·5 million. The cheque account now forms the core account of TSB personal services.

Credit Services The TSBs introduced personal lending in 1977. The motives for doing this were to widen the service range to the customer, to increase income and to raise the percentage of variable rate assets. In November 1984 total personal lending of the TSB banks including mortgage lending approached £2bn.

TSB Trustcard TSB Trustcard was launched in 1978. The company is a member of the VISA organization. At the end of 1984 the company had over two million cards in issue, which represents approximately 14 per cent of the total credit card market. Trustcard has a key role both in the expansion of credit services and in its use as a payment card.

Insurance Services TSB Group's insurance services are operated through TSB Trust Company Limited. Its core business is unit-linked life assurance, which is sold through a sales force of around 300 employees. The company also sells general insurance and operates a number of highly successful TSB unit trusts (managed by Central Trustee Savings Bank Limited). TSB Trust Co Ltd is the seventh largest unit trust management group with a 4·5 per cent share of the total market; it is also the second largest bank unit trust management company (to Barclays' Unicorn). Insurance is an integral part of TSB's move to a broadly based financial services group.

Instalment Credit Instalment credit activities are carried out by United Dominions Trust. TSB acquired UDT in March 1981. The two principal objectives for acquisition were to assist in the diversification of TSB Group's balance sheet and to increase TSB's service range through UDT's involvement in instalment credit, personal loans by mail and leasing business.

Commercial Business TSB introduced commercial business in 1979. The Group's broad thrust will be primarily in the small- and medium-sized business area although Central Trustee Savings Bank, which is a recognized bank and has operated as the City banking arm of the TSB Group, has substantial large-scale lending on its books.

Staff
The Group has 25,000 employees. The rapid changes of the last seven years have put obvious demands on all levels of staff. A key element in

TSB's progress has been a high commitment to training. Alongside a series of regional training centres operating throughout the UK, TSB opened a new £3m training centre at Solihull in July 1983. The centre monitors training standards of the regional centres and offers advanced courses to senior executives throughout the Group. For some time the banks, and in particular the operating subsidiaries, have also recruited expertise from outside to deal with the rapid advance in specialist areas and new services. In addition, the Group has a planned management development programme which systematically identifies potential within existing staff and possible gaps.

Retail network and technology
TSB has 1620 branches. Since 1976 the figure has remained broadly constant with selective openings and closures. During the eight years management has carried out a major programme of refurbishments and automation. However, in the richest part of the country, Southern England, TSB still remains relatively weak and the Group's current plans aim to address this problem. On the subject of opening hours, TSB was the first bank to introduce seven-day opening through a branch in Edinburgh in 1984. The Group is also unique in planning to offer a full service all day on Saturday at selected branches.

Technology plays a central part in TSB's strategy. As already indicated, TSB has one of the most sophisticated banking computer systems in Europe. A new computer centre for TSB England and Wales is currently under construction and, with the existing centre at Wythenshawe, will provide the bank with a single integrated on-line real-time facility throughout its branch network. To meet customers' growing demand for self-service facilities, the Group is developing an extensive range of customer-operated terminals. In the longer term, the Group believes that there is likely to be increased sharing of delivery systems by financial institutions, with competition centred on service and price.

Profitability and balance sheet management
At the same time as developing its range of services, the Group has had to establish a profits record, build up its capital ratios and reorganize its balance sheet. Each of these areas can be summarized in turn:

Profits In the year to November 1984 the Group made an audited pre-tax operating profit of £157m, which represents a return on capital employed of over 23 per cent. In comparison with the domestic operations of the London clearers, TSB shows the expected pattern of a lower gross margin due to TSB's lower proportion of commercial and fee income. However, TSB has a correspondingly lower cost ratio. A comparison of TSB with the domestic operations of the London clearing banks for 1983 is set out in Table 23.1.

Table 23.1   *TSB margins 1983*

	London clearers (%)	TSB (%)
Net interest income	5·1	5·1
Other income	2·5	1·0
Total income	7·6	6·1
Costs	5·2	4·0
Bad debt provisions	1·1	0·4
Total costs	6·3	4·4
Profit	1·3	1·7

Items are expressed as percentage of assets employed.

Capital adequacy From a gearing ratio of below 2 per cent at the beginning of 1976 the TSB retail banks attained an aggregate gearing ratio of 5·5 per cent in November 1984. This compares favourably with other UK banks.

Balance sheet management In the mid-1970s the TSBs had a significant interest rate risk because the banks' balance sheet mismatch (i.e. an excess of fixed rate assets over fixed rate liabilities) approached 40 per cent. This exposure took the form of a vulnerability to rising interest rates since the fixed rate asset portfolio was slow to respond to the need to pay market rates on deposits. A major objective has been to reduce this mismatch by expanding the percentage of variable rate assets. This has been achieved by the Group's expansion into retail lending and by shortening the gilt portfolio. At November 1984 the balance sheet mismatch had been substantially reduced.

The TSB Group reconstruction

The previous section outlined changes that have occurred in the TSB Group during the period 1976–84. Today, in terms of numbers of customers, TSB is one of the largest financial services groups in the UK. From the simple savings bank of the mid-1970s, TSB has developed the framework of an emergent financial services group. It has done this at a time when boundaries between institutions in the financial markets are rapidly breaking down, a process which is expected to gather pace over the next ten years. TSB has therefore laid a sound foundation for its future development in the 1980s and 1990s.

Despite the massive changes summarized in the previous section. TSB had still one major problem to resolve: its organizational and legal structure. In December 1984 the Government published a White Paper together with an accompanying TSB Bill. The purpose of this legislation is to allow TSB to move from its present quasi-federal structure to that of a conventional commercial structure under the UK Companies Acts. This will give the Group a more effective operating structure and also establish its ownership and accountability, neither of which was clear under the former legislation.

Following completion of the legislative process there will be a top holding company, TSB Group Plc. Under the holding company there will be four banking companies, the TSBs of England and Wales, Scotland, Northern Ireland and Channel Islands. In addition, there will be other principal operating companies including TSB Trust Company, United Dominions Trust and TSB Trustcard. It is intended that TSB Group Plc will issue shares with priority to customers and staff and obtain a quote on the London Stock Exchange. A summary of the new structure is shown in Figure 23.1.

Although the reconstruction will not be complete until late 1985–early 1986, the broad operational framework has been in place for some time. The four TSBs in Scotland merged in May 1983 and the ten TSBs in England and Wales came together six months later in November 1983.

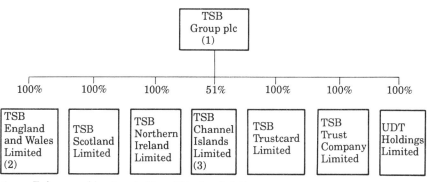

1   To be owned by shareholders following flotation.
2   To incorporate the operations of Trustee Savings Bank
    England and Wales and Central Trustee Savings Bank.
3   49 per cent to be owned locally in the Channel Islands
    (other subsidiaries will be wholly owned by TSB Group plc).

Figure 23.1   *TSB Group proposed structure. All limited companies are governed by the Companies Acts*

This brought the number of independent TSBs down from sixteen to four. By November 1985 the Group will have been operating in its proposed operational structure for two years.

TSB in the 1980s and 1990s

The previous three sections outlined the changes that have taken place to TSB's business and structure. As already stated, TSB's strategic aim is to establish itself as one of the major UK financial service groups. In looking at this final section, the following areas will be summarized:

1 TSB's approach to strategic planning:
2 Issues for the 1980s and 1990s.

TSB's approach to planning

Throughout the last ten years TSB management has continuously needed to look ahead to manage the shift from savings banks to financial services group. Planning in its widest sense has therefore received a high priority in the Group. In the period since the mid-1970s the precise conceptual framework has evolved to suit the style of senior management. However, the following underlying principles can be highlighted:

- The senior executives of the Group drive the planning process. It is the responsibility of the Chief Executives of each operating unit to prepare plans and obtain the approval of their Boards. To ensure co-ordination the Chief Executives meet both at full-day strategy 'workshops' and at regular operational meetings.
- Plans start from a segmentation of the market. In developing specific products the Group looks at a variety of segments based on combinations of age, demographic factors, sex and attitudes. However, in developing its strategic plan, the Group limits itself to around ten major strategic business segments which are made common across the Group.
- The plans are primarily geared to 'action steps' or operational plans. Operational plans are prepared to support targets in each of the strategic business segments.
- The operational plans are complemented by sophisticated manpower and financial models which allow a full range of 'scenario' planning.
- Throughout the planning cycle, the Group closely monitors the strengths, weaknesses and likely strategies of competitors and feeds this into the decision-making process.

To summarize, the plans are driven by senior management, based on a simple group-wide segmentation of the market and emphasize intended 'action steps'. The process is supported by modelling techniques and competitor and economic analysis. The approach to planning has taken a good eight years to evolve.

Issues for the 1980s and 1990s
In forming plans for the 1980s and 1990s key questions arise for TSB in common with other financial groups:

- What are the proper boundaries of an institution's business? In the financial revolution of the mid-1980s, organizations are rushing to create the 'international financial supermarket'. The lesson from industry is that companies should 'stick to their knitting' and beware of diversification. However, the problem for banks is that advances in technology have made it difficult for them to define their knitting. Are they 'high tech' retailers or conveyors of financial services?
- What do customers want from financial organizations? Advances in technology will allow new entrants into the financial services world. The winners will be those organizations which listen closely to the customer and deliver – at a profit – what he wants. Banks have not traditionally been good listeners!
- What will be the pace of technological change? The driving forces behind technology are the customer's desire for convenience and the costs of running a retail network. An organization needs to be in the forefront of technological developments and yet must not alienate customers by introducing untried systems which the customer is not sure he actually wants. We can all paint a picture of financial services in the year 2000 – the difficulty is to assess the pace of the change.
- Most important of all: How will the style of management adapt to the changing market place? As barriers between institutions become blurred the banker may need to become more innovative, more market-orientated, perhaps nearer to the retailer. This change in the style of an organization is easily said, but far from easily achieved. The winners in the year 2000 will possibly be those organizations which have affected the change.

24 The NFC buy-out: A new form of industrial enterprise

Sir Peter Thompson, Chairman, National Freight Consortium plc

When the employees of National Freight were offered the opportunity to acquire the ownership of their business, in February 1982, by buying shares, we had a vision for the future of the company. As I wrote in the Prospectus at that time, we believed, as we do today, that

by creating a company controlled and owned mainly by employees, we were launching a new kind of industrial enterprise. We believed that this would help to get rid of the conflicts between management and workers traditional to British industry: the 'us and them' attitude. In its place would be a new attitude of co-operation which should lead to improved efficiency, better prospects for employment and better profitability.

In working hard to put flesh on that vision, we also knew that commercial success was essential: not only to retain the confidence of our investors, most of whom worked in the business, but also to invest in the long-term future of the enterprise and, of course, to reward shareholders for their investment.

Our results for 1983–4, our third year of operation, demonstrate how successful we have been in building a strong, profitable and expanding business (Table 24.1). This success has been fuelled by record levels of investment in NFC, but the hidden 'plus factor' has undoubtedly been employee-ownership and, here again, we have worked hard to bring as many employees as possible into a share in the ownership: our most recent campaign, in March this year, resulting in a further 3000 members of our staff buying shares.

Employee-ownership and professional management have proved a very powerful combination, and there is no question in my mind that a company owned by a large part of its workforce has proved immensely

Table 24.1   *Dividends paid on NFC shares to date*

Date		Dividends paid (net) p	Amount of dividend per original £1 holding p
July 1982	Interim	4·5	4.5
Oct. 1982	Interim	4·5	4·5
March 1983	Final	3·0	3·0
March 1983	Interim	5·0	5·0
May 1983	Interim	5·0	5·0
Aug. 1983	Interim	2·5*	5·0
Nov. 1983	Interim	2·5*	5·0
March 1984	Final	2·0*	4·0
March 1984	Interim	3·0*	6·0
May 1984	Interim	1·5†	6·0
Aug. 1984	Interim	1·5†	6·0
Nov. 1984	Interim	2·8†	11·2
March 1985	Final	0·52‡	10·4
March 1985	Interim	0·56‡	11·2

* Dividend per share after scrip issue.
† Dividend per 50p share.
‡ Dividend per 10p share.

attractive to customers, not only as a concept but also for the expectation of better service from a highly motivated staff. While we are still seeing more buyers than sellers at each of the quarterly share-dealing days in our internal trading system, we are now having to look at the possibility of flotation on the Stock Exchange some time after February 1987; and, most particularly, at whether we can offer an attractive investment opportunity without losing the important advantages which we believe are inherent in our particular form of ownership and control. There is no guarantee that we will float, but I believe we have to offer the present shareholders a choice on which to vote at a future AGM.

Just what have we achieved, and how did we come to buy the business in the first place? Although the answers may not provide a blueprint for others, I think they have a great deal of significance for many parts of British industry, not least in the staff commitment which a real share in the ownership creates.

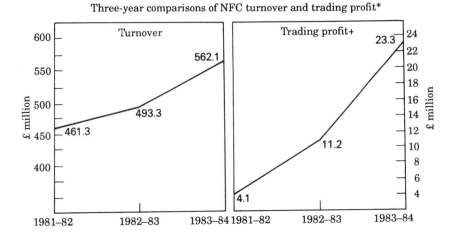

Three-year comparisons of NFC turnover and trading profit*

* 1981–82 and 1982–3 for 52 weeks 1983–84 for 53 weeks.
\+ Trading profit after deducting redundancy payments.
In 1983–4 costs of £1.3 m relating to properties held for disposal
were charged against profits on disposal of land and buildings.
In earlier years such costs were charged in arriving at trading profits

Figure 24.1 *How NFC turnover and trading profit have moved in the three years
since the buy-out*

The buy-out

When we bought NFC in 1982, 10,300 employees and pensioners bought
shares. Today we have around 16,500 such shareholders, almost all the
increase having come from more employees buying into the business.
NFC employees, pensioners and their immediate families hold 83 per cent
of the equity – the remaining 17 per cent being held by the syndicate of
banks which lent us money for the buy-out. Those who bought shares at
that first opportunity in 1982 have seen their holdings increase more than
twelve-fold in value, so even those who bought the minimum of a hundred
£1 shares have seen that investment grow to £1240. Meanwhile, dividends
have increased strongly year on year.

This increase in capital value (established quarterly by chartered
accountants Ernst and Whinney, in the absence of a Market quotation)
has been well ahead of the FT all-share index (see Table 24·1), so is the
growth in dividends. As indicated earlier, the improvement in financial
results, which have strongly affected the reward for investors, has come
increasingly from a considerable investment programme. For example, in
1983–4 we committed over £100m to the business – far more than ever
before. Much of this was to provide the property, vehicles and equipment

strong increase in profitability was accompanied by an improvement in the quality of profit (i.e. more from trading activities and much less from property disposals)

How the Consortium Performed

Profit and Loss Account for the year to 6 October 1984	1983–4 53 weeks £m	1982–3 52 weeks £m	% change
Turnover (sales of services or goods to customers)	562·1	493·3	+14
Less: Costs incurred (wages and salaries, hire of vehicles, fuel, licences, maintenance, depreciation, etc.)	536·5	477·0	+12
Trading profit	25·6	16·3	+57
Less: Redundancy	(2·3)	(5·1)	−55
Trading profit after redundancy	23·3	11·2	+108
Add: Profits on property disposals	4·7	11·6	−59
Operating profit	28·0	22·8	+23
Less:			
Interest on medium-term loan and overdrafts	(11·1)	(11·0)	
Overseas taxation	(0·3)	—	
Extraordinary items	(1·3)	(2·5)	
Minorities' share of profits	(0·5)	(0·1)	
Dividends, paid and proposed (including cost of Advanced Corporation Tax paid by the Consortium)	(4·3)	(2·6)	+65
Profit retained in the business	10·5	6·6	+59

to meet customer demand for dedicated distribution and other contract-backed activities. We plan to exceed this level of investment in the current year (1985) and have set ourselves a target of over £500m over the next five years to support the very strong growth (mainly at home but also overseas) which we are intent on achieving, not least as a basis for improved job opportunities, which we see as particularly important in an employee-owned business.

Last year for the first time we also covered all our outgoing from trading profit alone, having accepted from the time of the takeover that we would need to rely partly on property sales in the first couple of years. This situation has now changed, as the accompanying financial results table demonstrates (Table 24.2) not only have total profits increased very sharply but the quality of those profits has improved, with much the biggest contribution coming from our trading activities, despite heavy losses in one section of our business.

With the growth in revenue and profit we have not only been able to begin to invest in operations abroad as well as in the UK, but have had the confidence to create a challenging long-term strategy for the business, to which I return in greater detail later. First, let me remind you about our origins.

Where we came from

As Britain's largest transport, storage, distribution and travel business, NFC was shaped by a long-line of political decisions. The post-war Labour Government nationalized commercial long-distance road haulage; in 1953–6 a Conservative Government partially denationalized it, and Mrs Barbara Castle's 1968 Transport Act formed the remaining state road transport businesses into the National Freight Corporation, with the addition of the road haulage activities of British Rail, which became National Carriers.

The new Corporation operated from 1969 for ten years, initially with large revenue grants, then with chequered financial results: some small profits in one or two of the early years, heavy losses in 1975, and, after some structural and management changes in the following year, a slow growth to reasonable profitability at trading level.

When the Conservative Party came to power in 1979 the intention was to float us on the Stock Exchange and with this in mind the Corporation, whose assets were held mainly through forty subsidiary limited companies, was replaced by the newly created National Freight Company Limited, its equity share capital owned entirely by the Government. Plans for the flotation were upset by the economic recession and its effect on our profitability, and then crucially by British Rail shutting its collected and delivered parcels service for which our National Carriers provided vehicles and drivers (an almost immediate loss of over £20m in annual revenue).

The Government was therefore advised by its merchant bankers that a successful flotation could not be considered for some two years, which left it in a difficult position in view of its election manifesto. We sensed that they would seek some other way to sell the business and we feared, in particular, that it might be sold piecemeal or offered to a single purchaser who could well be more interested in stripping out the substantial property assets than in continuing to run a low-margin transport business.

There were still some 25,000 employees in the business (extensive redundancy made necessary by the bad trading conditions of 1980–1 had reduced the workforce from over 30,000) and we were concerned about their future as well as the possible effects on the business of the arrival of an asset stripper. It was at this point that a group of us senior managers began to consider whether we might mount a bid to acquire the company. Preliminary discussions with merchant banks made it clear that unless the management was prepared to accept a position where the bid was, in practice, an institutional one with the management simply providing a small percentage on top, two things would have to happen: first, the scope would have to be widened to include the entire workforce (to obtain not only sufficient finance for success but also to obtain commitment to the change of ownership); and, secondly, institutions would need to be persuaded to lend the majority of the purchase price without acquiring a majority of the equity capital.

The resolution of these two problems was to occupy the small group of senior managers concerned for over nine months but the principles which were established very early on, and which were subsequently published unchanged in the Prospectus, were:

- The business must be controlled by employee-investors.
- All employees, not just management, must have an equal right to invest.
- Investors should receive dividends in proportion to their investment.
- The business must be professionally managed with a board of directors responsible to the shareholders.

These were the main principles which distinguished our concept from a management buy-out on the one hand and a co-operative on the other. We had quickly come to see the possibility of creating a new type of industrial enterprise.

The ownership of shares in a business does not usually imply that the shareholder has any direct involvement in the running of the business: though there have been many creditable attempts over the years to involve employees more, especially through the issue of shares as an annual bonus or as part of a company saving scheme.

I see ownership in terms of the positive ownership of a piece of the company which varies in value as the health of the company fluctuates. For me it is important, indeed crucial, to see ownership of part of the business operating as a direct factor in the control of the business.

Government, bank and management reactions

In NFC we had long-established staff consultation procedures at all levels of the business, and equally well-established (and rare in the public sector), we had devolved decision-making. The management of its activities was through subsidiary operating companies, and profit centres at almost all the hundreds of branches, and this had important implications for the success of our particular kind of privatization. We had the first practical evidence of this when we brought together our top 130 managers in 1981 to put before them, in great confidence, our proposals to buy the business from the Government. A little while previously we had opened confidential discussions with Barclays Merchant Bank, who proved keen to help us, and in May, after some stringent financial and management exercises, we had put an outline of our plans to Transport Secretary Norman Fowler. He was delighted with what we suggested and gave the senior management group conditional approval to see whether we could sell the idea to the employees and make it work. At the same time he put his own legal and financial advisers to work on evaluating our proposals.

We had, of course, had to keep the NFC's Board informed of our proposals as they developed and, while the Board throughout maintained the correct stance of a body which had a legal obligation to safeguard the public interest in a state undertaking, it formally recognized our plans as perhaps the best for the future of the business and carefully 'held the ring' on behalf of the shareholder, the Government.

At the highly confidential meeting of our 130 most senior managers from headquarters and operating subsidiaries throughout the NFC, the reception (after the initial startled silence) was enthusiastic. Each participant was asked to fill in, anonymously, a questionnaire which simply asked three questions:

1   Will you be prepared to support the concept financially yourself?
2   How much, approximately, do you think you will be investing?
3   Are you prepared to endorse the concept and encourage your own people to take part?

Over 95 per cent said 'yes' to questions 1 and 3 and the answers to question 2 indicated that we should be able to raise the minimum equity which we had provisionally set at £5m. The amount from this group alone was likely to be well over £1m.

Armed with this reaction we were able to go back to the Secretary of State and make a firm offer, subject to the settlement of price and other conditions. So far as the government was concerned, they were sympathetic from the start about what we wanted to do, and we now had the banks behind us as well, subject to an enormous amount of detailed work in preparing the loan agreements and other complicated documents, and, not least, in arranging security for the medium-term loan which would provide the bulk of the purchase price. To give an example of the amount of paperwork and discussion involved, Barclays' original acceptance letter ran to nine closely-typed pages and was based on a scheme which it was hoped would avoid falling foul of Section 54 of the 1948 Companies Act, which came to haunt us over the coming months.

Put simply, Section 54 stopped people buying a company on the security of its own assets. It was designed to prevent fraud, but not designed to deal with the unique situation of employees trying to buy their company from the government with the government's blessing. It was that Section 54 which prevented NFC giving Barclays security on bank loans backed by its properties, and which sent us down tortuous alternative avenues: from which we were eventually rescued by the last minute appearance of the Seventh Cavalry in the shape of the Companies Act 1981. This measure was before the House as a Bill when our buy-out arrangements were nearing completion and it was brought into effect, not entirely coincidentally, in December 1981 just in time for Sections 42–44 to provide a route whereby loans from the banks could be secured against the NFC's properties, though in a rather complicated way in our case.

Back in May–June 1981, however, we had yet to discover the reactions of the rest of our management and all our other employees, the trade unions, the press and the public at large to our proposed buy-out. Since the Secretary of State, Norman Fowler, had set 18 June as the day on which he proposed to tell the House of Commons of our proposals to buy NFC, we had to ensure that our employees would be informed simultaneously, and we also had to tell the trade unions and the news media.

At very short notice we arranged for the printing of 25,000 copies of an information sheet for every employee, explaining the proposed buy-out in simple terms, and had these distributed in sealed bundles to all our branch managers with instructions that they were not to be opened until the afternoon of 18 June, but then ever employee was to receive one before close of business. Also at short notice, arrangements were made for senior NFC managers to brief the General Secretaries of the main unions having membership in NFC, and for a press conference in the City of London. Although this had to be set at the normally unpopular time for the press of mid-afternoon, we had an excellent turn-out, reflecting the good relations which we had built up with sections of the press over the years through a very open attitude towards the media, and also the lunch meetings with senior financial journalists in 1980 in preparation for the intended flotation. This relationship almost certainly played a part in the next day's press reports which, almost without exception, were enthusiastic; and most of the press remained supportive throughc·ut the whole of the buy-out period – and still do today.

The reaction of the trade unions was understandably less enthusiastic; three of the four main unions with members in NFC took the view that while they opposed denationalization as a matter of policy, our scheme was probably the best way forward in the circumstances. The fourth, and much the biggest, declared its opposition and campaigned against the buy-out.

This was a situation we had to live with but meanwhile we had some rapid communicating to do. We had set ourselves a very tight programme for the buy-out and, while the complex financial and legal issues were being tackled behind the scenes, we had to discover whether we could interest 24,000 employees and their families and 18,000 pensioners in putting up some money to help us buy the business between us. We started with six large regional meetings at which the leading members of our 'cabal' and myself put our proposals to the rest of our 2500 managers, with very much the same enthusiastic response which the senior managers had given.

A major communications exercise

We now had the task of educating, informing and persuading a large and geographically widespread audience that our novel proposition was in their best interests, against the background of the bankers saying, in effect: 'If you can raise at least four and a quarter million pounds between you, we will lend you the rest to pay the £53·5m purchase price and the attendant costs.'

Video was the main medium chosen for the mass communications exercise, which was not such an obvious choice in 1981 as it might seem today. The main practical considerations were that the equipment was fairly portable and simple to operate. More significantly, the philosophical choice of video was based on the need to communicate the enthusiasm and commitment of myself and my colleagues in far more locations than we could possibly visit; the fact that visual images were needed to put over a novel and complex message; and the simple fact that the television screen is such a familiar source of information.

There were multiple messages to get across; the basic facts about the buy-out proposals, the enthusiasm of the management team, the probable timetable, the nature of shareholding and its rights and obligations, and the variety and scope of NFC's business – since hitherto employees' main interest and knowledge would have centred on their own branch or company. Fortunately the resulting videotape did its job, and so did a second one dealing largely with questions and concerns raised by employees. It was shown just after the Prospectus had been issued, and so also dealt with share application.

Backing up the video thrust were printed progress reports, a booklet *Buying Your Own Company*, freephone advice sessions involving senior managers and, of course, the Prospectus itself. The latter was obviously a vital piece of communication and, in City terms, ours was a very odd animal indeed. We were determined that, even if all the usual legal and financial information had to be packed in, it would be accompanied by readable, illustrated material in plain English. The fact that over forty proofs were needed says something for the conservatism of the banking and legal professions and much for our obstinacy. In the end, I think we got it about right and it won considerable acclaim in the financial press for its clarity (Figures 24.2 and 24.3).

Waiting for success

The application lists for buying NFC shares (there were 6,187,500 Ordinary £1 shares on offer at par, payable in full on application) opened on 25 January 1982 and closed on 16 February. Interest-free loans of up to £200 for share purchase were made available to employees, and a target of £4·125m had been set as the minimum total subscription necessary for success.

At first the response was terrifyingly slow, but it soon became clear that we had a great success on our hands. Applications for over seven million shares were received and, though it went very much against the grain, the applications had to be scaled down and over £800,000 returned.

When people ask me about the relevance of NFC's buy-out success for other businesses I always stress the background from which we came as well as the unusual circumstances which gave us a window of opportunity. One of the most important was the fact that NFC never represented more than about 8 per cent of the market it was in, and this vulnerability to competition (unusual in the public sector) meant that managers were keenly aware of the relationship between productivity and profit. They were also aware of the relationship between effort and reward; some years ago we instituted performance target setting for the top hundred or so managers in the business, and this process has been extended to managers at all levels and, more recently, to clerical staff. As much as 12·5 per cent of a manager's salary can be dependent upon achieving agreed quality objectives during the year, while once-off bonus payments related to the achievement of cashflow and profit targets can be as much as 30 per cent

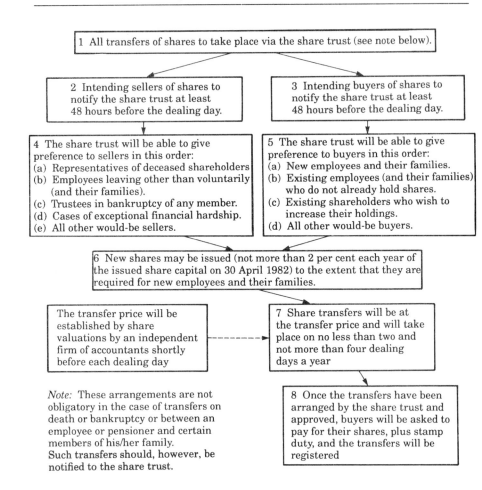

Figure 24.2 *An example of how diagrams were used in the 1982 Prospectus to put over complicated concepts – in this case, how the share scheme would work. The Prospectus diagrams were hand-drawn and printed in colour.*

of salary, depending on the extent to which targets are exceeded. Bonusing is in most cases on a work-unit basis so that many people share in achieving financial targets and benefit thereby. Such a background, I believe, made the acceptance of the risks and corresponding potential of shareholding itself more likely.

Involving the shareholders

Having bought the business, we resolved to involve our new 'owners' in a way that would set NFC apart from other large public companies. Shareholders (most of them employees) have been given opportunities to

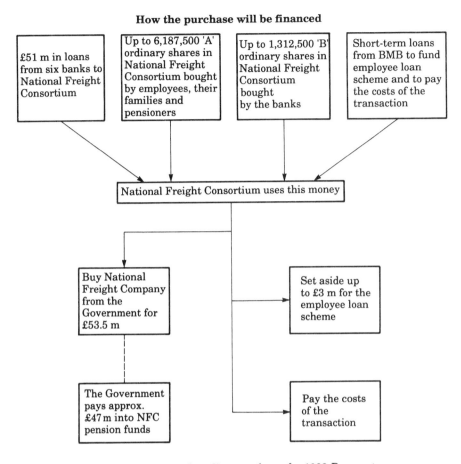

How the purchase will be financed

Figure 24.3 *Another diagram from the 1982 Prospectus*

give management their views. We hold quarterly shareholder meetings chaired by directors in eight regions of the UK; we have used MORI to survey all our shareholders' views about business development, dividend policy, shareholder communication, donation and sponsorship policy, shareholder representation and a host of other issues; we send them a quarterly newsletter about company progress and a range of shareholder matters; we deliberately structure our AGM agenda to promote discussion and the involvement of shareholders in policy decisions; and last year we had a postal ballot of all shareholders to elect a 'shareholder director' to represent their views at Board level.

Inevitably many of the questions raised in such forums are more about operating matters than about the wider direction of the business, but that is no bad thing. These people are close to the commercial roots and it can be daunting as Chairman to address an AGM knowing that the shareholders (and we typically have nearly 2000 at such a meeting) are closely involved and extremely well informed about what actually goes on at the workface. At our 1985 AGM we saw industrial democracy very much in action, with voices and votes used very effectively to decide significant issues – and not always in the way the Board intended. I see that as a strength of our policy.

While the shareholders have been quick to use their opportunities to comment, and to vote, they have also prove ! ready to be guided by the Board and professional management on issues where business experience and judgment are vital. For example, in accepting a modification of our original debt-reduction strategy (involving top priority for paying off our main loan) when we were presented with unprecedented business opportunities requiring investment in new resources.

Broadening the ownership

One of the subjects on which we have communicated and consulted with shareholders has been the widening of the share ownership among employees, which the Board sees as important. We have had AGM approval for two wider share ownership campaigns – in 1983 and 1985 – with new prospectuses, and these have brought over 6000 more employee-investors. We have continued to offer an interest-free loan for share purchase by new employees. Our policy is also to keep the 'entry price' low, so as the share value has risen we have split the shares three times to reduce the unit price. Few employee-shareholders have sold out (only 4 per cent last year) and, as Table 24.3 shows, buyers have been strongly out-numbering sellers in our internal quarterly trading. While this continues we can take the long view about whether or not to float NFC on the Stock Exchange, which in 1982 we undertook not to do for at least five years, and then only with the approval of shareholders in General Meeting. However, if the strong buying trend was reversed, this would obviously argue cogently in favour of broadening the market beyond NFC itself.

Whatever decision is eventually taken by shareholders, the need to retain the driving power of employee control is obviously going to be a crucial issue. We do not want to destroy the valuable thing we have created and become like any other transport company owned by the City, exchanging one set of faceless shareholders for another. I would also suggest that NFC in its unique new form has earned its exclusion from the political arena.

Meanwhile we have set our strategy for the next five to ten years after long and deep management discussion and a widespread consultation among shareholders. It is summed up in our new business mission:

NFC will become a broad based international, transport, distribution, travel and property group with a high reputation for service in all its

Table 24.3   *On the internal share market, buyers have continued to exceed sellers. This table shows the requests for shares at Dealing Days 3–10, covering 1983 and 1984*

Requests for shares at Dealing Days			
Dealing Day	Offered	Required	Offered as a % of required
1983— 3	49,548	374,473	13
4	169,184	348,486	48
5	135,815	208,320	65
6	266,042	317,987	84
1984— 7	169,098	524,193	32
8	109,326	421,648	26
9	148,300	300,433	49
10	170,335	327,768	52

NB. Share split after Dealing Day No. 6 discontinued.

activities. It will retain its commitment to employee-control and will use this commitment to expand into associated product areas where service levels are critical. It will have a participative style associated with first class results-orientated employment packages. It will seek increased employment opportunities and real growth of dividends and share values for its shareholders.

It is a strategy for growth, for high service levels and improved job opportunities, and particularly for a better balanced business. While investing more in UK activities than was ever the case when it was state-owned, NFC intends to put about a quarter of its investment into overseas activities, mainly in the USA where the returns from transport and distribution activities are about twice those in Britain. In the past NFC has been almost totally dependent on the UK for its income and the intention is to spread the risks and the returns internationally, so that we are no longer so dependent on the comparatively poor-performing home economy. And, while investing heavily in our UK transport and distribution activities and their modern-technology support, we are committed to developing our property interests and expanding our travel business – which is already one of the biggest agencies in Britain.

It is, I think, a measure of the understanding and support of our shareholders that they have accepted this broad view of our future direction. It is also a measure of how employee-shareholders are involved in a business whose ownership they are very conscious of sharing.

Long Range Planning journal articles

The list below gives first the number of the chapter and then the date of the journal issue in which the chapter has appeared as an article. Reprints of these articles are available from Pergamon Press, Headington Hill Hall, Oxford OX3 0BW (Tel: 0865 60285).

 1 April 1985
 3 June 1986
 4 June 1985
 5 December 1984
 6 June 1988
 7 August 1985
 8 April 1985
 9 February 1986
10 February 1988
11 October 1984
13 February 1988
14 October 1981
15 October 1988
16 December 1986
17 April 1988
18 April 1985
19 February 1989
20 August 1985
21 June 1983
22 April 1985
23 August 1985
24 October 1985

The authors and the publishers would like to express their appreciation of the cooperation of Pergamon Press in arranging this joint publication.

Index

Abell, D., 22, 28
Advanced Text Management
System (ATMS), 295, 298
American market, 178–80
American Telephone and
Telegraph, 121, 327–30
Ansoff, Igor, 285
Atlantic Richfield, 65, 66–8, 70,
74–5
Automation, factory, 134–5

Balance of payments, 58
Bank for International
Settlements, 60
Bell System, 322, 324, 327
Black & Decker Europe, 19–36
Boston Consultancy Group (BCG),
19, 35
Bottom-up planning, 8, 10, 206
Bridgestone Corporation, 221–34
British Airports Authority (BAA),
37–9
Budget process, 43, 152–3, 189
Bull, Compagnie des Machines,
122
Business Centres, ICL, 120–1
Business Development Planning,
214, 252–4
Business Plan, 13, 42–3
Business Portfolio Concept, 22
Business segments, 33–5
Business Systems Planning, 294–6,
310, 312
Business unit, 22–3
Buy-out, 342–50

Cambridge Associates, 252
Carlzon, Jan, 272
'Little Red Book', 269
Carrington plant, 81–92
'Cash cow' business, 33
Clean Air Act, 66, 67, 71
Collaborative ventures, 110, 111,
113
COMAU, 134
Communications, effective, 89–90
Competitiveness, 145, 146
Competitor profiles, 28
Computer-Aided Design Centre,
119
Computer hardware, 298–303
payback, 304–9
Computer introduction, 312–13
Computer Leasings Ltd (CLL),
115–16
Contents Addressable File Store
(CAFS), 119
Corporate culture, SAS, 261, 265–6
Corporate image, SAS, 273
Corporate philosophy, 262, 267
Corporate Plan, BAA, 39, 43–6
Corporate planning process, 20,
147–51, 153–6, 166
Cost reduction, 131, 134
Country risk assessment, 54–60
Customer service, MFI, 103

Data processing, 293, 309–12
Data validity, 23
Debt/GNP ratio, 58
Debt service ratio (DSR), 58

Debts, international, 48–51
  management of, 51–4
De-regulation, 321
Discounted cash flow (DCF), 10–11
Diversification, 168–72
Divestiture, 327–9
'Dog' business, 31, 34
Donnelley, Reuben H., 173
Dun & Bradstreet, 174

Education, *see* Training
Edwardes, Sir Michael, 122, 125
Employee-ownership, 340–1, 345–6
Entrepreneurs' role, 97–8
European Commission, 120
European Computer-Industry
  Research Centre, 122
Excellence Programme,
  Woolworth, 278–80
Executive directors' role, 144,
  147–51
External indebtedness, 56–9

Federal Communications
  Commission (FCC), 322, 327, 328
FIAT, 127–38
Financial planning, 43, 152–3, 189
Financial resources, MFI, 103
Financial targets, ICL, 112, 116,
  122–3, 125
Foresight exercises, 64–5
4M approach, 223–4
Fuji Photo Film Company, 251
Fujitsu, 111–13, 119, 120, 125

Gardiner, John, 109
Genba/Genbutsu principle, 228–9
Government, role of, 38–9, 108–9,
  112–13
Group Strategic Conference,
  Thomas Cook, 203
Group strategy, 147–51
Growth share matrix, 24–5
GTE Sprint, 321–31

Hedley, Barry, 22, 25
Housekeeping standards, 223

ICI, 143–56
ICL, 105–26
In Search of Excellence (Peters and
  Waterman), 219
Induction, 278
Industrial relations, 165, 274–6,
  289, 314
Information sources (for risk
  assessment), 60–1
Information technology (IT), 120,
  121, 155, 177–8, 289–304, 309–14
International Monetary Fund
  (IMF), 52–4, 61
International Thomson
  Organization, 168–82
Iran, political changes in, 55, 60
Issues management, 63–75

Japanese competition, 131

Key markets, 135–6

Laidlaw, Sir Christopher, 109, 120,
  122, 125
Leadership Through Quality
  Programme, 251–4
Less-developed countries (LDC), 48
Line management, 275
Liquidity gap ratio, 58
Lister, Noel, 93, 96, 99, 101, 102
Long-range planning, 19–20
Longer-term assessments, country
  risks, 61–2

Management by objectives (MBO),
  184, 224, 231
Management development
  programme, 269–70
Management organization:
  ICI, 143–4
  ICL, 108–9

MFI, 98–101
Rank Xerox, 248–51
Management processes, 256
Management role, 271–2, 277, 289
Management strategy, 6–16, 187,
  264, 268, 285, 289–90
Managers' training, 101
Manpower reductions, 82–3, 107,
  110, 128–30
Market and competitor analysis,
  26–7
Market development, 263, 323
Market preferences, 261
Market share, 330
Market value analysis, 270–1
Medium-term assessments,
  country risk, 60
Merchandise selection, 102
Mexico, debt problems, 48, 51, 53
MFI, 93–103
Midland Bank, 195, 202, 213, 214

National Freight Corporation
  (NFC), 340–53
National Westminster Bank, 47
Net funds, 190
Networks, computer, 300–3
Newspaper publishing, 179, 181
Norman, Sir Arthur, 183

Objectives/targets, BAA, 40
O'Brien, David, 246, 247, 252, 256
Office technology, 297–300
Oil prospecting, 174–6, 181
Operating plans, 210–11
Organization for Economic Co-
  operation and Development
  (OECD), 60
Organizational structure, 83–8,
  265, 281, 284, 286–7

Package vacation business, 171–2,
  181
Page Report, 332–3

Pay off matrix, 7–8
Personnel management
  Woolworth, 276–7
Philips International, 235–45
Picture of the Future, Our, Trebor,
  282–3
P–D–C–A cycle (Plan–Do–Check–
  Action), 228
Planning charts, 24–35
Planning horizons, 6
Planning cycle, Thomas Cook,
  202–7
Planning process, 18, 201–13,
  254–6, 338
Policy development, 66
Policy statement, 232–3, 239
Political risks, 60
Portfolio management, 19–23, 35
Post Office, British, 173, 174, 181
Preventive maintenance, 223
Pricing policy, MFI, 102
Priorities, business, 289
'Problem' business, 34
Product improvements, 119
Product strategy, 111
Productive organizational culture,
  80–92
Productivity, 164, 190–1, 212–13
Profitability analysis, 30–1, 116–17
Profitability growth/change chart,
  32
Project teams, 273
Public affairs functions, 73–5

Quality:
  demand for, 235–8
  improvement, 238–45
Quality Assurance (QA), 230
Quality Awards, Philips, 243
Quality control, MFI, 102–3
Quality Control (QC) circles,
  230–1
Quality standards, 222–3, 224
'Question mark' business, 31, 34

Rank Xerox, 246–57
Rationalization, 137–8
Recapitalization, 130
Recruitment, 165, 278
Redeployment Unit, Shell, 88, 91–2
Regulatory changes, 321–2, 328
Resource allocation, 214
Reward function, 10
Rights Issues, ICL, 112, 113–14, 116
Risk function, 10, 33, 47–8, 54–6
Robotization, 134, 135

Sales growth/share gain chart,
   28–30
Scandinavian Airlines (SAS),
   258–73
Scenarios, business, 5–6
Schewart cycle, *see* P–D–C–A
   cycle
Searle, Donald, 93, 96, 99
Segas (South Eastern Gas),
   289–314
Service management, 265
Shareholder involvement, 350–2
Share-ownership, 349–53
Shell Chemicals UK (SCUK),
   81–92
Shell Nederland, 11–13
Siemens, 122
Singapore Airlines (SIA), 157–67
Southern Pacific Communications
   Company, 322, 323
Southon, Arthur, 99, 101
SPRINT, 323–7
Staff recruiting, SIA, 163–4
Standard Telephones and Cables
   (STC), 125–6
Stanford Research Institute, 326
'Star' business, 33
Strategic planning, 3
   AT&T, 324–6, 330–1
   ICI, 147–51
   SIA, 167
   Thomas Cook, 210, 214
   TSB, 338
   WWF, 187–9

Strategy, *see* Management
   strategy
Strategy Review, Shell, 11
SWOT analysis (strengths,
   weaknesses, opportunities,
   threats), 186, 187, 188
Systems network architecture
   (SNA), 196–7

Targetting, 213
Technicians, changed role of, 84,
   86
Technological changes,
   telecommunications, 322–3, 329
Telecommunications industry,
   321–31
Thomas Cook Group, 194–215
Thomson Local Directories, 174
Top-down proposals, 9–10
Total quality control (TQC), 224,
   228–9, 231
Trade unions, 299, 348
Traffic forecasts, air travel, 40–1
Training, 226–7, 270, 312–13
   managers', 101, 277–8
   technicians', 86
Transform, 282
Travel industry, 157–67, 171–2, 181,
   196–201
Trebor, 281–8
Trustee Savings Bank (TSB), 332–9
Typing activities, re-organization
   of, 297

Vesper, V. D., 36

Wang systems, 299–302
Wilmot, Robb, 109, 111, 119, 120,
   125
Woolworth, 274–80
Word processing, 295, 297–300
World Bank, 60
World Wildlife Fund (WWF UK),
   183–93

Yellow Pages, 172–4, 181